Capital and Collusion

Capital and Collusion

THE POLITICAL LOGIC OF GLOBAL ECONOMIC DEVELOPMENT

Hilton L. Root

PRINCETON UNIVERSITY PRESS

PRINCETON AND OXFORD

Copyright © 2006 by Hilton L. Root
Requests for permission to reproduce material from this work should
be sent to Permissions, Princeton University Press
Published by Princeton University Press, 41 William Street,
Princeton, New Jersey 08540
In the United Kingdom: Princeton University Press,
3 Market Place, Woodstock, Oxfordshire OX20 1SY

LIBRARY OF CONGRESS CATALOGING-IN-PUBLICATION DATA

Root, Hilton L.
Capital and collusion: the political logic of global economic
development / Hilton L. Root.
p.   cm.
Includes bibliographical references and index.
ISBN–13: 978–0–691–12407–0 (cl: alk. paper)
ISBN–10: 0–691–12407–8 (cl: alk. paper)
1. Economic development—Political aspects. 2. Economic policy.
3. Developing countries—Economic policy. I. Title.
HD87.R66 2006
338.9′009172′4–dc22   2005045830

British Library Cataloging-in-Publication Data is available

This book has been composed in Sabon

Printed on acid-free paper. ∞

pup.princeton.edu

Printed in the United States of America

10   9   8   7   6   5   4   3   2   1

TO MY MOTHER

Contents

Tables and Figures

PART I

Analytical Perspectives

CHAPTER ONE

Risk, Uncertainty, and Social Progress

THE FUTURE IS, by definition, uncertain. But the developed world has many tools to quantify uncertainty and turn it into measured risk: that is, to calculate the probability of many types of events with some certainty. In fact, whole industries have come into existence to calculate risk and help people hedge against it. Reliable information about risk is so pervasive that individuals informally allow with virtually no reflection a whole range of indispensable household decisions to depend on cooperation with complete strangers. Developed countries can also count on social institutions, from private financial and insurance firms, to government welfare programs, to help manage risks, which are beyond the resources of a single household. As a result, people in the developed world respond actively to risk by marketing, developing, and financing new companies and products.

But similar ambitions fail in developing countries. Experts frequently explain this contrast by citing a shortage of capital—the developing world simply cannot generate the funds to break out of its cycle of poverty.[1] The conventional wisdom is that an absence of capital throttles the ingenuity of people in developing countries and prevents them from undertaking ventures that would improve their own welfare. Sophisticated economic theorizing equates development with capital accumulation and argues that the difference between the capital required by the country for investment and the capital available to it constitutes a financing gap.

To remedy the shortage, a wide range of multilateral and bilateral institutions—including the International Monetary Fund (IMF), the World Bank, the U.S. Agency for International Development (USAID), and the United Nations Development Programme (UNDP)—dispense aid to the world's deeply troubled and impoverished regions. Nevertheless, the very people targeted to benefit from these organizations' generosity often mistrust their interventions, breeding cynicism instead of hope. Nor have disbursements of a trillion dollars over the past fifty years to needy regions successfully breached the disparity between rich and poor either within one country or among nations.[2] Instead, gaps in wealth between the richest and poorest nations are at historic heights.

But the absence of capital is itself a reflection of other factors. This book attributes the wealth gap between developing and developed countries to the divergence between uncertainty and risk. Uncertainty refers to events about which knowledge is imprecise, whereas risk relates to events that can be assessed with some degree of certainty. Transforming uncertainty into risk is how countries grow rich. Lack of institutions that make managing risk possible is the root cause of the disparity in economic performance between developed and developing countries. Uncertainties grounded in the social and political systems of sovereign states, such as rampant public-sector mismanagement (which people living in developed countries no longer have to face), discourage households from engaging in activities that would harness their skills and capital.

Economic development begins with innovation that produces technological progress; that progress depends on an innovator's willingness to take a journey into the unknown. There is no question of such journeys for people living in developing societies; uncertainty over reaping the benefits of discovery makes such journeys unlikely and thereby keeps the pace of innovation low. Such journeys could only become routine in developing countries as in the developed world if developing-country innovators could assess the risk involved and therefore hedge against it. Without the tools to assess, for instance, the reliability of trading partners and the legal frameworks to form social institutions to cope with market risk, innovation and invention are unlikely.[3]

Measuring the social costs of these impediments to innovation is difficult; underestimating them, easy. When faced with such impediments, most sensible people simply forgo measuring risk and taking calculated chances. They withdraw into the arena where they can avoid uncertainty. Not surprisingly, this means fewer business ventures and also fewer basic risks taken by average households. This inherent conservatism means that both businesses and households only take those risks against which they can self-insure.

Developing-country households need better information about the risks they face and better tools for managing risks. Institutions that make market risk tractable expand the time horizons of economic actors. Developing countries rarely have private or social insurance for unemployment, retirement, workers compensation, intergenerational care, and disaster relief, so that people depend entirely on household savings, whereas either market or social insurance options exist in developed economies for all. If they are secure against basic market risks, households will learn to expand their frame of reference beyond their own endeavors. Once able to calculate the return on investments, they will pool their exposure to market risk by investing in the projects of other households. This is the essential step toward economic growth that people in developing countries are barred from taking. And if households cannot measure larger risks, they cannot take these steps.

Even as most households struggle, uncertainty does not prevent *all* members of a society from prospering. Many regimes have an interest in promoting uncertainty because it compels people to accept outcomes that allow only the ruler and a small band of cronies to prosper through secrecy, endogamy, and violence—defeating open, mutual endeavors by unrelated stakeholders. When households face the prospect that autocrats and their cronies will appropriate any gains they might make, the rationality of self-insurance is reinforced: be conservative; trust only those you know—and not all of them. For instance, households may invest in more children instead of in physical or human capital, but faster population growth slows the growth of per capita income.[4]

The disparities in risk management between developed and developing regions place a high cost on international investment and growth and result in the systematic undervaluation of assets in developing countries. It is the mandate of international organizations like the IMF and the World Bank to eliminate global gaps by imparting an anatomy of capital formation during the early stages of economic growth. Their charters permit capital to be lent but prohibit ventures into the politics of member states that are the very source of their capital inadequacy.[5]

By disregarding the political and social roots of poverty, organizations mandated to remedy global poverty may actually perpetuate uncertainty and contribute to the longevity of the governments that violate the rights and ignore the welfare of the people they govern. For example, an autocratic regime may agree to policies it will not enforce to guarantee the infusion of donor funds needed to reward its followers. Regime officials may agree to create institutions the donors advocate but ensure those institutions are diverted from their agreed-upon function once they are created. Since the government's books are rarely open to an independent external audit, donors are unable to track the deployment of donor assistance to monitor compliance.[6] Weak enforcement makes agreements with donors easy to game. In the future, donors, who have pre-announced aid targets, will be back to loan even more money to the same regimes—even if their policy objectives have not been met. After all, donors still have to justify the next year's aid budget.

So here is the conundrum of growth in the developing world: the very people who are in a position to transform uncertainty into risk are those who benefit from the current regime, and the organizations responsible for implementing schemes to foster growth are unable to address the root problem.

It is easy to blame reform failures on a lack of capital accumulation or an absence of domestic institutional capability. But to understand why capability is wanting in one region and not in another, we must examine the incentives of key social actors. Why do coalitions and leaders in one environment govern for prosperity, while in another they secure their own well-being at the expense of the people they lead? Leaders of East Asia's "tiger" economies, for example, built regime legitimacy by creating institutions that upheld their promise to share growth, which helped woo big business with assurances of social cohesion. Such innovations in governance, which implemented broad-based access to the benefits of development, helped East Asia to experience sustained economic growth.[7] In Latin America, by contrast, despite progress in democratization, substantive reduction of poverty and of inequality has not occurred. Leaders and regional elites secure their own welfare with shortsighted policies that undermine domestic economic sustainability. The roads, schools, health care, electricity, and property rights needed to give impoverished citizens control over their own lives are denied as threats to political stability.

This book begins where international organizations' missions end and explores the political arrangements that create incentives for political leaders either to foster growth or to steal their nation's wealth. It postulates that variations in economic performance among nations frequently stem from reversible institutional failures that encourage leaders to ignore the basic needs of all citizens. And it offers a way to break the poverty trap caused by perverse political incentives. *Capital and Collusion* contrasts the experiences of various regions and nations to ascertain the coalitional foundations of divergent strategies in economic development. It seeks both the causes of and the solutions to the problems of underdevelopment in the politics and social structures of sovereign states. Exploring the frontier between risk and uncertainty, it aims to offer readers a new perspective on the forces driving development in some of the world's fastest-growing regions.

Economic progress in developing nations requires significant and complementary innovations in social and political structures. Creating a political and social framework favorable to economic growth is often the greatest challenge these nations face. Yet developing countries are frequently advised to adopt models of economic institutions that can only succeed once appropriate social institutions exist. Enforceable property rights, for instance, often enjoy the status of being a necessary condition for economic development. The sustainability of the property rights requires social coherence and political accountability, since property rights can be overturned by the forces of social upheaval or confiscated by unchecked political discretion. The influence of the rich can compromise the property rights of the poor. The security of property rights in highly unequal societies is often enforced by military might rather than the rule of law. The property-rights regime is only as stable as the social and political foundations on which it rests.

When Risk Is Opportunity

Modern market economies provide many opportunities for the evaluation and measurement of risk, especially financial risk. If not for assumptions about the effectiveness of social and political institutions, many options for managing risk would be unavailable. Standard economic theory assumes that markets spread, pool, or assign a price to risk and can, over the long term, reduce, manage and reward it. This is a highly unrealistic expectation in most developing countries given that inadequate information obscures estimates of the economic value of private assets.[8] Whereas developed market economies possess many tools to pool, quantify, measure, and price risk, making it possible for them to reduce risk by reallocating it to those most capable and willing to bear it, the contracting parties in developing societies are prevented by asymmetric information from using the tools common to mature market societies.[9]

Individuals in developing countries do not have the option of taking remedial actions such as checking individual or commercial credit reports to overcome market imperfections and eliminate search costs or alleviate information asymmetries. As a result, they cannot trade many claims or risks. When these inefficiencies are paired with inadequate common knowledge and an absence of shared beliefs about valuation, market participants are rarely able to agree on an optimal contract for risk management. Rather than diversifying their portfolios at market prices, individuals choose to self-insure. As a result, household strategies for managing risk in developing countries vary significantly from those practiced in developed countries.[10]

A framework for capital markets in developing regions must go beyond the emphasis on market risk in financial theory to address the sources of uncertainty embedded in the political and social order. Unlike risk, uncertainty cannot be priced, and it therefore prevents many trades from occurring and may reduce or destroy the value of economic assets.[11] Uncertainty within an economic system is a market breaker; when two parties have widely divergent valuations of outcomes, they will be unable to agree on the terms of trade. Developing nations frequently avoid investments requiring sunk costs in favor of low-value short-term exchanges that discount an uncertain future.[12] Three sources of uncertainty—market, social, and political—prevent the economic calculation of risk and wreck the coordination of market activity.

The Trinity of Uncertainty in Economic Development

Noncompliance with contractual obligations—from private basic business contracts to tax collection by the government—is the most common source of uncertainty within the market system. Calculating returns on investments becomes difficult when individuals are uncertain about contract compliance. Institutions can mitigate uncertainty by monitoring the reputations of individual market participants and using the courts to make opportunistic behavior costly for perpetrators. In developed economies, institutions also provide innovators with capital from sources beyond their families by making it easier to know the probability of default of an individual loan. Applying the law of large numbers, institutions can facilitate the pooling of risk by providing information about the aggregate percentage of all loans that will default.[13] Such institutions, routine in well-functioning market economies, strengthen access to credit and shape risks into catalysts for development, yet they are in short supply in developing countries.

Avoidance and aversion, both a means of survival in the face of uncertainty, are the other side of risk and opportunity. When contract enforcement is weak, people respond by avoiding situations that require trusting a third party as well as the risk of investing in the projects of other households. Unfortunately, both of these actions are at the heart of economic growth. Households that avoid them violate the golden rule of investing, putting all their eggs in the same basket instead of diversifying in favor of a balanced and less volatile outcome.[14] All of us self-insure, but in the face of this uncertainty and immeasurable risk, developing-country households invest their resources in excessive self-insurance.[15] To insure against accidents or economic downturns, households rely entirely on their own resources and on informal networks of interpersonal obligations with neighbors and family members, constraining enterprise growth and avoiding business opportunities that might otherwise produce greater gains to society.

When households diversify their portfolios by investing in the projects of other households, the eventual result is the allocation of resources to the most effective or optimal manager.[16] Public markets for stocks and bonds eventually allow the Microsofts or General Electrics to emerge, buoyed by the investments of thousands if not millions of diverse households. When contract enforcement is undependable, however, firms reliant on the pooled capital of many separate agents cannot emerge. Moreover, overall risk in the economy will increase because those who invest only in their own efforts face the risk of losing everything if they fail. Diversification protects such households from the risk of losing everything when faced by a downturn in a particular sector of the economy. Contingencies that are small on the scale of the economy cannot be managed in the absence of insurance markets, and individual households forgo many socially advantageous transactions as a result of their risk-averting behavior. An absence of insurance markets or mechanisms for hedging risk is one of the great barriers to growth and prosperity in developing nations.

A second source of uncertainty in developing societies is policy discontinuity and social disorder that result from disparities in income distribution or from ethnic divisions. Uncertainty arises because predictions of social instability exhibit extreme variance. Experts frequently hold radically divergent views about the probability of social disorder and, depending on their background and training, view the same data through radically different lenses.[17] Thus, estimates of the frequency or intensity of social disorder are highly unreliable. Like estimates of climatic change, estimates of social volatility fluctuate radically; no agreed-upon basis exists to measure their probability. Uncertainty over the exact timing or intensity of disorder dramatically constrains investment decisions in suspect countries. The emphasis on short-term gain stunts the growth of productive enterprises or organizations and prompts the development of such organizations as mafias or private armies that arise to take advantage of the high returns resulting from an extremely unstable environment.[18]

A developed economy depends on organizations that enable individuals to undertake activities they cannot accomplish on their own by voluntarily placing their private resources into a common pool governed by an agent or representative body. Without effective social institutions, most households will choose to hold on to their capital. Pooling works best when members surrender personal rights to terminate or liquidate the collective entity.[19] No one wants to invest in an entity that can be abused by high-handed insiders. When individuals drop their liquidation option and submit to the will of the institution's governing body, they enable the formation of a self-determining entity.[20] They also enhance the validity of contracts with an external third party, making the enforcement of judgments against the collective entity more credible. For example, a legally chartered corporation that can only be liquidated after a majority decision of the shareholders can transact with other entities in the name of its membership.

In developing societies, by contrast, where recourse against the inefficient management of common resources is weak, individuals are reluctant to join an entity governed by unrelated parties and will not consent to surrender their rights to liquidate the organization.[21] If such an agreement is unenforceable, then the parties to it are right to suspect that they could lose all of their investment. Long-lasting enterprises will not exist without trust over how they will be governed.[22] Thus, uncertainty interferes with the formation of many joint endeavors, leaving many common goals unattainable.

A society without the capacity for independent institutions is left with a state that often uses its coercive organs of power to form a dictatorship. When only a few actors can hold the sovereign accountable, minority rights protection is weak. If the state fails to create a framework for coop-eration, then only organizations exercising violence can secure obedience from large groups of people.[23] In this regard, uncertainty is conducive to autocratic rule.

Polarized societies are unable to agree on sharing the fiscal burden to support optimal social investments—roads, schools, police, defense, or courts of law, for instance.[24] Social development stagnates if societies are unable to agree on the amount of these nontradable social goods that are necessary but are not provided through the market system. If a soci-ety creates insufficient quantities of social resources, it will produce fewer traded market goods, which then increases the likelihood of civil unrest. A society unable to divide up today's fiscal burden will lack the social resources necessary to cope with future needs. This risk is particu-larly prevalent in societies where a wealthy elite exists with little interest in paying taxes it might have to pay to provide public services it will never use.

Social polarization stemming from inequality or ethnic fragmentation also accounts for failure at economic policy reform. Populist efforts to reduce inequities result in frequent ruptures of policy continuity and in a lack of follow-through on policy initiatives designed to stabilize the macroeconomy. For example, no fewer than twelve elected presidents in Latin America who promised market reforms in the 1990s were unable to finish their constitutional terms; the resulting policy reversals under-mined the credibility of market reforms. In effect, these policy reversals occurred because sociopolitical stalemates prevented the Latin American societies from resolving debates about the level and distribution of taxes. Unable to tax, the governments borrowed from international capital mar-kets with devastating results for sound public finance.[25] By contrast, the dramatic opening of China's economy to market forces occurred with limited disruption because the benefactors of reform represented all strata of society. Hence, the expectation exists that the opening process will be stable and continuous, and those market reforms not already imple-mented will eventually be undertaken.

Consensus-building machinery allows governments to make bets on the future backed by their citizens. Social fragmentation that prevents consensual revenue collection and expenditure management is likely to leave the state with an inelastic revenue base. When new funding can only be raised through arbitrary levies enforced by coercion, governments face an uncertain future. Executable contracts or effective institutions for risk sharing in the marketplace will not be feasible until underlying social and political uncertainties are resolved.

A consensual budget mechanism is the best long-term social risk insur-ance.[26] The proposition that the legitimacy of collection has an important bearing on the effectiveness of collection enjoys strong confirmation by economic history.[27] Consensus about fiscal priorities among taxpayers lowers the cost to government of revenue collection. If this is so, then development policy must concentrate on establishing links between public credit and institutionally grounded consensus on national priorities. Making the government dependent on revenue from the entire citizenry is also the most certain way to encourage risk markets in developing countries. A government that depends on a broad-based revenue system will have strong incentives to avoid the economic logic of autocracy. Social disaffection, social strife, and social divides simply prevent the collective action necessary to transform household capital into the working capital of development in both the private and public sectors.

A third source of uncertainty arises when political agents use their discretion to pursue goals inconsistent with the needs of the social collectives they represent—when they represent themselves instead of their nominal constituents. To understand the consequences of discretion to potential investors in a developing country economy, consider a simple coin toss.[28] In this scenario, the probability of either outcome is 50 percent. But if political discretion enables one party to mint the coin according to its own specifications, the outcome to the other participant becomes uncertain, dependent wholly on the party in control. In this way, the exercise of discretion allows rulers to narrow their support base to a few key supporters, including ethnic and religious leaders, the military, secret police, technical experts, or a few wealthy business groups. With a narrow support base, leaders can hoard resources to purchase the maximum amount of loyalty.[29] The politics of exclusion gives leaders latitude to put resources to discretionary use, creating risk for nonsupporters and privilege for those whose goodwill is needed. Institutions that make holding office dependent on winning broad coalitions are the most credible way to constrain the excesses of executive discretion.[30] To court large coalitions, leaders must have as one of their gifts a capacity for economic policy. An irony of political development is that by creating a healthy economic environment in which private citizens can manage household risk with little direct assistance from government, the leadership makes itself dispensable and more susceptible to challenge. Leaders of small winning coalitions are simply unwilling to do so.

Autocracy and Underdevelopment

Autocracies litter the underdeveloped world. This is not coincidence. Insufficient public goods usually prevent autocracies from attaining their economic potential.[31] In fact, an autocrat stays in power longer if there is less economic development. Autocrats build support by providing special advantages to politically loyal firms even if that means channeling investment into projects that are not necessarily efficient via firms whose performance is not competitive. Attempting to improve policies and institutions that affect general market conditions does not provide a loyalty premium. For example, a leader does not create a special group of loyalists by stabilizing the currency; all citizens benefit. The social benefits of an information-efficient market clash with an autocrat's desire to maximize loyalty by rewarding followers with access to information, privilege, and justice.[32] Typically, autocratic regimes only enforce the contract or property rights of regime insiders, which cause the investment risks of insiders and outsiders to vary so extensively that only friends of the regime can take advantage of economic opportunity. At-large investors will avoid investments requiring political access or subsidies to be profitable.[33]

Firms that must operate without recourse to reliable contract enforcement demand protection from uncertainty in the form of rents from the government—such as monopolies, price-fixing, or subsidies—before investing. When government is besieged with efforts by firms trying to obtain such protection, a political marketplace that puts politicians in the driver's seat of the economy emerges, effacing the boundary between business and government. Politicization of access to market opportunities ensures a suboptimal level of investment, sealing the trap of underdevelopment.[34]

In an ideal society, everyone in effect insures everyone else. Households do not invest their entire savings in their own business; they pool their risks by owning shares in the businesses of other households. The resources of the entire society can thus ensure the mutual survival of the group. Autocracies, by contrast, are unlikely to provide a well-hedged variety of framework to anticipate crisis because the only crises that matter are those that threaten the regime's narrow political base. Thus, autocracies face uncertain futures because the rulers are unlikely to have access to adequate information to effectively allocate social resources. Only in the very long run when the ruling junta is faced with a catastrophe that threatens all of society does it address general issues of social welfare to prevent a political crisis from endangering its own survival.

The Postindustrial Productivity Gap

In a market economy, mechanisms such as bond-rating agencies, real estate appraisers, and insurance companies exist to price economic risk. If general economic conditions are the same for all firms, these mechanisms allow risk to be shifted to the most capable manager and each individual company can be evaluated according to its particular market performance. To establish specific knowledge about a company's state of health, an investor must be able to distinguish what part of company performance is due to management and what part is due to general economy-wide conditions.[35]

Market-based insurance cannot flourish in developing economies because risk bearing is thwarted by information asymmetry from both private and public sources.[36] To avoid government interventions, firms restrict information and underreport revenues, leaving insurance providers without tools for accurate assessments. Although these methods of opaque accounting may protect a company from governmental malfeasance, they prevent the valuation of a firm's potential. A second source of asymmetric information stems from corrupt governments that inaccurately provide information about the general state of the economy to the public in order to supply information for a particular group of cronies. When accurate information about individual market participants is restricted, the overall market is unable to price risk effectively, preventing the shifting of risk to those most willing and able to bear it.[37]

Risk coverage toils under an additional handicap in developing countries. Since no private party will insure against risks derived from the actions of government agents, and no market exists for risks due to government malfeasance, insurance contracts do not exist to protect against government favoritism.[38] Only in the political realm can insurance contracts between a government and the governed be written.[39] Constitutions and political institutions alone hold leaders accountable for the consequences of their policies.[40]

Regardless of culture, religion, or nationality, people are willing to take controllable risks. Without institutions to mitigate individual, social, and political sources of uncertainty, though, the market for goods and services lacks depth, scope, and liquidity. People view themselves as independent foragers, forgoing many possible gains from cooperation. Unable to manage ordinary risk, they are discouraged from seeking opportunity, thus they ensure that the future will be no different than the present. Instead of building, collaborating, or innovating for tomorrow, individuals plunder one another's current endowments.[41]

By contrast, efficient risk management allows an economy to exploit the full potential of gains from knowledge and innovation. The smooth-functioning machinery that spreads risk will encourage individuals to start new companies and to use knowledge-intensive resources to build products requiring prolonged incubation by innovators. Without effective risk allocation, technological innovation is suspended. Technological exploration inevitably creates a productivity gap between the societies that approach the technological frontier and those that fall behind. A postindustrial social order is emerging in developing countries in which access to information reduces market risks and allows individuals to undertake activities that once were the exclusive domain of a privileged few. Marx and Engels predicted that the struggle between the bourgeoisie and the proletariat—between the owners of capital and those who had only their labor—would one day produce a classless society. The access to information that has resulted from information technology has ended the dichotomy between labor and capital that characterized the first Industrial Revolution. In advanced industrialized societies, information technology and information access has become the great leveler, allowing workers to claim the residual profits of their own human capital.[42] Now, a postindustrial productivity gap increasingly separates developing countries, where social relations are based on tradition and hierarchy that restrict equal access to information about economic opportunity, from developed countries. The gap grows where new technologies cannot find sources of private investment capital because the relevant social institutions to support the contractual arrangements to manage and quantify risks are absent.

No matter how sophisticated an economy may be, no one can be adequately protected from the next natural catastrophe, the next outbreak of war, or the next jump in the price of some basic commodity such as oil or water. Although households in both developing and developed countries face these same unavoidable macrouncertainties, people living in developed countries enjoy some insurance from everyday risks to household income. For example, households in developed countries receive some relief from inevitabilities such as retirement, unemployment, and disability. Such insurance encourages acceptance of market outcomes. With foreseeable improvements in financial technology and new techniques in risk management, the gap in risk mitigation between developing and developed economies will widen.[43]

In developing countries, poor financial information foments volatility and uncertainty that make it difficult to assess assets and claims to future streams of income. The subsequent undervaluation of shares hinders investment and growth in enterprises. Insiders' practice of hiding information and assets from outside scrutiny makes attracting capital difficult. Insider manipulation of financial information fosters asymmetries of information between contracting parties, thinning the volume of trade and inviting opportunism. If not for the poor quality of information that frustrates the assessment of risk, market participants would take more risks to enrich themselves and their societies. When the market cannot distinguish between efficient and inefficient firms, the result is a so-called lemons discount, adversely impacting well-managed firms and increasing their cost of capital.[44] Owners end up seeking refuge in government patronage from an adverse business environment.

One result of the lemons discount is overburdened state systems result that lack the legal and institutional capacity needed to resolve conflicts ignited by growth. These overburdened states are unable to stimulate the institutional change needed to meet the demands that investors and citizens place on them. For example, when the private market provides no insurance against household risk, individuals end up depending on state-owned industries for jobs. People cannot risk losing the job they receive from the government because they cannot get insurance, education, or health care from the market.

The unequal distribution of financial assets across countries is one of the great disparities in world development. High-income countries with less than one-fifth of the world's population, account for more than 90 percent of world financial assets.[45] Low-income countries with at least one third of the world's population account for less than 1 percent of global financial assets. These cross-country differences in financial assets as a percentage of gross domestic product (GDP) contribute significantly to global insecurity. Thirty countries with a combined population exceeding 400 million have not received any private, long-term, nonguaranteed external credit since 1970.[46] Surprisingly, even the most impoverished of these countries rarely have a shortage of capital, yet capital is not available for growth because private savings rarely correlate with financial deepening.[47] Money not channeled into the financial system hides under mattresses and in teapots, creating a gap between a poor nation's savings and its investment.[48] Even in the best-performing emerging nations such as India and China, the financial system is weak, powerless to channel money to small, innovative firms. Emerging nations are better at duplicating the technology of developed economies than at duplicating their financial institutions.

Many policy makers ask if it is only rich countries that can support strong and healthy financial systems. It seems excessively idealistic to talk about the development of capital markets in inhospitable environments where people barely eke out a living, but the alternative, an ineffective financial system, is also very high in opportunity costs and futures lost. Without effective financial markets, economies are locked into a cycle of low expectations and low performance. One way to break this cycle is to actively initiate reforms to stabilize financial market activities and to encourage people to engage in them. This means tackling the failures in domestic governance and transparency that prevent emerging economies from effectively harnessing the resources of their own citizens.[49] Market economies without capital markets engage both wishful thinking and broken promises, creating grievances instead of opportunities.

Poverty and Uncertainty

A sharper awareness of why markets in developing countries do not respond to the standard expectations of capital theory can improve both long-term economic policy analysis and global stability. Economic models generally assume institutions already exist that provide regulation, oversight, and incentives driven by competition. But the emergence of such institutions is the very essence of development.

Mastering uncertainty through the provision of basic services such as health care, public roads, education, law enforcement, and property rights is critical to economic development; it makes people adaptive rather than opportunistic.[50] Health care that leads to longer lives and reduced infant mortality rates decreases social uncertainty.[51] Numeracy supports activities such as accounting that in turn build confidence in the manageability of the future. Although independence of the courts builds confidence in the legal system, impartiality is a consequence as much as a cause of development.[52] Property rights give people confidence about the future use of the wealth they create today and are essential to risk management, for without their enforcement, any investment is a gamble.[53]

Poverty reflects deep uncertainty about the future. The poor, whether they are Christian, Muslim, or Hindu, will tend to view their fate as being in the hands of God. The well-to-do rarely entertain equally passive views of the future. They are more likely to view their economic success as a result of will and ability, whereas the not-so-well-off consider almost every event in life a matter of luck.[54] Imelda Marcos of the Philippines, one of history's most colorful kleptocrats, was fond of attributing her great fortune to her superior intelligence, just as the power elite do in other societies.

All developing countries share the same central weakness. Living under deep uncertainty, people in developing societies cannot frame the most basic decisions about investment or consumption in relation to how the future will unfold. They cannot make decisions based on reasonable probabilities about the results of their actions, nor can they identify a feasible range of alternatives needed to plan and organize a better future. They can expect a shortsighted response from the people with whom they must interact: people who, like them, prioritize near-term goals rather than long-term ones. Poverty deprives households of the ability to take actions that have a long-term impact on the key variables in their lives. Faced with deep uncertainty about the future, they do not accumulate capital. The remainder of this book addresses how the world's most promising emerging nations transform uncertainty into risk to create opportunities that help their citizenry escape from poverty.

CHAPTER TWO

Social Foundations of Policy Credibility

SOCIAL INEQUALITY and economic performance of developing countries are linked by many pathways. Divided government, a frequent outcome of social polarization, prevents the establishment of a broad-based societal consensus about collective goals, weakens the credibility and durability of government commitment to policy reform, and undermines concerted action against governmental mismanagement.

Social inequality hinders growth by barring consensus on economic policy reform and undermines the legitimacy of policy making. Unequal distribution of wealth biases contracts between individuals by facilitating the informal influence of the wealthy few over formal institutions, impairing the legal system's impartiality. Inequality produces perverse incentives for politicians to cater to select groups of narrow supporters with private goods, reinforcing clientelism and fragmentation in the provision of public services. Social inequality hampers the civil service from operating on a meritocratic basis and instead encumbers policy implementation with patronage and influence. Governmental agencies, prevented from pursuing public agendas, are forced to rely on clientelistic channels of private influence. An outcome of divided government is a fiscal policy that is impaired by an absence of consensus on revenue collection and expenditures, making support for inclusive social objectives elusive.

THE CREDIBILITY OF POLICY REFORM

How did the high-performing economies of East Asia successfully introduce market-based, growth-oriented policies without the unrest that obstructs similar market reforms in South Asia and Latin America? Why do South Asian and Latin American leaders lack broad political support for growth predicated on market-friendly institutions so that at election time, incumbent politicians frequently decry the very policies they have implemented while in power? The relationship between anticipation, cohesion, and inclusion may explain why liberal economic policies succeed in one nation and not in another.

The success of policies for market-driven growth often depends on whether all strata of society believe they will benefit from the policies.

Governments seeking support for policies to open the economy face the challenge of making the policies credible (anticipation). To be credible, however, the policies must enjoy the support of large numbers of diverse social groups (cohesion). Cohesion is unlikely unless the benefits are perceived to be widely distributed (inclusion). Without these elements in place, market-friendly regimes will have difficulty establishing themselves and surviving.

Success in economic policy reform depends on the complex coordination of the expectations of diverse groups. Elites need assurances that their investments are protected from future confiscation. To reduce the danger of insurrection, leadership must convince the poor that they will benefit from future growth. Policy credibility results when those with veto power over policy change anticipate a better future by working cooperatively. Credibility exists when all groups, from elites to ordinary people, have assurances that their rights and properties will be respected.

Creating a credible economic strategy for future growth and investment is the most complex coordination problem in economic development. Consider how an exchange of money for potatoes at the market differs from a long-term contract where the quid pro quo is not specific and enforceable and where the time lag can be lengthy. Economic exchange involves promises that become increasingly believable as individuals learn to share a vision of the future. The prospects for broad-based economic cooperation expand when a community is united by ideology or by shared ethical principles.

Economic policy is the most promissory element of economic exchange that, like private investment, involves costs today for benefits tomorrow—with one important difference: future payoffs accrue to society at large and not to those leading the efforts.[1] Before broad policy responses to current dilemmas can persuasively influence the plans individuals make to improve their own futures, leaders must elicit trust by making economic policies credible and costly to reverse. Apprehension that government actors will break policy promises undermines compliance; individuals will ignore government regulations, expecting others to do the same. Reforming governments are thus hostage to a vicious cycle in which a lack of faith in the capacity to effect changes can be self-fulfilling.[2] External assistance rarely reconfigures the balance of power within a country because it allows the government to escape the need to negotiate with broad-based domestic coalitions and may actually concentrate power in the sovereign rather than in the people.

Shared common values or a shared vision of future objectives must be established to create the anticipation that working toward a common goal can produce a greater social good. Without a consensus on their objectives, institutions will lack coherence and be unable to inspire respect, legitimacy, or compliance. Successful policy reform requires more than just faith in the formal institutions or symbols of the state.[3] Leaders must be able to gain coalitional support to stay in office from the measures they undertake to implement reform.

Socially dysfunctional institutions endure because of dilemmas inherent in collective action, as explained by Mancur Olson.[4] When different groups are affected differently by reforms, they find little ground for consensus. By preventing collective action, inequalities interfere with a society's ability to make credible long-term commitments, which impedes economic policy reform.[5] If considerable trade-offs are needed to produce a social agreement, opposing parties are likely to protect their interests instead of moving toward collaboration.[6] Psychologists commonly observe that parties harden their differences when consensus is difficult to attain.

Observing the transformation of Germany and Japan after World War II, Olson argued that meta-transformations often occur in the wake of war or revolution which wipes the slate clean of residual interest groups and forces consensus.[7] Nevertheless, the experience of post-Soviet reform weakens Olson's point, and closer scrutiny of Japan and Germany's postwar transition indicates that prewar capabilities, such as the capacity for bureaucratic organization and key social networks, were maintained. Olson overlooked how some special-interest organizations facilitate market transactions and how a state, having annihilated redistributional private actors, may seek to maximize the welfare of governmental actors for its own sake. Moreover, many traditional societies practice clientelism even before avenues to the central government to pursue rent seeking are established. The clientelism of the past facilitates the rent seeking of the future.

Assuming a benevolent state that does not have its own motivations, strategies, and agenda, Olson posited that absent interest groups and states will act benignly in the name of social welfare. But history provides many examples in which interest groups prevent the state from becoming a predator. The failure of the Soviet Union to grow rapidly after its liberation from single-party communist control deflates Olson's key point about the deleterious role of interest groups. Despite the fact that Soviet leaders annihilated civil society, destroying all interest groups outside of the state, the post-Soviet state is too weak to act independently as a champion of market-enhancing policies. A weak state can easily be captured by distributional coalitions. If the entire fabric of civil society is destroyed, tyrannical and unstable outcomes are likely that empower quasi-state institutions, such as, warlords or mafias.

BUILDING A SOCIAL FOUNDATION FOR REFORM

Inequality can prevent economic reform from gaining political support.[8] During adjustment, countries that suffer from severe income inequality, real or perceived, may undergo political polarization. When adjustment packages appear to intensify inequalities, the fear of violent social reaction can cause investors to hesitate.[9] This is why countries with wide income inequalities find it difficult to attract long-term investment. When reform is given little chance of success because of inevitable social conflict, political coalitions in favor of reforms are difficult to sustain, sealing the development trap and ensuring the status quo.

The wave of beneficial macroeconomic reforms eventually undertaken in Latin America and India in the 1980s and early 1990s were precipitated by crises and enacted via internal administrative orders, with limited legislative scrutiny or debate. These technocratic reforms, including exchange rates, currency boards, and convertibility laws, did not make governments more accountable to citizens. They were undertaken to appease international donors, but in order to implement future reforms—such as trimming employment, slashing wages, imposing hard budget constraints, closing factories, providing ailing firms with exit options, and tackling education, agriculture, and infrastructure—popular consensus is needed.[10]

In Latin America, accountability for public-sector managers and politicians lags behind the less democratic regimes of East Asia because attention is given to monetary reform rather than to rebuilding the institutional capacity of the state. Public services, instead of being provided to all citizens, are provided selectively to reward or punish voters. Similarly, instead of improving court administration to simplify case-flow management, procedural reform of the courts is rarely carried out because reform adversely affects the leaders' ability to influence decisions of the court through patronage.

When citizens are unable to surmount great disparities in power and wealth by dint of education or entrepreneurial skill, a unifying set of economic policies is difficult to formulate. The majority will struggle with the privileged few, and policies will be supported according to their distributive impact. The expectation that a policy will intensify inequality makes its implementation politically divisive despite its intrinsic economic merit. Thus, great inequality will color economic policy making, preventing rational economic policies from gaining social consensus, as later chapters will illustrate.

When inequality is prevalent, initial social conditions are likely to constrain policy choices at the outset. Market-friendly policies found more fertile soil in China than in India because social conditions in China are more equal, so populist demands were absent in the initial implementation of liberal policies.[11] Vietnam has been able to accomplish more consistent international economic integration than India once the regime had established broad social foundations. In India redistributive battles interfere with moves toward opening the economy to the outside. Decreased social inequality also helps explain why market solutions enjoy more support in East Asia than in Latin America. In East Asia, social groups see their own interest being served from an expanded economy. The Latin American elite, whose interests diverge so dramatically from those of the majority, are threatened by competition. They can agree on making the monetary system work but not on creating opportunities that would shift resource distribution. Elites in East Asia fear social unrest if wealth is not spread, whereas elites in Latin America fear a loss of control if opportunities are widely distributed. There is also a geopolitical dimension to consider. Taiwan feared being overwhelmed by China if it did not succeed, just as South Korea feared being overtaken by North Korea. These fears created a strong sense of national purpose that was lacking in the Philippines and in Latin America, where anti-Americanism is not based on a sufficiently strong sense of menace to national survival.[12]

The Path from Social Inequality to Growth

Embedded inequality strongly influences how people view and shape their future. People living in highly unequal societies can rarely hope for or expect change.[13] In fact, studies conducted in Latin America, India, and the Middle East indicate the poor tend to view their status as an act of God.[14] Poor people who attribute their status to reasons beyond their control rarely feel obligated to support governmental change. This is one reason that social cleavages are not easily translated into politics.

Inequality tends to replicate itself in negative feedback loops, sometimes referred to as vicious cycles. These negative cycles create the expectation that today's poverty is inescapable and that tomorrow's consumption is determined by today's inequality.[15] Unable to save or to gain access to loan markets, the poor have few channels to improve their human capital.[16] As a result, parents have little to leave to their children, and the poverty continues. Tomorrow's human capital reflects today's distribution unless deliberate remedial action is taken. Social action to correct past injustices is best directed at distributing future wealth. The spread of schooling is an example of a policy that can increase income mobility across generations. Better schooling is a necessary but not sufficient condition for development. Even if a mechanism for eliminating income inequality through redistribution could be found, it is no substitute for fundamental institutional reform.[17]

INEQUALITY OF INFLUENCE

Inequality of influence is present in any society, but it is especially prevalent in poor countries where inequality often diverts institutions from their stated purpose and results in unequal access to judicial or political power. The inequality of influence can also be observed in the effectiveness of government agencies in developing countries. Agencies that do not directly affect the poor, such as telecommunications, financial ministries, or the central bank, tend to be more efficient than those that do. In the United States and Sweden, by contrast, institutions that protect the judicial rights of the poor are sufficiently funded to operate with some autonomy.[18] However, underfunded judicial and law enforcement services that typically suffer from excessive demand and insufficient access help translate inequality of wealth into inequality of influence as poorly paid police and judges are likely to be influenced by bribes.[19] The poor get less of everything provided by the state, just as they get less of everything provided by the market.[20]

The underfunding of public services permits the rich to convert their wealth into influence over the activity of public institutions. Even in a democracy with one vote per person, the wealthy can pay bribes to influence rule formation and implementation. They can capture institutions that ensure property rights, manipulate regulatory institutions, and lobby for anticompetitive measures; they can also influence discrete decisions such as zoning rules, licenses, import permits, and public procurements to private corporations; the wealthy can dominate contracts for public infrastructure, access to land titles, permits, and subsidized credits; and they can influence personnel appointments in education or public health.[21] Even so courts remain the most vulnerable to subversion since their performance is based directly on an expectation of impartiality by judges who are able to separate their private interests from their public role.

Vast class and economic differences compromise the possibility of procedural justice by allowing the decisions of the judicial system to be dominated by an elite group. In the Philippines, land reform was impaired when the valid claims of the peasants were ignored by their landlords and subsequently ignored by lawyers, judges, and law enforcement officers—all of whom were landlords themselves. For land reform to succeed, a society must have the administrative capacity to enforce the law. Land reform will not permanently influence the concentration of ownership unless it is complemented by measures to improve access to credit for buying land, agricultural inputs, or equipment. Favorable tax treatment of agricultural income is another hidden contributor to concentration. When tax laws and subsidies favor agriculture, wealthy farmers have a tendency to capture the benefits because they can best support the cost of lobbying the government for subsidies.[22] No surprise, then, that concentration returns even after land reform is undertaken.

A negative perception of the legal system's impartiality is a significant disincentive to use the courts or to engage in transactions that depend on third-party enforcement. Many economic opportunities are forgone because they become highly risky in the absence of impartial law enforcement. The lack of impartial legal adjudication poses a greater hurdle for would-be proprietors seeking to start new businesses than for established corporations. Concentrated ownership is a frequent response to weak law enforcement. In an environment of weak law enforcement, firms rely on political favors, and only a few will grow large. Countries with weak legal institutions are likely to exhibit concentration in sectors that in developed economies are owned by dispersed proprietors. Concentration in turn produces monopoly prices.

Proprietors that perceive bias in the dissemination of justice will conduct business in ways that deliberately avoid the use of the courts to redress grievances. When they lack confidence in the certainty of legal regulation, proprietors will view their security of property to be uncertain and direct their investments toward locks, safes, and security gates.[23] Investment in security is not technically underinvestment but distorted investment that does not create new productive capabilities, although it registers as GDP growth.

Tax compliance is perhaps the best indicator of confidence in the ability of a state to enforce policies. For example, compliance is higher in Chile than in Bolivia because Bolivians know that the state in unlikely to enforce existing legislation; by paying fewer taxes, citizens further weaken their institutions. Bolivia's insufficiently paid government officials are then more susceptible to the influence of the wealthy. A government unable to provide an effective civil service, in turn, cannot legitimize its request for taxation.

When firms perceive a bias in tax collection in favor of the politically privileged, they direct their investment toward operations that are opaque. Having underreported their earnings, these firms then face difficulties raising funds from external credit markets. To raise capital, their only choice is to selectively disclose their earnings to private sources of credit. In such environments, public debt markets are unlikely to exist; instead, lenders are likely to be tightly linked with borrowers. When proprietors are only able to borrow from a restricted network of their partners, their liquidity is impeded and risk diversification is stymied.[24]

When the Middle Is Missing

The middle class is the group most likely to lobby for increased protection against the risk of systemic market failure. The protection gained will create an environment more conducive to risk taking—as opposed to lobbying—for private benefits. The middle class is the basic constituency for strengthening the enforcement capabilities of the state, for demanding broad access to schooling, and, ultimately, for building a broad social safety net. A growing middle class provides support for citizen groups and the business community, monitors government services, and may even help to ensure that government jobs are awarded according to professional competencies instead of political favoritism. Accountable politics and civil administration may arise in response to these growing middle-class demands.[25] Without a strong middle class, however, there is unlikely to be a strong demand for effective systems of regulation, and there will be a shortage of individuals with the skills to provide necessary legal and accounting services.

To demand more accountability from government, the middle class must have something independent of state control and therefore difficult to tax. It must also possess some manner of acting as a collective. A middle class with independent control over resources the state needs might be granted a mechanism to express its collective interests, in the same way that a firm might willingly create a union. When the middle class derives its status from association with the state, it will play a less independent role in shaping the policies of the state.

When Good Policies Are Bad Politics

Where great inequality exists, a ruler can ensure loyalty by funneling resources to those who already have a grip on them. A leader improves his or her own survival prospects by ensuring that privileged insiders owe their advantages to political spoils.[26] As leaders eliminate rivals, they can keep more for themselves.

Good policies can actually be bad politics when massive inequality exists. For example, investing in public education can be a critical step in reversing the negative feedback loop of poverty. Numerous studies have reported robust results from investments in basic education and health.[27] Despite a strong record of productivity gains, political obstacles often prevent the adequate delivery of education.[28] Inequality affects the strategies of rulers by influencing the disbursement of public expenditures away from the poor and toward a select few in the form of private benefits.

Although investing in education, health care, and economic opportunity for the majority is good for general prosperity, distributing private benefits to a few key supporters buys leaders security of tenure.[29] As we will see in the next chapter, however, when leaders provide services to the middle classes, a chief property of those services is greater transparency, which exposes the foibles of leaders and makes their grip on office more tenuous.

So why is East Asia different? Why were good policies good politics in regimes that until the late 1990s did not enjoy electoral democracy? Why were some East Asian societies especially successful in achieving growth and social integration? One answer is that the threat of Marxist insurrection, rather than elections, motivated East Asia's leaders to extend benefits of growth to the lower income strata and to avoid blatant discrepancies in the distribution of wealth. With resourceful Marxist-Leninist parties at their doorstep ready to take power, leaders in East Asia did not have to face the ballot box to recognize the needs of the poorest citizens. Unlike East Asia, most of the world's developing regions do not face an insurrection constraint. They are threatened by competing elites, so managing elite competition is the focus of their survival strategies. If the leaders of Liberia or the Congo had to worry about insurrections by the poor, their behavior would probably resemble much more that of East Asia leaders. Societies equipped with the social and political mechanisms necessary for working cooperatively toward a common goal will be more capable of responding to a future crisis. A broad-based, society-wide bargaining process is the best insurance a society can have against uncertainty.

FISCAL CONSEQUENCES OF INEQUALITY

When analysts from developed countries regard the politics of developing countries, they frequently misconstrue fundamental disagreements over the size and composition of public expenditures with the normal politics of "horse trading" and swaps they are accustomed to in their own institutions. They overlook the fact that in developing countries a consensus on the boundaries of government action does not exist. Normal politics, however, requires establishing a basic consensus on the goals and functions of institutions. When institutions do not exist to reconcile dispersed interests, constituencies for private subsidies will form instead of coalitions for nondiscriminatory public policies, a distinction we will explore in the next chapter. Moreover, when consensus is elusive, parties will harden their positions, intensifying their disagreements. The most significant channel for social polarization to influence economic performance is through the political system in the form of divided government.

As already noted, ethnic and social polarization facilitates the capture of state institutions by highly concentrated elite interests who encounter limited resistance to their demands. This has fiscal consequences because groups with highly concentrated interests seek policies that will diffuse the costs of the privileges they enjoy. The only meaningful way to change the developmental prospects of a country in the grip of elite political competition is to rearrange the concentrations of power so that dispersed groups can act collectively to weaken concentrated interests. Unless concentrated interests are broken up, they will support spending programs from which they benefit but whose costs are borne by all taxpayers. For example, the inflated budgets for higher education among Latin American countries historically benefited a few but were paid for by the majority.[30] In developing countries, the social returns of investment in primary education are generally greater than the social returns of investing in tertiary education. The benefits to society of reducing the number of people with low skills are more important than that of increasing the number with the highest skills. Although society gets diminishing returns from investing in tertiary education, leaders have strong incentives to make socially inequitable expenditures that benefit those already secure in the exercise of influence. By contrast, education from early childhood through adolescence is a great risk mitigator for families and a significant source of equality for society. With the basic needs of children taken care of, parents have more money to invest in the household livelihood. In general, the provision of basic services such as health care, law enforcement, or public roads to all citizens contributes significantly to equality of opportunity and is an outcome that reduces risks for all members of society.

Inequality produces another adverse consequence for fiscal policy by increasing the use of debt financing from sources that are unaccountable for the consequences of repayment. Unequal societies are likely to acquire funds from outsiders who do not have the capacity to negotiate changes in the mechanisms of revenue collection. Without a consensus about the future direction of society, a government may prefer to borrow from outside sources. The burden of such debts is likely to be borne by those who do not directly benefit from expenditures made in their name. The costs of repayment are generally more broadly spread than the benefits accruing to the project. Thus, countries with a small governing coalition or "winning coalition" are likely to have high debt burdens for projects that do not provide future social resources.[31] A small group of winners has an interest in contracting for project loans from which it draws benefits, knowing that the country at large is responsible for paying back the debt. The resulting debt overhang reflects the misalignment of domestic political incentives. Debt overhang is frequently misunderstood by donors, who think they are reducing poverty by extending loans to some of the world's poorest countries.[32] Leaders will take risky gambles with their country's finances when the burden of risk lies with the powerless while the benefits can be distributed privately to key—typically tax-exempt—supporters.

During good times, when favorable terms of trade provide the government with a fiscal surplus, fractionalized societies have special problems convincing domestic interest groups to save the surplus to protect future spending.[33] The surplus is dissipated because each group fears that the others will spend it. When an economic downturn makes adjustment necessary, polarization makes consensus difficult to achieve. Each group prefers to wait and see if it can pass the buck of adjustment to rival groups, delaying action until the costs become unbearable and the nation's fiscal position is seriously compromised. The intensity of Indonesia's financial difficulties in 1997 reflected Suharto's efforts to delay systemic reform until private solutions for regime favorites could be found.

As the drama of inequality plays out, the credibility of government commitments to reform is undermined, making it optimal for governments to promise now but renege later. Governments then must pay a risk premium because of the possibility that future governments may repudiate obligations. Hence, investors ask a default premium when confronting untrustworthy governments to avoid higher debt-servicing costs. Governments may have to cut spending and raise taxes during a recession, which intensifies the damage caused by downturns. Interest rates can reach levels where repudiation is imminent when a government's commitment to pay is in doubt. Then the commitment problem has come full circle.

In 1918, Joseph Schumpeter warned of a crisis of the fiscal state due to pork-barrel politics that would make nations ungovernable. In the pork-barrel state, politicians defraud their constituents to buy the votes of special-interest groups.[34] The same tendency is stronger, not surprisingly, in developing societies where initial inequity in wealth distribution intensifies the distortions Schumpeter anticipated. Since polarized societies are unable to reach a consensus about their goals, government functions are distorted to enable politicians to buy votes rather than to implement policies and attain agreed-upon policy objectives.

In any society, politicians will attempt to enhance their own reelection chances by abusing financial institutions, but there will be more opportunity to do so in highly polarized societies where citizens are unable to agree on how to constrain the rulers. Unable to agree on a common framework for growth, politicians may try to win support by providing private goods, especially to highly unionized public sector workers. Developing countries display a distinct tendency for spending hikes the year before an election, creating political business cycles. These cycles originate almost entirely from payments of public money for the private benefit of potential voters. A new twist on the political business cycle was introduced by Macapagal-Arroyo during her reelection campaign in the Philippine national election of 2004: she allegedly instructed the internal revenue service not to conduct audits in the year before the election.

The World Bank's *World Development Report of 2002* noted that electoral cycles in fiscal policy are especially prevalent among developing countries. A study of the effects of elections on fiscal performance in 123 countries found that fiscal deficits increase on average by 1 percent of GDP in election years, with effects passed on for several years following the election. According to the report, a striking difference exists "between the magnitude of these electoral cycles in industrial and developing countries. Among developing countries, election year deficits were on average 2 percentage points of GDP higher. This discrepancy was due to greater rent seeking opportunities enjoyed by incumbent politicians in developing nations who took advantage of inadequate checks and balances on their behavior."[35] Developing-country incumbents had mechanisms to conceal the consequences of policy decisions from voters who were poorly informed about the broader economic consequences of policies. In the next chapter, we will find corroboration of this important difference between developed and developing countries, where debt accumulation and macroeconomic instability frequently reflect institutional differences, allowing politicians to govern through the dissemination of private goods rather than through policy outcomes.

SOCIAL CONFLICT AND POLICY REFORM

Growth that benefits one ethnic group in the same polity at the expense of others is likely to be contested.[36] Leaders who persist in policies that have a negative impact on the welfare of ethnic minorities may compromise the social and moral legitimacy of the institutions they will need to hold on to power in the long term.[37] Ethnically fragmented nations pay a growth premium. The examples of Malaysia and Sri Lanka illustrate that until ethnic quarrels are resolved, high-level development must wait. Since becoming independent, these two nations, with almost identical resource endowments and similar traditions of public administration derived from the British colonial model, have experienced vastly different economic fortunes. Sri Lanka was situated to become one of the leaders of the developing world, but its leaders pursued policies that discriminated against Tamil participation in government while allowing the government to control most of the economy. This meant few economic opportunities for the Tamil minority, igniting an opposition movement that has kept Sri Lanka embroiled in violence. If Sri Lanka's Sinhalese leaders had implemented policies that increased the size of the economic pie, they might have allayed the ethnic hostilities their language and other cultural policies engendered. In contrast, the leaders of Malaysia pursued policies of ethnic privilege but assuaged the hostility between ethnic Chinese and Malays by allowing both groups access to economic opportunity. Most notably, the Chinese acquired a safe haven in Singapore, which became an independent city-state, in sharp contrast to the opposition by Sri Lanka's Sinhalese majority to an independent or semiautonomous Jaffna. In 1970, Malaysia introduced the New Economic Program to promote full, productive employment and preferential university admissions for Malays.[38] It created new opportunities without threatening the economic wealth of the Chinese: the Malays gained while growth was broadly shared. As a result of unresolved ethnic conflict, Sri Lanka, which excluded Tamils from government service, languishes while Malaysia is among the most dynamic developing economies in the world.

The continuity of liberal policy reform in post-Pinochet Chile (after 1989) is related to the development of a formula for inclusive growth that reduced party fragmentation and social polarization. The first wave of market reforms in Chile was introduced by an authoritarian regime under General Pinochet in the form of shock therapy. Pinochet's radical policies opened a highly protected industrializing economy to market incentives, and state-led industrialization was supplanted in a draconian fashion by agro-extractive exports. Sustained macroeconomic growth was accomplished through the toll of deepening poverty and inequality. In their top-down manner, the Chilean reforms mirror familiar patterns in Latin America that precipitate resistance and backpeddling. Instead of overturning the market-friendly content of public policy, the Patricio Aylwin government that replaced Pinochet's socialized the benefits of reform.

After defeating the Pinochet regime in 1988 and again in 1989, Aylwin followed a strategy of growth with equity, emphasizing the inclusion of workers. Aylwin's reforms did not break with the neoliberal model. He increased taxes by 7 percent to sponsor social investment, introduced progressive direct taxation and value-added taxes, eliminated loopholes for the rich, and increased taxes on corporate income from 10 percent to 15 percent. The bottom 40 percent of the population received 65 percent of the new social expenditures. A "social investment and solidarity fund" supported an array of investments in the human capital of the poor, including public education, vocational training for unemployed youth, and funds for microenterprises. The public health budget was increased by 70 percent between 1990 and 1994. Family allowances and nutritional supplements increased, and targeted school-feeding and mother-and-child nutrition programs were introduced. Furnishing economic policy with a social dimension, these reforms strengthened the base of support for the neoliberal reforms undertaken by Aylwin's authoritarian predecessor. All parties wanted to avoid another authoritarian intervention like the one precipitated by the ideological bickering of the past. An effective civil service enforced tax compliance, making it possible for the government to sustain its promise and ensure broad-based growth with equity. Aylwin implemented policies to improve equity and smooth the social distribution of economic benefits without overturning the market orientation, thereby making Pinochet's reforms sustainable. Aylwin decided to buy in those who did not benefit rather than overturn the reforms.

Income equality enables leaders to pursue development policies that are economically rational and distributionally neutral. When equity is absent, growth invites destabilizing political conflicts, as often occurs in Latin America or in Africa. "Stop-and-go policy" cycles result. The poor oppose strategic behavior by the rich, and populist policies put a hold on growth.[39] Meanwhile, the ability of the rich to bribe politicians and the inability of the poor to avoid taxation distort incentives for investment.[40]

The success of Chile's reforms underscores how individuals will participate and support formal political and economic institutions when they are brought in. Without buy-in, however, income inequality creates incentives for individuals to avoid the formal economy and to seek alternative channels of political representation.[41] When both political and market institutions are poorly developed and provide unreliable services, both institutions will be avoided. Just as there is more market exchange in developed countries, there is also more political exchange. Thus, market and political liberalization are not substitutes but complements.

EQUALITY IN SUPPORT OF GOVERNANCE

How much progress in public administration can be achieved without social revolution? How much can be done through institution building? What is the relationship of institution building to social development? What social preconditions are necessary for bureaucratic rationale to prevail in society? These are questions long considered by Max Weber, who assumed a causal relationship between the equality of social conditions and the emergence of bureaucratic norms. Specifically, he presumed a close correlation between bureaucratic rationality and the leveling of a priori social status, but Weber failed to explain which came first. Under what circumstances will the rules of bureaucratic conduct overtake and level social differences? At some point, deeply embedded radical inequality is inevitably an obstacle to enforcing formal rules and processes.

In developing countries, modern bureaucratic management techniques are often deterred by the persistence of traditional notions of social status and paternalism. The successful application of modern bureaucratic principles requires a hierarchy based on merit rather than on social status. Equality of social condition makes it easier to establish bureaucratic efficiency and establish recruitment based on impersonal measurements of merit. For a bureaucracy to function, government workers must reject preexisting social roles in favor of those predicated on performance. When social and economic inequalities are rampant, career advancement of government personnel will inevitably be linked to social power and influence.

The Philippines has copied its civil service rules from the United States. Despite formal similarities, the practice in the two countries diverges radically because preexisting social inequality in the Philippines undermines bureaucratic standardization. In the Philippines, clientelism is perpetuated through emergency or confidential positions, pro forma performance ratings, or favoritism in reclassifying positions. Politicians will typically demand that temporary positions be filled outside of civil service criteria. Later, these positions are made permanent so that within the same agency, dual bureaucracies result, operating according to different rules of conduct. This compromise of standardization allows patron-client relations to flourish and engenders management by factions or cliques. When citizens seek bureaucratic services, they learn that "first come, first served" is not the rule. Instead, shortcuts and go-betweens are necessary to obtain routine services. When civil service entrance exams are given, they focus on general rather than specialized content, allowing for maximum discretion in the selection of candidates.

Malaysia offers a compelling contrast to the Philippines by demonstrating how relatively egalitarian social conditions can help modern management techniques take root in a society. Malaysia's leaders have prevented the official-citizen relationship from reflecting the inequality of social conditions by subscribing to the notion that the same rules apply within the civil service regardless of an officeholder's status as citizen.

To promote an ethos of egalitarian treatment, Malaysia introduced a Best Client's Charter in 1993, requiring government agencies to publicly formulate goals and to allow monitoring of their effectiveness. Each agency has a charter. The charters are premised on the idea that an agency's willingness to assist a client depends on rules, not on a civil servant's volition. The citizen need not play the role of supplicant but is instead a customer entitled to a recognized level of service. As a result, favorable action from a public official should not create a personal debt for the recipient. The charters' insistence on work norms, standards, and procedures thwarts government workers from soliciting bribes to expedite approvals of licenses or permits. Although a similar effort to develop a customer orientation based on a system of rules is urgently needed in many developing countries, their introduction is rare. Without special efforts to ensure that clearly stated rules apply to all, an applicant's background and ability to compensate the officeholder is likely to determine the quality of the bureau's response.

As this discussion suggests, the prevalence of vertical affiliations may have broad consequences for development. Robert Putnam observed that civic engagement is reduced when society is organized vertically into pyramids of patron-client relations. The "uncivic society" is typically characterized by the absence of "horizontal relations of reciprocity and cooperation." Vertical structures intensify social cleavages, Putnam concluded, whereas horizontal relations breed "honesty, trust, and law abidingness."[42] With different language, Putnam was making the same point about the key role of expectations in forging a basis for cooperation.

Modern bureaucratic management in the private as well as the public sector rests on the assumption that employees or citizens will interact as equals, not as patrons and clients, or governors facing petitioners. A modern bureaucratic state replaces vertical relations of authority and dependency with neutral, rule-bound decision making. Equality of social condition—access to status as well as income, health, and education—is the best groundwork for modern management techniques. In the absence of a fundamental equality of social condition, highly personalized relations of dependency can bypass bureaucratic norms and take precedence over the rights of citizens to equal treatment before the law. Citizens become petitioners, hoping to win favors from government on the basis of interventions by the strong and well connected. When citizens perceive that rules are made to be broken, the civic-mindedness of others cannot be assumed, social trust withers, and civic reciprocity is forfeited. Citizens can no longer distinguish private from public realms of action, and a basic pillar of the modern state is weakened.

Equality of social condition helps establish the basis for a shared moral vision of the mutual rights and responsibilities of citizens. When individuals enjoy equality of social condition, they are more likely to share the same opinions or to interpret events in the same way. This facilitates the establishment and enforcement of the norms of governance. The principle of equality, by making it easier for different strata to hold interchangeable opinions and perform interchangeable roles, makes it easier for the polity to adopt policies that enjoy mutual consent. As Tocqueville pointed out about democracy in America, "Equality of condition does not of itself produce regularity of morals, but it unquestionably facilitates and increases it."[43]

Self-enforcing economic relations based on a shared vision of moral responsibility are an important component of economic development. Forging a unified culture out of ethnic diversity helped Lee Kuan Yew's

Singapore enjoy social consensus about economic policy. Shared social understanding reduces transaction costs, thus increasing the range of possible economic interactions.[44]

WHAT SHOULD UNEQUAL SOCIETIES EXPECT?

Societies polarized by ethnicity or wealth can expect the poor to be trapped in a low-growth equilibrium, or poverty trap. They can expect difficulties in reaching a consensus on appropriate policies or frameworks for growth. Unsound fiscal policies, captured institutions, high external debts, and pet projects for the benefit of a few make it difficult to orchestrate plans for a common future.

Inequality of wealth leads to the inequality of influence, which in turn subverts the impartiality of institutions, weakens property rights, and leads finally to reduced growth. A cycle of negative expectations originating from inequities in the distribution of wealth raises doubt about the sustainability of policies that promote growth and creates the expectation that institutions are inefficient and corrupt. Entrenched inequality also nurtures the expectation that those who can gain most are those with the means to influence government most, encouraging investments in rent seeking.[45] Without trust in the state's ability to enforce its objectives, there is uncertainty about the future, which induces people to plunder for today rather than to coordinate and plan for tomorrow.

The cycle of negative expectations affects how people invest their time and make plans for the future. Anticipating a breakdown of cooperation ensures that the plans that individuals make for themselves privately will not be socially optimal.[46]

The good news for policy makers is that many methods exist for improving equity and growth. As examples in this book will show, countries are not imprisoned by autonomous social conditions or by initial conditions. Entrenched inequality can be converted into virtuous circles by adjusting patterns of public expenditure to close the social productivity gap. Reforms of education, of labor markets, of regulatory agencies, and of the judiciary can improve the economic opportunities of the poor more effectively than can direct or indirect transfers of existing wealth. Social polarization derived from inequality is a key source of uncertainty in developing societies and is a key determinant of economic success. By preventing the formation of broad political coalitions with similar policy preferences, it weakens policy credibility and reduces investment. Chapters 5 and 6 illustrate some of the many paths by which social polarization affects economic performance by comparing East Asian growth with that of Latin America.

Inequality, clientelism, and state capture all can lead to disunity and a lack of growth, but understanding how they do so depends on putting into place the final piece of the risk/uncertainty puzzle: the role of political agency. The impact of uncertainty on underdevelopment will come into full relief when we consider how political institutions influence the survival strategies employed by leaders.

Economic policy offers significant opportunities for countries to speed up or slow down growth. Under certain institutional conditions, however, economic policy is not the tool used by leaders to consolidate support for survival. In order to be implemented, the right policies for growth must also be the right policies for the survival of incumbent leadership. Good policy is not always good politics, as the next chapter will argue. Mao Zedong made himself into one of the world's most politically secure leaders by making China one of the poorest countries in the world. His Great Leap Forward (which left thirty million dead) stifled China's economy but helped Mao get the upper hand in the struggle for power within the Chinese Communist Party. Later his Cultural Revolution (three million dead) struck terror into the party and was a catastrophe for China's economy. Mao kept his country in turmoil but died in his bed having held more power over more people than any other leader in the twentieth century. The terrible consequences of his leadership are consistent with the economic logic of autocracy, and thus perpetuators of the world's greatest economic crimes often live to enjoy the longest tenures in political office.

CHAPTER THREE

Politics and Economic Structure

THE ECONOMIC LOGIC OF AUTOCRACY

THE EFFICIENCY with which markets spread information is a key variable for the liquidity and depth of capital markets.[1] An information-efficient market randomly creates opportunities for all members of society.[2] In a well-run market economy, participants constantly develop new measurements and reporting systems that enhance transparency. In this way, market participants can improve their own economic prospects while creating long-term sources of value for the entire society. The price system maintains its informativeness even if individuals are uninformed. An information-rich market eliminates the risks of being uninformed and unconnected, making everybody an insider by making no one an insider.[3] When the cost of information for general market participants increases, the value of being a government insider also increases.[4] Leaders can extract more rent from private producers by making access to information scarce.

When individuals are free to measure and report what creates value for their businesses, a leader will gain the information necessary to make economic strategies from which all citizens can benefit. When autocrats fail to promote the measurement and value of all economic resources, they deprive themselves of a basis for developing sound monetary, fiscal, and social policies. However, an informative price system creates economic opportunities that the autocrat cannot control. These opportunities are disseminated widely beyond the personal, private network from which an autocrat derives political backing. With broad access to ample information, private parties can master risk without the autocrats' assistance. To prevent this, an autocrat will attempt to limit the number of informed individuals, thus increasing the marginal value of the information he or she controls. Disorder and corruption are beneficial to many autocrats, providing them with opportunities to exploit some citizens while providing exemptions for others.[5] Efforts to dislodge dictators through trade sanctions frequently fail precisely because they provide opportunities for corruption in areas that the autocrat controls.[6]

Autocrats can earn a loyalty premium by selectively lowering the costs of information, for example, by allowing corruption to flourish and then protecting only special insiders. Cronyism or proximity to the ruler can reduce business risks for insiders and help them reduce the impact of corruption on their cost of doing business. Firms on the outside suffer from the corruption of those on the inside. Autocracy produces a convergence toward the survival of less-efficient producers as the more efficient firms are penalized in favor of producers with ties to the leader. When information is widely dispersed, by contrast, leaders lose direct control over the fortunes of citizens and the identity of a leader matters less than the policies he or she pursues. A competent manager will replace the "great leader"; the pomp of the court will give way to the efficiency of the bureau. An unremarkable Calvin Coolidge or Gerald Ford substitutes for Napoleon. What was once magnificent—the homes, extravagant clothing, uniforms, pageantry, and lifestyle of the politically empowered—become ridiculous.

POLITICAL SURVIVORS

The economic logic of autocracy presents a picture of awful but resilient regimes that entrench themselves while undermining the economy's well-being. The worst, abusive governments often survive far longer than their more benign, inclusive counterparts. Data collected by Bruce Bueno de Mesquita et alia shows that autocratic leaders who produce poverty and misery through the systematic distortion of information keep their job longer than those who enrich their country's citizens through stewardship of national institutions that produce trust and exchange.[7] Indeed, the eight countries consistently rated the most corrupt in the world—Congo, Iraq, Myanmar, Sudan, Indonesia, Syria, Pakistan, and Burundi—are those in which the political leadership has been relatively secure as measured by tenure in office. Only countries experiencing a complete breakdown in social order can rival an entrenched autocracy in generating extreme levels of poverty. The same data reveal that policy makers consistently overestimate the value of stability. Institutions that constrain economic risk-taking by failing to protect the property rights of proprietors disloyal to the regime are harmful to public welfare *because they are stable*. Among the world's most astute political survivors are malevolent kleptocrats who outlive their more compassionate, inclusive counterparts. What is good for the leaders is not necessarily good for the people.

In East Asia a number of dictatorships emerged during the cold war that promoted economic growth with equity. Those countries include South Korea, Taiwan, Thailand, and Indonesia. These dictatorships were constrained from plundering their populations by the development of input institutions that provided outlets for grievances and venues for policy dialogue with business groups. Moreover, the threat of communist insurrection supported by China provided a geopolitical incentive for East Asian leaders to legitimate their rule by succeeding at economic policy. The strength of the incentive coming from China is reflected in the fact that dictatorships exhibiting positive growth were largely clustered in East Asia. The unique characteristics of these regimes will be discussed in chapter 5.

Unlocking the Political Logic of Good Governance

Unfortunately, some of the world's longest-lasting governments are structured so that only small coteries of backers keep the leader in office, and these key groups support the politicians who best deliver resources to them.[8] The easiest way for political leaders to gain the loyalty of a small, exclusive subset of the population is by promoting nepotism, cronyism, corruption, and rent-seeking opportunities that impoverish many, distort the economy, but enrich the privileged few.

Autocratic political systems such as juntas and monarchies produce, on average, low growth, poor health, poor education, and few freedoms. They do so not because their leaders are inherently or personally disinterested in delivering good public policy for the citizenry at large, but because poor governance increases the length of time in office for the incumbent. Indeed, at all periods during their tenure in office, these leaders do much better at retaining their job if they undermine trust in markets by promoting black marketeering, corruption, and cronyism instead of promoting economic policies that lead to growth and prosperity. They can extend their stay in office by 25 percent on average if they support policies that are economically devastating to the majority of citizens.[9]

Autocrats typically retain power by winning the loyalty of a relatively small group of supporters in key positions, including those who control the military, the civil service, and the communications and information infrastructure, as well as key economic levers—and by keeping that core group as small as possible. In a poor country, an autocrat faces personal political risks by implementing policies that dissipate resources away from the few on whom he or she relies. The implementation of economic policies that protect and promote the property rights of all citizens, the rule of law, a broadly educated population, low taxes, and free trade entails political risk to the incumbent. It is not in an autocrat's interest for people to enrich themselves in ways over which he or she has no control.[10]

What distinguishes autocrats from benign rulers concerned with the prosperity of their country? Is civic-mindedness the answer? Bueno de Mesquita's quantitative assessments highlight the importance of political institutions that determine the inclusiveness of the regime. Inclusive governance promotes government spending on social policy by linking the longevity of the leaders to the welfare of the majority. Leaders who depend on a broadly inclusive political coalition do better at staying in office if they manage to promote exceptionally high growth rates. They do worse if, instead of growth, they promote rent seeking or black-market opportunities for friends and allies of the regime. Inclusive leaders who promote growth stay in office 15 percent longer on average than inclusive leaders who are less effective at economic policy and reduce growth rates. Remember that leaders of small winning coalitions that reduce their countries' standard of living actually enhance their own prospects of staying in office. Autocrats, on average, last in office twice as long as democrats.

The promotion of economic growth, political freedom, and social improvement must first and foremost benefit political leadership. Leaders who want to stay in office cannot be expected to undertake policies that harm their own prospects of political survival.

Rulers seeking a long tenure in office have an incentive to rule exclusively and to selectively spend resources only on those who have something the sovereign needs. When political survival depends on a large coalition of supporters, leaders can no longer maintain the loyalty of their coalition by granting personal privileges and benefits. Governments dependent on a large number of backers force leaders to compete by producing effective public policies (e.g., high growth, civil liberties, rule of law, transparency, etc.) that benefit everyone in the society. This does not mean that political leaders who depend on many supporters are immune from cronyism, corruption, rent-seeking, or even personal kleptocratic behavior, but rather that the opportunity for such economy-distorting behavior is much more circumscribed under inclusive political institutions than under exclusive institutions. Consider the occasional elected prime minister who steals the nation's silverware upon leaving office. What would such a leader have kept if not constrained by the oversight of nonexecutive bodies?

THE ECONOMIC CONSEQUENCES OF AUTOCRACY

In an efficient market economy, most people accomplish their economic transactions by passively referring to publicly available prices. Market-clearing prices merge people's desire with what is socially feasible, creating perhaps the greatest miracle of market organization. This is not so in an autocracy where a reduction in the informativeness of prices bars people from making optimal plans and allows leaders to increase their own authority and collect rents by arbitraging economic opportunity.

An economy grows if people are able to use today's capital to capture future value or future income streams. The willingness to purchase future streams of income depends on the integrity of today's information. Citizens will not invest in future streams of income if future access to that revenue is uncertain.[11]

If citizens bet on the future based on passively acquired information, more pooling of investment will occur, increasing the overall efficiency of the economy. In a well-functioning market economy, investors' portfolios are weighted toward passively acquired information rather than toward discreet sources of privately available information. The portfolios would be thinner and less adjusted to risk if individual investors depended on private information for all their investments.

If households were required to collect all the relevant information before making a particular investment, they would only be able to invest in areas where they had personal private information and would be reluctant to invest in the projects of other households. Households then would self-insure too much by saving excessively instead of investing their savings in the projects of other households, eventually exposing themselves to greater market risk. Investing everything in their own efforts, households risk losing everything they own at once during a market downturn. The availability of reliable public information allows effective managers of other people's money, such as Dupont, Boeing, and Microsoft, to find funding to expand their operations while increasing the wealth of their backers. Essentially, firms are less competitive and the economy carries more risk when diversification, pooling, and hedging are not widely practiced. Thus the uncertainty that results from the inconsistency of unconstrained sovereign discretion will result in idiosyncratic firm-, family-, or village-specific relationships. The specificity of these investments will impede the transfer of assets and the unbundling of assets into tradable value-added commodities, so the optimal amount of investment will not occur.

When available information fails to reflect the full assets of business, economic relationships will suffer. Ideally, we all want to live in a country where a leader's performance is assessed with a number that reflects the market capitalization of all national resources. In this regard, the complete equitization of a country's future value is the goal of economic development. With reliable public information, an equity value can be established for all property, allowing citizens to hold shares in the future according to their taste, plan, disposition, and goals regardless of their social identity. Ultimately, the quality of information can enable individuals to insure the expected future value of all their resources against ordinary market risks. This way each citizen can find a strategy to pursue his or her optimal plans. Similarly, it follows that a complete global market for all goods could exist if a country's resources were completely equitized. Then the same knowledge available locally to potential investors would also be available outside the country, allowing capital to flow to its best use all over the globe.[12]

AUTOCRACY AND THE MONETARY SYSTEM

The most decisive control exercised by government over the economy is authority over a nation's currency and money markets. Money represents the most fungible form of wealth. Authority over the creation of money can be used to generate loyalty and support on a scale that only ownership of national resources can rival. Very few leaders in the world today exert complete control over their nation's money supply and capital accounts. Leaders of the world's international financial organizations can take great pride in facilitating the convergence of developing-country financial systems toward international norms. If it were not for the gray-suited IMF economists, who made it difficult for member states to practice financial repression, this convergence would probably have taken much longer and would be much less complete.

In the 1950s and 1960s, developing-country governments frequently distorted the market for financial services by practicing financial repression. Ceilings imposed on nominal deposit and loan rates were lower than actual or expected inflation rates, discouraging investors from holding on to domestic financial assets while encouraging debt financing for unproductive purposes that lacked financial sustainability. Ceilings were imposed on the amount of credit extended by individual banks and within overall credit ceilings, and subceilings were established for various categories of loans. Simultaneously, a system of liquidity credits gave commercial banks subsidized rates to invest according to the goals of industrial policy. These policies depressed financial savings and promoted inefficient investment with subsidized capital. Credit repression was designed to help developing countries aid priority sectors, but because it allowed credit allocation to be influenced by political and other noneconomic considerations in the hands of unscrupulous leaders, it became a mechanism to channel funds into the hands of small winning coalitions, leaving behind a social legacy of crony producers in control of the assets of the world's poorest countries.[13]

As the twenty-first century opens, quickly available information about monetary distortions has undermined the feasibility of inflationary monetary policies and made it difficult for central banks and finance ministries to manipulate currency values. With the announcement of an impossible monetary policy, money flows right out of a country in currency trading, evident in thousands of decentralized transactions daily. Now that information from the global market place travels at the speed of light, leaders are discouraged from asserting their political authority to manipulate the national currency.

In today's world, global information standards determine where capital will flow; as a consequence, credit repression is rarely practiced, and interest-rate ceilings, credit ceilings, and loans to priority sectors have been eliminated in most countries. The removal of impediments to new entrants and of restrictions on foreign-currency payments has opened the financial systems in many countries to competition. Even so, reform of macroeconomic distortions has not necessarily led to steady and consistent economic growth. Countries must also construct an adequate institutional infrastructure for managing risk.

The emphasis of policy reform has shifted away from fiscal balances to questions about banking regulations, corporate governance, bankruptcy procedures, and contract enforcement. Along with being concerned with how much capital is flowing, policy makers now also question the structure and quality of the projects being capitalized. Investors are learning to seek evaluations of local institutions and legal frameworks and to avoid wasteful projects that benefit politically powerful groups without adding to the productive capacity of the economy.[14]

Forbearance of Public-Sector Mismanagement

In contrast to the chaos in public-sector management often exhibited in developing countries, the well-established and unifying theory of macroeconomics allows public-finance evaluations to follow a consistent set of principles that offer a benchmark to assess the finance ministry and the central bank. The accounting conventions governing monetary transactions are highly standardized. The formula for balancing revenues and expenditures lends itself to uniformity. In all countries, the nominal GDP is equal to private consumption plus private investment, net government spending, and net exports. The line between the overall fiscal balance and the financing line is drawn in the same place in all country budgets: total revenues, grants, total expenditures, and net spending are always above the line; financing which includes domestic bank and nonbank financing is always below. The overall fiscal deficit is defined and calculated the same way in every country and a consensus exists that fiscal accounts are best measured as shares to GDP. This makes it relatively easy to go from data to policy in public finance.

Differences in the quality of public-sector management that exist around the world are often overlooked because they are hidden behind a global convergence toward the same formal models that include civil service commissions, high courts, prosecutor's offices, and audit and budgetary agencies. Yet the management of these formal institutions differs dramatically from country to country. Take, for example, the creation of a securities exchange commission. It is widely acknowledged that an agency must have legal jurisdiction to be effective. Without financial independence from the central government, political strings can still be attached to the agency. We do not have to turn to examples from Uganda or Tanzania to see the subtle work of purse strings at play. In the late 1990s, the U.S. Congress reduced the budget of the Securities and Exchange Commission (SEC), an independent legal authority, diminishing the agency's ability to prevent conflicts of interest among auditors. Inflated profit statements were released to the public, which resulted in poor investment decisions. This interference was made possible by the dependence of the SEC on congressional appropriations for some of its revenues. Should we then be surprised to learn that regulatory bodies in developing countries rarely have financial independence and are frequently captured by fraudulent elites?

Experts on public finance are relatively interchangeable, and they can apply their tools relatively effectively to any number of countries. This allows the IMF to randomly assemble and send to any country in the world teams that typically include experts in the real, monetary, fiscal, and external sectors. In a matter of weeks the four-person team can confirm whether a country is in compliance with an IMF program and can then go to the next country. By contrast, the World Bank reports that in civil service, "the reform objectives have at times been unfocused, and occasionally contradictory. . . . There has been little consensus on what constitutes an acceptable approach to addressing each objective."

Evaluations of economic governance are intrinsically more difficult to assess than adherence to public-finance principles because of country-specific idiosyncrasies within civil service systems. Consider the differences between public administration and its sister discipline, public finance. Public administration does not offer a wide range of principles from which to diagnose defects and to precisely sequence a policy response. Unlike fiscal policy, in public administration it is difficult to state three discrete areas that alone need to be fixed or to identify three indicators of administrative fundamentals. Rarely does any one institution conveniently stand out as requiring remedial action. As the World Bank put it, "there is no single best 'model' of public administration."[15]

The skill sets of teams in public administration vary widely. Good knowledge of a nation's civil service requires an investment in specialized staff whose expertise is not easily duplicated in another country. Because it is country specific, expertise on public administration is hard to reproduce and is not easily interchangeable. The proliferation of transactions within bureaucracies is costly to monitor because it is almost always a black box known only to government insiders. Even when similarities exist, governments can always find ways to circumvent formal structures.

Within the civil service of a developing country, many avenues for corruption exist, because benefits allotted to government workers are not always monetized and may not show up directly in the wage budget. Financial management and accountability within the civil service is generally weak. Cash allowances and benefits may surpass basic salary—in Pakistan they can be 400 percent greater. Leaders can circumvent merit by diverting rewards to loyal officials, interfering with civil service discipline, ensuring that real compensation is beyond public scrutiny. Key data regarding the sectoral differences of wages and employment and the wage-scale differentials in various agencies are rarely transparent enough to inform policy choices. The compensation of officials most directly linked to sensitive areas of public-sector management is more carefully guarded than missile technology.[16] The roles, functions, and structures within ministries and agencies are not rationalized, and responsibilities are often allocated according to political caprice. Budgetary oversight is rarely vested in an unbiased independent authority or a parliament, and executives can bend the rules, sponsor favorites, and evade linkages between policy pronouncements and resource uses.

Policy makers find it difficult to decide whether poor institutions and mismanagement are a cause or a symptom of a nation's economic ills. Is bad management the source or the result of poor policies? We know that fraud always comes at the end of a process of economic decline, but did bad design exist at the outset or did this behavior emerge from mistaken policy? In the end, this determination is difficult to make.

Although mismanagement may not be the cause of a nation's financial failures, it is always present when nations fail. Forbearance and even encouragement of financial mismanagement, inappropriate political intervention in financial regulation, and an absence of market mechanisms to supplement the failure of state supervision all stem from the same source. Leaders obscure the economic consequences of policies that are designed to maximize other objectives.[17] From the standpoint of public interest, government policies that have negative economic consequences are often perceived as "mistaken" when in fact they may be intentionally designed to advance other goals of political leadership.

The inability to perform routine administrative tasks in developing countries is frequently attributed to the lack of funds or competence. For example, it is commonly maintained that the collection of taxes becomes easier as a country or region develops. Yet primitive conditions did not prevent the kings of England in the eleventh century from registering and monitoring all land in their kingdom. In 1085, William the Conqueror's Domesday Book registered the ownership and value of all real property belonging to his subjects. His cadastres were able to surmount the problem of record keeping more successfully than a large number of developing countries today, whose administrators fail to either register or protect property.[18] The kings of France in the seventeenth century were able to devise incentives for tax collectors to effectively identify and collect 30 percent or more of the production of agricultural communities.[19] Despite much greater capabilities, many modern governments collect a smaller fraction of or fail to identify total agricultural output. The laments of incompetence and inadequate resources by governments frequently hide intentional misinformation and low motivation. Officials in many countries create disorganization and deliberately underperform to aid corruption. It is not a lack of funds or capacity that causes "financial uncertainty, poor planning, unrealistic budgeting, inadequate record keeping, irregular accounting, overlapping responsibilities and institutional fragmentation."[20] Instead, mismanagement serves as a source of revenue generation, giving officials incentive to misbehave.

Public-sector weaknesses exist because they deliberately and strategically offer private benefit to leadership. Gaps in public accountability, weak internal financial and performance management systems, public procurement procedures, public-sector accounts and management information, regulation of corporate accounting, external public audits of government accounts, inadequate legislative scrutiny of audits, and inadequate public access to information are all readily correctable with fewer resources than it would take to build a highway or a dam. Such deliberate evasions of accountability are enmeshed in domestic political institutions protected by the doctrine of national sovereignty so that they are not a part of economic policy reform by external bodies that provide the funding.[21]

Another obstacle hindering the success of international efforts to transform the civil service is that multilateral organizations are usually under the jurisdiction of ministries of finance in donor countries, and they work primarily with central banks and financial ministries in client countries. Even when the finance minister champions legal reform, other ministries may have different goals. Governments frequently have conflicting objectives, and different ministries report to conflicting constituencies. Governments that want to rule through mismanagement can do so through a wide array of instruments, preventing a simple reform from achieving the desired goal.

Projects conceived as spoils for political cronies do not have to function or even be completed. For example, during the 1990s, the government of Sri Lanka could not determine its top twenty investment priorities, circulating instead a list of several hundred to multilateral donors, knowing that none would be completed. Rather than meeting a policy goal or providing a public service, public investments were selected to distribute private goods to political leaders often in the form of rents or side payments from the transactions needed to carry out the project. Sri Lanka's selection of public investments to support a particular boss or political power broker resulted in slow growth as well as in spending decisions unrelated to the population's needs.[22] Sri Lanka is just one among dozens of developing countries unable to invest for the future because it targets public investments to provide private benefits to regime supporters. Funding requests for projects that lack provisions for maintenance, and for which economic or commercial viability is never considered, contribute significantly to developing-country debts. Africa has lost almost a third of the $150 billion alotted for road construction due to the seepage of rents to regime stalwarts.[23]

The Achilles' heel of autocratic regimes is that government agents can shield misbehavior by not reporting the revenues they collect on behalf of the government. Once having let corruption flourish, it is difficult to prevent the dissemination of rents to parts of the officialdom over which the autocrat has weak control. The rights to corruption of those chosen cronies at the top may be sold to those lower down, reducing the ruler's take and diluting authority. The agents may develop sophisticated methods to divert resources from ever reaching the center, as occurred in the Soviet Union and contributed to its demise.

How can positive political economy be transformed into normative politics so that the bias of leaders to distribute private goods is transformed into the creation of public goods? Seizing a mismanaged public-sector from the clutches of a corrupt dictator means surmounting the prerogatives of sovereignty; international organizations are poorly equipped for such an undertaking.[24] Powerful domestic political rationales exist for the forbearance of public sector mismanagement. To understand this rationale, we must return to our analysis of the political foundations of the incumbent political regime. As the World Bank concluded, "continuing assessment of the underlying political feasibility of reforms are [sic] crucial for effective civil service reform."[25] The key issue for the effectiveness of external assistance is to strengthen domestic interest groups with a constituent interest in improving economic policy. When domestic political mechanisms are ineffective, it is very difficult for external bodies to constructively intervene.

Policy makers are increasingly aware that enforcement is the key to policy performance. Promulgation of good rules and prudential principles is not sufficient. For economic policy to succeed, policy makers must be mindful of why implementation occurs in one political context and not in another.[26] Development policy as a discipline took a significant step in the 1990s by recognizing the role of institutions. The next step is to make good institutional design incentive-compatible with the interests of political leadership.[27]

A Unified Approach to Economic Policy Reform

The ubiquity of bad policy is a central paradox of politics. When the number of backers is a relatively large proportion of the available pool— and all citizens are, in principle, potential backers—providing private goods will induce little loyalty: the number of recipients will reduce the value of such benefits. Autocrats rarely pursue wealth for purpose of consumption. Leaders who specialize in assuring a flow of private rewards will find they have a political crisis on their hands if they run out of resources to purchase enough loyalty to stay in office. Wealth is best salted away to prevent an economic crisis from becoming a political crisis. Such contingencies can force a leader to undertake reforms that might otherwise be avoided.

In small coalition systems, incumbents who promote growth are likely to diminish their term in office compared with counterparts who rule through disorder and plunder. Bad policy is good politics for the incumbent if it frees resources to invest in loyalty. In inclusive governments that rely on large coalitions, good policy is conversely good politics, because an incumbent's political survival depends on public-policy performance. Leaders of large coalitions spend more on producing good public policies to compensate for the weak loyalty they face from supporters, leaving less by way of a rainy-day fund (or secret bank account).

Leaders that depend on a majority of the population are likely to exhaust the supply of private goods before all the supporters are satisfied. Without an adequate supply of private goods, leaders must develop policy competence to win the support they need to hold office. Only then will leaders emerge who seek to create institutions revealing their policy competence to citizens. Institutional arrangements that allow inclusive governance significantly determine the likelihood of high per capita incomes, high growth rates, low levels of corruption, high levels of political rights and civil liberties, high levels of educational attainment, gender equality, low infant mortality, long life expectancy, and a variety of other economic, social, and political indicators of quality of life.[28] The irony is that the institutions that motivate good governance inevitably require that leaders put their own power at constant risk. When leaders improve transparency, they allow the discovery of small failures or inequities to shorten their tenure in office. This is a challenge their less policy-competent, autocratic counterparts do not face.

WHERE DO INCENTIVES FOR ECONOMIC POLICY COME FROM?

The key issue for the elimination of global poverty is to understand the political incentives of sound economic policy. The assumption that if only the government had sufficient knowledge of the structure of the economy it would act to make necessary improvements in social welfare leads economists to believe that if all the relevant knowledge is brought to bear and if advances in economic analysis are properly applied, poverty would be eliminated. This perspective makes economists susceptible to linking dictatorships with efficiency and growth. The more intractable problem is that those designing and implementing government policies have incentives that are inconsistent with social welfare. When policy makers exhort poor countries to create an environment conducive to growth—correcting overvalued exchange rates, reducing import barriers, eliminating state-owned industries—they often ignore the political motivation that accounts for these seemingly inappropriate and inept policies in the first place.[29]

The notion that what makes large groups of citizens better off also makes politicians better off is true under highly restrictive institutional settings. Only when their jobs depend on policy competence will leaders want the results of their policy performance to be transparent and measurable, their contracts to be enforceable, and their promises to be credible.

The first challenge of development rests in the creation of institutions that align the interests of rulers with the interests of all those they govern. This brings us back to the conundrum concerning the role of policy advice: rulers may actually decrease their hold on power if they follow the policies most consistently advocated by economists. So the first challenge of economic development is political: building institutions that make leaders accountable to citizens. Yet economic policy reform generally starts from the proposition that leaders have everything to gain from helping their countries grow. From this perspective, the primary task of economic policy is to enlighten political leaders. However, this assumption is challenged by the very simple observation that the leaders of the world's most successful nations have lower prospects of remaining in office than their counterparts who mismanage and destroy their nation's economic futures.

Why do so many leaders ignore the abundantly available good policy advice about economic development?[30] The answer is that the policies most likely to lead to prosperity often differ from those most likely to keep leaders in power. To put it bluntly, leaders are able to stay in power by ruling badly. The only durable resolution of this tension is to build domestic political institutions that reward rulers for policy performance. The next generation of reform will be an experiment in designing institutions that demand policy competence from political leaders.

CHAPTER FOUR

An Amazing Economy of Information

THE FINANCIAL SYSTEM

A FINANCIAL SYSTEM transfers assets, pools capital, reduces risks, increases liquidity, and conveys information.[1] Deep, liquid, and robust financial systems are essential to the long-run effectiveness of market economies.[2] In times of crisis, a financial system must respond quickly to changes in market conditions and continuously reallocate resources toward more-effective uses and users. To ensure the greatest social value, a financial system must also be blind to the political identities of market participants.[3]

An efficient financial system pools resources and allows savers to achieve increasing returns to scale on their investments. It reduces risks and increases liquidity by concentrating the application of capital toward priority projects that yield both social and private returns. Sanford Grossman describes a well-run financial system as an "amazing economy of information." To assess the operation of this "amazing economy" tools are needed that measure how effectively resources find their way to the most innovative projects and users. According to Rajan and Zingales:

> The right measure would capture the ease with which any entrepreneur or company with a sound project can obtain finance, and the confidence with which investors anticipate an adequate return. Presumably, also, a developed financial sector can gauge, subdivide, and spread difficult risks, letting them rest where they can best be borne. Finally, it should do all this at low cost. . . .
>
> In a perfect financial system, it will be the quality of the underlying assets or ideas that will determine whether finance is forthcoming, and the identity of the owner (to the extent it is orthogonal to the owner's capability of carrying out the project) will be irrelevant. Because our focus is on how easy it is to raise finance without prior connections or wealth, our measures of financial development will emphasize the availability of arm's length market finance.[4]

Liquidity within a well-run financial system contributes to technological change and facilitates the flow of capital to high-return, capital-intensive long-run projects. Without a well-run financial system, resources will flow into projects with little uncertainty about the timing and settlement of transactions. However, this leaves high-return, high-risk, and long-run projects starved for funding. For this reason, many economic historians argue that the industrial revolution had to wait for the financial revolution of the eighteenth century. Having capital and having a capital market are not the same thing. Capital markets are needed when the entrepreneur is different from the investor.

Professional financial intermediaries mobilize savings by helping investors to identify the most promising projects and the most capable managers, so that innovators can concentrate on developing new products. Today, developed financial systems offer a wide diversity of capital instruments that enable people to take chances on new ideas and to match money with talent. Among the capital-market options that exist for entrepreneurs to borrow against future earnings are junk bonds (high-yield, high-risk debt instruments),[5] securities (ownership of equity in the corporation),[6] angels (professional investors using their own money to make early-stage investments), venture capital (investors of their own and other people's money; their high-risk, high-reward portfolio is a small part of the larger portfolio held by other, usually institutional investors), initial public offerings (first-time shares that are sold publicly), and leveraged buyouts (using existing assets and cash flow as collateral to obtain funds to buy out a portion or all of the existing management).[7] The vast decentralization of capital instruments within a developed financial system allows risk to be matched with those most willing and most able to carry it, enabling companies to choose the financing most suited to their market structure. Financial markets do more than redistribute risk. They provide feedback mechanisms that allow entrepreneurs to obtain information about investments. An entrepreneur would still seek out the capital markets for their informational value even if he or she had all the funds necessary to accomplish his or her goals.[8]

A deep and liquid financial system must have information at its disposal to facilitate the selection and the monitoring of funds. Financial development is to the economy what development of the cerebrum is to the human body: it is the most important producer, processor, disseminator and user of information. The quality of this information determines how effectively the financial system allocates resources. Financial markets are, in essence, information markets.

Accurate and timely information about company performance increases the liquidity of the market. The rate a company must pay for its funds, or its cost of capital, is determined by the availability and quality of information about risk. Market participants want firms to state the corporate mission, disclose the results of their operation, and equitably distribute the residual commercial benefit to stakeholders. Market participants also want to know that sound judgment exists in the custodianship of corporate assets and that those assets are used in a socially responsible manner (consistent with accepted norms concerning the environment or labor). Investor confidence depends on reliable performance reports. When verifiable information is not available, increases in the cost of capital shrink the market for goods and services. Reliable information on a timely basis is the lifeblood of capital markets.

The quality of information available through private disclosure increases market depth and liquidity, and benefits all citizens. Governments, according to Joseph Stiglitz, must provide consumer protection through disclosure laws, because "without such protection, capital markets might not work effectively. If investors believe that the stock market is not fair, then they will not be willing to invest their money. The market will be thin, and firms may have greater trouble raising capital. Honest firms are hurt by the potential presence of scoundrels."[9] Governments that protect investors, Stiglitz implied, make capital markets function better and prevent the market from drying up. He emphasized that individuals and the market both benefit from prudent government regulation, but he did not suggest going back to the development consensus of the 1950s, when the leaders of the developing world substituted the role of government for that of the financial system.

Ultimately, the information gathered and released within a financial market fulfills the two critical properties of a public good. First, the consumption or use of information by one party does not detract from its use by another (it is a nonrival). Second, once the information is created, an individual may not be excluded from enjoying and employing it (it is nonexcludable). Improvements in the management and accountability of firms result from external monitoring, yet those providing the monitoring do not capture these benefits.[10] Economic development requires a satisfactory solution to this dilemma if economic actors are to make optimal social contributions.

This public-goods dilemma acquires global dimensions as capital flows more freely around the world. Today, no developing-country risk is too great for the collective resources of the world to effectively manage. Assistance to South Korea and Mexico by the IMF in the 1990s, considered to have been a "massive bailout" (each received less than 5 percent of its domestic GDP), probably exceeded no more than one-half of one-10,000th of global GDP.

With greater global risk insurance, collective resources will be more efficiently allocated. However, divergent domestic prudential standards prevent the development of global protection. The source of these discrepant domestic standards is sometimes benignly attributed to gaps in knowledge about best practice. But, considering multilateral organizations and their extensive efforts to provide up-to-date assistance to countries in need, ignorance becomes hard to rationalize. Adequate knowledge, then, through international financial networks, is available to overcome these gaps in performance and can occur at little direct cost to government.

THE FINANCIAL SECTOR AND ECONOMIC DEVELOPMENT

If external funds are available, owners will have an incentive to create a transparent management structure in order to attract finance. Thus, financial markets encourage a convergence toward good firm governance. For example, to convince potential investors who seek professional custodianship of their capital, firm owners may separate ownership from management. Firms that fail to attract external capital will be outperformed by those competitors who, by virtue of having adapted standards of good governance, can attract more capital. In a world of effective capital markets, firms that persist in less-transparent structures will be unsuccessful competitors, and their growth will be stymied.

Difficulties arise in developing economies because firms do not face the incentives provided by a well-developed financial system and are often better off limiting disclosure. In fact, a lack of access to market information is consistent with the normal evolution of private business in developing countries. An accurate view of company ownership and capital structure is typically hard to come by. Furthermore, concepts of ownership, boundaries between sectors, and clarity in corporate organizing methods are often absent. Accounts may misrepresent the true financial position of firms, as they rarely provide financial data on pretax profits, fixed capital, or working capital, making the rate of return on capital difficult to assess. The underreporting of assets, although hostile to the development of a strong market, actually has an important economic motivation and is, in fact, a rational calculation in the face of uncertainty.

The fears of government opportunism, an inability to register because of inappropriate legal codes, and an absence of suitable categories of incorporation give firms incentives to underreport or misrepresent financial data, the number of employees, and assets. An opaque tax system further encourages underreporting. Although an absence of necessary market information prevents firms from realizing their market potential, lack of adherence to standards of transparency enables a nimble response to regulatory and policy uncertainty at the cost of creditworthiness that would bolster potential investment.

When it is difficult to ascertain who owns the assets, who controls the firm, and how management decisions are made, private enterprises find it difficult to attract external financing. Unable to provide clear title to assets or transparent documentation of financial assets, which creditors need in order to assess prospects for repayment, borrowers face increased costs of capital. Barred from achieving their optimal scale of operations, firms get stuck in the first, more informal stages of organization. In Brazil, the large number of mom-and-pop enterprises gives the impression of a highly entrepreneurial population, whereas the real reason for the proliferation of small-scale enterprise is the lack of capital for business expansion. To cope with uncertainty, owners seek close ties to the local bureaucracy and conduct transactions informally to avoid opaque regulations, but the failure of mature private enterprise development reinforces a dependence on large government-owned, inefficient operations.

Political leadership is needed to foster the convergence of domestic firms toward international standards of good corporate governance. Leaders who provide incentives for firms to correctly define their assets will increase the size of the market by lowering the cost of capital. When they provide incentives for disclosure and open corporate governance, leaders create economic value for the entire citizenry. Expanding the amount of and access to market information is perhaps the single greatest economic public good a leader can provide. A leader provides this good by ensuring that prices are an effective guide to scarcity in an economy. Economic development is adversely affected if prices lose their informational efficiency and reflect political access rather than market scarcity.

Despite the social benefits of good governance, leaders in many of the world's most impoverished countries do not take action to enhance the informational content of prices. They distort value by providing under-the-table benefits, subsidies, or licenses to favorites so that the costs of doing business are not the same for all players. Once this occurs, private investors have no reason to consult a company's business plan before deciding to invest, and will instead seek information about the proximity of regime leadership to company management. Once access to leadership becomes essential for deal making, it is easy to mistake longevity of leadership with sustained economic performance when, in fact, leadership longevity is the enemy of performance. In many cases, highly autocratic economies become so dependent on the personal well-being of their ruler that the value of assets collapses almost immediately upon rumors about a leader's frailty. Growth rates in the Philippines, for example, collapsed when rumors of President Ferdinand Marcos's poor health began to circulate, as many firm owners owed their good fortune to close ties with the dictator. In fact, the dependence on strong leadership can never compensate for the absence of independent contract enforcement.

DOES FINANCIAL STRUCTURE MATTER?

Leo Tolstoy is known to have remarked that among happy families remarkably little difference exists, but among unhappy families, no two are unhappy for the same reasons. Like Tolstoy's happy families, the financial systems of developed economies such as the United Kingdom, the United States, Japan, or Germany function according to the same principles. Essential functions may be allocated differently among the various institutions, however. For example, in the United Kingdom and Germany, banks sell securities, insurance, and real estate; own nonfinancial firms; and are owned by nonfinancial firms while the United States and Japan have barred their banks from doing so. Differences among well-regulated financial systems also exist in the size of the financial system relative to gross national product (GNP), in the relative importance of commercial bank assets, and in commercial bank assets relative to equity market capitalization. Although a bank in one country may not be the same as a bank in another, well-regulated institutions exist to offer these services in developed financial systems. Regulatory and supervisory infrastructure can be effective regardless of what shape the financial sector takes. Among ineffective financial systems, the reasons for poor performance are numerous, as different possible relationships exist between individual, social, and political risk. A World Bank survey of investment climates around the world found

> enormous variance in the nature and severity of different types of constraints across countries and regions. It points up the limited value of engaging in global generalizations regarding the severity of a particular constraint. It also suggests the importance of unbundling generic clusters of constraints; for example, regulatory or governance constraints always will exhibit different manifestations and components and their severity and effect will vary across countries—even where, on average, the generic constraint is rated similarly across such countries.[11]

One reason for diversity in failure is that financial development is extremely sensitive to initial conditions, and as in meteorological models, small differences in initial conditions produce wide swings in outcomes. How to supplement the paucity of computational data to capture these differences in initial orientation is a basic conundrum in the economic analysis of development. Eventually, with the use of supercomputers, computational models will exist that can compensate for uncertainty and can map complex path dependency.[12] But until such models are available, narrative must fill the gap in our cognitive abilities.

The financial system was once lamentably viewed by policy makers as an appendage of the real economy: a mere channeling device to the real sector with no independent impact on the economy. As noted, this view encouraged leaders to substitute government allocation for the role of the financial system. Since the early 1980s, the emphasis has shifted among policy makers to view government as merely a facilitator of financial market development. This new orientation leads the way for policy makers to identify practical measures for building an efficient financial sector.[13] This new consensus emphasizes the role of a legal framework that includes a court system and a flow of information based on sound accounting and auditing, and sound supervision and regulation.

The costs of investing in the infrastructure of governance, regulation, and transparency for capital markets would be quite low if countries simply adopted international standards. Inexpensive computers, for example, have replaced costly physical infrastructure to run a capital market. However, it is not for lack of knowledge or of funds that many promising economies lack appropriate financial institutions to ensure prudential regulation and supervision. Grossman's "amazing economy of information" is a product of social and political forces as much as an outcome of effective financial institutions. Furthermore, essential differences in the allocational efficiency of various financial systems are a consequence of political action. Yet, an information-rich financial market will eventually enable businesses to survive without dependence on political powers, which is why financial systems and their development are good for people and bad for dictators.

THE FUTURE OF CAPITAL

One of the greatest gaps in global development is the discrepancy in the financial capacity of countries around the world. As noted earlier, high-income countries with less than one-fifth of the world's population account for more than 90 percent of the world's financial assets.[14] Low-income countries with at least one-third of the world's population account for less than 1 percent of global financial assets. These cross-country differences in financial assets as a percentage of GDP contribute significantly to global disparity and instability.[15] Thirty countries with a combined population exceeding 400 million have not received private, long-term, nonguaranteed external credit since 1970.

Financial markets among all the regions covered in this book are bank dominated. Investor confidence in capital markets is undermined by lack of faith in price discovery and settlement mechanisms, and by the belief that the markets are run for insiders by insiders. The opaque nature of financial disclosure supports the perception that companies are managed to benefit a few majority owners. The investor base in emerging markets is not broad enough to sustain strong independent intermediaries that are equipped to evaluate and buy securities on behalf of a broad client base. As a result, the belief that free markets function more effectively than regulated markets has lost favor and has been replaced by an emphasis on institution building. Many policy makers conclude that missing institutional capacity can be supplemented by government action and argue that erecting such a mechanism can be done at a low cost by simply mimicking what works in developed market economies.[16] Yet even after capacity building is attempted, the investor base remains too narrow to sustain a demand for adequate regulation to protect all investors. Domestic reformers seeking to improve stock market regulation and accounting find few necessary allies such as self-regulatory trade groups of trustees, accountants, or lawyers. Without coalitional backing for their effective operation a regulatory framework for the evaluation, mobilization, and allocation of capital—no matter how sophisticated—will not succeed.

In the following chapters, we will explore the social and political reasons for the weaknesses of coalitional support for capital market reforms and try to offer solutions. We will see that the future of domestic capital markets in developing countries will not depend on copying the regulatory structures of successful nations. Institution building is of no avail without broad-based domestic support for independent surveillance and supervision.

PART II

Regional and National Complexity

CHAPTER FIVE

Closing the Social Productivity Gap in East Asia

THE ASIAN FINANCIAL CRISIS of 1997 was a rare historic turning point with ramifications that went far beyond the financial sector. Financial crises are frequent occurrences and common to all economies, though most are quickly forgotten.[1] Some, like those that precipitated the French Revolution or the New Deal, have lasting social and political consequences. The crisis that erupted in Asia was just such an event, speeding up history and consolidating political developments already under way. The crisis also illustrates the difficulty of defining the boundary between capital and collusion, considering the embeddedness and interconnectedness of state, social, and financial institutions.

As a result of the crisis, all affected governments collapsed, with the exception of that of Malaysia.[2] While some collapsed peacefully through elections (Thailand and South Korea); others collapsed after disruption (Indonesia had four leaders in five years, and the Philippines jettisoned a corrupt president in midterm after riots). With the exception of the Philippines, all of the succeeding administrations were more democratic than their predecessors. The wave of democracy occurred in societies in which democratic institutions and practices were embryonic and only weakly capable of promoting and sustaining far-reaching reforms. Only in the Philippines, where the impact of the crisis was weakest, did the pace of democratic reform stay at precrisis levels. The crisis also had geopolitical consequences, shifting the region's center of gravity from Japan to China, which gained credit for avoiding competitive currency devaluation, while Japanese banks withdrew from the region, offering no solace to crisis stricken neighbors. Denied investment from their richest neighbor, the region's economies now turn to China's expanding economy for hope and opportunity (See figure 5.1.) Japan holds $1.2 trillion of the region's $2 trillion of nonperforming loans after a decade of unconvincing efforts toward restructuring.[3] The crisis may also have precipitated a rift between the region and the West, highlighting differences in economic organization that will be discussed in this chapter.

The economic crisis of 1997 initially boosted groups that advocated greater democracy and good governance. However, subsequent elections, especially in Thailand, seem to have reversed this initial tendency. The growing influence of money on politics mars efforts toward democratic consolidation. A symbiotic relationship between business and politicians

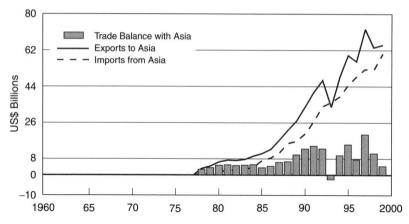

Figure 5.1 China's Growing Trade with East Asia. Source: WEFA; IMF

has allowed the reversal of many necessary procedural reforms that were established since 1997, as well as the forestalling of campaign promises of greater democratic accountability. Candidate and vote buying, corruption of government officials, and fraud are salient features of political campaigns. Although administrative reforms increased local and regional autonomy, financial interests at local levels tightly bind political representatives to the beck and call of local elites. The rise of Thaksin Shinawatra, a fabulously successful businessman in Thailand whose businesses began with government licenses, is the symbol of the new corruption/symbiosis in which wheeler-dealer capitalism takes precedence over patient and purposeful technocratic tinkering. Stability is secured at the price of accommodating local firms with political connections. Rival politicians view Thaksin's landslide electoral victory as the defeat of the spirit of Thailand's most democratic constitution, written four years earlier. Rivals allege that Thailand's biggest media and communication network, founded by Prime Minister Thaksin and controlled by his family, uses the company's profits to enhance the fortunes of his political party. They further assert that the good fortunes of the family's financial holdings since the election dramatize the intimate connections between profit and power. If governmental decisions in favor of companies linked to the prime minister's family give investors incentives to favor shares in companies that are connected to the prime minister, how can citizens be expected to hold public interest above selfish intent? Thailand is not unique. In Asia's new "crony capitalism," the bureaucracy plays less of a guiding role, reducing policy continuity and the predictability of rule enforcement. The era of state-led growth seems to have given way to business interests leading the state.

East Asia's Bad Old Ways

The character of Asia's emerging democratic practices can be traced to the autocratic institutional foundations of the "Asian miracle." During the pre-democratic, high-growth decades, the unifying theme of policy was shared growth, making everyone a winner. East Asia made its great leap forward by closing the social productivity gaps between different social strata. Fearing enemies at the gate, elites throughout East Asia made short-term sacrifices in authority, rents, and privileges in order to improve the living standards of the rural poor and the working class. To ensure national survival, the need for collaboration among different social strata led to inclusive policies that required sacrifice and coordination to produce broad-based benefits. The resulting social cohesion, unique in the developing world, helped motivate East Asian populations to learn, to innovate, and to absorb new ideas. The contrast with other regions will be highlighted in the subsequent chapters.

East Asia's high-growth-stage institutions are characterized by an efficient centralization that gives the head of government effective authority. Convinced that economic failure could lead to national disintegration, the leaders of East Asia's high performers gave technocrats influence over economic policy.[4] Core economic planning units reported directly to the head of state. Unlike centralized communist regimes that considered the existing social system to be expendable, governments in East Asia, relying on family networks, allowed social actors to be the instruments of the society's technological potential. As a result, preexisting social institutions assumed most welfare functions, and family values and family business networks became the basis of economic and social coherence. South Korea's strongman Park Chung Hee captured the essence of this partnership in his slogan "the modernization of the fatherland." No revolutionary social transformation ensued as it did in China—no new system, no overthrow of the existing order, only a healthy upgrading of existing structures and ways.

Instead of uprooting, the region's Confucian Heritage in the style of China's Cultural Revolution, East Asia's leaders took the gentle path of modernization. Initially considered an obstacle to capitalism because of their emphasis on bureaucratic authority and the low status of business, Confucian traditions were modernized to link a loyal bureaucracy with a cooperative business sector; unity was based on continuity of culture. Existing social elites played a key role in expanding societies' technological frontiers.

In contrast to autocratic regimes in which leadership exploited uncertainty to create regimes of domination and exploitation, East Asian leaders used their bargaining power to make effective promises rather than threats. They minimized their own flexibility to strengthen the credibility of their policies.[5] Such East Asian leaders as Chiang Kai-shek (1950–1975), Park Chung Hee (1961–1979), Lee Kuan Yew (1959–1990), and later Mohamad Mahathir (1981–2004) enhanced the credibility of their commitment to shared growth by establishing merit criteria for entrance and recruitment, constraining their own discretion to dismiss and appoint officials at will. Bureaucrats were designated a flow of benefits comparable to the private sector.[6] This reduced incentives for corruption, prompting officials to consider the virtues of impartial career service. In South Korea, export contests supervised by bureaucratic authorities were established for the allocation of investment capital to those firms that could produce letters of credit for export sales. Impartial bureaucratic referees were necessary for the export yardstick to allocate credit effectively.[7]

Another way that leaders minimized flexibility was through the creation of an effective business and government interface to improve collaboration on business-friendly fiscal policies. Business councils constrain under-the-table dealings and ensure that above-the-board channels exist for firms to influence the state. Habits and institutions of collective-interest representation are a legacy of the councils, but strong ties between government and business can easily foster cronyism.[8] It has long been argued that the state can make a significant contribution to economic growth. The commitments East Asian leaders made to establish durable limits on government discretion show how the state can stimulate growth and structural change.

In East Asia, government-sponsored credit schemes for business and industry were balanced by improved access to jobs, housing, health care, and education for ordinary workers and citizens. Unfortunately, many firms that had been sheltered for decades with political access and subsidized credit became hothouse flowers, feeble and uncompetitive. Continuing to support these firms involved unappetizing choices and high social costs, but ignoring the deterioration of established and prestigious firms was not an easy choice, either. International efforts to impose financial discipline by exposing distressed international assets to takeover by foreign capital have fueled a regional nationalist backlash against multilateral institutions. This backlash has launched a regional dialogue to explore prospects for greater regional cooperation and integration.

Many of Asia's institutional weaknesses stemmed from the same sources as its strengths. To jump-start the economy, governments placed emphasis on developing bureaucratic and executive capacity rather than on creating legal and judicial structures. None of the key players—politicians, bureaucrats, or big business—favored diverting time or energy to endow a source of authority that could contravene state development goals. Foreign trading partners or investors did not regret the absence of an independent judicial forum because they counted on business-savvy heads of government to get them licenses and agreements and to resolve disputes promptly. A call from an embassy to the executive branch of government was usually all it took to remedy the disputes. These policies worked so long as leaders depended on economic success to legitimize why they and not someone else should lead. That someone else—the communist party, with its ambitions for total societal overhaul—was always in view as a potential alternative to a government that failed to deliver. The insurrection threat weakened with China's transition to an economic competitor. In parallel with China's new orientation, domestic political challengers within East Asian states evolved from revolutionary contenders into electoral ones.

Once the age of the dictators that began in the sixties ended, first in the Philippines in 1985 and later in South Korea and Taiwan, the weaknesses in legal and judicial structures began to reveal themselves. Many firms, both domestic and foreign, have reported more difficulties doing business as the dictators' bureaucratic methods of contract enforcement deteriorate, and legislative bodies resist strengthening rival power brokers. Legislators characteristically prefer a bureaucracy that is ineffective so that more opportunities to intervene on behalf of special clients will exist. As a result of the transition to democracy, patronage is gaining a foothold over bureaucratic efficiency.

Underdeveloped Financial Systems

Underdeveloped financial markets are another consequence of the state-centered high-growth strategies of the seventies. On the upside, many non-traditional small savers were given access to the formal banking system through the development of a postal savings system in the Northeast, and access to agricultural banks, especially in Thailand. Nevertheless, savers faced a limited choice of placement for their savings, since the government dominated credit allocation. A weak marketplace for financial services, equities, and bonds[9] diminished outside oversight of company management.[10]

Banks were the primary conduits of funds to new industries. Powerful banks have many advantages in the early phases of growth.[11] They have the potential to induce firms to reveal information and pay back debts. Firms requiring staged financing often depend on banks to provide additional funding as project needs emerge. Market-based sources (stocks or bonds) are less capable at sustaining long-range commitments during the early stages of development. Financial intermediaries, such as venture capitalist or investment banks, do not usually exist to fill the void between entrepreneurs and savers, and venture funding cannot gain a foothold without an elaborate set of preexisting financial institutions.

Depending on banks has a downside. The consequences of the Asian crisis (1997–98) were aggravated because financial assets were concentrated in a few inefficient banks.[12] Banks can resist disclosing information and collude with their clients to interfere with competition. They can extract information rents from firms and reduce incentives to undertake profitable projects. Capital market alternatives to bank financing could have better protected East Asian companies from the impact of the crisis. Market-based financial systems can foster competition and create incentives for firms to invest in research.[13] But the system of financial intermediation that had emerged in East Asia lacked one of the most notable underlying characteristics of capital markets: information transparency.

The financial systems that supported state-directed investment strategies presented an additional impediment to financial development. When governments undertake the credit risk, banks need not worry about quality of their portfolios and need not perform adequate due diligence to assess the quality of the balance sheet.[14] Companies have access to credit according to their size and power, rather than their cost and efficiency.

Closed systems of production, another legacy of the high-growth period, contributed to poor business decisions. In the United States, people trade with companies they find in the phone book. East Asian firms choose partners with which they have prior relationships. To protect against opportunism, companies buy from and sell to companies with which they are integrated within a network (i.e., *keiretsu* in Japan, *chaebol* in South Korea). They often engage in cross-shareholding (owning shares of each other's companies). Earlier in this book it was argued that closed networks were designed to protect firms from extractive states. What made East Asia's high performers different is that bureaucratic guidance transformed these closed networks into agents of national modernization that led the process of growth.

A society capable of supporting sophisticated arm's-length trade will also be able to support sophisticated hierarchical firms, but as market economies develop they frequently depend on intermediate bodies to supplement weak arm's-length markets. The Japanese *keiretsus*, and the South Korean *chaebols*, and the government-chartered trading companies of early-modern Europe are all examples of such intermediary bodies that coordinate exchange in the absence of a fully developed and independent legal system. Business groups provide access to capital and information to supplement underdeveloped markets.[15] They can help stem problems that arise from imperfect intermediary goods markets, and the unrelated diversification of business groups is an alternative to portfolio diversification. Although business groups supplant poorly performing economic institutions, they pose a dilemma to subsequent development in that the boundaries between firms and those separating firms from the state are unclear.

At the outbreak of the 1997 crisis, East Asian economies had many features that sharply distinguished local business practices from the norms among the Western economies that were funneling money into East

TABLE 5.1
Transparent vs. Opaque Markets

Transparency	Opacity
Arm's-length contracts	Relational contracts
Competitive sourcing	Bilateral monopolies
Supplier switching	Dedicated suppliers
Litigation remedies	Self-help remedies
Liquid claims	Illiquid claims
Hierarchical firms	Nested firms—inside contracting
Clear firm boundaries	Business groups—*keiretsus, chaebols*
Contingent contracts	"Lump-sum" contracts
General licensing	Specific licensing
Standardized accounting	Idiosyncratic accounting
Labor mobility	Dedicated labor

Table courtesy Greg Lablanc.

Asia. In East Asia, relational contracts prevail over arm's-length contracts, and bilateral monopolies are more common than competitive sourcing. Instead of supplier switching, dedicated suppliers to one buyer are commonplace, private remedies substitute for litigation. Business groups lack clear firm boundaries. Licensing tends to be specific rather than general. Accounting is idiosyncratic rather than standardized. Instead of having mobility, labor is dedicated to a specific employer. In fact, exchange systems in East Asia are opaque, and claims to the ownership of economic resources were highly illiquid.

Due to weak financial infrastructure, financial decisions in East Asia suffer poor quality of information. This can be attributed to the region's preference for administrative governance over law-based governance. As a result, the region's financial markets rely on related-party transactions that are subjected to a less rigorous assessment than that applied to arm's-length transactions. Off-balance-sheet financing is rampant. Excessively leveraged large firms survive at the expense of smaller, more innovative enterprises.[16] Stronger legal and judicial foundations are needed if corporate ownership is to become more public. The contrast between transparent and opaque systems is illustrated in table 5.1.

The characteristics on the two sides of the chart rarely are interchangeable, making a transition from one set of structural features to the other very difficult.[17]

The high-growth formula became the target of a sharp Western critique virtually immediately. East Asian economies went from being the darlings of the international investment community to being instant pariahs. The transition from "miracle" status to catastrophe in less than a decade was abrupt and painful for several Asian nations. The rapid shift in perception suggests that Westerners had only a dim understanding of the countries

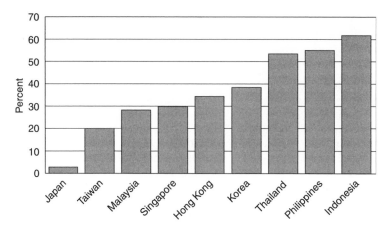

Figure 5.2 Rational Sins: Ownership Concentration—Top 15 Families

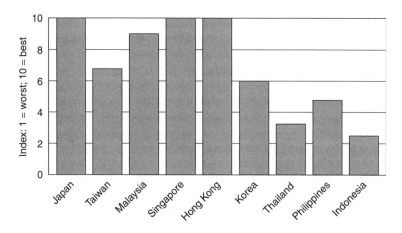

Figure 5.3 Rational Sins: Legal Framework—Efficiency of the Judicial System

they invested in. Global companies driven by the fear of being left out were willing to sacrifice profit for growth just to establish operations in East Asia. Many global companies established branches, affiliations, or plants and equipment just to be sure they got there before their rivals did. In the financial sector, traders with little experience in the region undertook much of the portfolio trading, resulting in catastrophic overinvestment.

Overnight, East Asia, the world's leading emerging market, developed a high-risk investment climate. Foreign investors discovered invisible barriers to entry in the customs and practices of closed production systems. They suddenly began protesting discrimination through expropriation,

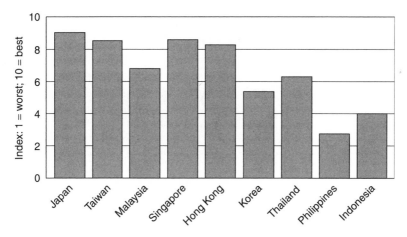

Figure 5.4 Rational Sins: Legal Framework—Rule of Law

discrimination by extraordinary taxation, and unequal access to justice, whereas earlier they were content just to gain access to the local market. Unlimited opportunity suddenly was transformed into rampant corruption. But the lack of transparency and accountability in government and corporate operations was nothing new in the region. Therein was the paradox: *if the old ways were all that bad, why did they work so well for so long?*[18]

Figures 5.2 through 5.5 reveal how well East Asian corporate structures are adapted to their actual environment. High levels of family ownership correlate to low-quality public sectors: the concentration of ownership strongly correlates with a weak rule of law and a high level of corruption. These strong correlations indicate that the concentration of wealth in Thailand, Indonesia and the Philippines results in high levels of information imperfections that produce informal personalized networks that, in turn, thwart the development of arm's-length markets.[19]

The corporate history of the United States provides a useful comparison. Family businesses dominated U.S. business development into the late nineteenth century, yet in the United States today, almost all large companies are publicly owned. According to Berle and Means "in 1929 only 88 of the 200 largest corporations were classed as management controlled, by 1963 169, or 84.5 per cent, were so classed. And in 1929, 22 corporations were classed as privately owned or controlled by the owners through majority ownership, while only 5 were so classed in 1963."[20] The dispersion of stock ownership and the separation of ownership and control made possible by the development of capital markets was essential to the transition of family firms into publicly owned firms.[21] Berle and Means concluded:

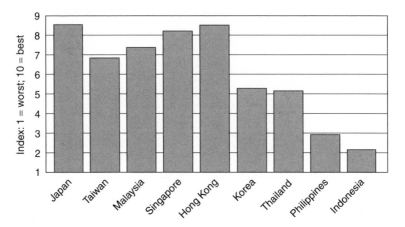

Figure 5.5 Rational Sins: Legal Framework—Corruption

The Fords and the Mellons, whose personal wealth is sufficient to finance great enterprises, are so few, that they only emphasize the dependence of large enterprises on the wealth of more than the individual or group of individuals who may be in control. The quasi-public corporation commands its supply of capital from a group of investors frequently described as the "investing public." To secure these funds it must commonly avail itself of an open market in its securities—usually by listing shares on a stock exchange, or, less importantly, by maintaining a private or "unlisted" market. So essential, in fact, is the open market to the quasi-public corporation that it may be considered almost as characteristic of that type of corporation as the separation of ownership from control and the great aggregation of wealth.[22]

Private capital markets allow publicly owned (shareholder-owned) firms to grow faster than family-owned firms, but when primary capital markets are less developed, family businesses are bigger, they last longer, and attract less investment than firms in economies with more-developed capital markets.

When their journey to industrialization began, significant differences existed between the social and economic institutions of East Asia's high performers and those of the pioneer developed countries. To jump-start their economies, Asian governments used the power of the state to bolster the family economy. By supplementing family access to credit with government access, family firms increased to great prominence. Modeled after the Japanese/German bank-based example, the jump-starters grew large companies but missed a key development stage, in which professionally managed firms gain financing through arm's-length, impersonal transactions outside the family.[23] Another consequence of privileged political access was high concentration of corporate ownership, which facilitated lobbying of the government.

The corporate revolution that resulted in the separation of control and ownership in the U.S. economy was not matched by a similar development in the East Asian economy because legal foundations and legal recourse against the original owners is weak. Legal machinery in East Asia is not sufficiently developed to prevent abuses stemming from the concentration of corporate ownership. As a result, abusive practices that were rife in the early U.S. corporate history persist in East Asia. Small groups of owners line their own pockets by profiting at the company's expense rather than by making profits shared by diffuse owners. A similar trend toward concentration in the United States was broken during the New Deal. In the U.S. economy today, individual wealth generally consists of shares in enterprises in which no individual owns a controlling fraction: the larger the company in the United States, the more its ownership is likely to be diffuse. Why has the dispersion of ownership, a continuing process in the United States, only barely begun in East Asia?

East Asians favor an extensive role for the state in the economy to ensure that pressure can be applied on firms to respect broader social concerns. To protect the wider interest of society and to counterbalance the concentrated influence of a few enterprise owners in each sector, citizens of East Asia want the state to directly oversee and direct company management. However, the financial crisis of 1997–98 has compromised the states' ability to supervise the private marketplace. The bureaucratic apparatus that was useful before the crisis to curb abuse is vulnerable to capture by a small group of families who now own most of their countries' production assets.

After the crisis, the downside of the Asian approach became painfully apparent. The concentration of ownership among a small number of families impeded the postcrisis rebound. Companies stayed in business by issuing bonds backed by short-term cash flow to finance current expenditures, but have found it difficult to raise funds privately for long-term capital expenditures. Weak capital markets and the dependence on banks for financing inhibit restructuring. Distressed assets are hard to sell, and buyers are difficult to find. Potential buyers underprice the value of the assets because much of the value to the local owners derives from family or political connections to state banks—and this cannot be transferred to third parties.

Indonesia had the most difficulty recovering after the crisis, whereas South Korea's greater institutional capacity made its recovery easier. Let us compare Northeast and Southeast Asia to see why.

Northeast Asia and Southeast Asia Compared

Vertically integrated conglomerates with relatively explicit property rights dominate the corporate ownership structure in Northeast Asia. In South Korea and Japan, for example, corporate shareholders, banks, or nonbanks can hold controlling stakes in a company.[24] It is common for one company to hold a controlling share of another company that in turn owns a controlling share of the first company. Thus, two conflicting impacts on firm valuation result. Such an arrangement intensifies supervision of management, forcing management to take notice of other firms in the group. However, cross-monitoring also enables collusion between firms and protects them from the market for corporate control.

There is a buffer of depositor protection in Northeast Asia that does not exist in Southeast Asia, because the governments control the banks in Northeast Asia. In Southeast Asia, private banks tend to control the central banks. In Southeast Asia, a small number of prominent and connected families own firms through social networks that make the property and ownership structure murky.[25] The telecommunication sector in the Philippines necessitates using a genealogist rather than an auditor to uncover inter- and intrafirm activities. Another important difference in supplier-distributor relationships exist between the Northeast, where suppliers and distributors are often incorporated in conglomerates, and the Southeast, where they follow more informal channels comprising loosely connected families with few registered or legally identifiable ties.

Much of the difference between Northeast and Southeast Asia in their recovery from the financial crisis reflects regional differences in capital base and financing sources. In the Northeast, banks are incorporated in conglomerates (Japan) or are government-backed (South Korea), but in Southeast Asia, financial institutions are typically related to the families that own the companies.[26] Privately owned banks must be constrained from using deposits to invest in ventures from which the bank's owners privately benefit. Close ties between banks and companies foster bad business decisions, as bankers invest in projects in which they own shares or derive profit and disregard projects that offer the highest returns to shareholders. Furthermore, a bank owner that is also a firm owner is likely to invest in his or her company instead of in one with the best business plan. Savers will also lack appropriate services, because a family banker has no incentive to find the best return on capital. Relationship-based loans have a lower rate of repayment than arm's-length transactions because financial institutions will only reluctantly enforce sanctions on related companies that do not perform.

The banking sector can contribute to growth by monitoring management if banks have proper incentives. But before the crisis in South

Korea, the incentive for monitoring was very weak. Intermediaries did not develop the necessary skills in credit analysis, believing that the government insured the financing requirements of the conglomerates and implicitly underwrote their risks. Since the banks did not choose projects or make decisions about which firms should expand, very little monitoring occurred. Lacking an incentive to independently assess the plans they were financing, banks did not acquire the skills necessary for effective loan assessment.[27]

One other perversity in ownership structures was exposed to scrutiny as a result of the crisis. In South Korea, Japan, Indonesia, and Thailand, control of a conglomerate can be achieved with substantially less than a majority ownership of shares.[28] Even with a small ownership stake, a small group of owners can acquire control rights to a firm's cash flow and can extract benefits from the firm that reduce the firm's value at the expense of other shareholders. The *chaebols* are family-owned companies that maintained contractual relations with shareholders who rarely receive the same bundle of rights as family owners. Frequently, shareholders exercise virtually no control over the wealth they contribute. Much of the South Korean financial crisis can be attributed to distortions in decision making that flowed directly from such opportunities of profiting at the expense of the corporation.[29] The interests of the family networks that control the *chaebols* via elaborate cross shareholding mechanisms can be counter to the interests of the other shareholders and counter to the interests of the public.[30]

The financial crisis of 1997 revealed how conglomerate organizations can prevent the efficient measurement of unit productivity. Conglomerates can hide inefficient units from shareholder view because the measurement of the separate inputs to total output is sometimes unclear, and resources within a conglomerate can be distributed without correlation to productivity. Although the *chaebols* behaved this way to protect themselves from outside scrutiny, management could not make the best decisions with regard to resource allocation within the firm. Profit-making operations were used to attract funds that were in turn diverted into loss-making sectors, making it difficult to establish share prices.[31] In the United States, many vertically integrated firms faced this same measurement quandary and responded by spinning off units or contracting out activities that once were performed within the firm.

Conglomerate structures allow dominant players to expropriate rents from junior partners by prohibiting junior suppliers from seeking more profitable outlets, such as doing business with large competitor firms.[32] The dedicated supplier, in response, may underinvest in opportunities not supported within the network, knowing they will be unable to find funding for a new project that is not favored by the dominant group. Small firms cannot improve their future by establishing a relationship with firms outside of their group. For example, when General Motors decided to build cars in Thailand, it had difficulty accessing supply networks that already serviced their Japanese competitors.[33] This loss of opportunities by small enterprises during good times may be the price of survival in hard times.[34]

Government/business relationships vary from Northeast (Japan, South Korea, and Taiwan) to Southeast Asia (Thailand, Indonesia, the Philippines). Malaysia falls in between, and Singapore can be added to the Northeast model. In the Northeast, the governments play a planning and supervisory role in order to reduce the transaction costs of coordinating information flows between firms and across sectors. The Southeast fits the definition of cronyism, whereby government officials draw profits from private-sector activities they supervise. The private and public interests of officials are never distinct, and good governance over private-sector firms is difficult to achieve. The lack of distinction between the private and public roles of the bureaucracy distorts the market and adds political risk to ordinary business risks. Southeast Asia has had a more sluggish recovery because institutions there do not protect public interests but are geared to protect the private interests of regime insiders and those that have market power.

Economic reform and corporate restructuring in Indonesia, the Philippines, and Thailand require broad social changes because of the salience of personal relationships in business, where communal rather than legal sanctions apply for misconduct. By contrast, in North East Asia, particularly in South Korea and in Japan, where well-defined and enforceable property rights exist, more-effective corporations will emerge if obstacles to minority shareholder accountability are removed. If the region succeeds in lowering barriers to transparency and increases the accountability of corporate control, explicitly owned assets can be more easily conferred to outside investors. This will entice greater investment and risk-taking and help disperse the concentrated ownership of the nation's wealth-producing assets. For these reasons, investors bet more willingly on South Korea's recovery than on Indonesia's.[35]

Precrisis institutional differences also explain why the IMF programs and related structural-adjustment loans and programs extended to South Korea, Thailand, and Indonesia differed significantly in their concentration on corporate governance.[36] The emphasis was strongest in South Korea, where the IMF provided significant financial support for corporate governance reforms as part of the government's responses to the crisis. Corporate governance reform was viewed as a mechanism to enable market forces to redefine Korea's industrial structure. In Indonesia, by contrast, the first and second letters of intent[37] only briefly referenced corporate governance, and those reforms played a modest role in the overall Indonesia reform program, whereas concerns over corporate debt restructuring and state enterprise reform were paramount. Barry Metzger argued that these differences in emphasis arise from a concern with "the institutional frailties of many government agencies with principal responsibility for implementing the program, and corruption affecting those agencies." The IMF did not believe that corporate governance reform could play a central role in remedying the structural weaknesses that had contributed to the Indonesia crisis because "[c]orruption and 'crony capitalism' were much more deeply entrenched and intertwined in Indonesia."[38] As a result, the essence of the program in Indonesia was about public governance reform. The initial letters of intent for Thailand are similarly silent on the subject of corporate reform. In Thailand, the focus is on financial-sector restructuring, the rehabilitation of banking, other financial institutions, and the privatization of state enterprises.

CREATING A COALITION FOR ECONOMIC REFORM IN INDONESIA

Underestimating the effects of poor institutions on competition, many economists believed that the liberalization of an economy would disadvantage firms with strong explicit ties to the ruling party. In the late 1980s and early 1990s, Indonesia allowed foreign ownership of stocks, reduced tariffs and import surcharges, deregulated banking, and privatized several state owned companies (i.e., Indosat). Bureaucratic obstacles to investment, such as the number of permits required to start a business, were reduced. The liberalization did not cause firms with ties to Suharto to lose their comparative advantage.[39] The powerful families did not suffer relative to independent firms; instead, connected firms obtained more analyst coverage and were considered to be better partners, and international capital migrated to connected firms.

In a society in which family comes first, the First Family comes before all others. Under Suharto, members of the First Family used their position to dominate contracts with foreign firms seeking to invest in Indonesia. Their place on the board of directors of both foreign invested and domestic companies provided assurances within an insecure legal environment against capricious treatment by low-level bureaucrats. Investors believed that contracts, concessions, and investment approvals would be easier to obtain by involving the First Family members. Large international investors, such as Japan's NEC and Sumitomo; America's Hughes Aircraft, Ford, and Union Carbide; France's Alcatel; Germany's Deutsche Telekom; and Switzerland's Nestlé, all formed partnerships with the president's relatives.[40]

Indonesia's First Family helped investors reduce the costs of gathering information. The Suhartos' involvement augmented investors' confidence because the latter could expect that the family had information about the economy or about forthcoming political decisions that competitors lacked. It also reduced information and transaction costs, and provided assurances against expropriation and bureaucratic caprice, thus creating value and a sense of protection that further boosted investor confidence in Indonesia.[41] The legacy of resentment left by Suharto's cronyism continues to be an obstacle to further liberalization of the economy.[42]

Indonesia's weak institutions strengthened firms that were related to the president, creating a backlash against further liberalization both among the smaller, privately owned firms and among the populace. This resentment has nurtured a mistrust of foreign capital and foreign ownership. Lingering mistrust made it politically difficult for Abdurrahman Wahid and his successor Megawati Sukarnoputri to gain coalition support for increased market liberalization.[43] Those most sympathetic to greater foreign engagement in the economy tended to be member of Suharto's former party, Golkar, and were not part of Megawati's governing coalition. President Megawati's first priority was to hold Indonesia together, she was partial to those groups that opposed openness and detached from groups that advocated a liberal economy for fear it would escalate social tensions.[44] During the electoral campaign of 2004 all the leading candidates emphasized nationalism and aloofness from transnational capital.

PROGNOSIS FOR THE FUTURE: RESISTANCE TO CHANGE

Throughout Asia, the grip of money on politics prevents the clean up of the political order. Costly political campaigns makes candidates dependent on the wealthy few for help to get elected, in exchange for favors. Consider the dilemma and misfortune of the Philippine president Joseph Estrada in 2000. He campaigned on a promise to provide his poor supporters with shares in the nation's wealth producing assets, but he depended on the owners of those assets for the money with which to buy the votes of the poor. It is easy to blame his fate, impeachment, criminal prosecution, and disgrace on his lack of morality, but it is plausible to argue that Estrada, caught in a system that divides society into those who can outsmart the system and those who cannot, could find no legal way to help the poor who championed his political career.[45] The failure of his successor, Macapagal Arroyo, to implement meaningful reform suggests that the Philippine political crisis goes beyond the need to replace the person at the top.

Despite the allegations of misdeeds, Estrada pointed to polls that showed 44 percent of the poor population in disagreement with the calls for his resignation. Allegations of corruption against Estrada had a limited effect on his core constituency because they lived in a world where the difference between legal and illegal behavior is difficult to define. The poor doubted that the "soft coup" staged to replace Estrada would remedy the source of their misery. In the Philippines, Southeast Asia's most unequal society, discrepancies in wealth are rarely due to a difference in ability but rather to a disparity in rights. Few Filipinos are optimistic that even good economic policies can close this gap.

Throughout East Asia, expensive political campaigns distort the policy goals of government. In Thailand, where vote buying is prevalent, the costs of political campaigns are reportedly four to five times higher (relative to average incomes) than those in the United States.[46] In Asia, especially Southeast Asia, the advent of "democracy" in a society cemented by patron client ties involves the exchange of gifts for votes.[47] Thus, traditional patronage politics is more costly than United States-style television campaigning.[48]

CREATING AN ELECTORAL MACHINE IN THAILAND

After Thailand's blatantly corrupt 1995 and 1996 elections, voter vociferously demanded political reforms to curb electoral abuse. These demands crystallized in a number of muscular reforms that included an election commission, an independent National Counter Corruption Commission (NCCC), a Constitutional Court, an Administrative Court, a National Human Rights Commission, term limits on legislators, restrictions on party switching, and a directly elected senate. Nevertheless, the national election of January 2001 that followed the reforms produced an electoral majority for a politician who flaunted his contempt for the new institutions. The winner of the election, Thaksin Shinawatra and his Thai Rak Thai (Thais Love Thais) Party, was alleged to have misrepresented his income on his income tax returns, flaunting his disregard for the newly founded NCCC.

Candidate Thaksin made party switching a lucrative business, offering legislators that could command a strong network of local canvassers transfer fees along with a supplementary salary for switching to his group. Leaders that could swing whole factions from one party to another might receive the most profitable concession of all, a prime cabinet post.[49]

To win an absolute majority when no party had even reached one-third in any election year since 1979, required mass appeal. Thaksin promised the rural masses one million baht in microcredit development funds, a debt moratorium for farmers, and a public health-care scheme that treats all ailments for a token thirty baht. Previous politicians appealed to mass voters by promising roads, schools, hospitals, or airports to local constituents. Thaksin's approach ensured votes along party lines rather than local lines. He implemented all of the major elements of his electoral platform in one year. However, Thaksin's critics point out that he is redistributing enough to the poor to secure social peace, but not enough in education, the environment, and technology for tomorrow's new opportunities. Nor has Thaksin applied his mandate to necessary reforms of the civil service, police, military, health, and local administrations.

Thailand's strategy for cleaning up its postcrisis debts through a policy of helping debtors stay in the game exemplifies the government's opportunistic approach to economic policy reform. In order to make politically directed loans to regime supporters, Thaksin ensured the new and independent watchdog agencies had little room for maneuvering. Although the goal is pro-Thai, firms are encouraged to restructure rather than sell off assets to foreigners at bargain prices; friends of the regime benefit at taxpayer expense.

Yet, it is simplistic to refer to the rise of Thaksin as the resurrection of crony capitalism. By shifting the source of patronage, Thaksin reinvented local politics, weakening the basis of old-style provincial elections. Substituting personal bonds of local clientage with a direct universalistic relationship with the central state, he offers the rural masses policy outcomes and assets that directly improve their lot. These enticements induced local elections across Thailand to run on party lines for the first time. Inflated construction profits that once ended up as bureaucratic graft were reduced as money politics became big-money politics so that local players can no longer play.

During the years when Thais could expect a coup every two years, the bureaucracy was one continuity in government. Weakening the bureaucracy makes it easier for political victors to secure personal deals, but it compromises the legitimacy of institutions, since the legislature, like its counterparts throughout Asia, has few means to scrutinize or challenge deals that are promoted by the executive.[50]

Will Thaksin's combination of nationalism and populism set the trend for winning elections in Southeast Asia? If his formula for electoral success becomes an example, then the regional economy will face new risks, the greatest of which is that populist promises will fail and voters will be left disillusioned with democracy. Thaksin's supporters argue that where corruption is concerned, the difference between Thaksin and the Democrats he defeated in 2001 is only cosmetic. While espousing accountability, they were in practice rent seekers and vote buyers, no different than their precrisis predecessors: Thaksin is more direct; he does not preach what he does not practice.

All observers agree that Thailand for the moment has found a path to stability while its larger neighbors in Southeast Asia have all lost their footing.

THE DRIVERS OF CHANGE

The problems of Thailand and the Philippines are emblematic of changes that are taking place throughout the region, where governments that once enjoyed unchallenged authority have become hostages to corporate elites. It is a conundrum of democracy in the developing world: aspiring leaders cannot get elected if they pledge to reform economic policies that benefit elites that hold the purse strings.

The erosion of the states' power makes it difficult to gain support for economic policies that benefit the whole society. Even with Western lectures on the evils of state-led development ringing in their ears, many East Asians have mixed feelings about having central bureaucracies hand over power to the corporate sector. The problem is not bureaucracies with too much power but legal regimes that are too weak. Many East Asian countries lack the smooth-functioning legal systems usually associated with high-growth economies, and they have instead relied on able bureaucrats to fill the gap. With bureaucracies losing power, and legal systems still weak, good governance suffers. Public authorities find it hard to enforce contracts, and investment flows are diminished. In Suharto-era Indonesia, for instance, investors knew that the strongman and his Chinese cronies—if properly cultivated—would safeguard investments and enforce contracts.[51] That personalized mechanism vanished from the scene along with Suharto, and no one really believes that Indonesia's attenuated legal system can adequately uphold the integrity of contracts as effectively.

In thinking about economic reform, the region's policy makers must first restrain powerful firms and individuals from buying politicians and bureaucrats. In 1961, General Park Chung Hee, the South Korean coup leader began his tenure by throwing wealthy conglomerate owners in jail. The leaders of the same firms openly resisted the democratically elected President Kim Dae Jung's efforts to promote corporate restructuring and put an end to "crony capitalism."[52]

The hard truth is that authoritarianism in East Asia, whatever its sins, did foster well-developed organs of public administration.[53] East Asia's democratic governments face a large task of institution building before they can hope to implement national development policies with the effectiveness that once flowed from the top-down models of the past.[54] Democratic governments must find lawful, peaceful ways to stop wealthy minorities from distorting public policy to serve their own ends. Civil society, regrettably, still suffers from an authoritarian hangover (social mobilization always required government approval), and so in this crucial struggle its effectiveness is limited. Civil society groups tend to be too thin on the ground, too poorly organized, and too weakly represented to ensure that public institutions are used to uphold public interests rather than to maintain the power of ruling coalitions. In most of Asia, the middle class is too small and too financially weak to demand accountable governance or to establish a political ethos based on public performance and civic virtue.

The absence of a strong civil society to counterbalance the power of the wealthy is also a big reason why democratically elected regimes in East Asia are failing to deliver equity to their citizens or to implement effective reform programs. Economic power is concentrated in firms with a history of political connections—a condition that lends itself to corruption. Corporate owners and officials, anxious for continued special treatment, can and do tempt judges, politicians, civil servants, and other agents of the state with huge bribes. The wealth that these corporate interests dispose of is itself the result of previous government interventions in their favor. The current holders of this wealth know that paying for more such interventions is their key to continued fortune. The result is popular frustration, resentment, and, ultimately, political instability, locking many Asian societies into a struggle for elite survival in a battle between "old regime," precrisis wealth and new democracy.[55]

The drivers of change include increased international exposure and greater access to international media. The region is plugged into international coverage of events that take place around the globe and the outside world is an observer of events that occur within East Asia. Compare the limited coverage by the international media of Indonesians who died in the struggle that brought Golkar to power in 1965 with the benign, relatively bloodless turmoil that led to Suharto's departure in 1998, which received extensive worldwide coverage. In the Philippines, assassinations ordered by Malacanang Palace allowed Ferdinand Marcos to impose and maintain martial law with little international comment. Today, riots in Indonesia or the sacking of a finance minister in Malaysia is international news that draws the attention and rebuke from the heads of friendly governments who never uttered a word publicly about the more heinous political assassinations linked with Marcos.

Another driver of change is growing importance of foreign direct investment, which has increased relative to the passive portfolio investment characteristic of the precrisis period. Direct investors have a stake in domestic policy outcomes and are involved in their formulation. English is the business language of Asia, not Chinese or Japanese, and its spread offers access to a global culture of accountability. Asia is vigorously thrusting itself into the information age. Twenty percent of the people who use the Internet regularly are in the Asia-Pacific region, compared with 26 percent in Europe, despite its much higher income. China is on the way to becoming the largest telecommunications market in the world. Capital markets are imposing discipline and accountability on firm management. Civil society is gaining experience and organization, and the middle class is growing. All of these changes make going back to the past impossible.

Ending Labor's Privileged Status

The absence of a social safety net for dependent labor is a source of tension in the region and a cause of a basic difference between East Asian and Western views on the relationship of the state and the private economy. East Asians embrace personal norms of conduct based on competition but reject limitations on the state's role over the private economy. They accept the behavior associated with competition but do not seek to emulate the norms that are characteristic of Western industrial enterprises. The origin of this discrepancy lies in the different social contract between labor, management, and government that has evolved in East Asia.

The original contract can be viewed as an understanding between labor, management, and state that the burden of labor risk would be internalized by enterprises that received government support to avoid provocations of labor unrest. The state, in effect, protects jobs by restricting layoffs, which shifts the burden of social support and the risks of wage dependency to the enterprise sector. Labor markets, as a result, suffer from rigidity.

Today East Asian economies, Japan included, no longer enjoy a consensus about the relationship of the state to the private economy. Yet East Asians are ambivalent about the need for public protection of dependent workers because they are reluctant for both fiscal and cultural reasons to substitute the state for the role of the family. And pressures to repeal existing labor protection are mounting because after the financial crises of 1997, firms are less willing and are less well equipped to absorb social risks in order to preserve the social order. However, governments are reluctant to relax those laws because they feel unable to provide social protection out of public resources. An expansion of the state's social role would require additional sources of revenue that would increase government expenditures as a percentage of GDP, with obvious consequences for the region's global competitiveness.

The East Asian crisis has often been compared in its economic impact to the Great Depression in the United States. But seven years after the Great Depression, the relationship between the individual and govern-

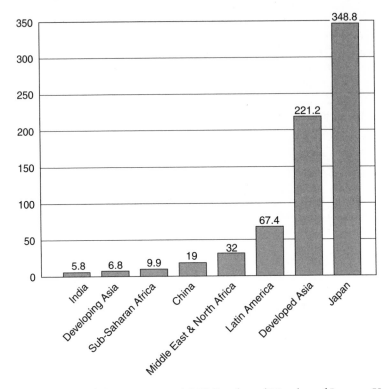

Figure 5.6 Personal Computers per 1,000 People and Number of Internet Users (number of computers 0–350). Source: WB

ment was unalterably transformed, as some responsibility for market risk was transferred from the individual to the state. A similar transformation has not taken place in East Asia. In the industrial sector, companies with state support absorb most of the risk for economic downturns, passing that risk on to taxpayers and consumers in the form of higher prices for manufactured goods. A shift in the locus of responsibility for dependent workers would have a significant political influence on the structure of the state. It would alter the relationship between government and people, turning citizens into taxpayers instead of wards of an enterprise state that muffles the voice of individual citizens. This is a change whose time has not yet come.

PUBLIC RISK MANAGEMENT IN EAST ASIA

One of the key sources of East Asia's success lies in the efforts of political leaders to mitigate the sources of economic, social, and political uncer-

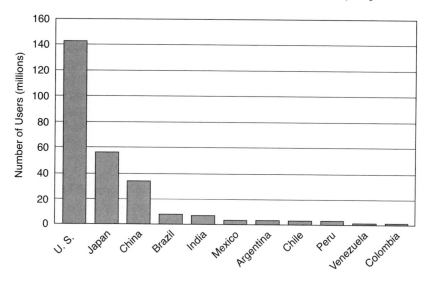

Figure 5.7 Number of Internet Users. Source: WB

tainty in economic development. The state's success in mitigating these uncertainties is why East Asia has been the most promising developing region, with strength in the sectors of the world economy with the greatest yield curves and the potential to attract high-quality investments.[56] A commitment to closing the social productivity gap sharply distinguishes East Asia from Latin America, South Asia, the Middle East and Africa. (See figures 5.6 and 5.7.)

In India and in much of Latin America, corrupt bureaucrats have not updated the land titles of rural households for generations. Without proper titles to their land, farmers are denied access to electricity, bank loans, and government welfare subsidies; rural property rights and market access for small landholders was a government priority in East Asia.

The fiscal, monetary, and trade policies of East Asia's high performers provided strong encouragement of sound market conditions that allowed for the calculation of economic profit. Unstable macroeconomic policies were avoided in East Asia through rural development policies that compensated for indirect taxation on agriculture (overvalued exchange rates and tariff protection of nonagricultural goods) with investments in rural infrastructure.[57] Rural investment is essential to equity because it reduces the disparity between urban and rural sectors. Rural people will often migrate to the cities for employment, worsening the unemployment situation. Building rural infrastructure, including schools, roads, and health facilities, prevents massive migration to cities, which are often unequipped to handle massive inflows of people.

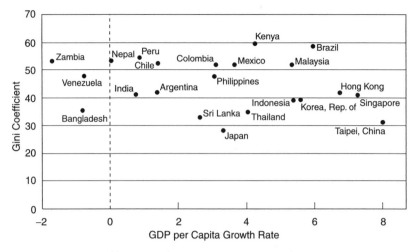

Figure 5.8 Gini Coefficients and GDP per Capita Growth Rate (1971–80)

East Asian leaders based their commitment to growth on broad social foundations to mitigate social risk. They championed policies that offered broad benefits to the rural population, such as the land reforms made possible through the recognition of de facto land ownership in Japan, South Korea, and Taiwan.[58] In Hong Kong and Singapore, public housing became the urban surrogate for land reform. East Asian countries spent more on primary health, did better on immunization, invested more in primary education and had the best primary-school completion rates of all developing regions. They especially encouraged female literacy. Although they were still low-income countries, both South Korea and Taiwan did more to support primary-education completion than did any other country at their income levels. They led the region—and the region led the developing world—in levels of public spending on primary education. Similarly, East Asia did more to provide quality public health and reduce child mortality, as illustrated by a superior record in child immunization and high levels of spending on public health. East Asia's high performers also improved access to sanitation and potable water. These efforts reduced income disparities and the resulting demands for redistribution through consumption subsidies. The figures on income inequality and growth show that the countries that have both high growth and low income inequalities are clustered in East Asia. (See figures 5.8 and 5.9.)

Government-backed postal savings accounts give small savers a secure venue to take money from teapots and put it into the banking system. In all these ways, East Asian regimes reduced uncertainty for individual citi-

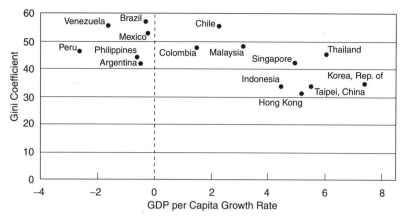

Figure 5.9 Gini Coefficients and GDP per Capita Growth Rate (1980–91)

zens and won support for market reforms, reducing the long-term danger that social movements would contest the regime's legitimacy and topple the government. Social disparities and household economic insecurity in Latin America and India by contrast, produce wide swings in economic and fiscal policies.

How did the high performers accomplish what so many others merely promised? Comparisons with other developing regions show that East Asia's high performers established a lead over all other developing regions in the predictability of the public sector. Unconstrained executive discretion is a source of political uncertainty with a detrimental economic impact in developing nations. In East Asia, leaders were generally willing to restrain executive discretion and tie their own hands by allowing economic policy to be carried out by able bureaucrats who were recruited through competitively administered exams, thus owing their promotions to merit-based assessments of their performance in office. Merit as criteria for appointment and promotion helped improve the competency of government, by reducing executive discretion. The region's leadership combated corruption within the civil service by employing a range of incentives for civil servants to use their positions to promote long-term social objectives rather than short-term personal benefits. Effective public-sector management has enabled governments to plan and implement sound policies. (See figure 5.10.)

Although East Asian societies were not governed by a legislature, deliberation councils were established that forced economic elites to operate within clearly defined rules. The councils established rules for leadership to gain a consensus on economic policy that would otherwise have been impossible without a legislature. These councils legitimized government

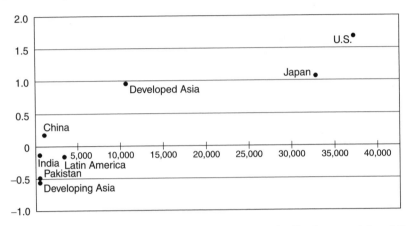

Figure 5.10 Government Effectiveness vs. Income Level (effectiveness –1.0 to 2.0; GDP per capita 0 to 40,000). Data source: WB and ADB

economic policies and granted private-sector participants some influence over the rules governing their sector. The consultative framework performed a commitment function and provided economic actors with assurances against sudden policy shifts. Consultative routines made the economic property rights of the private sector more durable, binding sovereign authority to a set of rules governing economic policy making.[59] In effect, a state/society interface built on a framework for rules to govern discretion tied the hands of East Asia's leaders. The rule-bound framework for working with the business sector made it difficult to pursue arbitrary or predatory agendas, and many leaders such as Korea's Park Chung Hee and Singapore's Lee Kuan Yew did not acquire personal fortunes while in office. They flaunted their personal austerity rather than their wealth. When conducting economic policy, they operated within channels that were well understood and consistent. With regard to their reputation for separating their public and private roles they set an example that differed dramatically from that of the leadership in the majority of developing countries.

NEW POLITICAL RISKS

Policy advice like that offered in this book cannot stimulate popular action to wrestle power away from corrupt elites, but it can alert international agencies about the need to alter the balance of power between the population and the leaders. East Asia faces new risks to the quality of public-sector governance at a time when inequality is on the rise. With the exception of South Korea and Thailand, inequality increased between 1990 and 1997 in all countries in the region.[60] A new round of institution building is needed to protect many of the accomplishments of the high-growth period because in its initial stages, democracy weakens the state. In contrast to the United States, the pillars of the postcolonial East Asian states are bureaucracy and state control over finance, rather than the powers of legislation, taxation, and mediation by the legal system.

Having met the first set of challenges in building equitable and stable market-based societies does not ensure that the state can protect the rights of all citizens through elections. Many regional governments have poorer scores on governmental effectiveness following the introduction of democracy; their capacity to plan and implement policies to continue the tradition of inclusive development is feeble. Elected leaders have increased their personal authority at the expense of bureaucratic impartiality, and improvements in the rule of law are insufficient to compensate for a less capable bureaucracy. Political corruption increasingly influences bureaucratic performance in Indonesia, Thailand, and Malaysia. South Korea's executive retains many of the powers acquired during the dictatorship. (See figures 5.11–5.13.)

East Asia must avoid becoming like other rapidly democratizing developing regions, in which the representation of poor people has increased but services for the poor have not. Politicians in young democracies may selectively provide social services to supporters with political clout, making services for the poor worse than those provided in nonelected single-party states like China or Cuba. Will East Asia's democratically elected leaders, like Thailand's Thaksin, provide only enough redistribution to protect social peace but not enough to ensure access to tomorrow's opportunities?

Prospects for strengthening the effectiveness of the democratic state face a formidable barrier. Wealthy citizens can buy the loyalty of politicians and delay much needed changes. How can political contenders who make themselves unpopular with the veto-bearing barons of power hope to get elected? What is to prevent interest groups from pulling the strings of politicians who depend on the resources of the wealthy few to be reelected? Will the rise of money politics lead to the next generation of reform or to repression? Although democracy has made Asia's developmental contradictions more visible, it promises a more viable future than going back to the past when all it took was a call to a dictator to get things done.[61] Will Asia's leaders find the foresight to match their ambitious economic objectives with equally ambitious political restructuring to bolster governmental effectiveness with a new round of institution building to strengthen the state, the political parties, and the organizations of civil society?[62]

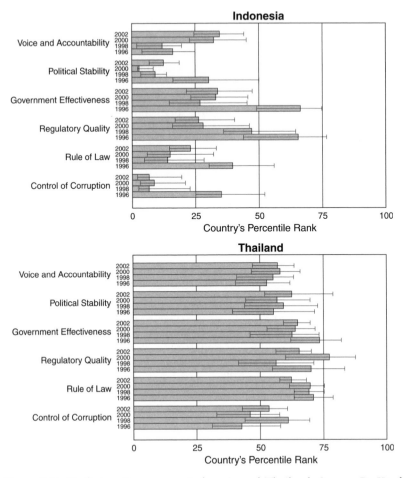

Figure 5.11 Declining Governance: Indonesia and Thailand. Source: D. Kaufmann, A. Kraay, and M. Mastruzzi. 2003. Governance Matters III: Governance Indicators for 1999–2002 (http://www.worldbank.org/wbi/governance/pubs/govmatters3.html)

A new nationalism is sweeping across Asia, bearing many new risks for the economy. This new nationalism is a response to the post-1997–1998 crisis, when new constitutions increased the access of transnational capital to domestic assets, something that aroused visceral opposition throughout the region. Many of the champions of the new nationalism view the IMF interventions of 1997–98 the way their ancestors viewed Western gunboats and troops a century earlier. The constituency for the new nationalism has emerged most strongly in Southeast Asia, where Thaksin of Thailand forcefully articulates the backlash against the imposition of foreign rules and regulations. He argues against regulatory bod-

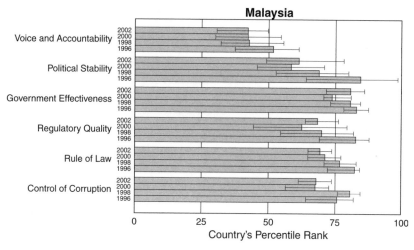

Figure 5.12 Declining Governance, Declining Voice: Malaysia. Source: D. Kaufmann, A. Kraay, and M. Mastruzzi. 2003. Governance Matters III: Governance Indicators for 1999–2002 (http://www.worldbank.org/wbi/governance/pubs/govmatters3.html)

ies or rules that tie local business up in knots so that foreigners can seize their assets. His biographers affirm that Thaksin "mentions rights only as an irritating foreign imposition. He views the rule of law as subordinate to 'management'"[63] He asserts that the post-1997 constitution, with its emphasis on increased transparency, checks and balances, decentralization, and citizen empowerment, hinders local firms and governments from mobilizing national resources for the purposes of investment and growth. This orientation finds fertile soil among East Asian businesspeople who never accepted the Western view that they were crony capitalists. The pejorative implications of the Western critique are deeply resented. The new nationalism espouses a different self-image, in which local businesses are survivors in a difficult environment, and owe their success to methods that make local business sense. To protect domestic competitiveness against transnational capital, they seek stronger control over the state.

After all, East Asian business practices arose as rational solutions to the problems of business organization and structure, specific to the environment in which they were nurtured. Since the high-growth years of the 1970s and 1980s, the international environment has evolved in ways that put it at loggerheads with local market conditions. A conflict between local and international practices and conditions is the crux of the dilemma these businesses now face. Old practices are harder to justify and more difficult to maintain. To cope with this change East Asians are looking inward and to each other to find solutions for the region's future.

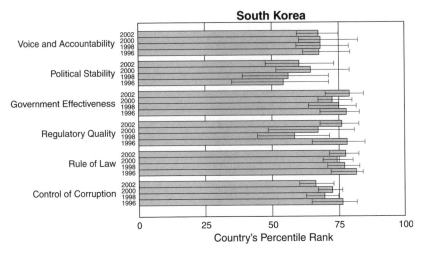

Figure 5.13 Governance Paralysis: South Korea. Source: D. Kaufmann, A. Kraay, and M. Mastruzzi. 2003. Governance Matters III: Governance Indicators for 1999–2002 (http://www.worldbank.org/wbi/governance/pubs/govmatters3.html)

The new nationalism has a strong pan-national component that envisions greater regional cooperation. The first steps toward the new cooperation are currency swaps, followed by an Asia bond and later legal harmonization of regional capital markets. Will these new instruments work? Can the new financial instruments succeed before the underlying fundamentals of such markets—primarily information transparency—are firmly established?[64]

East Asia still suffers the same weakness it had before the crisis, weak capital markets. This has led to the dominance of Western financial institutions in providing capital market services in East Asia to the benefit of regional companies that accommodate global standards. Support of information transparency in East Asia still falls far short of what is necessary for regional capital markets to reduce regional market risk. The bulk of company shares tend to be held by institutions with strong business ties to company owners such as banks, life insurance companies, and holding companies. Ownership concentration hinders the creation of an informational infrastructure needed for capital markets to flourish. Insufficient access to information infrastructure is at the core of this gap between East and West. The question that no one can answer is whether the creation of instruments can precede the establishment of market fundamentals. Without a regional surveillance mechanism, can a regional bond market prosper? Should the instruments for enhanced financial intermediation be created simply because it is a step in the right direction? What are the conditions under which capital markets can be self-governing and self-enforcing? The future financial stability of East Asia may depend on answers to these questions.

CHAPTER SIX

The Price of Exclusion

LATIN AMERICA'S EXPLOSIVE DEBT

INVESTORS LURED to Latin America during the 1990s by the siren song of economic reform, deregulation, better government, and privatization are wondering in 2004 why the region is again ranked highly vulnerable to a financial calamity. Frequent trips to the financial emergency rooms of the world do not seem to have brought about permanent change. No wonder frequent visitors, such as Argentina and Brazil, doubt whether the prescribed medicine, liberalism coupled with macroeconomic stabilization by dint of fiscal austerity, is really suited to the ailment. Most of the political leaders and parties that introduced liberal economic policies during the 1990s are out of power. Will the decade-long experiment in liberal economic policies be overturned as rapidly as it was introduced? Although Latin America's leaders embraced the high-risk market-enabling policies of more developed regions, they lacked the capability to spread the risks of market activity to those most capable of bearing them.[1] Instead of risk allocation, they engaged in risk redistribution, transfers that distorted economic incentives and placed a burden on the treasury without promoting productive behavior to replenish what was transferred.

What the financial doctors seemed to have overlooked was that the region's social and political foundations are not stable enough for the patient to endure the prescribed medicine. In most Latin American countries the gap between richest and poorest remains among the worlds widest.[2] (See figure 6.1.) By almost every known indicator, Latin America is the most unequal of the world's developing regions with the exception of sub-Saharan Africa. (See figure 6.2.) The richest 10 percent of Latin America's population earn 48 percent of total income compared with the 1.6 percent earned by the poorest. (See figure 6.3.). In developed economies, the top 10 percent nets an average of 29.1 percent of total income compared with 2.5 percent for the bottom. The region's average Gini coefficient for the 1990s, 0.522, contrasts sharply with the Organisation for Economic Co-operation and Development (OECD) average of 0.342, Eastern Europe's of 0.328, and Asia's of 0.412.[3] Latin America's averages are comparable only to Africa. The poorest 20 percent of Latin America's population receive only 3 percent of total income; the wealthiest get 60

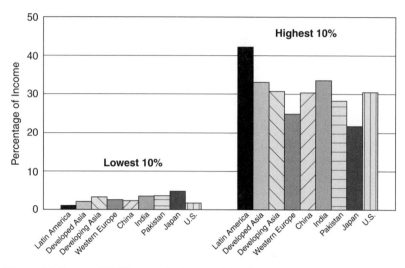

Figure 6.1 Regional Differences in Income Distribution. Source: WB

percent. The poor still represent a steady 35 percent of the total population despite periods of economic growth. The lives of the region's rich and poor have virtually nothing in common except that both are highly mistrustful of government. By international standards, the absence of trust in institutions is unusually high and all members of society, regardless of income, share in this mistrust.[4]

Liberal policies—grafted onto a society with no shared sense of social engagement—draw shaky support. Essential decisions concerning trade, education, taxes, and social insurance garner weak political consensus. When the consequences of policy reform are dramatically different for citizens at different economic strata, dramatic swings in the economic platforms of political parties make fiscal consensus elusive. Social tensions caused by income inequity increase the possibility of an ex post reversal of reforms. Social instability expresses itself in skyrocketing crime and a general contempt for mainstream institutions and their representatives. Inequality in developing countries does not always lead to political tension, but it can render institutions incapable of shifting risk to those sectors and individuals best able to support it.

Rather than closing the income gap, economic liberalism in Latin America revealed the inadequacy of institutions. To attract international investment leaders reduced deficits, stabilized exchange rates, built up financial markets, expanded trade opening, liberalized foreign direct investment (FDI), and undertook extensive privatization. But even after attracting considerable investment leaders did not use the opportunity

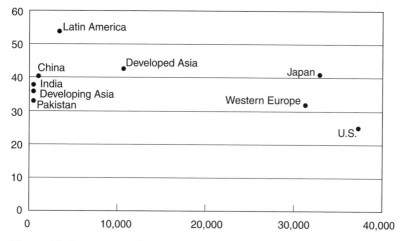

Figure 6.2 Income Distribution vs. Income Level (Gini coefficient 0–60). Data source: WB

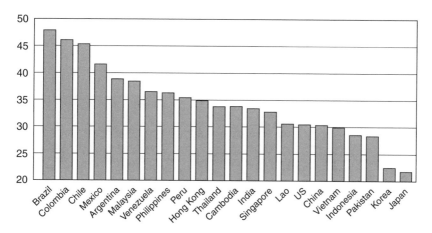

Figure 6.3 Percentage Share of Consumption: The Wealthiest 10 percent (percentage share 20–50). Data source: WB and ADB

to improve basic services such as health, education, communications, or transportation infrastructure. Property rights, basic needs, infrastructure, improvement of courts and laws and improvement of institutions were all neglected. (See tables 6.1 and 6.2.) Despite macroeconomic improvements, governmental ineffectiveness reduced the developmental impact of investments so that not all strata of society benefited. (See figure 6.4.) The region's human development in 1975 was stronger than developed Asia's; however, by 2001, developed Asia had surpassed

TABLE 6.1
Scorecard of Economic Reforms in Selected Latin American Countries

	Argentina	Brazil	Chile	Colombia	Mexico	Peru	Venezuela
Public Finance	0	2	3	3	3	2	0
Tax/budget reform	2	2	3	1	1	1	0
Exchange rate	0	2	3	0	3	2	0
Financial market	0	1	3	2	2	2	0
Trade opening	1	1	3	2	3	2	0
FDI liberalization	1	1	3	2	2	1	0
Labor reform	0	1	2	1	0	1	0
Pension reform	1	0	3	1	2	1	0

TABLE 6.2
Scorecard of Economic Reforms in Selected Latin American Countries (continued)

	Argentina	Brazil	Chile	Colombia	Mexico	Peru	Venezuela
Privatization	3	2	3	0	2	1	0
Deregulation	2	2	3	1	1	1	0
Property rights	0	1	3	1	1	1	0
Basic needs	0	0	3	0	1	0	0
Infrastructure	1	1	2	0	0	0	0
Good laws/courts	0	1	3	0	0	0	0
Good institutions	0	1	3	0	0	0	0
Total score	11/45	18/45	43/45	14/45	21/45	15/45	0/45

Source: Milken Institute, 2000.

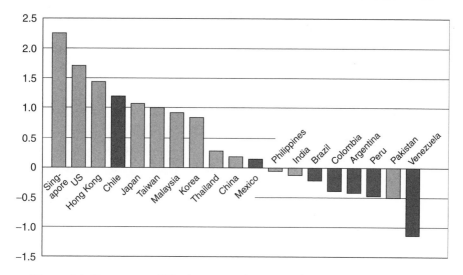

Figure 6.4 Government Effectiveness (index: 2.5 = best, −1.5 = worst). Data source: WB

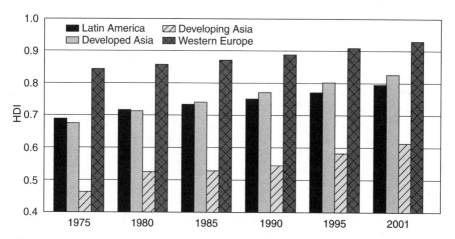

Figure 6.5 Human Development Indicator—Overall Ranking. Data source: UN

Latin America. (See figure 6.5.) Weak accountability arenas allowed the caretakers to steal what they were mandated to protect. (See figure 6.6.) Consider the legacy of Argentina's champion of market-friendly reforms, Carlos Menem: allegations that he personally profited from illegal arms shipments and bribes marred his two terms in office.

When macroeconomic meltdown threatens the ruling elite, the political powers on the continent were willing to turn policy over to the tech-

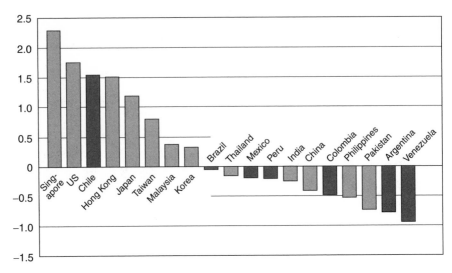

Figure 6.6 Control of Corruption (index: 2.5 = best, −1.5 = worst). Data source: WB

nocrats. Economists who advised both the international institutions and private investors did not scrutinize the basic integrity of the institutions necessary to ensure the outcomes they envisaged. While agreeing on the merits of necessary macroeconomic policies, they typically overlooked the elaborate public risk-management regimes that made these policies acceptable in already-developed countries. Greater social insurance would probably provide breathing space to respond more effectively to macroeconomic shocks. But broad-based safety nets and distributionally inclusive risk-management institutions have never been high on the regional policy-making agenda.

The failure to address the sources of social tension undermines the effectiveness of sound macroeconomic advice. By raising doubts about the durability and momentum of ongoing reforms, social conflicts drive money out of the region and leave macroeconomic reforms in disarray. Risk-allocation capabilities are necessary to make reforms more acceptable to those most vulnerable to the forces of change.[5] For the government to manage risk, it must first be trusted to conduct the affairs of state in an impartial manner.

From Crisis to Crisis

The connection between institutional weakness, distributional conflict, and volatility is a constant of Latin American history and the events in

Brazil of 2001–2002 highlight that connection. Consider the dangers of economic collapse during the presidential campaign in Brazil's 2002 election. Apprehension about policy reversal led Brazilian financial markets to panic when the leftist candidate, Luiz Inácio Lula da Silva, started to lead the center-right candidate, Jose Serra, in the polls. Lula's ascendancy created uncertainty about postelectoral monetary policy because his policies defied recent market reforms and threatened a sudden shift to the left. He called banks "parasites," and referred to foreign investment as "international extortion," and vowed to "interrupt the immense drainage of resources overseas" caused by foreign debt payments. The fear of policy reversal that chilled the investment climate in Brazil drove money abroad, weakening the currency. A knee-jerk reaction of capital flight greeted his initial success at the polls.[6] Investors anticipating a debased currency sold *reals*, in effect causing what they feared and risking a cycle of wage demands and inflation. Previous IMF bailouts to Brazil took into account only macroeconomic issues as if these were not rooted in political stratagems. The bailouts were designed to bolster investor confidence that adequate reserves existed to defend the currency. These interventions did not take the political dimension into account and were often contested and sometimes repudiated in the political arena. A capital infusion from the IMF allowed the government to buy time with creditors, and allowed the politically connected to escape at a better exchange rate than the average citizen. Political favoritism at the central bank's exchange desk ignited claims that the IMF interventions subsidized capital flight—the exact opposite of what it was intended to accomplish—and thus embroiled the IMF in local political disputes.

The IMF's 2002 agreement in Brazil was different from previous agreements in two significant regards. First, the IMF obtained an agreement from candidate Lula before the election to abide by the terms of the loan should he be elected. Second, the funds would be divided into tranches delivered both before and after the election to ensure compliance. This restored investor confidence, stemmed the capital flight and allowed Lula to win the support of an otherwise skeptical business community. He ended up with a victory that included influential members of the business community in his coalition, and he began his presidency with a wellspring of goodwill, having helped the country avoid a financial crisis even before being elected. Lula looked responsible and the IMF looked like it had learned a great deal from previous agreements that neglected discussions with members of the political opposition. Of course, a long road ahead faces Lula, who must now deliver the benefits of economic growth to the many poor voters whose support enabled him to win the election. To trim inherited deficits, he will have to get tough with his core supporters, and this will only be possible if he succeeds at convincing the privileged minority to bear a larger share of the nation's debt burden. In other words, Lula's success will hinge on his ability to woo investment from the business community by delivering social cohesion. But does he have the resources to provide more inclusive policies while eliminating budget deficits?

During the nineties, a decade of market reforms in Latin America brought neither prosperity nor civility to the region, and greater global economic integration seems as distant as ever.[7] Although Brazil has the largest economy, has the potential to steer the entire continent, and is the largest recipient of foreign lending and investment, its financial instability is emblematic of the region's woes. Since the election of market reformer Fernando Henrique Cardoso as president of Brazil in 1994, public debt soared from 29 percent to 60 percent of GDP, demonstrating how successful Cardoso had been in instilling confidence. Nevertheless, income per person has grown annually by a slow 1.3 percent. While Cardoso, his central banker Arminio Fraga, and finance minister Pedro Malan score outstanding grades from the international banking community, the cross-border loans they attracted, totaling $140 billion did not stem the stagnation of living standards. In fact, income per person has improved by less than 9 percent since 1980. Growth has not been an independent source of institutional improvement and consequently, has not created confidence among average Brazilians that the future will be any better than the past.[8] Lula appealed to these doubts by saying the country was suffering from the "speculation and greed of half a dozen bankers," and he asked if liberalization was a trick to pay foreign banks for loans local firms could never access. In Lula's words, "we are facing a serious crisis that was aggravated by eight years of a mistaken policy, of an administration that sold 76 percent of Brazil's assets through absurd privatizations."

Do Brazil's debts exceed its prospects for growth? Although economists tend to view the answer to this question strictly as a macroeconomic issue, politics influences the answer. An indefinite future of high interest rates raises distributional issues that arouse dissent. The question of whether Brazil can swallow more debt is influenced by the fact that Brazil's potential is marred by dangers arising from having the worst income inequality in the world. It is a country in which additional doses of macroeconomic austerity exacerbate existing inequality, making economic reform politically destablizing. If there was a sense among Brazilians that the benefits as well as the burdens of additional debt were equally shared, international lending programs would be better received by a wider subset of voters.

The country's anemic capital markets poorly serve Brazilian firms, making the benefits of global trade elusive. Domestically, Brazil's companies can generally only borrow for periods of six months or less. Unable to find adequate capital at home, large Brazilian companies (mostly oil, telecom, and banking) seek recourse by issuing bonds on international markets where they are lucky to get 21 to 22 percent a year for thirty-month bonds. Short-term financing becomes the order of the day, disregarding one of the cardinal rules of investing—do not finance long-term assets with short-term credit. Firms that must renew their financing frequently are less capable of dealing with shocks than firms that have access to long-term debt. The private sector ends up with a mismatched balance sheet in which, just like the government, it carries excessive short-term debt when it really needs access to long-term credit.[9]

Borrowing from overseas to conduct business domestically, firms are exposed to another liability. *Reals* sold for dollars to repay loans drive down exchange rates. A steep decline in the value of the local currency makes the debt more difficult to service. A downward spiral ensues, as firms sell more *reals* to cover foreign-currency debt payments, and the declining currency makes loans even more costly. With an export sector that is a mere 10 percent of Brazil's GDP, debt compared to exports stands at an unsustainable 400 percent; the annual external debt service ratio to exports is 90 percent (or about one-fifth of emerging Asia's average.) In this context, Brazil's private-sector dollar-denominated debt contributes to Brazil's deepening financial vulnerability.

One reason for the inadequacy of domestic capital markets is that firms must compete for finance with the government. In 2001, Brazil's treasury issued US $23.55 billion in bonds. During the same year, companies were able to raise only US $2.09 billion from international markets. Investors enjoy the high-yielding risk-free returns on government paper and tend to ignore the stocks and bonds of private-sector sources. As the growth of public debt drives interest rates into double digits, the private sector must pay more for capital.[10] As we will see, asymmetric information problems in financial markets, currency balance-sheet mismatches in government, and weak financial-sector regulation are interrelated and unlikely to be resolved in isolation. Fiscal laxity, weak lending practices, and imprudent financial-sector behavior all stem from the politics of inequality in influence, recognition, and wealth that allow clientalistic practices and abuses of power to go unchecked.[11]

Weak capital markets constrain large numbers of the population from contributing to economic growth in Latin America. (See table 6.3.) A Milken Institute study of access to entrepreneurial capital in 98 countries ranked Chile 29, Panama 34, Argentina 45, Peru 50, El Salvador 54, Honduras and Mexico 64 (tied), Bolivia 67, Brazil at 69, and Guatemala at 70. Costa Rica, Colombia, Venezuela, Ecuador, and Paraguay finished at the bottom at 82, 84, 87, 88, and 89 respectively. "Equity markets are particularly narrow in Latin America; the ratio of the number of firms [publicly traded] to population is roughly one third of the world mean,

TABLE 6.3
Latin America's Financial System in Comparative Perspective (1999)

	High-income countries	Upper-middle income countries	Lower-middle income countries	Low-income countries	Latin America
Population	17.8	11.4	37	33.8	8.3
GDP	80.5	9.7	7.2	2.6	6.2
Bank assets	93.2	4.5	1.3	1.0	2.2
Equity market capitalization	93.4	4.0	2.0	0.7	1.6
Bond market capitalization	96.8	2.1	0.7	0.5	0.8
Total financial assets	94.3	3.6	1.4	0.7	1.1

Source: Milken Institute Policy Brief (2002).
Note: Economies are divided among income groups according to 1999 GNI per capita, calculated using the World Bank Atlas method. The groups are: low income, $755 or less; lower middle income, $756–$2,995; upper middle income, $2,996–$9,265; and high income, $9,266 or more.

whereas the ratio of the number of IPOs [initial public offerings] to population is more than 10 times smaller than the world mean."[12] Table 6.2 shows that Latin America's financial system is smaller than the average of middle-income countries. It has a smaller percentage of GDP than is the norm.

Financial intermediation in Latin America is dominated by commercial banks that are heavily concentrated and lend mostly to large customers. Consumer credit is scarce, stock markets are small and illiquid, and the margins between borrowing and lending rates are high. Before the law changed in 2001, banks in Mexico were not permitted to make loans to small businesses or to entrepreneurs. The absence of a method to valuate property in order to collateralize loans keeps the number of loans low. The size and age of a firm become important qualifications in loan considerations. Firms tend to be old because they are not subject to pressure from innovative newcomers.

Established producers are protected from the threat of emerging entrepreneurs because new firms that would be capable of challenging the status quo are unable to find financing. The security enjoyed by established firms comes at the cost of job growth and competition. Only in Chile, the region's best performer, does credit from the banking sector to the private sector exceed 50 percent of GDP. In Peru and Argentina, the ratio is around 20 percent. The region's capital markets are highly segmented, from midsize firms borrowing at 25 to 40 percent to the smaller firms facing rates of 60 percent. The small debt load of Latin American firms contrasts sharply with that of East Asian firms. UBS Warburg estimates the ratio of debt-to-equity was only 26 percent in 2001. This can be compared with Japan's corporations, which maintain debt-to-equity ratios of about 277 percent. In South Korea, ratios were about 300 percent (with extremes of 600 percent) when they peaked in 1998, down to 198.3 percent in 2001. The heavy dominance of debt finance by banks, combined with weak equity markets and low debt-to-equity ratios, results in volatility: to support high interest rates, firms require a higher rate of return than would otherwise be the case, filling bank portfolios with high-risk projects. Business deals that would ordinarily be financed in a world of stable capital markets go unfunded.

Over the past thirty years, Latin America's macroeconomic volatility surpassed that of any of the other emerging markets. By late 1980s, the region's average annual rate of inflation approached 1,500 percent per capita, and income declined by 10 percent relative to the early 1980s. Macroeconomic-instability erodes savings and undermines broad pledges to honor contracts. Unfortunately, potential investors, whether domestic or international, perceive fiscal discipline to be reversible, and for every Cardoso there is a populist Lula just around the corner. The fears of policy reversibility increase the cost of the government's capital finance. Thus, fiscal discipline that is not credible may be more costly than none at all.

Unable to plan for the future by saving today's abundance for tomorrow's shortcomings, countries end up with fiscal adjustments that are "procyclical": Latin America's finance ministers typically cut spending during recessions and spend rather than save during boom times, whereas fiscal policy should be designed to protect against volatility. They violate the golden rule of sound fiscal policy. In Latin America, Chile is a rare exception, having adopted fiscal rules that encourage positive countercyclical policies during good times. With procyclical financing, the region ends up with excessive budget cuts to reduce fiscal deficits during recessions, which exacerbates the consequences for the poor. Health and education spending are often the first to go, producing equity losses that are difficult to recover during upturns and making the region's poverty even more intractable.

Weak institutions, improper regulations, and misaligned incentives poorly equip Latin America for a market-based financial system.[13] Budgetary procedures are nontransparent, property rights for both fixed and movable property are inadequate, and the laws do not provide adequate security for loans made against collateral. Paul Holden's research has revealed that bankruptcy proceedings are long and the number of independent legal actions required to collect overdue debt is prohibitive. Only a small fraction of the value of any asset can ever be recovered.[14]

Poorly functioning legal systems and the lack of good credit information, even for the region's elites, undermine small-enterprise development in Latin America. Complex regulations, inconsistently enforced, prevent businesses from acquiring legal status. Many entrepreneurs start out in the informal sector because start-up procedures for independent businesses are cumbersome. Once they embark on informal-sector activity, the transition to formal status is elusive. Excessive regulation makes the cost of going formal exceed the benefit, but remaining informal makes it difficult for firms to find sources of outside capital. As a result, societies like that of Brazil enjoy a large number of small, family-owned firms with little chance of growing into mid- or large-size operations.

GOVERNMENT DEBT ON THE RAMPAGE

Although Latin America's citizens put aside large sums to invest, the private sector still starves for funds because citizens' savings pay for government debt. In Argentina, Brazil, and Mexico—three of the region's four major capital markets—government debt is a huge part of total debt capitalization. Chile remains the exception. Another indicator of the region's financial weakness can be measured by adding the debt of central governments held by banks. In 2003, the claims on central-government assets as a percentage of total bank assets was 55 percent (for the region); in Brazil it was 28 percent, and in Mexico 22 percent. The average for middle-income countries is between 10 and 15 percent.[15]

Mutual funds should consist of a broad basket of shares from many different enterprises and sectors. In Latin America, however, the legal form of mutual funds is used to invest in government liabilities. Fund managers are often ordered to invest in government issuances and may have to trade good assets for government issues. Banks in Argentina that lend to the government were even allowed to default on their depositors. Portfolio managers are discouraged by government policy from diversifying their portfolios, and so their behavior diverges from standard financial theory.

Extensive government borrowing has the net effect of driving the private sector out of the credit market, weakening Latin America's financial markets. Banks become huge depositories of government risk, compelling people to save in international currency, creating a permanent savings deficit. Other avenues of investment are sealed off by a lack of supporting institutions. For example, equity markets are weak because of inadequate corporate governance that fails to protect minority shareholder rights. With the exception of Chile, which has strong shareholder rights, Latin American countries have higher ownership concentrations than the world mean. Despite a growing awareness of the need to make legal changes, weak enforcement persists. Toothless watchdog agencies cannot monitor company accounts thoroughly, and companies have no incentive to disclose since they then become vulnerable to expropriation. In Brazil, regulators can even be sued privately for their actions as civil servants. What better way is there to paralyze their activities? The regulators are not intrusive when needed and are unpredictable when unneeded.

Most Latin American economies depend on banks whose collapse could devastate the entire financial sector. When asked why investment banks or brokerages do not set themselves up as market makers, the usual answer is volatility. The market is never stable enough for a market maker to emerge from the private sector. But another reason exists: the concentrated monopoly power of a few large firms in most industries impedes the ability of investment banks to underwrite mergers and acquisitions.

Government policy makers now openly discuss extending maturities on corporate debt issues, creating new equity instruments, encouraging a secondary market for corporate debt, protecting the rights of minority shareholders, and strengthening the administrative independence of the region's regulatory agencies. However, the big industrial interests oppose reforms of corporate governance and depend on their informal ties with politicians to obtain subsidies and favorable interpretations of the regulations.

Moving away from the financial sector, long lists of institutional failures have not been corrected during a decade of macroeconomic adjustment. These include a general absence of predictability in budgeting and rule making and significant delays of audits of government and private-sector accounts. Unfortunately, a lax regulatory environment that increases the risk of socially costly bank failures is favorable to some interest groups and their political sponsors.

It is widely acknowledged that the relative absence of fiscal discipline shapes Latin America's financial markets. For progress to be made on fiscal and budgetary transparency and an effective financial infrastructure, a consensus is needed on creating a more competitive economy and society. This requires trust. Latin America's enormous income disparities have ruptured the bonds that unite society around causes requiring austerity and fiscal restraint.

The weak fiscal positions of government often stem from the use of public money to dispense a wide range of private benefits through vast patronage networks, ranging from lucrative business contracts to keep the rich happy to plentiful jobs for the poor, such as municipal trash collectors. Thirty one percent of Latin Americans polled in a major UN Development Programme (UNDP) study reported that they knew of someone who had received "privileges"—typically a government job or handout—thanks to connections with a political party in power.[16] Patronage is a way of sharing with the poor, but it does not compensate for weak social cohesion, and it does not produce policies conducive to general economic growth.

ARGENTINA'S ROAD TO RUIN

Perhaps the most rapid and successful economic reforms in Latin America occurred under president Carlos Menem in Argentina when the lifelong populist brought in economist Domingo Cavallo with his 300 or so "Cavallo Boys."[17] In 1991, Argentina bet its future on a set of ideas that enjoyed strong endorsement from international policy experts. They made their currency convertible with the U.S. dollar, keeping one dollar in reserve for each peso printed. This concept came straight out of the economic textbooks as a modern-day equivalent of the gold standard, and it provided Argentina with the means to reign in inflation, which had reached 200 percent a month. With confidence in the currency restored, money started to find its way back to the banks where it could be used to fuel economic growth. Banks from all over the world opened branches in Argentina. Outside investors were attracted by high rates of return coupled with regulations that facilitated the movement of capital into and out of the country. At its peak, $800 million entered Argentina every month.

The dollars in Argentinian banks made Menem very popular, but he did not use that popularity to take the critical step of increasing taxes to pay down preexisting debts and to reduce inflated government services. Instead, he expanded government programs and thus compromised government's fiscal position by increasing government jobs and subsidies. Menem, the great reformer of monetary policy, created an army of shadow employees who were actually political mobilizers for the ruling Peronist Party. As one observer notes, people kept showing up at government agencies expecting jobs that did not require being at work every day. The strengthened economy only inflated the patronage system, despite massive privatizations of government-owned enterprises. The telephone, water, and gas companies, railroads, the post office, and the national airlines all were privatized, but the number of government jobs did not decrease, staying at about two million, the same as in 1990. The *Los Angeles Times* reported: "The spending spree was especially brazen in Buenos Aires province, home to a third of Argentina's population where Eduardo Duhalde, the province's governor, was Menem's top rival in the Peronist party. Their political rivalry was fought, for the most part, with government money." Duhalde offered constituents whatever he thought would purchase more votes. His rival Menem tried to outbid him in dispensing largess. "Menem, for his part, had control of a discretionary fund called

'Advances from the National Treasury,' or ATNs. Friendly city governments have access to the ATNs. . . . They would find any excuse to ask for an ATN. Theoretically, they had to present a written project, but there was no accounting," the *Los Angeles Times* reports.[18]

Patronage remains insurmountable in Argentina. One term of austerity to get Argentina back on its feet was followed by a second term of deals to drum up political backing, rolling back the good policies that provided the credit to borrow in the first place. A full second term of misgovernment forced Menem's successors to decrease salaries and dramatically increase taxes to cope with the large deficits they inherited. One World Bank study ranks Argentina as the world's most corrupt country according to GDP per capita, yet even at the peak of his reformist zeal, Menem never undertook reforms of Argentina's public sector to improve the quality of public services or to prevent political appointees at the top levels of the civil service from deciding who gets electricity and phone service. Menem did little to correct the cheating that cost the government 40 percent of its expected revenues. He never stopped spending programs and slush funds that politicians use to buy power. Privatizations did little to improve competition or efficiency. Although his government started with popular reforms, it never proceeded to build constituencies and political support for the less-popular reforms that were essential to better manage the public sector so the economy would function at its capacity. Argentina needed the reorganization of government but instead it received macroeconomic reforms that did not relieve uncertainty about law enforcement. Without shared values, institutional mechanisms to forge consensus are still hollow and do not build self-enforcing social norms that foster entrepreneurship, trust, and respect for legality.

Opacity Is Good for the Fox

Argentina's spectacular collapse in 2001 made it a poster child—or some would say, whipping boy—for faults such as inflated public-sector payrolls that are endemic to the region. Large public-sector budget deficits throughout the region reflect the prevalence of private patronage provided at public expense. Institutions create fiscal illusions that contribute to the pervasiveness of this pattern, and nontransparent fiscal transfers temporarily hide long-term social costs. Domestic constituencies to improve overall competitiveness are absent, and necessary reforms are rarely implemented. Powerful segments of society enjoy opacity, explaining why their governments hesitate to strengthen the legal foundations for long-term contracting and the management of financial risk.[19] But opacity may only protect the powerful from the powerless temporarily. Moreover, the region's politics are further complicated because when economic interests are not in league with the state, they are in competition with the state.

Globalization has not helped the region to find a solution for its divisive politics. Instead, access to global financial markets actually reduces the cost of perverse domestic political incentives. Because countries can borrow easily in overseas markets, they can avoid making difficult fiscal choices at home. In fact, large deficits in the 1970s coincided with international financial market access. The easy access to international funds allowed the region's strongest economies to borrow from overseas capital markets without making the necessary changes in domestic governance. (See tables 6.1 and 6.2.)

Fiscal Consequences of Social Polarization

Proportional representation allows deeply divided social groups to support deeply partisan political parties that are the main source of Latin America's severe policy failures. Meaningful institutional reform arouses distributional conflicts that inflame the region's politics. Polarized societies produce single parties that promote strong partisan ideologies. Partisan conflicts over how to resolve issues of fiscal policy cause boom-and-bust cycles that heighten uncertainty about policy continuity.

Like most of its neighbors, Argentina tolerates giant tax inequities that are often endemic to emerging nations. Direct taxes are difficult to levy both because the wealthy oppose such levies and because the inherent administrative costs of direct taxation are very high. As in most poor countries, Latin American governments instead rely on indirect taxes, which are typically regressive and fall most heavily on the poor. Such indirect levies are highly distortionary and difficult to increase.

The absence of a social consensus for tax reform is the key reason for big borrowing. It is much easier to borrow money than to settle vast ideological differences over systemic tax reform.[20] Until a consensus is reached that eliminates the sources of the states' weak fiscal position, financial markets will demand a risk premium from borrowers. The resulting underdeveloped financial markets bar many citizens from making a contribution to or enjoying the benefits of economic growth, which is why populism endures.

Many leftist candidates, despite earning a nationwide following, strike fear into the hearts of investors who dread a resurgence of populism in economic policy. However, the liberalism of the 1990s is linked with the continuing concentration of wealth and therefore weakens the legitimacy of governments associated with open market policies. The region's radical inequality fosters insurrection, not cooperation, and makes heroes out of those who, like Bolivia's Morales, throw stones at the symbols of corporate power. A brave new political realignment is needed in which capital, labor, and farmers collaborate on a social contract that restores legitimacy to the political processes. Affording Latin America's inhabitants access to capital and opportunity will require a reconstruction of the region's states from their social foundation up to their regulatory and administrative systems but reforms stop at macroeconomic adjustment.

Latin America and East Asia Compared

East Asia frequently gets credit for having relatively good economic policies. But those policies were hardly original. They succeeded because of East Asia's bureaucratic capacity. The same economic policies in Latin America would have floundered without the bureaucratic capacity necessary to foster this development.[21] The weakness of Latin America's implementation capability is sometimes linked to the structure of its economy, which is dominated by the export of raw materials. Whether the concentration on raw materials is a consequence or a cause of the region's poor governance is open to speculation. Figure 6.7 indicates the preponderance of unfinished-good exports in Latin America as compared with the other emerging markets discussed in this book.

A 1995 study by twelve Latin American economists for the Inter-American Development Bank pointed to a number of critical shortcomings in the region's governance, mostly the absence of those factors that made the East Asian Tigers successful. For example, the study concluded that "the complexity of administering a centralized [bureaucratic] system, processing information, and issuing orders on time cannot be resolved given the present capability of public administration in Latin America."[22]

In a further study, Philip Keefer and Stephen Knack estimated the effect of bureaucratic quality, corruption, the risk of expropriation, and contract repudiation on average per capita growth from 1960 to 1989 and found that each variable has a significant and independent effect on per capita growth rates.[23] A comparison of the quality of the judiciary, the degree of transparency in government (or lack of corruption), and the quality of the national bureaucracy in Latin America and East Asia shows they are highly divergent. Latin America has some of the weakest institutions among the countries in the sample, and, relative to East Asia, its institutions continue to deteriorate.[24] The medians for Latin America are in every case below those of East Asia's high performers, reflecting the inefficiency, ineffectiveness, and corruption of the civil service.[25]

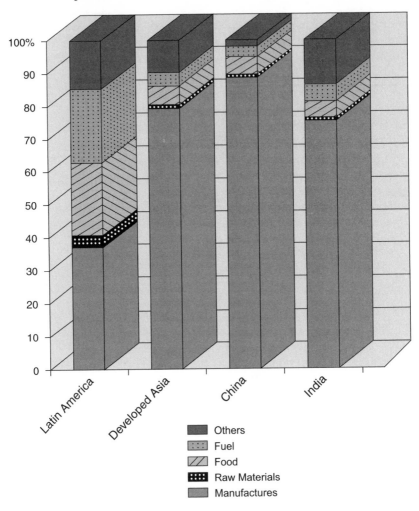

Figure 6.7 Share of Merchandise Export

Although variation exists throughout Latin America, Chile and Costa Rica's effective bureaucracies are the exception rather than the rule in the region.[26] Chile has accomplished more in government reforms generally than its neighbors. The Chilean government is highly centralized and effectively oversees taxation and regulation of programs from the capital; and considerable administrative responsibility to local citizens exists outside the capital, local administrators are in close contact with the people they serve. Shortcomings remain: government funding for local programs is sometimes inadequate, and evaluations of programs need to be improved. Each year Chilean bureaucrats are evaluated on the basis of dedication, capacity, and other matters, but the standards are often unclear; the processes lack transparency. Although it outperforms its neighbors, the bureaucracy in Chile is not as efficient or independent as in East Asia's high performers.[27]

The typical Latin American approach to getting things done remains in the strongmen or "caudillos" in varying forms—military, presidential, and, more recently, ministerial.[28] To implement their programs, elected political leaders depend on nonbureaucrats because the civil services and governance in Latin America generally are not up to the task of initiating or implementing reform. Even in Chile, politicians depend on political appointees, who constitute 15 percent of the bureaucracy. One of Mexico's early market reformers, with long experience in his country's bureaucracy, wrote in the mid-1970s that "perhaps no other group can be as detrimental to reform as the bureaucracy itself."[29]

Macroeconomic policy reforms are politically less secure in Latin America than in East Asia due to social tensions. Inequality encourages voters to opt for radical redistribution, and populist subsidies discourage investment and trade.

Unlike in East Asia, where credible institutions and a relatively equal distribution of assets encouraged public support for continuity in economic policies and strengthened the existing institutional structure early on, in Latin America the incentives were structured so as to encourage redistributive demands and policy swings on the one hand, and the conducting of most economic transactions outside of the system of formal rules on the other. In Latin America, redistribution has been limited to intermittent short-term income transfers, and asset ownership remains highly unequal. This unequal distribution of assets, coupled with weak public sector institutions, has resulted in weak confidence in government policy, and encouraged rent seeking or tax evasion by key economic actors, and populist economic promises by politicians. Over time this eroded the capacity of institutions to deliver public goods and services effectively, and therefore public faith in them.[30]

The organs of government that serve the poor lack administrative capacity—for example, record-keeping practices, typically taken for granted in developed nations, are weak. Without reliable data, it is difficult to evaluate current administrators, departments, and programs and to implement services such as sanitation, building inspection, and urban planning. Central governments cannot monitor the use of funds in the provinces or municipalities. Governments are thus unable to conduct the programs that most people count on to give them a fair chance at success.

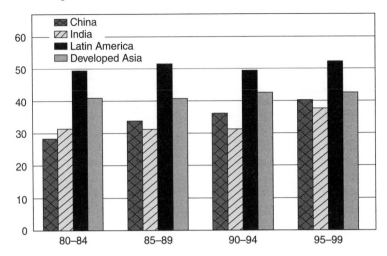

Figure 6.8 Changes in Inequality over the Past Two Decades (Gini coefficent 0–60). Data source: WB

Better public risk management is one of the reasons East Asian nations have overtaken their counterparts in Latin America and have eliminated the advantages in living standards that Latin Americans enjoyed until the 1980s. The governments of East Asia's high performers took on the dual role of social and financial risk mitigator.[31] Governments in East Asia provided businesses with financial functions that are often privately provisioned in developed economies: they provided households with basic health, education, housing, and property rights to land. By making the promise of shared growth credible, governments reduced both market and social risk.[32] In contrast, Latin American governments took risks in the name of the sovereign but passed the benefits to well-organized or well-connected regime supporters. Where East Asian governments took measures to mitigate individual household market risk by providing secure property rights (title to land), predictable fiscal policies, and access to the formal banking sector for all social groups, Latin American governments did virtually none of the above. Where East Asian leaders followed policies to share the benefits of growth widely, Latin American governments allowed the highest levels of income inequality in the world. (See figure 6.8.) Where East Asian governments contained government discretion by subjecting policy implementation to effective bureaucratic agencies and business councils, Latin American leaders used the civil service as an employer of last resort, ignoring merit as a criterion for appointment in order to pack the civil service with political backers.

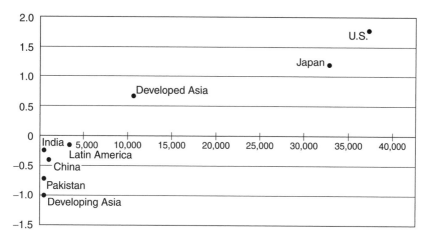

Figure 6.9 Control of Corruption vs. Income Level (index: 2.0 = best, −1.5 = worst). Data source: WB and ADB

Latin American nations can learn much from East Asia about building bureaucratic capabilities. The market reforms that have made the most progress in Latin America were imposed by dictatorial decree (i.e., Chile under General Pinochet) or by technocratic agencies of government that deal primarily with the macroeconomic system (i.e., Argentina and the Cavallo Boys). Although they have improved general macroeconomic indicators, Latin America's reformers have been reluctant to remove mechanisms in public-sector management that allow leadership to influence the behavior of subordinates through personalized off-budget transactions. As a result, when their standard of living is taken into account, Latin American governments are often among the most corrupt nations in the world. (See figure 6.9.)

The comparison of Latin America and East Asia allows us to assert something essential about the DNA of successful countries: social equity and economic productivity are complements, and one cannot be forsaken in favor of the other.[33] East Asia's commitment to social cohesion separates its development experience from Latin America's unsteady patterns of growth.[34] Rapid growth with equity allowed East Asia's leaders to reduce the expectations of policy discontinuity that deter long-term investment in Latin American countries.[35] Broad-based public risk management shifted the horizons of investors toward projects with long-term yield curves.

A dearth of human capital explains Latin America's most glaring current difference with East Asia. Slowness in establishing universal free schooling, literacy, and numeracy results in a social productivity gap. In its tardiness, Latin America seems to be following in the footsteps of Spain and Portugal, which were also latecomers to a belief in mass education. The percentage of the population engaged in knowledge and service work is noticeably smaller than in North America or East Asia. Most of the population remain in manual labor. "In comparison with other regions of the world (and taking into account the differences in the level of development of the economies), Latin America has approximately the same relative amounts of physical capital, and is more abundant in natural resources but poorer in human capital. Exploiting natural resources generates rents that go to a few hands, with little employment and, as a rule, with few incentives to create new productive activities."[36]

Extremes of inequality cause the erosion and eventual failure of impartial institutions, making redistributive policies appealing and locking Latin American countries into a cycle of low capital investment and underdevelopment. Biased institutions that increase social polarization perpetuate the unequal distribution of assets and undermine the promise that the future will be better. A government that is not to be trusted as an impartial monitor cannot effectively reallocate risk, shift it from one group to another, or spread it across a larger number of people. Instead of managing risk effectively, regional governments provide redistribution through patronage mechanisms, eventually depleting the public treasury and, in fact, creating more risk. Patronage becomes a surrogate for a reliable state-based system of social security. It draws its appeal from the need of citizens to find succor in times of need and deprivation. Locked into a battle about the rights to redistribution, the populations of Latin America are discouraged from venturing into profitable trade and investment. Prevented from engaging in risk-rewarding activities, citizens do not generate the wealth needed to ease the burden of inequality and poverty.

In April of 2004, the United Nations reported that Latin Americans would support an autocratic government if it improved their lives. According to its report, "Political institutions which have lost credibility and the persistence of poverty and discrimination together have created a situation which makes these democracies vulnerable."[37] The study concluded that corruption, poverty, and economic crisis has discredited democracy: 56.7 percent of the 18,600 people polled in eighteen countries said they believe that economic development is more important than democracy, and 54.7 percent said they would support an authoritarian government if it proved able to resolve economic problems.

On the bright side, all of the region's economies posted positive GDP growth in 2003 for the first time in more than a decade. Presented with an ideal time for governments to pay off debilitating debt, the governments of the region used the positive economic climate to launch a spree

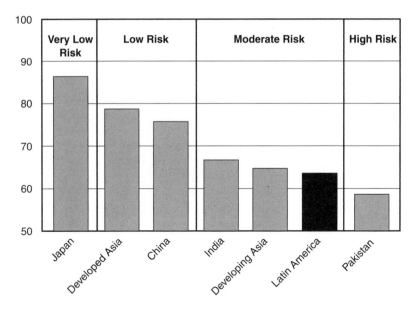

Figure 6.10 Country Risk—Composite Risk (composite index 50–100). Data source: ICRG

of international borrowing, profiting from the low lending rates. Why are the region's leaders ignoring the need to ensure against future risk by reducing the debt-to-GDP ratio to manageable levels? Certainly they understand that acting prudently to pay off debts when times are good will reduce the pain of another boom-and-bust cycle. Over the past twenty years, the region already has lost its technological advantage and its lead in human development over developing Asia because of poor financial management. It can hardly afford to see its international competitiveness further eroded by another spree of debt ending in another boom-and-bust cycle. Excessive borrowing in foreign currencies by national treasuries will prevent the region's private businesses from finding capital to invest and grow. Instead of furnishing credit for business expansion, the region's banks continue to earn their living by handling government bonds.

The region's political leaders must find a consensus for necessary financial reforms so they can raise revenues to reduce the debt through tax reform. Governments paralyzed by low levels of popularity and low levels of trust have not undertaken the necessary tax reforms. A weakened economy prone to a growing distributional conflict threatens democratic stability, creating political risk that deters international investment. If mismanaged the recovery of 2004 will stimulate the cycles of civil unrest and make Latin America the most volatile and uncertain region in our sample after Pakistan. (See figures 6.10 and 6.11.)

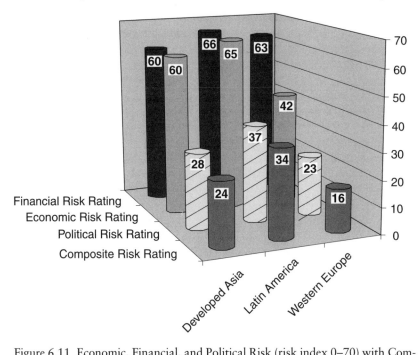

Figure 6.11 Economic, Financial, and Political Risk (risk index 0–70) with Composite for Regions (January 2000 to March 2004). Note: Reversed notation (i.e., the higher the number the greater the risk). Data source: ICRG

In retrospect, it is widely believed that what went wrong in Latin America was that the region's leaders had the wrong priorities in the 1990s, putting macroeconomic reforms before institutional reforms. The analysis offered here suggests a different perspective. It does not refute the critical need for administrative and judicial reforms but emphasizes addressing the highest source of uncertainty first in order to implement the most sustainable sequence of reforms. In Latin America, the greatest uncertainty stems from the threat of distributional conflict and the inability to correct social imbalances. Once the uncertainty in the social system is mitigated, it will become easier to identify the next sequence of reforms. The first priority must be the implementation of social reforms to allow the region to fully utilize its rich domestic resources to solve its own problems. The necessary resources to pay down the region's debts and restore financial stability are stashed in banks all over the world in the private accounts of a handful of the region's wealthiest citizens. A new wave of populism, inspired by leaders who point to injustices in the international order to explain their nation's plight, only diverts attention from the region's true source of weakness: the domestic political economy.

As a consequence of divided governments that reflect the region's social polarization, Latin American governments are rarely able to reach a consensus about spending priorities, and they collect insufficient revenues to cover the expenditures they do agree on. The poor refuse to pay taxes for services they do not receive, and the rich, have no incentive to pay for services they do not use. One solution is to increase the share of direct taxes imposed on the rich, but governments fear the revolutionary implications a shift in the share of current income payments absorbed by taxes might have for the social organization of Latin American states. Governments in the region lack the self-assurance to expand their taxable capacity, which leaves most Latin American states in a permanent fiscal crisis, with their citizens' savings safely harbored overseas.

CHAPTER SEVEN

Why Not India?

NEW CENTURY, NEW COUNTRY

IN THE LATE 1990s, after nearly fifty years of neglect, the international business community discovered India as an investment opportunity. India's promise emerged after a decade of strong economic growth between 1994 and 2003 increased its GDP by 5.95 percent each year, and GDP per capita rose from $352 to $558 in 2003 and 2004, illuminating India's promise.[1] Should this trend continue, India's domestic private sector coupled with its strength in the service sector will exert a forceful influence on world economic growth. Already a global player in software, India has strong prospects in global outsourcing services. Growing middle-class consumption promises to bolster the expansion of the domestic housing market, automobiles, and information technology. Improved telecommunications will enable firms from all over the world to open operations in India. India has an increasingly open market economy, modern accounting standards, wide use of English, an active stock market, and low wages. And India enjoys the "advantage of backwardness," the expectation of rapid convergent growth as it catches up with more-developed, slower-growing economies. As labor shifts from agriculture to nonfarm activities, gains in productivity are inevitable. As a manufacturing base for the export of textiles and automobiles, India combines both low labor costs and advanced skill sets in engineering, giving it cost advantages over major international competitors in capital-good production.[2]

India already contributes 3.8 percent of global GDP growth, making it the fifth most important contributor. Since 1991, its market reforms have progressed steadily, taxes have been flattened, barriers to entry have come down, interest rates have been deregulated, and private-sector banks have been introduced. These efforts to unshackle the economy have the potential to make India one of the world's largest and fastest-growing countries, whose growth, along with that of China, is likely to have a larger overall impact on the global economy than did the rapid growth of Asia's tiger economies in the post–World War II period.

However, India's rosy future is clouded by the deep discrepancies between the fortunes of the growing middle class and the lagging rural sector. The world's largest clusters of poor people live in India. (See figure

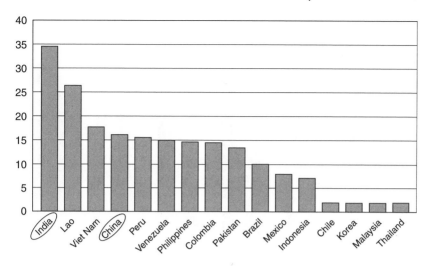

Figure 7.1 Proportion of Population (in percent) Living on Less than $1 a Day.
Data source: WB and ADB

7.1.) The poor made themselves heard in the spring of 2004 when the leader of the incumbent Bharatiya Janata Party (BJP), which championed privatization and economic policy reform, was trounced in efforts to win an early election. The defeat plunged the Indian stock market into its largest freefall in its history, losing 17 percent of its value in a single day. Yet investment optimism has not woken up to the dreary poverty of India's masses. The supporters of the ousted BJP maintain that rising expectations created by growth led the rural poor to rise against the incumbent. This view ignores the fact that incomplete markets for social risk represent one of the great failings of India's emerging market economy.

The benefits of India's economic transformation have yet to reach the two-thirds of its population who are trapped in a stagnant agricultural sector without adequate irrigation or power. The entire technology industry employs fewer than one million people, but 40 million Indians are registered as unemployed, highlighting the gap between the growing middle class and those who are excluded from it. About 45 million of India's 180 million households have telephone lines, and only 26.1 million of India's one billion people have mobile phones. Close to 300 million Indians live on less than $1 dollar a day, and only an estimated 659,000 households have computers—a far smaller proportion than in East Asia, China, or Latin America. (See figure 5.7.) India's high-tech ambitions rest on a narrow social base. It remains a country in which nearly 200 million people lack access to safe drinking water and more than 700 million lack proper sanitation facilities. (See figure 7.2.) The gap between the intractable poverty of India's predominately rural population and the developing

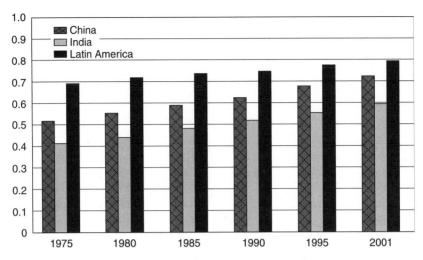

Figure 7.2 Human Development Indicator—Country Ranking. Data source: UN

sectors of India's economy is a product of the strategies employed by India's political parties to exercise political power through the management of a vast patronage machine. Information technology escaped from the tangled jungle of regulations: politicians left it alone because initially it offered few prospects of government employment or patronage.

India is widely perceived to be a political success, and despite its economic disappointments, it is a rare democracy in the developing world. India's poor choice of economic policies, however, is politically motivated. Despite the strength of India's primary democratic institutions, poor public-sector governance puts India's market reforms at risk. The obstacles to the performance of the public sector result from the relationship between the government's centralized administrative institutions and political party competition. That poisonous nexus is responsible for the largest bottleneck to India's future economic health: its ballooning deficits and soft budget. Patronage politics and the quest for spoils stimulate interventionist economic management that eventually leads to massive fiscal deficits.

THE FOUNDERS' LEGACY

Jawaharlal Nehru, India's first prime minister (1947–64) placed India firmly on the path of democracy. He encouraged parliamentary debate, stood for internal democracy within the Congress Party, maintained a politically neutral civil service in the British tradition, and fostered judicial independence. He encouraged a free press, championed secular over sectarian legal codes, and firmly entrenched civilian control over the military to prevent Bonapartism. The political structures he installed and nurtured made India a unique and resilient democracy among developing countries. Despite his exceptional commitment to democratic governance, India's growth pattern during its first postindependence generation was not exceptional.[3] To the contrary, output growth per worker is now squarely in the middle of all developing-country averages. India's entirely mediocre performance is very discouraging to those who wish to link democracy with economic growth.

The spirit of democracy in India must struggle against elitist institutions, politics, and social policies. In the early years of independence, political power belonged to the upper castes, and officials of upper-caste backgrounds dominated all Nehru's national cabinets. This elitism cannot be attributed to any personal failures in leadership. Elitism is so deeply rooted in India's history that it is difficult to pin responsibility on its founders or any other set of individuals.

Elitism strongly influences economic policies and the means of implementing those policies in India. Like Gandhi's, Nehru's economic outlook was shaped by the struggling economy of the pre–World War II era of the Great Depression. India's founders attributed the hard times of their youth to the open economic policies that exposed India to the effects of depressed global conditions. To avoid being battered by forces they could not control, India's founders adopted a highly interventionist government and closed their economy, hoping to generate internally the huge investment the growing economy needed. Nehru looked to the example of the Soviet Union and engaged India on a path of state-supported industrialization that reinforced the role of elite business groups, who were drawn into webs of political patronage. Like the Soviet Union, India focused on heavy industry that had declining value in the emerging global economy. New industries, entrepreneurialism, private-sector initiative, and engagement in the world economy were stifled, leaving India's industries without any comparative advantage. Planners told investors where to invest, what technology to use, what was to be the size of the plant, how it was to be financed. Then the battle for licenses to import capital goods and raw materials began, with dozens of clearances required from state-level officials who controlled access to power, land, sales tax, excise, and labor regulations. The planners even limited the entry of firms into "frivolous" sectors such as toys or cosmetics. They limited firm expansion with stifling labor regulations that seem to benefit the working classes. However, powerful unions compelled government budgets on education and health to be spent on salaries rather than on students or patients. The planners further curtailed imports by imposing the highest tariff levels in the democratic world, curbed remittances of foreign exchange, and kept all of the nation's financial resources under their own control. Looking back, it was a mistake to deny Indian firms the right to compete in export-oriented activities that could have generated foreign exchange and established patterns of engagement in the world economy. Overlooking such benefits, politicians established control over the commanding heights of the economy and used the vast powers at their disposal to help get themselves elected. This left an economy with antiquated labor laws, high internal and external tariffs, a bloated and inefficient public sector, a corrupt civil service, deficient physical infrastructure, and rampant poverty.

A process of liberalization that began after the fiscal crisis of (1989–91) attempted to mitigate and eliminate the control "Raj."[4] Nevertheless, a decade later, the government's 2003 budget continued to support a jungle of tax breaks, dodges, exemptions, and twists that strangle private enterprise and drive initiative in the direction of evasion rather than disclosure. Inefficient roads make importing steel from Europe to Mumbai cheaper than carrying it from nearby Jamshedpur. Indian industries pay three times more for power than China's, small firms face forty different inspectors a year, and every new power project requires a minimum of eighteen clearances. Industries slated for privatization are still under administrative control despite its debilitating impact on government deficits. Rajiv Gandhi admitted in the late 1980s that less than fifteen paise from every rupee spent on rural development actually reaches the rural poor. About forty thousand villages do not have sanitation facilities, and private power generation is an idea that has come and gone because the chronically indebted state-owned industries rarely pay their electricity bills. Politicians still lure voters with the promise of subsidized power, driving private providers away.[5] Archaic laws, like the Factories Act, which requires the provision of drinking water in earthen pots rather than in water coolers, remain.[6] Such regulations end up as nuisances that are irregularly enforced because the state does not have the capacity to ensure speedy judgment in court.

Why has it taken so long for India's economic potential to become a major factor in global economic calculations? One of the reasons that India has not performed up to its potential is that it failed to realize its obvious advantage in labor-intensive industries. Unfavorable tax and interest rates, intrusive enterprise regulation, and rigid labor laws strangled enterprise growth. Because of the adverse climate for enterprise creation, company governance has been below par. Few Indian companies meet international standards of accounting and shareholder protection, and even fewer meet standards for registration on the New York Stock Exchange.[7]

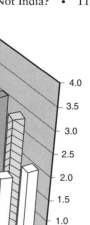

Figure 7.3 Economic Freedom Across Regions 1995–2003. Note: Heritage Foundation 1 (most free) to 5 (least free).

Why is India's strength in information technology, a sector that requires skilled labor, if India's average educational level is low? India's most obvious advantage with a labor force dominated by young unskilled workers should be labor-intensive manufacturing activities. Yet investment in industry is sluggish, and the formal service sector which accounts for nearly 50 percent of India's GDP resists foreign investment, leaving many workers unemployed.[8]

In relative terms, India's liberalization has not significantly shifted its global status as one of the world's laggards. After more than a decade of liberalization, India's rank is 121 of 156 countries in the annual rankings of economic freedom around the world. (See figure 7.3.) Among the world's sixty-two democracies, India is in the bottom tier for economic freedom. Trade policies have the highest level of protectionism, average tariffs are 29.5 percent, and 715 products require import licenses.[9] Of course, relativity is key. Tariffs are down from 300 percent in some sectors, and licenses for imports once covered over two thousand products. In a study of globalization, India occupies 61 out of 62 countries for overall economic ranking, 53 for personal ranking, 55 in technological ranking, and 57 in political ranking.[10]

Despite India's importance in software programming in 2003, it has little part in the global production chains that are increasingly important in regional East Asian trade. Its inward-looking economy attracts little foreign investment, and it plays a smaller part in world trade today than it once did.[11]

After independence, India's development strategy enjoyed the endorsement of policy leaders throughout the world, and India seemed poised to assume the intellectual and moral leadership of the Third World. Fifty years later, many developing nations view India's experience as proof that development and democracy are incompatible. Today, many compare India to East Asia and conclude that the moral of the story is to first get rich and then democratize. Leadership of the developing world has shifted to East Asia, and India is no longer sought out for its advice or education. In October 1996, India contested Japan for one of the five nonpermanent seats on the Security Council of the United Nations and was beaten by a 142–40 margin.

India has had no shortage of exceptional economists and social reformers. Yet, its internationally acclaimed universities, intellectuals, economists, and statespeople were unable to correct India's direction even after it became clear that the ship had veered off course. India's omnipresent state sector did not promote growth as well as East Asia's high-performing states, nor did India's highly trained bureaucratic elite identify or implement social and economic reforms. India started out with a strong set of laws on the books and ended up with rule by powerful individuals, going from institutional to personalized power. These patterns have undermined many established certainties in the world of development policy. How did a country seeking to show others the way to development itself become a model of mediocrity with few imitators? Why is India's civil service system, designed to recruit the best and the brightest by objective criteria, unable to define and solve social problems? How did a political system that began with highly unified central administrative machinery and a political party with a clear national vision end up with personalized, fragmented parties that offer patronage instead of policy directives?[12] How did a political culture that began by espousing nonviolence eventually breed endemic political violence? The answer lies in the linkage between electoral politics and public administration.

INDIA'S "TAMMANY HALL" SYSTEM: TO THE VICTOR, THE SPOILS

India's Congress Party dominated electoral competition during the first twenty years after independence. Created by India's founders, the party was founded on principles of self-dependence, self-reliance, cooperation, nonviolence, communal cooperation, and participation built from the grassroots level. Its leaders were reputed to be incorruptible; many earned their reputations for integrity by having served prison sentences for the cause of national independence. Yet, fifty years after independence, prime minister Narasimha Rao was convicted of corruption but has not served a prison sentence.

India's leaders from the very outset adapted quickly to the reality that poor interregional communication and high levels of illiteracy made it difficult to get the message of policy results through to the large Indian franchise. Most Indian voters lack the resources to overcome communication, travel, and language barriers in order to gain knowledge about policy outcomes.

To overcome barriers to informed voting, the Congress Party created a patronage network that empowered or co-opted local power brokers, or "big men," offering access to governmental services controlled by the party[13] in exchange for their local influence to gain electoral support. A chain of individuals, or brokers, which stretched from village to state and eventually to the capital, made the Congress Party an irresistible force.[14] Under Congress rule, patronage coexisted with centralization and single-party rule. Patronage followed new rules since the emergence of divided government and the rise of the BJP as the dominant party.

In the mid-1960s the Congress Party's chain of power deteriorated, and numerous scandals began to tarnish the halo it had earned from its central role in the independence movement. In addition, the party's association with privileged elites promoted opposition parties to mobilize previously dormant sectors of the population. This mobilization intensified the competition for spoils, as new group identities were forged to serve increasingly narrow social or political purposes. With the exception of Marxist parties, politicians competed by offering spoils rather than ideology. Politicians linked an individual or a group's identity with the likelihood of receiving benefits from the state as a reward for political participation.[15] Gurcharan Das wrote that competitive politics has created "vote banks" that strengthened caste consciousness. He adds that caste associations "have begun to behave like modern interest groups, competing for spoils in a democracy."[16] Sectarian social identities were politically cultivated in the chase for spoils. By 1967, its inability to deliver goods to the many newly mobilized sectors of the population lost Congress Party its majority.

Congress Party politicians failed because the demand for spoils was greater than the supply, and an inability to provide basic services made the party vulnerable to attack from all sides. Alternative parties were generally led by charismatic individuals focused on private goods[17] rather than on issues.[18]

To understand why the politics of patronage is unsustainable, imagine a scenario in which a majority party (group X) diverts resources for electoral purposes to expand its patronage base, and this recurs until no more resources exist for expropriation purposes. The majority party must restrict its patronage base until eventually the increased demand for rents (e.g., increased numbers of patrons/clients) exceed the party's supply of resources. To challenge group X's majority, losers from group X join a new party (group Y). However, if most goods in the economy have already been allocated for patronage, group Y may promise to expropriate and redistribute group X's patronage benefits to satisfy its own constituents. Conflict is especially likely if the majority of group Y's constituents defect from group X. Group Y must represent its constituency by expropriating from group X, which leads to squabbles. As Atul Kohli reports, "The state's resources, therefore, no longer constitute the functional resource that at one time helped grease the Congress machine. Competition over state-controlled resources increasingly is what many contemporary political struggles are all about."[19] As the growth of the state crowded out other alternative economic activities,[20] conflicts over spoils erupted in violence and social unrest.[21] Competition for access to resources produced political conflict because no party could meet the demands it mobilized.[22]

How Politicians Exploit Ethnic Fragmentation

Bloc voting allows a few barons of power to control large numbers of voters. In the predominantly rural states such as Bihar and Orissa, the poor, who depend on upper-caste landlords for their livelihood, cannot afford to vote independently of the wishes of their patrons. The village "big men" must in turn be loyal to patrons they depend on higher up, so that a senior member of the patronage chain ends up controlling a large number of votes. Candidates for political office can assemble the votes for an electoral victory just by backing a few key clients. Thus bloc voting allows democratic selection processes to be circumvented by small coalitions.

As noted, ethnic fragmentation is a strong incentive for bloc voting to emerge. The imams of the prominent mosques in India employ the logic of bloc voting to control the votes of their followers simply by issuing a fatwa. For example, before the national election, the contending players would turn to Old Delhi's Jama Masjid to influence the imam's call to the Muslims to vote for a particular party. Political observers believe the imam's edict helped turn the Muslim vote against Indira Gandhi in the post-Emergency elections.

Muslims were on the same side as the Hindu Nationalist Jan Sangh, the BJP's earlier avatar, in alignment against Indira Gandhi. Gandhi learned her lesson, and when she faced midterm elections in 1980 she personally went to Jama Masjid to meet the imam and regretted in writing the excesses of the Emergency. Obligingly the imam extended support to her for her comeback elections. Since then fatwas from religious figures and caste heads are an important convention around elections. For example, to counter Jama Masjid, the imam of Fatehpuri Masjid at the other end of Chandni Chowk backed the other side.

Bloc voting in Indian elections closely mirrors the logic of North America's Tammany Hall system, which drew its support from Irish-American populations in late nineteenth-century American cities.[23] Politicians who could get out the vote were supplied with the means to help out-of-luck constituents survive difficult times. Since anyone who wanted access to succor in times of need had to be counted among the party's supporters, the poor could not vote independently. They sold their votes to the machine to be protected from economic risk, allowing their patrons to deliver a large bloc of votes that kept the machine in power. By avoiding personal economic risk, voters sacrificed the hope of good economic policies for the promise of a handout during hard times. In this way, the North American constituents of the Tammany machine were no different than the poor landless farmers in India. In both cases, individually rational strategies for survival in the face of risk produced collectively irrational and unstable social outcomes that allow the wealthy barons of power to exploit the weakness of the poor. It took big government welfare systems to drive Tammany Hall–style politicians out of business in American politics.

In India today, as in the United States during the nineteenth century, wealthy businesses desiring government support for licenses and permits are a principal source of funds for political parties. Because voters strategically elect candidates who are most likely to provide private benefits, a generous supply of funds is needed and corporate financial support is the logical source for these patronage funds. In India, control of state-owned sectors is a source of spoils that did not exist in the United States. Patronage politics has had a more detrimental effect on the economy in India because to maintain state-owned industries, the government subsidizes electricity at great public expense.

Bloc voting also makes it difficult for candidates who stand for the public good to defeat rivals who specialize in the discreet service of narrowly defined ethnic enclaves. If their bloc leaders lose, citizens must forgo their expectation of private goods. If the candidates of rival blocs prevail, entitlements already gained can be redistributed. A politician promising to clean up the corruption has little appeal in the logic of bloc voting because if the good-governance candidate wins, voters benefit regardless of who they voted for. In India's winner-take-all electoral system, being a loser can be extremely costly, but so can winning because patronage networks eventually run out of resources.

Bloc voting is unstable because voter loyalties change in the pursuit of the best private payoffs. To maintain loyalty, party bosses find that they frequently deplete their sources of private goods. As these supplies are depleted, winning coalitions have to accept public policy instead of private payoffs. In this regard, political competition will hopefully move the Indian voters toward a demand for better public policy and fewer private goods.[24]

How Patronage Works in India

At election time, politicians need to hire a large number of rank-and-file political workers to get out the vote. These workers build networks of personal relationships, obliging as many people as possible to vote. Favors must be provided to voters so that they will remember incumbents at election time with their votes.

Because of rules that prevent firing government workers, each government increases its size and control over the economy. This sharply contrasts with the Tammany Hall system, in which all city workers could be fired with a change of regime, preventing entrenched interests from prevailing. Civil service systems arise to prevent patronage. Once civil servants are protected by civil service rules, they should be indifferent to who wins an election. Politicians who cannot hire their supporters or dismiss the appointees of other parties have little discretion over the disbursement of spoils. In this sense, patronage systems and civil service systems are usually opposed. However, in India this opposition was circumvented, and instead the civil service was subordinated to patronage.

The civil service rules frustrate politicians because they cannot dismiss the appointees of the previous government and therefore cannot control government payrolls—an important cause of inflation. Paradoxically, less control over the macroeconomy and limited job creation in the private sector makes patronage essential for politicians who wish to garner the support of voters.

Government service contracts are another source of funds enabling politicians to purchase political support. To maximize these opportunities, politicians need information from bureaucrats about future construction sites, new factories, and public buildings. Kickbacks helped one Tammany-type boss, Atulya Ghosh, develop an efficient machine: in exchange for public contracts, Calcutta businessmen made contributions to the city's Congress Party that were channeled into services to the better-off influential people in the city and into resources to build party support in the countryside.[25] With the help of local bureaucrats, Ghosh successfully purchased the votes necessary to remain in office.

Control over the allocation of urban land is another key political resource. One of India's most famous corruption fighters, K. J. Alphons, described the agency he works for, the Delhi Development Authority (DDA) as "the most corrupt institution in the country." Those who corrupt it, he added, are "nearly all the top politicians in India." They help illegal builders grab DDA land to build unauthorized buildings that range from the shanties of the poor to the shopping centers for the middle class to the mansions of the rich, all built on government land with false documentation obtained through high-level political complicity. Moreover, Alphons reported that nothing gets built, legal or illegal, without a bribe.[26] Presumably, politicians who are bribed must share their rewards with the civil servants who have the power to control licenses. Politicians have the power to control postings that determine which bureaucrats have access to fees for their services.

Even access to woefully inadequate health-care services was turned into a patronage good the access to which depended on political intervention. A politician from a ruling party in an appropriate political council can and is expected to command executive agencies to do things for his constituency. It is common practice among property holders to negotiate tax value with the assessor to reduce the estimated value of property. Master-plan roads can be diverted to avoid the property of the town elite. Money can even improve the level of daily services (e.g., mail delivery), which can be sped up through contributions from those who want to ensure that government employees do their job. The telephone repairperson, of course, has options: a line may be repaired "immediately," "soon," or "in due course." The postman may deliver a letter with "extra effort," "speedily," or "regularly," depending on the bribe.[27] Even routine opportunities to collect bribes allow for networks of corruption to emerge that eventually revert to the politicians who control the postings.[28] In this sense, even the most mundane corruption at the bottom—the venality of the official who sells postage stamps—is connected to the corruption at the top.[29]

When bloc voting prevails, voters can no longer depend on services being available to all citizens. Candidates who stand for universal client needs have little chance of supplanting the candidates who appeal to ethnic blocs, because voters cannot afford risking their sources of patronage by allowing a rival bloc to win. General service delivery will deteriorate, leaving the poor powerless since they cannot afford to defect to a rival bloc out of fear of further reducing their access to benefits. When clientelism takes over service delivery, the selective distribution of rewards leaves much of the population without adequate services. For example, politicians may prefer to keep prices for infrastructure services below the cost of recovery. They may use their power to appoint company directors and supply public subsidies to ailing enterprises in exchange for commitments to supply favors that include excess employment, below-market tariffs to selected clients, or the targeting of new investments to garner support for a particular constituency. Spiraling costs and deteriorating service quality result, leaving much of the population without adequate services. When cost recovery is circumvented, the providers depend on budget transfers, which the politicians control. In the absence of transfers, the providers may choose to cut back service.

Citizens respond to the rationing of their access by supporting those politicians who favor them. As already noted, the politicians who attract the votes are those who link their clients to services. Candidates who advocate universal access find they have a weak client base because all citizens benefit from universal access even if they have not voted for the good-governance advocate. Voters who lose their patron lose access to private goods, and the losing party has no way to penalize the provider for poor service. In a clientelistic system, politicians who advocate universally accessible public goods will have less appeal than those who offer rationed access of private goods to supporters.

From personalization to deinstitutionalization to corruption, the evolution of police and educational services illustrates how the personalization of authority—achieved through deinstitutionalization—inevitably leads to venality.[30] In India, venality refers to the selling of discretion in the performance of duty.[31] Because the police control access to the ballot box, chief ministers can use the police force to extend personal political control and to help influence votes.[32] The police help to influence votes, as individual citizens are dependent on their services, and control over police personnel administration ensures that the party boss, his cronies, and constituents are all protected. What began as a strategy to enhance political control has had unanticipated and unfortunate consequences. An ill-trained, venal police force rarely provides the high standards of evidence needed to convict felons. Fines and arrests are lucrative sources of funds, encouraging venality and leaving the police force unable to provide basic law enforcement.[33] Although in the long run, patronage politics is inherently unstable, how and when it will be replaced is uncertain.

The seemingly benign recruitment of teachers is also a source of spoils. Highly decentralized school boards offer excellent patronage opportunities. Since teachers are paid by state governments, political bosses hire teachers based on their political loyalties. When teaching appointments are political, government inspectors (also political appointees) have no incentive to supervise teachers effectively.[34] Instead, they collect bribes from teachers who do not report to their classrooms but collect individual payments from students for private lessons. This leaves many schools in rural districts empty and many children uneducated.

Ordinary citizens suffer the most from political patronage because of its interference with social welfare. Politically elected officials personalize and deinstitutionalize the system of service delivery and rob the state of its ability to solve problems in a rule-bound fashion. Leaders who come to office by virtue of their personal appeal are likely to rule by fiat rather than by means of regulations and established procedures.

By far the most important conflict between patronage politics and development is the decay of public services. Police and fire services, clean streets, and schools with teachers are not provided. Services that can be distributed selectively are more desirable than those that go to everyone. Without selective services, politicians have little pull on election day.

India's "Hindu, i.e., mediocre, rate of growth," as coined by Raj Krishna, is the economic outcome of a political dilemma. Personalization of authority erodes party discipline, and voters lose power over politicians. Patronage politics sustains personal power but robs politicians of their power over the administrative machinery at all levels of government, making incumbents vulnerable to failure and defeat. With politicians regularly being voted out, the electorate has begun to look for more durable outcomes than patronage so that politics has become more policy and governance focused.

One of India's strengths in the battle against corruption, well hidden from public view, are the agencies that audit and monitor governmental accounting. India enjoys relatively good access to information about the government budget. The accounting documents are accessible and at a glance offer an overview of the main central government aggregates. Budget estimates report the budget as well as revised estimates for the preceding year's budget, and information on general government data is available but only after a time lag. However, this delay, caused by the slow preparation of state budgets, is due to the lag on transfers from the central government.

The comptroller is effectively separated by a firewall from the auditor general responsible for auditing government accounts, so the accounting function is independent of the audit function. The independence of the Controller General of Accounts (CGA) is established in the constitution, and it has gained an international reputation for its effective oversight in keeping the offices of accounting and audit distinct. This type of institutional security is not found in countries like the Philippines or Indonesia, where government budgets are leaky buckets whose malfunctions are veiled from public view and are rarely noticed by businesses working in the country. India's leaks are in visible places where the public and the bureaucracy interface. Bribery rather than internal theft is the main source of distortion, and the effects of their visibility are devastating to the political order.

POLITICIANS STRUGGLE TO CONTROL THE BUREAUCRACY

In the early days of independence, India's elites took control of public administration from the British. Few members of the society could meet the rigorous educational requirements for entrance into the higher branches of the bureaucracy. This generated resentment on a massive scale as the elites used economic privilege and social prestige to their advantage.[35] In an attempt to dilute the elite character of the civil service, political leaders recruited officials from the poorer elements of society to create a broader, more representative service. In both Pakistan and Sri Lanka, politicians went so far as to dismantle the independent civil service commission and eliminate the elite civil service corps.

While trying to endow the country with a federalist constitution, India's founders left intact the centralized system of administrative control introduced by the British to hold the nation together. As a source of political unity, it has succeeded but still maintains a poor record in promoting development. The Indian government was not as iconoclastic as its neighbors and did not risk abolishing the elite corps of civil servants, thought to be the steel frame that held the nation together. India's federalism was constrained by an interlocking system of administrative, legislative, and judicial arrangements, binding the central and state-level governments and limiting the amount of local control. India's central government relies on its own administrative personnel to carry out programs and exercise authority in the states. The elite cadre of officers, Indian Administrative Service (IAS), is a key tool in maintaining central control of essential decision making. IAS collects revenue, regulates scarce commodities, and implements the five-year development plans. Dispatched by the party that controls the central government, the IAS restricts the states' right to recruit and control their own civil servants. While this system may create a far-flung empire with minimum personal and transaction costs, it hides necessary economic and financial information.

India's politicians learned to control the civil service by manipulating its rules rather than by dismantling it entirely. Moreover, as will be seen, once elected to national office, politicians find that a centralized, elite bureaucratic corps represents a thick, liquid market for the sale of lucrative bureaucratic posts.

An important transition occurred in the relations between politicians and bureaucrats over the course of India's first thirty years as a democracy. After independence, politicians depended on the expertise of the bureaucrats to govern and provide policy leadership. As the key source of policy advice, bureaucrats dominated the politicians. Unsurprisingly, political masters resented being neophytes before a sophisticated elite corps of trained civil servants, and the politicians attempted to assert a more active role that they believed to be consistent with the nation's democratic ethos.[36] The politicians gained an additional advantage from the inability of the civil service to deliver services effectively to the population, thereby creating strategic opportunities to stand up to the bureaucrats on behalf of the people. Helping constituents secure a contract, or find a place in a school or hospital, was a way to win electoral support and do something useful. Accustomed to looking down from great heights on the people they served, the bureaucrats in India and throughout South Asia viewed this new political aspect of administration as interference.[37]

A stalemate was eventually reached, the politicians remonstrated the rigid rules and regulations of the bureaucracy, and the administrators denounced political interference just as the politicians began to intervene even more.[38] Although they seem to accept the supremacy of political leadership, bureaucrats still openly blame the ministers and political leaders for all the ills of public administration.[39]

RULE-BOUND AND UNACCOUNTABLE: CAN IT BE BOTH WAYS?

The conflict between bureaucratic and political forms of authority exists in any society. A bureaucracy, by its very nature, will seek to establish its professional authority through secrecy, keeping its knowledge and intentions from the purview of the uninitiated outsider.[40] It warmly welcomes poorly informed political interests and typically resists attempts by political sponsors to gain knowledge by means of independent experts or interest-group collaboration.

Politicians seek to win votes by promising to control the bureaucracy. The politicians justify their quest for greater authority on the grounds that the bureaucracy was never suited to its vast responsibilities; the bureaucrats' tendency to prioritize the enforcement of rules over the pursuit of outcomes gives the politicians a justification to directly manage government agencies.

The incentives for bureaucrats to be distant and rule-bound come from the same source. Because they control information, bureaucrats can screen out information not conducive to their own interests. They can produce information that suits them and then get their political sponsors to believe it. Political leaders know the information is biased but do not have alternative sources of information. To overcome this familiar bureaucratic pathology, politicians have to intervene in a discretionary manner.

Getting a relative into a hospital, getting a license to open a food stall, getting a job, a telephone, a train ticket—all may require political intervention. Effective handling of such requests is a good way to build up electoral loyalty. The bureaucrat, as master of red tape, engenders the politician as "fixer."

The bureaucratic system inherited from the British was initially designed to be apolitical, with appointments and promotions based on merit. Hierarchy, extensive written rules, and merit appointments were all in place. Clear lines of authority did not end in the hands of politicians but in an independent civil service commission established to enforce the rules. The service worked by the standardization of procedure down to every trivial detail, the rules and procedures governing every aspect of behavior were fixed by centrally established codes. The design was classic and thoroughly well executed. However, it quickly produced the pathologies of excessive hierarchy, most notably an absence of accountability. The officers seemed high-handed because the rules ensured that they were accountable to no one but themselves. Designed to be apolitical and established to eliminate political interference, the classic administrative model produced a lack of accountability in the name of neutrality.[41]

THE POSTINGS MERRY-GO-ROUND

In India, an independent civil service commission determines the rules of bureaucratic service. Flaws emerge, however, in what seems to be an airtight design. Laws may prohibit the discharge of civil servants and restrict promotions, but they do not restrict politicians from intervening in postings.

Central authorities rarely use their power over postings to impose their will on the states. Instead, they allow local officials to control the career paths of the local bureaucracy.[42] By giving local leaders control over transfers, chief ministers at the center can consolidate leaders of local factions and give them the tools necessary to cultivate an electoral constituency. Ministers of the central government need a pyramidal support base— at the constituency, state, and central levels. Members of the legislative assemblies (MLAs) at the state level are needed to bring in the votes. A chief minister sitting in Delhi who loses the support of the state's MLAs is likely to be replaced. In exchange for their support of the chief minister, local politicians typically gain the right to control transfers within their respective communities.

Local-level politicians build networks of loyal followers in the local bureaucracy, who in turn target services for individuals whose support is needed to win national elections. Without local control over the disposition of IAS transfers, community politicians would lack many of the key assets under the thumb of the IAS.[43]

The district is the basic unit of politics and administration within the state government, and the IAS collector, as the head of the state apparatus in each district, presides over all district authorities. The collector's power is derived from authority over a range of resource collection and allocation. The collector can appoint public-service personnel on a short-term basis into jobs with significant political implications. In most states, the collector has power over postings, transfers, and issuing licenses for "fair-price shops," all of which are of great interest to local politicians. As part of the government's food distribution program, the fair-price shops are designed to make food staples available to the poor. The state government issues ration cards for essential commodities in fair-price shops, where food is sold at subsidized prices. Even so, the foods most commonly sold are not the coarse grains wanted by the poor. Fine and superfine rice is more frequently available than common varieties, and about a quarter of sales are in sugar, a commodity not demanded by the poor. In some regions, 90 percent of the poor have no access to the shops, which generally carry the goods demanded by the groups being wooed for their electoral support.

Jean Dreze wrote:

> In 1994–95 the 50th round of the National Sample Survey highlighted another disturbing aspect of the nutrition situation in India: there is no food security system worth the name. At that time, the main plank of public intervention in this field was the "public distribution system" (PDS). Access to PDS was supposed to be "universal," but in practice, only a privileged minority of the population was covered. For instance, in India as a whole, barely one-fourth of the survey households reported buying food grain from the PDS at that time. Further, access to the PDS was heavily biased against the poorer states, against rural areas within the poorer states, and even against poor households within specific states or areas. In states such as Bihar and Uttar Pradesh, only four per cent of all households were buying food grain from the public distribution system in 1993–94.[44]

The collector plays another significant role: deciding, in some instances, which cases will be heard by the courts. Collectors decide, for example, on actions taken against smugglers of essential commodities.[45] These decisions have had significant political implications.[46] Fortunately, with controls ending, smuggling too is disappearing.

When the posts are politically sensitive, members of the bureaucracy are generally chosen because of their personal loyalty or expected compliance with those in power. Technocrats are sent to positions that require expertise. These are unlikely to be the "wet posts" from which the rupees pour. Instead, technocrats are routed to dry posts where personnel learn to interact with international officials and are kept out of the lucrative departments that allocate licenses, subsidize goods, or can raise money by black-market sales. Political control over postings to sectors such as transportation, public health, civil supplies, land development, and construction licensing promotes corruption because of the attractive opportunities for kickbacks.[47] Once these opportunities are removed through the truncation of the "permit raj," new forms of corruption such as defective bidding procedures for awarding government contracts may arise to replace the old corruption. The assumption that corruption can be combated through liberalism is without empirical basis. N. Vittal, a former chief vigilance commissioner of India, reported:

> Political corruption is seen as one of the most significant sources of corruption and the root of the culture of corruption in our country. In fact, our entire political process and the system of election depend on black money. Every candidate in an election from the lowest to the highest level needs money. 40 percent of India's GDP is black money. No wonder that Indian politics also has a significant association with black money. It is not as if the politicians or those who participate in politics want to be corrupt. Many of them are good professionals and would probably earn more professionally if they do not spend time in politics. There are also other genuinely committed social leaders who may not like to handle black money. But over a period of years, a new culture of "political honesty" has grown in which while the political leader, at least at the individual level, may be honest, and is forced for the sake of the party to raise funds even from questionable sources.[48]

A Thick, Liquid Market for Corruption

While politicians can gain considerable rewards from controlling the system of transfers, they have no direct knowledge about the value of a particular post or potential output in terms of bribes or kickbacks. As a result, politicians will allow the bureaucrats to compete by auctioning the posts to the highest bidder. The price offered by the seeker reveals the value of the post.[49] To maximize the amount of revenue collected, these auctions are held frequently, increasing the incidence of transfers.

The auctions allow bureaucrats to bid for the most desirable "wet posts." Because posts vary significantly in how much private benefit can be extracted, there is considerable competition among managers. The most corrupt managers have the money to compete for the most lucrative posts. Efficient managers are those who maximize their yield through side payments rather than those who provide public goods. The system fosters innovation to improve the private yield on posts but gives little incentive to produce widely distributed public benefits.

The answer to why a highly elitist and centralized civil service is maintained in sharp conflict with India's democratic aspirations lies in the side payments politicians derive from a highly concentrated, liquid market for the sale of administrative posts. As in any auction market, the larger the number of buyers, the higher the asking price. An increase in the concentration of bidders heightens the value of the posts, especially because bidders are often insiders who alone know the value of the positions.

The evolution of the civil service in India demonstrates how institutions can be diverted from their intended usage by subtle shifts in the rules that govern them.[50] Although merit recruitment and seniority promotions were not tampered with, discretion over postings allows politicians to circumvent the intent of the original design. Bureaucrats are now shifted from post to post much more frequently than efficient job performance would justify.[51] Excessive mobility adversely affects the capacity of the bureaucracy to provide leadership; continuity of expertise is disrupted and production of private rather than public goods is rewarded. Politicians rarely discuss the motives for transfers; this ensures that favors for key constituencies can be kept secret. Secrecy in the awarding of posts also prevents civil servants from influencing decisions about postings and discourages group representation of civil service interests.

Competition over rewards and posts is intense, but the wrong kinds of output are maximized. Since a successful post holder is one who acquires funds to move to a more lucrative post, he or she must specialize in distributing goods and services privately to maximize kickbacks and bribes. To prosper, bureaucrats focus on activities other than those fostering development.[52] Thus, bureaucrats become specialists at mismanagement, working at cross-purposes with the laws and institutions they oversee. Unable to use the bureaucracy to achieve policy objectives, politicians are powerless to effect meaningful reform.

As long as the present system exists, the frequent transfers of personnel among posts will continue. Politicians cannot opt out of corruption because they must sell positions to get reelected, and although the market does involve transfers from post to post, politicians are only able to evaluate performance based on the amount a manager can pay for a transfer. Because an efficient manager in this system must maximize private goods to stay competitive, avoiding corruption is difficult.

A symbiotic relationship exists between the politicians and the bureaucrats, in which each holds the other responsible for the powerlessness of government to carry out meaningful public sector reform. Who is to blame? The real culprit is the continuous expansion of new and attractive posts for which only bureaucrats may apply. Many defenders of the postings system view it as a way to punish incompetent subordinates and replace them with more efficient managers. Although this is not by itself a bad practice, it becomes corrupt when conducted without any reference to actual performance ratings and output accountability. Panels that represent citizen and government interests are necessary to correct the arbitrary character of the present system. The current transfer system does not eliminate corrupt officials; it only moves problems to other locales. Periodic assessments to improve efficiency have included recommendations for major changes. The Santhanam Committee recommended reforms as far back as 1964, but its proposals have yet to be acted on. The politics of getting elected explains these delays.

THE OBSTACLE OF STATUS

Just as India's elite bureaucracy conflicts with the country's democratic aspirations, a rigid hierarchy of job classifications frustrates the intentions of the nation's founders to build grassroots democracy. Attempts to achieve community objectives through elitist management are a contradiction in themselves, especially considering the perverse incentives that discourage the delivery of social services to the poor.

India's system of public administration features high firewalls between senior management and rank-and-file bureaucrats: status distinctions are heavily emphasized and career mobility from bottom to top is highly restricted. A communally oriented system would feature flat pay scales and bonuses paid for group accomplishments; instead, India's highly legalistic system inhibits face-to-face transactions, thereby reducing informal channels of communication between ranks. Subordinates are given limited responsibility for even the design and implementation of production processes at the microlevel.

Beginning with job classifications, the Indian system does not link incentive compatibility with developmental tasks. It is highly centralized and legalistic, sharply distinguishing between officers and subordinates; only officers can be promoted. Thus, 98 percent of the staff running irrigation canals has no promotion prospects. The Public Service Commission assigns the seniority of officers on the basis of an initial examination, referees' reports, and a five-minute interview. The initial ranking is binding for a lifetime and determines all subsequent promotions. Out-of-step promotions based on skills are opposed. Because current judgment of one's merit is less relevant, diligence at an individual level does not pay off. There is no reason for subordinates to struggle to improve skills or to gain access to training opportunities since once a coefficient in the hierarchy is assigned, an officer only moves up according to seniority. In-service training, which could provide an objective basis for judging current performance, is not related to performance and it is rarely available. About 2 percent of Indian employees have promotion prospects. In East Asia the percentage is much higher, in Korea, for example, 35 percent can dream of promotion on the basis of merit. The morale of people subjected to this kind of stratification suffers.

Indian civil servants lack identification with place and have few incentives for teamwork. Hierarchy and formalism isolate workers from each other, forcing them to look to the center rather than cooperate with co-workers. Since senior officers rarely work their way up the ranks, they are unfamiliar with the tasks of those at lower levels of the system. Pay differentials, then, are not based on demonstrated differences of skills or knowledge or quality of work, which only encourages subordinates to mistrust their supervisors. Authority is more legitimate when based on demonstrated competence in service. In India, status substitutes for knowledge.

Vertical differentiation is more pronounced in Indian bureaucratic organization than in comparable East Asian organizations to the extent that in India, rank can be predicted by dress; even recreation and eating are strictly segregated by rank.

> In 1963–4, a top ICS [Indian Civil Service] Secretary in New Delhi received 63 times (3,500Rs compared to 55Rs per month) the amount earned by a common messenger. The comparable differential for Pakistan 38.96%, or the USA 7.24% is far less dramatic. The high and the low were somewhat less far apart in the early 1980s, but the differences were still very marked. Top Secretaries in India are earning more than 10 times the amount that central government employees earn, whereas this differential in the United States remains half that amount. Senior IAS officers also occupy sumptuous government bungalows, are driven by chauffeurs, and saluted by armed guards as they enter secretariat buildings.[53]

With extreme vertical stratification, information does not spread easily to the top. As a result, detection of noncompliance in India is low. Typically, subordinates will say they did not get a telegraph in time to attend a particular meeting or that resources were unavailable. A culture of mistrust results and problems get worse before being attended to. Low trust in management inhibits conscientious efforts and discourages the discussion of problems with superiors. Existing levels of performance are maintained—nothing is ventured and nothing is gained.

Poor management practices also cause weak workplace solidarity. India's vertical authority structures, characterized by legalism, pretensions to neutrality, universality, carefully enumerated rights, and rule-based personnel codes all engender low-trust relationships between members of the bureaucracy, sharply dividing those at the top from their subordinates. Status obstacles inhibit cooperation and undermine trust. Those who passed through the exam system look down from great heights on those at the bottom. Hierarchy gives senior managers the ability to pit subordinates against each other. Suspicions and unwillingness to share data about local conditions result so that those in the higher reaches of the hierarchy have only limited local knowledge. Awareness that those at the top do not play by the rules encourages those at the bottom to do the same. Furthermore, frequent transfers of personnel prevent the development of relationships and thus the transfer of information.

"Playing it safe" behavior was inspired by a colonial leader who decided to concentrate administrative power in the hands of a small group of elite administrators because he could not trust the rank-and-file. In this context, a gulf separated the few strategic officers who made the rules from the workers at the lower levels. Extreme stratification in the bureaucracy conflicts with the assumptions on which Indian democracy is built. Combining democratic political authority with effective bureaucratic administrative authority has proved to be the Achilles' heel of India's development.

A system that provides limited citizen satisfaction provides many reasons why politicians must intervene. However, their interventions do not increase accountability to the actual recipients of government services because the interventions themselves are inevitably ad hoc and discretionary.

The Long Shadow of the "Permit Raj"

Although the reforms of 1991 made the permit raj obsolete, its legacy casts a long shadow over India's future. Many weaknesses of Indian business reflect the legacy of the closed economy: an inability to separate ownership from management, a lack of business strategy, a tendency to expand into unrelated sectors, inadequate investment in employee or product development, insensitivity to customer satisfaction, weak marketing, and backward technology and corruption. All of these habits acquired during the permit raj make it difficult for India businesses to create large-scale nonfamily business organizations.

With the bureaucracy caught in a web of corruption, businesses too found it difficult to escape the same web. Government control over the commanding heights of the economy drove entrepreneurs seeking essential permits, licenses, and loans into the hands of politicians. Politicians, needing money, arrange for the delivery of licenses to businesspeople who then depend on politicians for legal protection for offering bribes in the first place. For example, prosecutors are directly controlled by ministers and are not expected to follow an independent line; therefore, politicians may prevent investigations or block judicial authorities from taking action. United Press International reported, "Lack of accountability and patronage of a few corrupt politicians and greedy businessmen have made the Indian bureaucracy a law by itself. So much so that, reportedly, it even made a former prime minister admit that: 'Indian administrative-government officers have created such a steel frame around them that even the might of the state can't dismantle it.' "[54] Because the legal system is plagued with delays and filled with political appointees, the business community does not see the judiciary as offering much of a check on the politicians.[55] It is widely believed that nobody with influence is convicted. Corruption, as the Indians often say, is built into the system.

Politicians may ask financial institutions to support a firm's existing management in the event of a takeover threat or when the firm lacks adequate collateral, which is a frequent occurrence.[56] Because murky deals are best for generating unaccountable funds, an absence of adequate accounting occurs, making it difficult for firms to verify their assets. Hence, corporations often find they require political backers to arrange credit from the state-run banking system.[57]

Political parties could demand public contributions, since companies are allowed to donate up to 5 percent of their net profits to political parties. However, the parties prefer to collect money on the side to avoid seeming beholden to business and to avoid shareholder endorsement of such expenditures. It is in everyone's best interest for company managers to possess discretionary funds to obtain discretionary interventions. The system is hard to beat since all decisive players benefit, and the voices of shareholders and citizens are never heard. The system of corruption is so pervasive that in a study of the global competitiveness of 49 countries, the World Economic Forum ranked India number 45 in the honesty of government officials, 44 in the effectiveness of laws to protect shareholders, 46 in the ability of boards of directors to ensure corporate honesty, 45 in the ability of board's to protect shareholders' interests, and 40 in tax evasion.[58]

East Asia's economic success stories often include the important role played by industry organizations that help government planners define and implement policy and reduce individual deals or exceptions at the same time.[59] By contrast, India's decision making has rarely benefited from a system of advisory bodies of economic or social actors. Until the 1980s, the ability of professional business associations to unify interests across firms of the same industry was weak, and as a result, industry was not involved in the selection of general sector- or economy-wide policies. Instead, business leaders transacted business with government officials on a personal basis, which meant that no two members of an industry or of an interest group were treated the same way.[60] Atomized relationships, designed to facilitate the exchange of favors, was an outcome of patronage politics.[61] The expectation that rivals will seek political favors motivates others to do the same and prevents firms from acting as a group to impose policy consistency on government. As a result, India's private sector had little direct influence over public policy until the 1980s and previously was unable to prevent or modify the introduction of a single major redistributive policy.[62] Kochanek, a leading specialist on Indian business organization, asserted that the business community in India was prevented from acting as a unified lobby nor of pursuing a long term policy to achieve well-defined objectives.[63] Since industry did not act as a group, the government did not bargain collectively with industry. During the '50s, '60s, and '70s, the Associated Chambers of Commerce and Industry (ACCI) represented foreign multi-nationals and the more managerial firms of Bombay, led by Tata's. The Federation of Indian Chambers of Commerce and Industry (FICCI) were dominated by the Marwari firms that moved from trade to industry in the last half of the nineteenth century. The Federation of Associations of Small Industries of India (FASI) represents the small-scale sector. The three organizations often have sharply divergent views and were unable to generate a homogeneous perspective or to articulate a consistent set of interests or values. In the '80s the Confederation of Indian Industries emerged as an effective organization, with offices around the globe, and FICCI has become more effective and more representative.

India's Private Sector Adapts to Uncertainty

Critiques of India's protectionist economic policies emphasize the supply side and single out the country's planners and politicians for maintaining high tariff walls that protect central planning and import substitution.[64] Ideas with regard to trade policy have changed radically in India since the early 1990s. However, the demand side seems more intractable, more deeply rooted, and longer term than the supply of bad ideas, which have been corrected by experience and cross-country observation.[65] The market for trade protection is still active because firms have developed structures and strategies for accomplishing goals domestically that hinder their ability to compete internationally. The structures, systems, and procedures of management evolved to cope with domestic political risks, such as weak policy credibility and random government intervention. The weakness of the private sector then creates the demand for protectionism.

The weakness of India's private sector has many sources. Government firms often fail to pay debts owed to private companies.[66] Ad hoc regulatory interventions and arbitrary tax collections are forms of governmental discretion that can wipe out a firm's capital.[67] Successful firms often have something to hide; it is hard to imagine how success could have been achieved if serpentine rules had not been broken. This means managers in the private sector cannot escape vulnerability to political manipulation. Companies must have black money on hand that can only be accumulated through tax evasion or black-market operations to circumvent government controls or to make necessary contributions to political parties. Firms can expect that a political party representative will ask for specific amounts under the threat of raids by either the revenue intelligence director or the enforcement director. The threat of a raid by income tax authorities is supplemented by more routine demands for payment by inspectors and licensing authorities and became just another cost of doing business. Many firms established offices in Delhi to gain access to the market through the purchase of exemptions, licenses, and patents to perform ordinary investment decisions.[68] Large private groups were able to buy their way out of the regulations; for them, private/public collaboration typically took the form of private bribery. Tax rebates, price preferences, and exclusive rights to manufacture certain items could all be arranged but the price could not be disclosed. Many of these rights were sold to "ghost factories"—small-scale units that exist only on paper, designed to secure licenses, permits, and quotas that are resold. The negotiations between the firm and the bureaucrat for such rights were private and could easily be reversed when political power or bureaucratic postings had shifted.

To avoid tax raids, which can shake even the most seemingly stable operations, businesses adapt ownership and decision-making structures to maximize secrecy. Information about assets and activities is hoarded, accounting procedures and ownership structures are arcane, and the books are cooked. The firm's liabilities are not publicly available, taxable assets are disguised and the identity of investors and ownership structures are kept secret. All of this dissimulation leaves minority shareholders vulnerable to abuse by company management.[69] In fact, the *Investor's Guide* of India's *Economic Times* reported: "There is hardly a company that can resist the temptation or even the pressure to indulge in some amount of financial manipulation. The only difference is the degree to which accounts are played around with."[70] The need for secrecy, which generates high levels of firm-specific capital, are all rational, risk-reducing responses to regulatory uncertainty. Keeping secret the information concerning the assets and liabilities of individual firms limits a market for claims on their liabilities or assets, and secrecy also delays the evolution toward professionally managed, rationally structured administrative hierarchies.[71] The government contributes to information scarcity because officials jealously guard the information that is the source of rents, preventing the introduction of institutions that can quantify, measure, spread, and pool risk.

Despite the availability of technical expertise and skilled labor, firms avoid investment in managerial and financial technologies that facilitate the separation of management from ownership.[72] Instead of formal, large-scale organization, formal dynastic arrangements through intermarriage often seal business deals. This is understandable; nepotism is a rational form of human resource development in the absence of accurate reporting and weak information disclosure. Relatives closely identify their interests with the owners because they know that they will not be able to find equally good positions elsewhere. Relatives are notoriously difficult to control since they know they cannot be replaced with employees who are equally loyal. When the supply of competent relatives is exhausted, management may be unwilling to expand the organization. Thus, while nepotism is an efficient control device, it has the distinct disadvantage of linking firm size and capabilities to the size and capabilities of the ownership clique.[73] The firms that prospered under the permit raj are parts of family holding companies with opaque methods of accountability such as the Birlas, Tatas, Modis, Goenkas, and Sahara; these groups dominate the traditional industrial sectors and hold shares in a diverse portfolio of enterprises.[74] It remains to be seen if under the new regime these firms will be able to assert family wealth over shareholder value. The old business houses lack focus; having extended into unrelated activities, they lack core competencies. Many signs exist that a new generation of entrepreneurs will supplant the stalwarts of the past. In terms of market capitalization, forty-five companies have been forced off the list of the top one hundred. Indian managers now have to lower costs to compete with cheaper imports and to increase the equity value rather than depend on licenses that restrain competition. But powerful groups among the nation's politicians, bureaucrats, and business houses threatened by liberalization are committed to rallying the populace to prevent their more nimble competitors from capitalizing on global trends. The reform agenda is blocked by the force of organized labor, which opposes the privatization of loss-making public-sector plants; farm lobbies resist terminating subsidies for power, fertilizer, and water; thousands of state inspectors on the payrolls of state governments still hold on to intrusive rights to inspection; and the industrial bourgeoisie still resist competition. But the main culprits for India's laggard reform process are the social imbalances that cause dramatically unequal access to opportunity created by liberalization. India's social imbalances mean that opportunities from removing the barriers to growth will be concentrated on a small minority of already privileged people.

BUSINESS REPUTATION AND LIBERALISM

It is often repeated that India's business elite lacks ideological legitimacy. Decades of circumventing the rules have given business in India a bad name. This is partly due to intrusive economic legislation that made the economic calculation of profit-seeking businesspeople into quasi-criminals who have to break the law to simply conduct business. Between 1964 and 1969, the government appointed four committees that questioned the market power of India's largest private firms.[75] Businesses were prosecuted for producing more than their licenses allowed. When Vicks increased its production during a severe flu outbreak, it was subjected to investigation for having surpassed its quota. Government bankers routinely requested kickbacks in exchange for loans made to private businesses. Licenses were required for the import of capital goods and raw materials, each giving some regulatory authority an opportunity to collect under-the-table fees. Government officials determined where investments should be made and in which sectors, as well as the size of the plant and how it could be financed, and then collected a fee before granting the required permits. Businesses were under constant attack in Parliament, by the bureaucracy, and in the media, as they were held responsible for the bribes they were forced to pay in order to conduct business. Because of the obstacles in India, businesses had to invest abroad, further arousing popular ire. No surprise then that, in popular opinion, business practices are often mixed with criminal and antipatriotic practices. This is not fertile ground for liberalization.

In 1991 the government, in a matter of weeks, eliminated decades of control. The government led by Prime Minister P. V. Narasimha Rao (1991–96) did indeed take decisive steps to liberalize the trade and foreign investment regime as well as the industrial-licensing rules. Industrial-licensing regulations were simplified, and protective tariff walls were slashed.[76] The reforms included an initial devaluation of the rupee and subsequent market determination of exchange rate, abolition of import licensing (with the important exceptions of restrictions on imports of manufactured consumer goods and on foreign trade in agriculture), convertibility (with some notable exceptions) of the rupee on the current account, reduction in the number of tariff lines as well as tariff rates, reduction of excise duties on a number of commodities, some limited reforms of direct taxes, abolition of industrial licensing (except for investment in a few industries for locational reasons or for environmental considerations), relaxation of restrictions on large industrial houses under the Monopolies and Restrictive Trade Practices (MRTP) Act, easing of entry requirements (including equity participation) for direct foreign investment, and allowing private investment in some industries hitherto reserved for public-sector investment. The reforms mean that owners can expand existing businesses or start new ones without government approval. The Directorate General of Technical Development could no longer dictate which technology is appropriate. Raw materials and key components can now be imported without a license. Manufacturers can now choose between an Indian and foreign supplier. A National Renewal Fund for assisting workers currently employed in enterprises that will be scaled down or closed altogether was established. Reform of the financial sector included simplification of the interest rate structure with the elimination of interest rate floors on large loans, replacement of fixed-term deposit rates by an interest rate ceiling (still falls short of a floating market-determined rate), reductions in government preemption of loanable funds and monetization, and improving the capital position of the banks.[77] As a result of these reforms, it is possible to imagine that more open trade and pathways to the global economy will provide lasting prosperity, but corruption still stands in the way. Instead of restraining corruption, these reforms initiated a new wave of corruption and a heightened sensitivity to the deeply embedded corruption of the past.

CORRUPTION UNLEASHED

Corruption causes the breakdown of service delivery and intensifies communal violence, the prominent role of the black market, and the government's inability to effectively collect taxes. A government that is unable to implement basic programs has a credibility deficit. How can a country liberalize its economy while undergoing a crisis of governability? Unable to either enforce the law or provide basic services, how can the government be expected to direct liberalization to benefit all parties? If it has performed badly in the past—when basic services were not delivered despite numerous reforms and governments—why should citizens believe government will do better next time?

Until the mid-1990s, the international development community, donors and borrowers alike, were indifferent to the link between corruption and underdevelopment. A consensus existed that corruption was inherent in developing-country administration: honest governments were a luxury only developed nations could afford, and efficient administrations would emerge when domestic demand emerged with them. Until the 1990s, notoriously corrupt governments received development assistance with hardly any reference to the widespread misuse of public funds. Analysis of underdevelopment rarely confronted corruption except anecdotally. How did rampant abuse of public resources avoid disclosure, analysis, and response for so long? The cold war played a role, but so did professional economists who provided scientific support for ignoring corruption, elaborating a number of reasons why corruption does little economic harm during development. Corruption may even be a good thing, some believed, when it lubricates unwieldy administrative machinery that might otherwise grind to a halt. Indifference was also justified on the grounds that no evidence existed that corruption was a quantitatively significant component of GDP. This brand of developmental stoicism drew on Karl Marx's observation that the early stages of capital accumulation thrive on inequality and are inherently unjust. Even Marx's capitalist critics were willing to accept the bitter pill: no corruption, no development.

This stoicism was reinforced by the notion that East Asia's prosperity is proof that dirty practices do not prevent growth. The generalization about East Asia is inaccurate: the high performers—Singapore, Korea, Taiwan, Hong Kong and Japan—all aggressively tackled bureaucratic corruption before undertaking economic reform as a way to establish the credibility of government in the eyes of their citizens.[78] Studies undertaken by the World Bank confirm that corruption is less of an impediment to business in East Asia than in South Asia.[79]

No national government has been reelected successively in South Asia during the 1990s, the decade of economic liberalization, because no one was able to control corruption. Contrary to what the apologists have claimed—that corruption is a Western invention—the poor voters in these countries know what corruption is and will rise in furor against those politicians who practice it. Pakistan's Benazir Bhutto was brought down twice on charges of corruption. Pakistan's prime minister, Nawaz Sharif, was deposed twice on charges of corruption. India's Congress Party was undone on charges of corruption; Prime Minister Rao has been convicted and many of his top cabinet members are facing criminal investigations. The impetus for the 1996 political reversals of the Congress Party in national and local elections was corruption driven.[80] Sri Lanka's Chandrika Bandaranaike Kumaratunga of the People's Alliance Party made corruption a cornerstone of her successful attack on the rule of the United National Party. In Bangladesh, the Awami League defeated the government of the Bangladesh Nationalist Party (BNP) on the grounds that the BNP had abused public trust. In all of these elections, opposition parties can cite the corruption of the previous government to gain political advantage. The elections on the Asian subcontinent are unambiguous on corruption: scandals erode popular support for government and produce political crises that cost leaders their jobs. In a democracy, corruption is difficult to hide and will instead be publicly examined, discussed, and debated.

POLITICAL CORRUPTION AND CAPITAL ACCUMULATION

Throughout the first fifty years of India's history, firms adapted management practices to maximize secrecy so they could outwit regulators, but without a transparent balance sheet, long-term businesses confidence was undermined. Willful efforts at misinformation make businesses vulnerable to assaults on illegally accumulated wealth. A continual target of political uncertainty, the business sector is denied public support and is not invited to play an open role in policy making. Weak institutional support for business is overcome by strong personal relationships between businesspeople and politicians. However, deals that depend on the right connections can easily be overturned when a new government appears.[81] The threat of a counteroffensive biases firms from undertaking long-term investment.

Firms know that when government changes hands, the contracts consummated under the previous administration may be reconsidered. To entertain long-term investing, investors frequently require government subsidies or guarantees of monopoly to offset the political risk. If each new government or minister overturns the contracts of its predecessor, private investors will only make short-term investments by requiring the government to subsidize large capital expenditures and further crowding out the private sector.[82]

Thus, corruption is a political problem with economic consequences: opportunities are lost, innovation is deferred, and entrepreneurialism and investment are aborted. When citizens perceive that the government cannot credibly commit to the implementation of policies designed to increase economic growth, the government loses support, and reelection becomes improbable. The possibility of a political crisis brought on by corruption may further raise doubts about the durability of agreements with the government.[83] The cost of these distortions cannot be captured in strictly quantitative terms as a percentage of output. Corruption prevents the establishment of a credible policy environment, which is crucial to the success of economic reform.

PRESERVING THE HOST: HOW CORRUPTION AND DEMOCRACY COEXIST

Surveys of business opinion indicate that since liberal economic policies were introduced in the early 1990s, complaints about corruption are at an all-time high. In the World Bank's World Business Environment Survey comparing various impediments to business growth, corruption was named the greatest constraint on business development in South Asia.[84] Comparing region by region, the study reported that the percentage of firms citing corruption to be a major obstacle to business growth was highest in South Asia.[85] Transparency International ranked India at a low of 83 among 133 countries in its Corruption Index of 2002.[86] South Asian managers spent more time addressing the application and interpretation of the laws than did managers from any other world region.[87] When asked if it was common in their line of business to pay some irregular additional payments "to get things done," more than 65 percent of South Asian firms reported this was often the case, the highest frequency in any world region.[88]

Dismay over corruption arises at the very time that core democratic institutions seem stronger than ever. The Presidency, the Supreme Court, and the Election Commission, as well as numerous regulatory institutions, seem more robust in their efforts to safeguard the nation's democratic legitimacy. In the 1990s, an activist judiciary, for the first time in the nation's history, held politicians accountable to the law. Several state ministers were indicted and sent to jail. These indictments have increased the stature of the Supreme Court, raising the hope that the Election Commission, the Auditor General, the Supreme Court, and the Presidency will be the foundation for the progressive moment that will revitalize India's democracy.[89]

Why has corruption, as bad as it has been, not killed the host? The purveyors of corruption share an interest in protecting the institutions in which they have a stake; hence they have learned to practice corruption while promoting anticorruption activities. Ironically, the people and organizations that corrupt India are often the very ones who also work to ensure that democracy endures; corruption has domesticated rather than destroyed Indian democracy.

A constant need for increasing access to patronage caused new social forces to mobilize. In stage one of India's economic consolidation, an import-substituting, state-dominated economy gave politicians the economy's commanding heights. In stage two, liberalization opens new opportunities for corruption and rent seeking to replace the old depleted ones. Liberalism gives the ruling party new opportunities for illicit income, opening up vast territory for insider trading and for the manipulation of the secondary market for privatized government assets. Oddly, in both stages, corruption is the impetus for democracy to gain deep social roots. As Robert Jenkins asserted, "the consolidation of Indian democracy itself rested upon the creation of a pool of state spoils for which established and emergent groups could contend, using the new political system at their disposal."[90] Ironically, exploiting the state for resource allocation helps democracy survive in India, as each new group that is politically mobilized exploits the state for privilege and advantage. Without access to corruption, many powerful groups in Indian society would find little to admire about democracy. Opportunities for corruption might even be greater for these groups without democracy.

India's democracy has been strengthened by another sweeping change that ended the supremacy of the founding Congress Party (1996). Under the Congress Party leadership, the dominant business houses depended on a top-down system of redistribution. The Bharatiya Janata Party reversed the order and won over a number of states from Congress. Providing state governments with responsibilities over local resources provides state leaders more patronage ventures.

Although democracy has acquired social roots in India, liberalism has not. Liberalism lacks a deep supporting vision, and politicians at election time are thus likely to dissimulate their support for liberal policies. As Gurcharan Das put it, "none of the political parties has tried to sell economic reforms to the people. Most politicians believe, however, that the reforms are necessary. Hence, they have tried to do them through stealth."[91] There is only one solution to this dilemma. Economic reform must be combined with the provision of public services to protect the majority of households from economic insecurity. Macroeconomic stabilization and privatization must be combined with a public sector able to deliver health, education, sanitation, and the protection of women.

India without Democracy

Robert Barro made an important contribution to the study of democracy: mounting considerable data demonstrating that democracies without prior economic development tend not to endure. His work implies that democracy is a luxury good that only rich countries can afford. Barro explicitly stated that poor countries would be better off investing in the rule of law rather than in elections.[92] He exhorted that the pursuit of democracy at any price is nothing more than a temporary romance. Although based on extensive cross-country testing, Barro's advice is ill suited to India. In fact, the one point all Indian political parties can agree on is that democracy is good for India, protecting it from the extremes of ethnic violence and social exclusion.

India's beleaguered democracy may seem to confirm Professor Barro's skepticism about premature democracy until we consider what India might have become without democracy. We do not have to search far to find an appropriate counterfactual. We need only to look next door to Pakistan, which became an independent country at the same time and

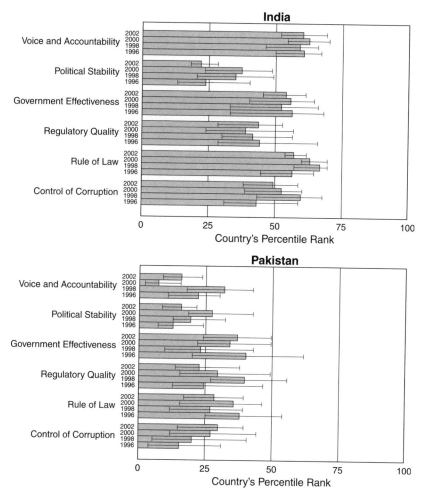

Figure 7.4 Governance: India and Pakistan. Source: D. Kaufmann, A. Kraay, and M. Mastruzzi. 2003. Governance Matters III: Governance Indicators for 1999–2002 (http://www.worldbank.org/wbi/governance/pubs/govmatters3.html)

shares many cultural and administrative patterns with India. Most notably, it shares with India its ethnic rivalries, its elitist culture, its weak civic traditions, and the same British administrative and civil service traditions. Nevertheless, Pakistan took an authoritarian path. In every category of governance—voice and accountability, political stability, government effectiveness, regulatory quality, rule of law, and control of corruption—India has done better than Pakistan. (See figure 7.4.) Being dependent on the personal charisma of its leaders, Pakistan totters on the abyss of disintegration and threatens the entire subcontinent as it unravels. We will turn to the creation of modern Pakistan after a brief digression to compare India with China.

India and China: Constitutional Foundations Compared

Although China is as high in risk for foreign investment as India, China is a magnet for continual investment. Why has India not inspired the same level of investor enthusiasm as China, despite its similar overall risk?[93] India's greatest strength is largely intangible and rests in the survival and sophistication of its democratic institutions. However, India's constitutional strengths are overshadowed by its weak social performance. Its social structure and lack of attention to human capital pose serious restraints to India's progress as a market economy.

India's democratic institutions can take credit for a number of major improvements in national well-being. Literacy, among many social indicators, has improved, and in many parts of the country the supervision of education has been decentralized. Significant steps have been made to open the economy and to direct public spending toward productive sectors. The exchange rate regime has been liberalized and capital markets improved; these changes represent a consensus achieved in the framework of democratic institutions concerning the importance of competition to improving the economy.

Democratic accountability has acquired new mechanisms. Several states have incorporated information technology to improve public access to information about the activities of government and to speed up governmental decision making. Andhra Pradesh introduced "smart governance," which includes video conferencing with farmers and administrators. In Bangalore, government agencies voluntarily cooperate with citizen groups to produce a report card that measures performance, allowing improvements to be tracked on an annual basis. Public agencies are rated on criteria that include availability of information, speed of service delivery, frequency of red tape, and side payments. The report card serves as a platform for public discussion with the government. Also in Bangalore, a citizen-action task force funded by industry analyzes the impact of public investments and helps government to decentralize the budget. Citizen oversight includes the supervision of road works. Similar citizen partnerships with the government exist in Delhi and Baroda. In Calcutta the mayor governs with a corporation council. Punjab has introduced laws that make public procurement more transparent. Community management of the local water supply and participatory irrigation management are occurring in several states. "Right to information" legislation, breaking traditions of governmental secrecy inherited from the colonial government, is gradually winning the support of state governments. Karnataka has introduced an ombudsman. To overcome the politicization of civil service transfers, Karnataka posts transfer data on a public Web site and subjects transfer requests to a cadre management committee.

National reforms have also significantly improved the institutions of governance. Campaign finance laws now limit contributions; the tax returns of political parties are now public documents, and a freedom-of-information law similar to that of the United States has been passed. National-level deliberation councils with business now actively engage in meaningful dialogue with government officials. The National Law Commission has drafted a corrupt public servants act that calls for the forfeiture of property acquired through graft. The posting of criminal records of elected officials is now mandatory, making it difficult for criminals to buy their way into elected office. Throughout India, an explosion of Web sites on government has occurred. Local education committees in many states exist in which local communities share responsibility for the recruitment, pay, and retention of teachers. Contrary to the experience of numerous other countries, India's movements toward a mature democracy are not confined to the middle class.

Governments in India have become adept at weathering very difficult times without resorting to Bonapartist antidemocratic posturing. Despite the hostility of its neighbors and the recurrence of caste and intertribal violence, faith in institutions overshadows uncertainty about national survival. By successfully tackling external security threats and facing down militant religious extremism, democracy gives India its first durable political unification.[94]

India has successfully transferred power at both the national and state level relatively smoothly and can be expected to do so without the risk that any of the major parties will refuse to abide by the outcome of an election. A significant failure actually marked a great success in India's history. When the once all-powerful Congress Party that had ruled for forty-five out of the first fifty-four years was defeated in elections, power was peacefully transferred despite support for the party among dominant social and economic elites. Because a consensus exists among all relevant parties on the indispensable role of democratic institutions in shaping public policy, Indians do not look to East Asia for models on how to solve their problems. The match between the nation's constitution and its people's aspirations are India's greatest strength. In sum, democratic debate and a relatively free press renders India's failings highly visible; its strengths often go unnoticed.

In China, political stability is firm but not supple. For example, if the military opposed a candidate who was favored by other members of the Politburo, the succession would not be smooth and the successor would be insecure in office. When held behind closed doors, a selection process cannot inspire confidence in an established pattern for selecting future presidents. If challenges arise from within the Politburo, the political security of the entire nation will be compromised—an unthinkable scenario in India, where politicians have learned to share power without degenerating into chaos. This is why many of the world's most forward-looking investors consider the threat of discontinuity in China, due to its incomplete political transition, to be the greatest single danger facing the global economy.

Political challenges to the authority of central government officials are becoming more common in China but still do not follow any predictable constitutional process. This does not prevent shocks to the system that may arise from a lack of predictable procedures. The Communist Party's ability to govern effectively from Beijing is deteriorating and is likely to continue its downward slide for the foreseeable future. How far down it slides can ultimately affect national law and order because they are tied to the fate and fortune of the Communist Party. In India, by contrast, no party exercises a decisive influence on the nation's fortune as state and party boundaries have significantly matured. Thus, India may have stronger prospects for institutional continuity than China. When political opposition does arise in China, it may take the country into uncharted regions and begin a period of turmoil, whereas opposition to a sitting government in India does not threaten the underlying continuity of India's political institutions. However, where basic risks to economic security faced by the population are concerned, China has much to teach India.

HOW TO BUILD A MARKET ECONOMY: LESSONS FROM CHINA

Market economics enjoys a more modest constituency in India than in China. Yet, despite its shortcomings, India maintains more of the institutions that economists generally believe are essential to a market economy, including protection of private property rights, third-party arbitration of commercial disputes in the courts, and the constitutional separation of the judiciary from the executive branch. Nevertheless, the strength of India's institutional endowments has done little to win over large-scale support for markets among India's masses. The key difference between China and other wishful liberalizers like India and Latin America is that China eliminated flagrant social injustices in distribution before engaging on the path of economic reform.[95] China's transition to a market economy began after programs in education, health care, and land reform eliminated basic deprivation. For example, China introduced the "household responsibility" system in 1978, allowing farmers to market their surplus and retain the profits after landlordism was eliminated through collectivization. In many areas of India, such as Uttar Pradesh, Bihar, Madhya Pradesh, and Rajasthan, old landlords still dominate and the highest income inequality coexists with the lowest levels of education and health care. Where the landlords are strongest, the population tends to be most skeptical of market allocations, which are often perceived as the source of inequality. The human development disparities between China and India are quite striking. India is far behind China in terms of the proportion of the population living below the international poverty line: 44.2 percent versus 18.5 percent. Infant mortality rates are at extremes with India at 71 per thousand births and China at 30. Also the proportion of low-birth-weight babies in India is more than five times as high as in China. The literacy rates of adult females in India is merely 34 percent, while in China it stands at 68 percent. The adolescent literacy rates in China are even more significant. Adolescent females and males are highly literate, at 92 and 97 percent, respectively. In India, by contrast, a sharp disparity exists between adolescent females and males in literacy rates.[96] Having equalized the social endowments of the population in advance of liberalization, market outcomes carry greater legitimacy in China than in India.

China's pre-reform investments in human capital were made without the ample budgetary and administrative resources of an industrial economy. Thus another key lesson of China's experience is that the basic needs of the population can be adequately addressed while the standard of living is still very low.[97]

Economists Amartya Sen and Jean Dreze have stressed that China's market reforms raised general income levels because they rest on a foundation that preceded market reforms, including basic literacy, basic health care, and the protection of female employment rights.[98] Basic education ensured wide participation in the benefits of a market economy, and eradicating illiteracy helped promote market opportunities. What good is a machine to a worker who cannot read the instructions to make it run? Sen and Dreze alluded to another important difference between India and China: China's leaders promoted labor-intensive economic activity that enabled wide social participation in the process of economic growth. India's planners, who instead focused on capital-intensive prestige projects, eschewed many of the labor-intensive manufactures, such as toys for export (which provided mass employment in China's transition) and heavy industry (which provided limited employment).

Among a population that lacks basic social security, the perception that liberalization will only magnify the persisting inequalities must be eliminated. The political commitment of China's leadership to eliminate deprivation gives leaders the credibility to pursue market reforms. Furthermore, in China there is little fuel for a revolt against the owners as a separate elitist caste because there is little difference in class or social origins between the entrepreneurs and the workers in China's economy.

Leaders in both India and Latin America that encounter class-based opposition to liberalization might do best to reconsider the trickle-down approach.[99] How can liberalization be a unifying ideology when one part of the population cannot satisfy its basic needs?

India Shining, but Not for All

Economic policy reform in India has yet to win a decisive electoral mandate. Both the Congress Party in 1996 and the BJP alliance in 2004 were defeated in the polls because they failed to establish political support at election time for the economic reform process they championed while in office. Having led India since 1998, the incumbent BJP considered victory a foregone conclusion on the grounds of its economic success, which included statistically impressive growth, information technology and telecom prowess, and the promise of global superpower status by 2020. Yet, to large numbers of India's voters, the government's "India Shining" campaign was a reminder that India does not shine for all.

To understand why liberal economic platforms do not carry broad appeal in India, consider why economic policy reform has a stronger constituency in neighboring China. The following thought experiment would help conceptualize the different levels of appeal enjoyed by open markets. Imagine that, at birth, individuals can choose to be a free, rational, and self-interested, but ignorant of their place in society. They would know neither their fortunes nor the distribution of assets given by nature such as intelligence, strength, or beauty. Would it be better to be born in Vajpayee's shining India or in China's socialist market economy?

An individual who is born in China has a better prospect of surviving infancy. India's infant mortality rate is more than double that of China (31 per thousand vs. 67). (See table 7.1.) A person can expect to live longer and therefore enjoy the benefits of reform in China, where life expectancy is 70 compared with 63 years in India. A person born in India has a 21 percent chance of being chronically undernourished compared with 11 percent in China. A person born in China has greater access to basic health care: 85 percent of China's population has access to essential drugs, compared with only 35 percent in India, and China has 62 physicians per 100,000 people, compared with only 48 in India. Basic education is more readily available in China, where the gross enrollment rate (of primary, secondary, and tertiary education combined) is significantly

TABLE 7.1

China or India?

2001	China	India
Gross Domestic Product (GDP)	1.2tril	.477bil
Financial Assets as a percentage of GDP	269	166
GNP, PPP, $ billion	5,027	2,930
GDP per capita, PPP, $	4,020	2,840
Surface area, thousand sq. km	9,598	3,287
Population density, people per sq. km	136	347
Population, millions	1,272	1,032
Population growth rate, average annual 1980–2001/2001–15	1.2/0.6	1.9/1.3
Female % of labor force	45.2	32.4
Children 10–14 in the labor force	7	12
Exports of goods and services / GDP, %	25.8	13.7
Poverty, population below $1/$2 a day	16.1/47.3	34.7/79.9
GINI index	40.3	37.8
Adult illiteracy rate, % Age 15 and above	14.2	42.0
Primary pupil-teacher ratio	22	40
Maternal mortality ratio, per 100,000 live births (1990–98)	55	410
Anemia, % of pregnant women, 1985–2000	52	88
Child malnutrition, % of children under 5, weight/height	10/17	47/46
Births rate, per 1,000 people	15	25
Infant mortality rate, per 1,000 live births	31	67
Life expectancy at birth	70	63

Data source: UNDP Human Development Report 2003 and Milken Institute.

higher in China (73 percent) than in India (56 percent). The chances of being literate in China are 83 percent, compared with 56 percent in India. Literacy significantly increases the odds of being able to benefit from new job opportunities that result from liberal reforms. The UN Development Programme's human development indicators rank China at 87th in the world and India at 115th. A similar disparity is reflected in UNDP's gender development indicators, which rank China at 76th and India at 105th.

China's stronger investments in human development provide its population with greater individual prospects to benefit from economic reforms than those available to Indians. China's masses look at the nation's new highways with the expectation that one day they will own a vehicle of their own. To an average Indian, likely to be born and to die in a sector of the economy that sees no direct benefit from the economic transformation, new roads will be enjoyed by others. What good is shining new technology to those Indians who can neither read nor write?

Speeding up India's global integration highlighted how much of India is being left behind. Take, for example, the state of Andhra Pradesh. Its leader crowed of transforming the regional capital, Hyderabad, into a world-class cyber-city. That boast, however, is a mockery to farmers who suffer from insufficient irrigation and routine power outings. Nearly three thousand farmers in Andhra Pradesh, where only 40 percent of the state is irrigated, committed suicide to avoid facing the humiliation of bankruptcy and starvation. The state's elected leader, Chief Minister N. Chandrababu Naidu, an icon to the Davos crowd, was trounced in a defeat that presaged the end of the BJP.

Many people will draw the wrong conclusion that the defeat of the BJP indicates the hazard of putting economic policy reform up to a national plebiscite. BJP's failed efforts to hold on to power while promoting reform will mistakenly be contrasted with China's Communist Party, which has suppressed dissent and speeds economic policy reform forward without elections. Pakistan's military dictator, General Pervez Musharraf, is the first to draw this wrong message from Vajpayee's defeat. He is reported to have said that the only successful models in the developing world were countries with long periods of stable, semiauthoritarian rule. The general conveniently overlooks the fact that most countries in the developing world that enjoyed long-term autocratic rule experience negative growth and rampant corruption. The East Asian countries that Musharrraf had in mind were highly consultative regimes that emphasized shared growth with strong investments in primary education and health care, the opposite priorities of Pakistan's authoritarian regimes.

Support for China's Communist Party comes from its success in economic policy, because a wider percentage of China's population benefit from economic reforms. Public support for market-based resource allocation in China, as in East Asia, is built on healthy human development prospects. The wealth-sharing mechanisms introduced by East Asia's high-performing governments offer its leaders the freedom to implement economic reforms. Whereas Indian farmers are crippled by policies hostile to rural development, East Asian leaders emphasized providing basic services to the rural sector. China, for example, relaxed government control of agriculture before opening other parts of the economy; rural areas in India have been excluded from reform. Monopolies over agricultural markets prevent farmers from getting better prices for their efforts. A drought in agricultural investment during the five years of BJP rule resulted. The inequitable distribution of basic services, in India as in Latin America, deprives a large number of the population, making liberal reforms divisive and arousing resistance by well-mobilized antimarket political parties.

The reemergence of the Indian Congress Party raises many concerns that it will seek redistributive justice before growth. The Congress Party builds its appeal by promising subsidies, higher taxes, and continued state ownership. Its leaders pledge to slow down privatization by keeping profitable state-run companies such as the state-run oil companies from the auction block. This makes investors apprehensive. They have good reasons to be suspicious of a party that campaigned without a coherent economic policy platform. Reform will go at a slower pace, but a greater danger to efficient resource allocation is the Congress Party patronage machine that is quickly gearing up with no meaningful laws to restrain its operation.

The new government named sixty-eight ministers, including twenty-nine cabinet ministries, to satisfy coalition allies that seek senior posts. Laloo Prasad Yadev of the Rashtriya Janata Dal Party of Bihar, although facing charges of corruption, was named railway minister. These coalition linchpins, unlike the new prime minister Manmohan Singh, do not bring technocratic ingenuity to the table and are instead interested in supplying supporters at home with private benefits. The cabinet's bloated size reflects a government constructed to provide rewards for all those who helped bring out the vote.

To ensure that its victory is not a defeat for economic progress, the Congress Party must convince followers that liberalization can work for all. The party took the first major liberal reform steps in 1991 but was defeated in the next election for its failure to sell reform to its own followers. Then it backed down from responsibility, taking the position that international pressures compelled the opening of the economy. To succeed this time, the party must unify the path of economic policy reform with efforts to tackle mass poverty, ignorance, and disease, much of which owes its origins to the past policies of its former leadership.

The real challenge for India's new governing coalition is to forge a policy-based coalition that is market friendly and inclusive. A partnership with India's communists surprisingly can be an opportunity, because communist parties in India mix policy with patronage. Together they must give India's poor a greater stake in future growth by improving primary education, health, sanitation, and housing. But this will not happen without strengthening India's weak democracy with laws and institutions that promote accountability and limit corruption. Political parties are not subjected to rules that require mandatory disclosure of accounts statements. This absence mirrors the general absence of transparency about the functioning of the government. Ultimately India's politicians and policy makers know what they must do, but ensuring those politicians carry out what they promise and that their intentions do not break down in the process of implementation requires introducing governance driven by policy performance rather than patronage.

The political quake in India rattles global economic policy. The decimation at the polls of India's pro-reform ruling party heightened the volatility of share prices in stock markets throughout the developing world, as many governments employed similar policies to attract private investment. Along with India, finance ministries around the world reduced their short-term debt, made capital markets more attractive, floated their currencies, and enjoyed current-account surpluses. But to accomplish macroeconomic stability, they cut health and education budgets and reduced public spending on infrastructure and did not provide the poor with effective governance institutions at the local level. The fall of the BJP is a cautionary tale for all of these governments. National leaders elected amid great hopes of reform have become unpopular in Latin America as well, where macroeconomic medicine administered during the neoliberal consensus of the 1990s is being rejected amid a widespread belief it has not delivered hopes of affluence and social mobility to the region's dispossessed.

To gain broad support for economic liberalization among the poor people of the world, human development priorities such as education, health, child nutrition, and women's rights must be added to the list of economic priorities that includes trade, fiscal, monetary, and industrial policy. Governments that sponsor economic success by increasing the risks to ordinary people are likely to be ousted by parties, like India's Congress, that lead a populist campaign. Ignoring the fate of two-thirds of India's population that live in crumbling rural communities to cater to the 1.5 percent that own stocks reveals that the defeated BJP and its constituency made poor estimates of social and political risk. Investors in emerging markets around the world have much to learn from this mistake. Inclusive development, East Asian style, is more sustainable in the long run.

CHAPTER EIGHT

Pakistan on the Edge

PAKISTAN'S CHARISMATIC ambassador to the United States, Dr. Maleeha Lodhi, was among the first high-ranking visitors to visit the Bush administration's newly assembled international team at the U.S. Department of the Treasury in the spring of 2001. Her reputation as one of Washington's most dynamic and charming ambassadors preceded her. After the usual salutations to the new administration, Ambassador Lodhi immediately got down to business by raising the issue of Pakistan's International Monetary Fund accounts:

> LODHI: As you know, we are in compliance with the terms of our latest IMF agreement. We have met the deficit reduction targets set by the agreement. Only in one area, raising revenues, have we not succeeded in meeting expectations.
> UNDERSECRETARY JOHN TAYLOR: How did you bring the deficits down?
> LODHI: By cutting or freezing social expenditures.
> UNDERSECRETARY TAYLOR: Could you not find anything else to cut?
> LODHI: We would give consideration to restoring social spending but we need help on renegotiating the terms with the Paris Club creditors.[1]

The ambassador's response to Undersecretary Taylor's questions captures the essence of Pakistan's managerial or governance dilemma. After the meeting, the Treasury Desk Officer said that there was one question he would have liked to ask: "Why, Madam Ambassador, do you expect us to love your people when you do not?"

During the cold war, the United States cultivated a relationship with Pakistan to foil Soviet access to the Middle East. When Pakistan temporarily lost the status of a frontline state after the cold war ended, the United States emphasized democratization, and its support for the military coup undertaken by General Musharraf in 1999 was lukewarm.

The attack on the World Trade Center once again made Pakistan's role, as a soft Islamic state, essential to United States security to help counter religious fundamentalism. But can Pakistan be a counterterrorist center in Central Asia or will it become a terrorist sanctuary? Pakistan has already proven to be an unreliable ally. Much of its unreliability is due to domestic instability. Poor domestic governance cripples Pakistan, and poor eco-

TABLE 8.1
Literacy Rates in South Asia, Developing Asia, and China 1980, 1990, 2000.

	Female Literacy Rate			Male Literacy Rate			Adult Total Literacy Rate		
	1980	1990	2000	1980	1990	2000	1980	1990	2000
Pakistan	13.89	20.15	27.90	40.42	49.25	57.40	27.82	35.40	43.20
Cambodia	39.08	48.79	57.24	74.36	77.73	80.16	54.63	62.02	68.01
India	26.54	35.92	45.39	54.57	61.87	68.36	41.03	49.32	57.24
Indonesia	59.36	72.51	81.94	79.06	86.70	91.78	69.04	79.51	86.81
Lao PDR	32.44	42.76	53.35	63.79	70.26	76.21	48.18	56.52	64.79
Vietnam	82.02	87.07	86.90	93.32	93.97	93.90	87.27	90.35	90.30
China	54.35	68.89	86.53	79.03	87.20	95.14	67.06	78.29	90.92

Source: Pakistan UNESCO.

nomic management that is designed to give a small wealthy elite control over the nation's resources blights its strategic dependability. State failure—a strong possibility—could come slowly or suddenly and make Pakistan an outlaw and threat, a base for international terrorism and a disseminator of nuclear weapons technology. Its ability to become a normal state, at peace both with itself and its neighbors, will depend on whether it can find a way out of its governance dilemma.

To help Pakistan live up to the strategic mission, Western donor nations have contributed large amounts of aid to stimulate economic growth and poverty reduction. Unfortunately, the aid frequently fails to reach the poor because of Pakistan's failing public institutions, which ensure a gap between social returns and private incentives. In this regard, Pakistan enjoys the company of a large number of failing states. Among the members of this club, Pakistan alone possesses a considerable nuclear arsenal, and therefore its problems cast a long shadow on the future of Asia. Yet, the donor community openly courts and indulges the perpetrators of public mismanagement, assuming that Pakistani leaders do not know better. In reality, the leaders do not suffer from a lack of knowledge, but from a lack of incentives to serve the public.

Pakistan's per capita military expenditures are probably as high as those of any country in the world. In social indicators, however, Pakistan is among the worst performers in the world, and in many districts, female literacy is below 5 percent. When compared with the other developing countries in this study, Pakistan's literacy rates are the lowest and the discrepancy between female and male education is the largest. (See table 8.1.) Considering Ambassador Lodhi's background in nongovernmental organizations (NGOs) and investigative journalism, she is well informed about the distortions in public expenditures that cause Pakistan's disappointing development experience. The internationally respected research by Pakistani economists, including Mahbubul Haq, has publicized the human tragedy.[2] Clearly, at the upper echelon of the government, senior officials know how to connect Pakistan's inappropriate policies with their disastrous social consequences.

Pakistan's uneven development record has its roots in governance failures and inappropriate institutions, intentionally devised and deliberately sustained. Why does its leadership choose to maintain inappropriate institutions while failing to build institutions that would maximize general social welfare? The answer to this question lies in the realities surrounding the types of coalitions that have formed and attained political power.[3] Institutions that allow politicians to lead while preserving the impartiality, permanence, and expertise of a public bureaucracy are deliberately sabotaged, and political leaders are left with many opportunities to exercise discretion without accountability.

Pakistan's institutional failures allow small governing coalitions to effectively distribute resources according to the goals of political decision makers. Broad-based distribution of economic surplus decomposes the governing coalition and increases the political power of groups outside the coalition, making it harder for the regime to stay in power.[4] Because politicians fear shifts in the social balance of power, they oppose policies that would help society prosper.[5]

SETTING OFF ON THE ROAD TO DISCRETION

Pakistan's political history is marked by an inability to find a constitutional consensus on the limits of state power. Five constitutions have been written since its independence: one inherited and four more-recent creations (1956, 1962, 1972, and 1973). Between 1958–62 and 1969–71 there was no written constitution, and from 1977 to 1985 the constitution was suspended. A restored constitution served after 1985 but was abrogated by a military coup in October of 1999. The absence of an enduring constitution reflects a lack of common vision about the country's future direction. The concept of granting elected bodies the authority to scrutinize the budget or to hold the government accountable for how revenues are spent has been excluded from all of Pakistan's constitutions. This opacity in financial management allows incumbent politicians to hide transfers of government funds to members of their winning coalition. As a result, Pakistan's political parties have not created broad-based support for national policies.

1947–1958: The Parliamentary Period: Constitutional Merry-go-round and Political Vacuum

During the parliamentary period, Ali Jinnah became the autocratic leader and president for life of the Muslim League.[6] Ali Jinnah made his position the most powerful in the country. It soon became a model for autocratic rule in which the "doctrine of necessity" became the hallmark of Pakistani jurisprudence.[7] During the first decade after independence, the Muslim League leaders made few attempts to link provincial or national leadership with the grass roots. By selecting former members of the Indian Civil Service as provincial governors, Ali Jinnah extended political authority to Pakistan's Civil Service, unlike India where political authorities eventually overtook the civil service.

Pakistan's political parties have been personality driven. Just as the founders of the Muslim League depended entirely on the leadership of Jinnah, subsequent parties have also been vehicles for the ambitions of powerful individuals. Keith Callard explains: "political parties in Pakistan [bear] little resemblance to that of most other democratic countries. Politics has begun at the top. . . . politics is made up of a large number of leading persons who, with their political dependents, form loose agreements to achieve power and to maintain it; . . . political parties . . . have not turned their attention toward the primary voter."[8] Khalid Arif asserts that "Pakistan's political parties are also barely democratic. Few have held in-house elections on a regular basis."[9] Nonpersonalized, meritocratic authority exists only in the military and civilian bureaucracies.

Constitution making reflected political incentives. The 1956 constitution gave extensive emergency powers to the president and constitutional protection to the highest civil servants.[10] During this period, no leader could risk alienating the bureaucracy, one of the few well-organized groups in the society. Even politicians ideologically committed to transforming the elitist character of the Civil Service of Pakistan (CSP) required bureaucratic support during the years when no constitution or government lasted more than a year.[11]

1958–1969: Ayub Khan: Pakistan's First Dictator

On October 7, 1958, two years after being introduced, the constitution was abrogated and martial law was declared. Field Marshal Mohammad Ayub Khan became prime minister and ruled under martial law as president.

Ayub's military government supported a policy of official nationalism with highly centralized decision-making structures that have since been used by every subsequent government to rationalize centralized control over governmental decision making.[12] Unfortunately, nationalist ideals have not substituted for bureaucratic performance and have only created more opportunities for the exercise of discretion by regime officials.

To hold power, Ayub crafted a working partnership between the military and the CSP.[13] While allowing the four hundred–odd members of the CSP to dominate every locus of governmental authority, he kept military officers firmly in his governing coalition through the disbursement of economic privileges. To ensure full compliance from both groups, Ayub offered land allotments to officials who maintained his power and allowed former generals and army officers to become indispensable to businesses as lobbyists. With ample opportunities for enrichment, neither party felt threatened by the other, and a working partnership emerged among the two groups.[14]

Ayub enhanced the administrative capacity of the CSP by offering bureaucrats training in the economics of public administration, finance, and accounting, thus adding to their liberal arts backgrounds. In general, advanced training was showered on senior civil servants, regardless of their cadre, making it all too explicit that their abilities were deemed far more valuable than those of the rank and file.

Ayub only made one exception that compromised the CSP's authority; he allowed the planning commission to bypass the CSP in the formulation of economic development programs. Since Ayub used state resources to forge alliances with business groups, a small tightly organized bureaucratic apparatus was useful to target the distribution of costs and benefits for maximum political impact. With a small bureaucracy at the top controlling all major posts, Ayub efficiently directed resources to his coalition members. The green revolution increased agricultural output on medium and large estates, allowing Ayub to bring medium-sized landholders into his orbit. The majority of rural dwellers had no land, and the urban masses, who similarly received very little, were to become major props for Bhutto, the man who eventually overturned Ayub's policies.

While in power, Ayub provided the unemployed with public jobs and created new government agencies without a clear division between the new and existing agencies. These actions, in addition to previous reforms, considerably weakened the integrity of government, removed reliable measures of performance, and increased dependence on the elite CSP.

Ayub discovered that collecting rents from a small group of large firms is more efficient than collecting from a large number of smaller groups, so he showered benefits on a small, tightly knit group of firms that could be closely monitored to assure political loyalty. All of Pakistan's subsequent leaders have maintained a small elite civil service, which allowed government to target the distribution of costs and benefits for maximum political impact. Keeping the knowledge circle small kept favoritism behind a wall of secrecy and helped hide the effects of corruption. In the development field, there are still a large number of people who believe that it is important to overlook corruption in favor of rapid growth. However, in Pakistan, the primary reason that corruption during this period of high growth was not destabilizing was that it was highly concentrated among a few people and the public had no channels by which to learn who was getting what as a result of governmental malfeasance. The repercussions of the patterns of corruption that began under Ayub surfaced later, fostering anti-Western critiques of the relationship between elites, international organizations, and the United States.

Ayub's party, Convention Muslim League, became no more than a label for his colleagues in power: a metaphor for favoritism and nepotism, a device for Ayub to control the disposition of resources and the loyalty of those who held them. Ayub encouraged his sons in the military to resign their commissions and enter industry and trade. The bureaucracy was directed to issue permits and licenses to Ayub's favorites. Those who were not part of the ruling clique bought permits and licenses from regime insiders at black-market prices, which had a corrosive impact on elite coherence since their purchasers had few loyalties to Ayub.[15] Husain pointed out that "The flourishing of the black market in import licenses, and the need for political connections to ensure access to cheap credit and fiscal incentives, paved the way for a private-public sector relationship where clientalism and patronage predominated." Rent-seeking behavior was legitimized throughout the economy, creating a class of industrialists who could enjoy monopoly prices for their subsidized, untaxed products and helping to create large pockets of private wealth and low tax revenues.[16]

Pakistan's evolution toward oligarchy is virtually a classic model of the political economy of national economic failure. Elites play a vital role in early economic development by reducing transaction and information costs. Political motivations keep the concentration of wealth in the hands of a small number of business families so that government can easily control the political loyalties of those with access to resources. However, the absence of growth and prosperity for nonelites sowed the seeds of discontent.[17]

Since the governing coalition was small in relation to Pakistan's economy, providing private goods to win this group's support did not at first undermine the economy. In fact, under Ayub's leadership, the country's positive growth rates were the envy of the developing world; macrogrowth was measured at 6 percent annually during the 1960s. Nevertheless, economic inequality increased, the share of wages in industrial output declined, and a few dozen families reputedly dominated the country's industrial wealth.[18] While the elite espoused a growth-friendly policy, few resources went to the poor in the form of public goods, such as education, health, or public housing. To avoid alienating its landholding support base, the government shunned land redistribution. Education and public health languished. LaPorte summarized Ayub's social and economic policies as reflecting "a preference for preserving elite privileges; changes that did occur were of a minor, gradual nature and did not infringe upon the prerogatives of the conservative coalition that supported Ayub."[19] In fact, Pakistan's era of great economic growth exacerbated social inequalities, a pattern that contrasts sharply with the East Asian pattern where the fastest-growing countries experienced declining inequality. In Pakistan, growth was essentially a private good for the elite, setting the stage for the populist policies of Bhutto to repudiate the Ayub legacy.[20] As Robert Looney explained, "this period of rapid economic growth generated a great deal of economic tensions: Regional and class inequalities increased, while large segments of the population experienced failing standards of living. The concentration of income was particularly disturbing. Twenty-two families owned 66 percent of industry, 97 percent of the insurance sector and 80 percent of banking. Only 0.1 percent of landlords owned 500 acres or more, yet they owned 15 percent of the country's land."[21]

1972–1977: Zulfi Bhutto: Patronage for the Masses

The rise of Zulfiquar Ali Bhutto exemplifies how a change in the governing coalition can produce a different set of economic policies and beneficiaries of government spoils. Bhutto set Pakistan on a straight course toward fiscal irresponsibility by reorganizing the bureaucracy and beginning the process of redistributing unearned income toward the bottom levels of society.[22] In 1973, Bhutto purged 1,303 civil servants over national television without providing any opportunity for redress or appeal. This was a one-shot mass dismissal, where punitive measures were applied without uniformity and without establishing institutional norms or standards of surveillance. Even during the days of martial law, such high-handed methods had no precedent, and the means of direct intervention by the chief executive eroded the last vestiges of integrity in the civil service.

The Establishment Division issued several acts that helped to concentrate power in Bhutto's hands, including the Civil Service Act of 1973, the Service Tribunals Act of 1973, and the Federal Service Commission Act of 1973.[23] The 1973 Civil Service Act ensured that the president could easily create and fill civil service positions, bypassing standard procedures. Oftentimes, postings were assigned to individuals who did not meet the minimum merit criteria. A national pay scale was adopted, weakening the pay structure advantage enjoyed by CSP officers, and all services and cadres were integrated into a unified service intended to give equal opportunity to all. The reservation of certain posts in the central secretariat for members of the CSP was discontinued and replaced by the District Management Group (DMG). Horizontal mobility among cadres was introduced, provisions for lateral entry established, and vertical movement between cadres was acknowledged. Opportunities were also opened for talented individuals from the private sector. The president drew broad public sympathy for his reforms from the public, who perceived the existing bureaucracy as elitist, inefficient, and corrupt.

The most significant encroachment on civil service neutrality is perhaps the most esoteric. Before 1973, civil servants could resort to writs of the high court to protect their constitutional rights, but after that year, the constitution stated that no court could any longer have jurisdiction over service matters. Instead, special tribunals would handle grievances.[24] However, because bureaucrats and retired judges generally staffed these service tribunals, the independence of the civil service suffered.[25]

Under the pretense of opening the civil service to talent, the president staffed newly opened positions according to his own discretion. The reforms allowed the president to control appointments, dismissals, retirement, recruitment, promotions, and grievances. Between 1973 and 1977, the Establishment Division approved 1,374 officials into the civil service—about three times the norm of the old system based on strict examinations.[26] The chaos of the lateral entry system demoralized the service. One senior civil servant made the analogy of "black ink dropped into clear water, never again to be clean." Since the appointments were primarily in one of three services, the police, the DMG, and the foreign service, their nonmerit impact in these sectors was strongly felt into the 1990s.[27] Favoritism opened the doors to graft, and the politically protected thought of themselves as above the law. By participating in the 1977 general elections, the newly appointed bureaucrats flexed their muscles, smearing the service's apolitical reputation.[28]

It is widely conceded that the reforms politicized the bureaucracy and that lateral recruitment and horizontal movement facilitated control by Bhutto's political party.[29] Bhutto's reforms created, in effect, a system in which power holders could easily build a base of amenable decision makers, which explains why his reforms have not been systematically reversed. Each new government welcomes the opportunity to intervene in appointments, transfers, and postings. In fact, the practice has become essentially reform-proof because it creates a cohort of like-minded people with no interest in apolitical, merit-based promotions.

Bhutto attempted to develop a coalition among the middle and lower classes to counterbalance the traditional elites, the military, civil service, and the industrialists. Patronage, through an enlarged public sector, was the mechanism used to craft this new coalition.[30] He encouraged workers to demand higher wages and land grants,[31] and he dismissed leading military figures and bureaucrats who would not follow his orders. Broad-based patronage networks also required a significant economic base. To expand his sources Bhutto selectively nationalized large firms owned by elite families and gave the government further opportunities to buy their support.[32] Although his support base was different, Bhutto, like his predecessors, controlled all aspects of national existence with one driving goal—creating coalitional support to sustain personal political power. Bhutto demonstrated little interest in creating a political party that could carry on without him. The Pakistan People's Party (PPP) was "essentially a coalition of forces that have been kept together by its charismatic leader within a loosely defined party framework."[33]

The 1970s was Pakistan's lost decade. Unlike the leading economies of East Asia, Pakistan did not make the shift toward an export orientation but instead linked nationalization with import substitution to maximize patronage opportunities. Pakistan's economic growth took a nosedive as nationalization drove capital out of industry into land, as Bhutto's broad-based patronage proved economically more costly than patronage for the elite had been.[34] Introduced as a challenge to elite institutions, Bhutto's policies quickly degenerated into spoils-based rule, differing from previous regimes in that Bhutto directed some spoils to specific groups of the poor while leaving the privileges of the elite essentially intact. "Except for a handful of dedicated workers who truly believed in the socialist principles espoused by the PPP, most of its elected ticket in 1970 were former members or supporters of Ayub's Muslim League. The circle was fully completed at the time of the 1977 elections, when almost all the tickets were awarded by the PPP to former Muslim Leaguers, the majority of whom by now crossed over into the party in power."[35] Building a personalized system of control based on the ruler's ability to dole out mass patronage had significant fiscal implications, as it led Bhutto to use deficit financing to a greater extent than his predecessors.

Politically, the decade of Bhutto was also lost, as democratic institutions did not mature.

1977–1988: ZIA UL-HAQ: LIVING DAY BY DAY

Following the violent military coup of 1977, a white paper was released that publicized Bhutto's abuse of administrative reform. Nevertheless, this recognition of abuse was not a commitment to reform, nor was it an attempt to turn back the clock, and despite his military background, Pakistan's new leader, Zia, did nothing to change the basically personalized style of rule that had resulted from the slow but steady erosion of bureaucratic capacity. Zia chose not to exercise his opportunity to restore the integrity of the civil service. By maintaining a civil service that enjoyed weak constitutional protection, Zia held a pliant instrument for the resumption of autocratic control.

Zia stopped the nationalization of the economy, but he did not return property to its original owners. Fear of losing one's factories was gone, rumors no longer circulated that the homes of recalcitrant citizens might be nationalized, but confidence in the neutrality of government did not return. The banking system remained in government hands and was used as a passive instrument for financing government deficits and allocating credit according to government plans. Controls over the financial sector became a surrogate for the inability to collect taxes, which led the country further down the path of indebtedness without accountability for policy choices.

Although Zia clearly wanted to distance his regime from Bhutto's administrative reforms and regain the support of the civilian bureaucracy, he did not encourage administrative reform but only tinkered with Bhutto's policies. He gave the civil servants discharged by Bhutto hearings and reinstated many with payment of salary arrears. Once in the system, officers under Bhutto depended on political advocates for postings. Zia, by contrast, rarely meddled in recruitment below the top twenty people. He restored performance evaluations and training; he abolished lateral recruitment and expanded reservations for military personnel in the civilian bureaucracy but did not reinstitutionalize the CSP or the concept of reservation posts for the successor DMG. Most significantly, he did not restore the constitutional protection enjoyed by the civil service before Bhutto. The only recourse for settling grievances continued to be by tribunal judges, who did not have tenure and could be sent home at any time. Civil servants never regained the kind of protection once provided by their access to the writs of the higher courts. The act that brought the courts into existence barred them from handling a wide range of issues.

An outstanding change under Zia was the recruitment of military personnel into civilian service at unprecedented levels so that the civilian bureaucracy appeared to some as a junior partner to the military regime. Army officers were inducted on a separate quota of their own, allegedly on criteria of loyalty rather than on administrative or professional skill.

During the first two decades of independence, Pakistan's religious leadership did not share any leader's power. Pakistan's leaders before Zia were explicitly secular, but Zia gave religious leaders their first taste of power with four cabinet posts and the provision of external support for religious parties. Unable to win the hearts of the urban classes, Zia built an Islamic base, using religious allies to keep him in power, building religious schools and mosques, and creating a dual legal system. He introduced the Islamic requirement for charity, the *zakat*, 2.5 percent deducted annually from all bank deposits. *Zakat* committees were created and given discretion over the disbursement of *zakat* funds, providing the president's religious allies a local power base. His introduction of religious law (*Hudood* law) gave bureaucrats, politicians, and police discretion over whether offenses would be tried under religious law or secular law. Although the courts were the same, the laws of evidence and punishment were different. For example, adultery is punishable by death under religious laws but not under secular law. The resulting confusion gave government officers enormous power over offenders, fueling corruption and providing a powerful instrument of political and control.

Although Zia came to power through a coup and had the military behind him, this position was unstable since he never stood for election to a fixed term. Because of this, Zia never considered long-term reforms. Significant decisions during the Zia years were made by a very small number of generals with no overarching vision or policy objectives other than staying in power. Zia and his generals never considered long-term reforms because Zia did not want to risk losing the support of any existing interest group. From Zia, Pakistan's democratically elected leaders inherited a system of public administration in which incentives to act in the public interest had evaporated.

Geopolitical events provided Zia with resources to consolidate his reforms without ever having to consider their lack of internal support. The Soviet invasion of Afghanistan made Pakistan essential as a depot for supplies to anti-Soviet forces. After 1982, assistance from the United States totaled around $5 billion, and Pakistan became the third largest recipient of U.S. aid in the 1980s.[36] Imports funded by remittances and foreign aid increased without efforts to promote exports.[37] Few noticed that Zia's attempt to legitimate his illegal rule was sowing the seeds for fundamentally anti-Western coalitions that would eventually transform Afghanistan and Western Pakistan into a bastion of religious fundamentalism. Zia leaned increasingly on radical religious elements for support and brought about the eventual alliance between radical Islam and military rule under Musharaff.

Under Zia, Pakistan lost a decade to religious obscurantism. Just as women were making gains throughout East Asia, deepening their nations' human capital, Pakistan embraced regressive patriarchal notions of confining women to home (*chaddar* and *char diwari*), complemented by a repressive dress code. Puritanical revisionism made the military rule an anathema to the educated classes, further consolidating the divide between Pakistan's two nations. Japan, China, and Korea have shown how nations can modernize and still take pride in their own culture. Pakistan's treatment of women sacrificed equity, social cohesion based on modernization. Political and cultural repression went hand in hand with the imposition of theocracy from the top and military rule. A small privileged elite and a discontented mass are the consequence.

1988–2000: DEMOCRATIC ELECTIONS, AUTOCRATIC SYSTEMS

A popularly elected government took over at the end of 1988 and promptly appointed an administrative reforms commission. However, the return to civilian governments did not take Pakistan off the path of illiberal governance. Pakistan's elected rulers embraced predatory governance and the institutions that nurtured it. A similar fate has befallen each of Pakistan's subsequent elected governments. Although one reason why governments fail is the inadequacy of the machinery for formulating and implementing policy, no democratically elected government has been in power long enough to decide on a course of reform action. Despite fourteen years of democratically elected governments, the previous administrative system designed to consolidate centralized authoritarian rule experienced only minor modifications. The subject of administrative reform has been the topic of more than thirty commissions, committees, and working groups during Pakistan's first fifty years of independence, but none has received adequate political follow-up. Policy performance has never been an avenue to political power in Pakistan. World Bank economist Ishrat Husain offered a thoughtful assessment:

> What is most puzzling is that the forms of government—democratic, nominated, directly or indirectly elected, dictatorial—did not matter. Nor did the professed ideological inclinations of the government in power—liberal, conservative, Islamic, leftist, rightist—make any significant difference to the general thrust of this model. The PPP governments—supposedly leftist, liberal, and populist in orientation—performed as badly as the rightwing, conservative governments of the Muslim League. The Islamic dictatorship of Ziaul Haq was in no way distinguishable from the modernist, secular dictatorship of Ayub Khan. The politicians, military and civil bureaucrats, and some co-opted members of the religious oligarchy and professional and intellectual groups dominated the scene under every single government. The faces did change from time to time, various relatives did appear or disappear over a specific period of time, but the stranglehold of this elite group,

accounting for less than 1 percent of the population, on the affairs of the state has remained unscathed. The capture of the institutions of the state and the market by the elite is complete.[38]

Bhutto's reforms diluted the monopoly and exclusivity of the civil services in 1973, but he did not create a classless, unified civil service or end widespread administrative corruption. Inexpensive venues of speedy redress of citizens' grievances against public officials were never introduced.[39] Although it served different purposes under different governments, one group—the CSP and its successor, the DMG—controlled the central planning bodies of the state.[40] Many observers believe that this elite corps of the civil service controls Pakistan's political leadership. Pakistan's politicians have constantly complained that they are thwarted in their policy-making efforts by the power of an entrenched public bureaucracy. This is a gross exaggeration. Bureaucratic privilege has endured because it has never posed a direct challenge to political leadership.[41] Government derives much of its support by employing bureaucratic discretion to disburse patronage. Since bureaucratic discretion is a key to the exercise of political power, the many reports calling for a more accountable bureaucracy and of the CSP in particular were "buried by the country's political bosses."[42] Although the bureaucracy itself is generally blamed as the chief source of resistance to administrative reorganization,[43] reluctant politicians maintain the status quo.

INSTITUTIONAL FAILURES BY DESIGN

Those who come to public office in Pakistan typically deplore their inability to use the apparatus of government for reform. To surmount the obstacles, leaders have sought to concentrate a preponderance of power in the executive. The absence of effective systems and procedures at the lower levels has led to overcompensation through the continuous centralization of functions in the highest institutions. However, strengthening executive authority does not correct the absence of the systems and procedures of efficient governance.[44] Local institutions are underfunded, poorly staffed, and inefficient. Responsibilities must be delegated to lower levels in order to decongest the upper levels where it is often impossible to effectively make decisions. Until then, undersupervision, undermonitoring, and undermanaging will continue to erode public discipline and morality.

The bureaucrats complain that ministers micromanage departments and politicize recruitment; the politicians lament that too many rules are used to protect bureaucratic perks. Politicians argue that bureaucratic discretion and arcane rules of business in the bureaucracy prevent the implementation of policy. In actuality, no party has the power to change the fundamentals that determine their actions; they must function in an administrative system over which they have no control. Politicians, elected officials, and now military officers are unfamiliar with how the system works, and as outsiders, they have limited knowledge of the process or the people in the bureaucracy. The patterns of poor governance are outcomes of reversible institutional failures. Beginning with the decay of the civil service, examples of the breakdowns follow.

The civil service has absorbed thousands of unemployed citizens when no jobs existed in other sectors of the economy. Thousands of ill-trained people are dumped into the system, discouraging managers who cannot cope with their sheer number and low skills. The absence of precise duties and responsibilities, moreover, makes supervision and coordination difficult.

Where policies exist, they undermine rational management. For example, wage policy has never been linked to job descriptions, and the responsibility level in the civil service is not matched by remuneration. Equal benefits at the same level of grading are not maintained. A job can be upgraded many times without the job description being altered, the qualifications amended, or the command expanded.[45] Removal from appointments can occur without a review process or justification. Perquisites are attached to appointments—basic salary is a small component of total remuneration—thus, change or transfer may be tantamount to a demotion. Because perks are associated with individual assignments, having no assignment causes a noncompliant or politically undesirable officer considerable economic hardship.

Senior officials routinely bypass lower-ranked decision makers, because as we have seen, there is weak support at the lower-levels of the administrative services. Lower and middle levels of management are generally unclear about their responsibilities, and standard operating procedures, where they exist, are generally antiquated. With functions assigned to lower levels so unclear, decisions cannot be made. The lack of tools and authority at the lower levels is not recognized; rather, lower-level personnel are considered untrustworthy and are surpassed even in routine decision making. Minor decisions end up being sent to the highest level in the ministry.

Civil service reviews are not transparent: the appointment and transfer criteria are opaque, and discretionary waivers are commonplace. Since job descriptions and qualifications are rarely linked, performance evaluations are difficult. Most evaluations are nonspecific in nature and do not identify any performance target or fulfillment of job description. Managers are not evaluated for the performance of specific tasks or for meeting stated targets. Years of service substitute for objective performance evaluations and are frequently the only yardstick in assessments.

In-career training is generally considered a waste of time, since postings or promotions do not require qualifying exams or the assessment of training institutions. Training courses are generally not followed by examinations and rarely qualify applicants for better positions.

Subjective measures of job performance have been found unsuitable because modern organizations neither specify nor measure the precise behaviors desired from subordinates. Pay-for-performance systems generally depend on objective performance evaluations. Pakistan's subjective civil service evaluations produce a lack of trust, which explains why Pakistan's military avoids them.

Extensive red tape and obsolete laws provide ample opportunities to collect bribes. Weak budgetary accountability allows for the persistent misallocation of government resources, such as plots of land, loans, timber rights, and vehicles. Middle agents are common in government decision-making structures. Accurate government data are rarely available, as exemplified by the fact that no census was taken between 1981 and 1998 although one was due in 1991. The absence of current census data made it possible to disregard increased urbanization, which would decrease the power of the rural magnates. No autonomous commission like the federal ombudsman exists to review complaints against the government by civil servants. Conflicts of interests are ignored. For example, the financial interests of civil servants and members of Parliament (MPs) are neither recorded nor open to public scrutiny. The regulatory authorities enforcing them generally frame the rules. Definite functions are not assigned to particular ministries producing an ad hoc mix of functions and a lack of coordination. Successive governments without integration of functions or a defined, unified structure respond to the chaos they face by adding on ministries and subunits.

Facilities for long-term strategic planning are absent. No agreed-on formula exists for approving or evaluating public investments. Developmental projects are not chosen in reference to long-term developmental objectives, nor are they evaluated in terms of publicly documented strategic objectives. Though the planning and development department has the authority to approve projects, politicians maintain discretionary use over the funds and often disburse them without reference to national or local objectives. In sum, planning and budgeting are generally disassociated.

FEDERALIST IN NAME ONLY

Central leaders fear that a lack of cooperation from local governments will lead to national disintegration. As a result, local units of government were kept on a very short leash by weak provincial governments, firmly controlled by the central government.

The central government's control over personnel and financial resources removed a layer of accountability from provincial government.
Central secretariats dominate policy making and provincial governments
are left with virtually no control over strategic administrative positions.
The deputy secretary and the board of revenue, the final appeal bodies in
provincial tax disputes, are both centrally appointed, formerly from the
CSP and now by the DMG.

The provinces depend on federal grants and taxes doled out by the
federal government. They lack financial autonomy and have limited powers to tax, which only strengthens the ability of the center to undermine
provincial security. The president can declare an emergency and efface
any semblance of provincial independence. Presidential orders go directly
to the governor, who carries them out through the centrally selected administrative hierarchy, thus circumventing accountability to elected national or provincial legislative bodies.

Beneath the provincial level of governments, local initiative and administrative capacity have languished. A federally appointed district officer can
easily withdraw the few powers that local authorities maintain. This officer
can, for example, abolish local boards, remove local staff, grant exemptions from local taxes, suspend any local regulation, and block any actions
that are locally initiated. Local institutions depend on the provincial governments for the bulk of their finances and can rarely make or implement
their own laws. Municipal administrations are further handicapped by the
absence of local police and local courts to enforce the laws that do exist.

While local governments are criticized for lacking integrity, the real
source of impropriety is the lack of rules needed for accountable local
governance. For example, mechanisms to scrutinize expenditures and to
subject local governments to judicial review are absent.

Development plans are generally handed from provincial governments to
local bodies, which are uninvolved in the planning stages. When more than
one central government agency is involved, the chances of implementation
failure are significantly magnified. Since high-level intervention is necessary
to resolve almost every local problem, many local issues are neglected.[46]

Elected local bodies are routinely dismissed by provincial governments
based on political considerations and subsequent elections are delayed for
years. The rights and authority of Pakistan's provinces exist only to the
extent that they serve the interests of the central authority.

DEMOCRATIC FAILURE

Democracy has failed in Pakistan because mechanisms to counterbalance
the head of state are virtually nonexistent. Cabinet appointments are tools

used to buy votes of political coalitions and rarely reflect the technical competence of the appointee.[47] For many years, the head of state had the power to censor the press and to detain citizens or legislators.

In 1998, an attempt to transfer power to elected officials did not include the transfer of power to judicial officials. Ignoring the recommendation that the judiciary be separated from the executive branch, federal and provincial governments tightened their hold on the magistracy in 1988.[48] The executive branch of government reviews local laws in place of the judiciary, and businesses are left without means to find redress from corrupt politicians or to protect property rights through proper judicial enforcement.

Swift and inexpensive justice is not available to all. Judges are overburdened, salaries are low, cases drag on for years, legal education has deteriorated, and government officials often use their power to evade legal proceedings altogether. As a result, elected and appointed officials are not personally liable for their actions. As Tariq Banuri concluded, "there is a widespread feeling in the country that you cannot receive justice, nor protect your basic rights to human dignity, unless you are powerful and well connected."[49]

Financial management is not subject to legislative oversight. "The consideration of the relative priorities among the various ministries with relation to the total amount of available revenues was left to the higher civil servants." The budget figures "cannot be related to anything the legislator or the administrator can see and identify, and it is almost impossible to establish a sequential relationship between a vote and an end result. Since the administrator did not have a current accounting system which could be easily related to program accomplishment, it was difficult for any system of quarterly allotments to have meaning."[50] In addition, penalties for not meeting targets do not exist. As a result, supplementing a budget is always possible, as accountability for project performance is weak. Moreover, auditing of accounts is essentially meaningless because few credible and independent auditors exist, and processing delays are often used to evade accountability.[51] There is virtually no way to measure whether budgetary outlays attain the objectives for which they were designed. Democracy so conceived had no chance of delivering quality services or infrastructure to the people of Pakistan.

Managerial Dilemmas

To prevent the country from disintegrating and to combat the centrifugal forces threatening national unity, Pakistan's leaders created a command hierarchy that rules through central government ordinances and decrees, depriving local governments the possibility of taking initiative. Once created, the hierarchy is vulnerable to the information asymmetries that inspired the hierarchical design in the first place. Those in subordinate jurisdictions or positions within the central hierarchy do not have incentives to share information needed by senior management to make informed decisions. Strategic nondisclosure is a major barrier to hierarchical performance. It affects intrajurisdictional decision making and intradepartmental decision making within the bureaucracy, and it shapes the response of the private sector to economic incentives. Also, by preventing the effective use of local information and capacity, it builds pressures for regional disintegration.

Huge discretionary power at the center, an absence of standardized methods or formal procedures, and poor delegation to lower levels of administration weaken the effectiveness of hierarchy and undermine the government's ability to implement and enforce policy.

"Inbred" Information

Resistance to sharing information with the public has deep roots in the colonial tradition. Despite more than fifty years of independence, the Pakistani government still enjoys a monopoly over public information and independent committees and rarely allows access to state documents or recommendations. The bureaucracy is guarded from public examination, can conceal its errors, and is not reprimanded when it does not perform in the public interest.[52] As a result, publicly available information is generally suspect. "Information processes were closely linked to familial connections and sources and were not strongly based on any institutionalized process."[53] LaPorte pointed out that Pakistani elites were surprised by their defeat in the civil war with Bangladesh, although defeat was predicted by Western reports. The reluctance to accept information from sources other than family, friends, or connections to the bureaucracy was the cause. When access to information is a privilege, group-inspired unreality—groupthink—results. Since outsiders are denied access to government reports and proposals, alternative proposals are not available.

Hidden information in hierarchies is a principal obstacle to effective governance for Pakistan's leaders. Superiors cannot get the information they require to set goals and expectations for subordinates, because subordinates gain extra income from the strategic use of information. While coercion, fines, the confiscation of profits, jail, and even execution can correct improper actions, those who falsely report information are harder to condemn. An inability to trust information results in a groupthink that produces radically distorted worldviews unmodified by an objective standard of publicly accepted truths. It is difficult for superiors to gain access to information known to their subordinates, and no obvious punishment exists when the information is denied. Public administration is ineffective because incentives for information to reach the top do not exist.

Lower-level officers also have no incentive to tell government about the merits of a particular project or policy and will instead misrepresent the merits of a project to protect private rents. Thus, in the selection of investments, subordinates act according to the private benefits they derive from the project. Because no arrangement exists to reward subordinates for the best resource allocations, central leaders must determine the merits of a project on their own. Unfortunately, project defects are not discernible without trustworthy sources of local information. For example, the central government may not learn that educational standards are plummeting until several years after the policies, procedures, or steps that led to the decline were put in place. Aggregate data about decline become available long after the decline has set in.

Because local officials do not have incentives to report accurately on the value of resources they possess or the real use of the resources they control, central officials cannot get reliable information about the level of tax receipts that can realistically be expected or about the optimal choice of capital investments.[54] However, there is no reason to assume that the federal government would respect local interests either, since central power knows no constitutional boundaries. Subordinates that anticipate self-interested actions by their superiors will deny information. Hence, the center does not have sufficient information for the effective choice of public investments. The goal for Pakistan's new leaders must be to compensate subordinates for disclosing information by creating an efficient incentive system through access to training for career development and granting local autonomy in the choice of local revenue assignments and expenditures. Incentive-compatible schemes to induce cooperative behavior from subordinates require tying the hands of executive authority to explicit and predictable constitutional limits.[55] The end result is that even when Pakistan's leaders agree to certain policy objectives, the capacity to ensure compliance is lacking.

BUSINESS AND GOVERNMENT: THE VEIL OF SECRECY

The information scarcity that results from unaccountable bureaucratic discretion has had important long-term consequences for the industrial development of Pakistan. Frequent irregular intervention by government officials induces secretive business practices.

Pakistan's bureaucracy enjoys a high level of control over industrial and commercial policy making, as the concentration of power over resources lies in the hands of only a few government ministries. This provides the government with far-reaching powers to create patronage but little control over policy outcomes. The government has the power to shape the scope, pattern, and pace of development by determining the establishment, size, location, and type of industry.[56] The central government's control over foreign exchange allocations, taxation, and tariff policy provides additional leverage to groups who support the regime. With prerogatives to introduce or limit the entry of new firms, governments could affect the level of competition and solicit bribes from those who benefit from favorable action.[57] Pakistan's governments concentrated resources on industrial planning but neglected essential government functions such as crime control, education, and law.

A discretionary tax code allows government to investigate, harass, and even arrest businesspeople. Income tax investigations, criminal cases, or arrests under security statutes can arise without notice. At any time, firms can be prosecuted for filing incorrect tax returns, black marketeering, dealing in illegal foreign exchange, or hoarding wealth abroad. The first Bhutto openly stated he often resorted to such tactics to keep business in line politically, and his daughter employed this authority almost entirely for personal aggrandizement. In addition, government controls over economic statistics make data on growth and investment public after they are no longer relevant.

Governmental discretion ranges from providing inputs below their opportunity costs to cheap wages and curbs on unionization, cheap capital from low-interest loans, import licenses, and overvalued exchange rates that make imported machinery cheap. A liberal fiscal policy, tax holidays, and generous price policies for infant industries, combined with corrupt and inefficient enforcement and widespread tax evasion, often provide start-up capital for entrepreneurs. Access to government largesse via political proximity is often the most important source of investment capital in the private sector and the single biggest factor in industrial success. Government contracts, industrial and commercial licenses, cheap foreign exchange, subsidized agricultural inputs, trips abroad, low-interest loans, and low-cost land are the benefits of particularistic relationships in Pakistan. The government could alter the economic fortunes of its critics simply by denying access to patronage, but government officials often keep some of the benefits for themselves. However, it is difficult to assess the political proximity of rival groups, as firms cannot determine the costs rivals will incur to gain government favors. Incomplete information about a rival's political influence makes cooperation across sectors and between firms difficult and prevents business from exercising a collective influence on policy. Incomplete information results in incomplete markets.

The dictatorial power of government has made it difficult for financial markets to impose discipline over company management. Without well-functioning stock markets, the savings of the small saver are not brought into the productive sectors of the economy. Since tight information management is essential, businesses are typically family affairs. Even when corporations are formed, actual control generally remains with family members. Family-owned and family-operated organizations dominate formal corporate structures.

A managing agency system is one common adaptation to uncertainty because it allows a large number of individual companies to be controlled by a small family group, with a single family member dominating the management team. Interlocking family ownership with representatives of closely linked families on the board of directors is also common. Such family control of executive management positions allows companies to reduce their vulnerability to political manipulation by allowing insiders to tightly control information. Under- and overpricing inputs and outputs often occurs so that firm owners may appropriate profits without sharing them with nonfamily stockholders: "the stock market value of the company seldom reflects the true value of the company nor do the shareholders get their proper share. As a result, the market is not able to exert its discipline on management, nor is the small saver able to invest fully in the development of business and industry."[58]

Business groups in Pakistan have no organizations to constrain government discretion. The government plays one business against the other to prevent collective action, diminishing the business communities' advisory and advocacy capacity. The government acts secretively, refuses to discuss issues, and does not welcome the input of business councils. Advocating a critical view of government policy could lead to withdrawal of individual benefits, which makes participation in business associations highly risky. Dominant families stand aloof from business associations, concentrating instead on their contacts for individual benefit, such as credit, foreign exchange, and industrial licenses, which embroils their fortunes in the fate of the politicians whose favor they enjoy.[59]

One consequence of crony-capital accumulation is public resentment of business, making business activity an easy target of populist and religious attack, the most dramatic example being when Bhutto attacked the families that Ayub had enriched. Populist pressures against business are rooted in the perception, not unfounded, that industrial and commercial wealth has its origins in crony deals with the government. With opposition groups having a reservoir of resentment toward capitalism to draw upon, it is difficult for the government to muster broad public support for economic liberalization.

WHY PAKISTAN'S POOR INSTITUTIONS THRIVE

Successive governments have acted in ways that decrease general social welfare and make Pakistan a dangerous place to live and to conduct business. How have these governments retained power despite the adverse economic consequences of the policies they advocate? Poor policies create less wealth to go around but maintain the governing elite. The government can then stay in power, providing private goods for its supporters by using government mechanisms to dispense spoils. If a government exhausts its capacity to raise more revenue, a geopolitical crisis seems to conveniently emerge and foreign donor funds keep the system from collapsing.

Economists use the notion of Pareto optimality to hypothesize a competitive market economy. In such an economy, policies are chosen that make all better off without making some worse off. Under the rule of small numbers, policies that are Pareto optimal may make it harder for the regime to satisfy the decisive coalitions that brought it to power. Regime supporters instead are paid off through access to the fruits of corruption, which politicians can control, as they control the courts, regulatory bodies, and career paths of the bureaucracy. A small dominant coalition need only consider the effect of a policy in terms of its own utility and act in ways that disregard the well-being of the nation. Avenues for profit maximization are benefits reserved for the governing elite and their supporters, while social consideration is often viewed as a cost, as is illustrated by the comments of Ambassador Lodhi at the beginning of this chapter. Under Ayub, for example, industrial wages were a small proportion of expanding industrial profits. Social output and organizational efficiency of the public sector is evaluated in terms of firm profits captured by leadership and distributed as spoils. Compensating the coalitional linchpins is part of the cost of doing business, while the welfare of the general population is a cost if it interferes with the profits of the governing coalition.

While Bhutto expanded the concept of the rule of small numbers by introducing patronage for the masses, he did not eliminate the need to make substantial payoffs to the elite. Despite his objective of winning small farmers, he never disregarded the large landholders. Instead of broad wealth-enhancing policies, political survival through the disbursement of patronage goods remained the rule. Bhutto just extended the flow of benefits to levels beyond economic capacity.

The logic of patronage-driven politics allocation conflicts with assumptions common to neoclassical economic models about individual behavior. In standard economic models, coalitions with other traders are unlikely to change the competitive forces that shape prices. A neoclassical actor is a price taker who can accomplish little through collusion or boycotting the market. The market provides all the necessary information to make profit-maximizing adjustments that create an effective investment portfolio. A neutral third party legally enforces property rights, and owners clearly define rights to all acquired prices and quantities, so that economic agents can maximize profits without knowing the names or families of particular trading partners. Competitive forces drive the market to efficient outcomes, and political organization is not needed.

In a patronage economy, individuals form capital according to their particular political connections. When political access determines economic outcomes, coalition formation is essential to economic success. Firms do not interchange their expertise and are unaware of the government's strategies and goals. Both sides limit information dispersal and disguise motive, which reduces the amount of publicly available information. Furthermore, government business relations are characterized by strategic misrepresentation to prevent taxation that may put them out of business. Profitable firms may find that the government wants to share their good fortune. Benazir Bhutto was known for taking shares of companies that depended on the government for licenses to do business. Thus a cell-phone distributor might find its import licenses at risk unless the president was given a share of the business. When political proximity determines the terms of trade and relative prices of scarce commodities, gains from exchange will not be exhausted and specialization and cooperation will be undermined.

Trade based on complex coalition formation engenders conflict over property rights and decision-making authority. By giving market power to favorites, economic success engenders political rivalries and instability. Defectors from the political coalition to which they are connected may lose their property rights. If a regime changes hands, the property rights of the dominant coalition may be altered, elevating the stakes of political competition so that political assassinations and violence become routine. The political leadership is unable to provide economic stability because the fringe benefits needed to keep a governing coalition together in Pakistan have continuously increased. A small military elite first expanded to match the size of the civil service elite. Knowledge about the private perks needed to sustain these elites was limited to a small inner circle within the government. Monetary advances to build houses, buy imported cars, and purchase land at cheap rates, employment of relatives, and land schemes in the names of wives and relatives all added to the weight of corruption that the economy had to bear and created secrets that had to be shielded from the eyes of the public. Since each new regime needed its own set of loyal supporters, the top grew heavy, and the weight of the layers of privilege increased the economic burden. Of course, the government had to assure its supporters that they would not suffer retribution if ever they were caught or singled out for attention, so anticorruption devices were deliberately weak. Tax evaders and corrupt government officials are rarely prosecuted, which further undermines government legitimacy.

Regimes that cater primarily to narrow elites are rarely able to collect information about discontent or project failure, since they see only loyalists who will tell the regime what it wants to hear.[60] Those with negative comments find their benefits removed, and those not with the majority have no reason to believe that government will solve their problems. A government that does not provide basic law and order but enriches those who exercise power is not likely to gain broad respect or admiration. Why should people pay taxes to a government that has become inconsiderate of their welfare?

PARALYSIS

Since 1988, each of Pakistan's four democratically elected governments (under Benazir Bhutto, 1988–90; Nawaz Sharif, 1990–93; Benazir Bhutto, 1994–97; and Nawaz Sharif 1997–99) was terminated by an outside order. The first three were annulled by constitutionally legal actions taken by the president. Until amended by Prime Minister Sharif in 1998, the constitution allowed the president to end the government and call for new elections. Sharif hoped that by abolishing this mechanism he could ensure his grip on power. Instead, as the catastrophe of his leadership began to unfold, a military coup led by Pervez Musharraf ended Pakistan's fourteen-year-old democratic travesty in October of 1999. The military travesty that has supplanted it suffers from the same crippling paralysis and inability to make difficult decisions.[61]

Sharif pushed Pakistan toward an elected dictatorship, steadily eroding all independent bodies and institutions. By the time Sharif's government fell, the army, Pakistan's last independent institution, seemed like an island of integrity in a deeply corrupted country.

Democracy in Pakistan produced governments incapable of protecting citizen's basic rights. No actions were taken by either Nawaz Sharif or Benazir Bhutto to confront open evidence of rampant mismanagement and the outright theft of resources. Their immobilized regimes inspired hostility and alienation, and drove the population to seek nonsecular answers to their daily problems.

In his attempt to acquire total political control, Sharif tampered with every functioning institution, from local government to the court system. The "rubber stamp" Parliament did nothing to stop the destruction of the country's governing institutions. In fact, Sharif's Parliament, composed primarily of feudal landlords and industrialists, many of whom bought their way into office, was less representative of Pakistan's people than the military. In the end, his move to dominate the military led to his fall.

Instead of using his majority in Parliament to promote effective economic policy reform, Sharif exploited it to consolidate his personal power. In the process, he helped a small minority plunder the country's economic resources. Rich landlords and industrialists like him were free to default on taxes and loan repayments and to steal electricity. Six months before being ousted, he had to turn over the collection and management of the country's electrical system to the military. Instead of compelling wealthy landlords to contribute to the national treasury, he allowed the landed aristocracy that received between 6 and 10 percent of national income to pay no taxes. Only one million Pakistanis paid taxes, less than one percent of the country's 130 million population.[62] He did not stop the hemorrhaging of the banking system and ignored publicly available lists of defaulters. In fact, he continued to ration credit through political access and allowed those who acquired loans to default. Musharraf's government disclosed that Sharif misrepresented tax data to the International Monetary Fund to obtain money the fund might have otherwise withheld.

The more Sharif tried to tighten his grip, the more the country slipped out of his control. Conflicts between Sunni and Shiite Muslims led to frequent violence and killings. While Pakistan was coming apart internally, it exported terrorism to its neighbors as far away as Russia and the Philippines. Many people turned to fundamentalism as a last hope for law and order.

The successful economies of East Asia have all graduated from aid dependence. Only in the Philippines, which is failing but is not dangerous, does aid exceed 1 percent of gross national product. In Pakistan, aid exceeds 2.5 percent, which suggests that it provides a substantial part of public investment. If dictatorship were to take Pakistan down a course of self-reliance and to establish connections with the world economy, then Pakistan could become an instrument for genuine development. However, this requires making difficult decisions that affect the distribution of power.

Pariah status and the loss of bilateral donor assistance motivated strong rulers such as Chiang Kai-shek and Park Chung Hee to create viable economies in Taiwan and South Korea. If forced to depend on its own resources, Pakistan might also have to reform its economic policies and develop internal accountability mechanisms in exchange for cooperation and eventually revenue. If a viable economy were the source of government financing, Musharraf would be obligated to make deals with the urban middle classes instead of turning them away in favor of anticapitalist mullahs. But external assistance gives him the means to avoid facing the debt burden he inherited while providing fresh funds to win additional coalitional support. Without donor resources, Musharraf would be faced with little alternative but to restore the integrity of the civil service, to allow local governments to function, and to give the judiciary independence. With donor funds flowing in, the general need only promise to reform. Promises buy him a reprieve from action.

Geopolitical imperatives make Pakistan the world's third largest recipient of development aid since 1960. Since 1988, Pakistan has negotiated consecutive IMF arrangements for achieving macroeconomic stabilization but has been in compliance only once, meeting deficit reduction but not revenue collection targets. Despite an unconvincing record at abiding by the terms of agreements, in September of 2001, Pakistan received an IMF arrangement that doubled the one expiring the same month because the world worried about the stability of the regime.

Among the many inconsistencies of the donor policy toward Pakistan is a promise by the Asian Development Bank of $300 million in direct budgetary support to reconstruct the judiciary. This money was awarded without benchmarks or concrete measurements of current performance. Most remarkable, considering how much is known about the decay of Pakistan's judiciary, is that no explicit promises were extracted guaranteeing the political independence of the judiciary to counteract its corrupted state. A focus on improving the judiciary may seem like the most direct route to improved compliance but experience suggests that the perceived fairness and legitimacy of the law is essential to compliance. The ability of Pakistani's politicians to abuse the law suggests that the political process is where the real work must be undertaken.

Even more surprising to those who follow the evolution of donor rhetoric is that the largesse—which included additional funding, write-offs of old debt, and the restructuring of Pakistan's entire stock of $12.5 billion sovereign debt from the Paris Club—was offered without guarantees by Musharraf on two issues the donors have most aggressively championed as essential to sound development policy.[63] The donors did not make new funding conditional on the dismantling of gender-discriminating legislation. Yet, they are firmly convinced that Pakistan's discrimination against women is an egregious violation of human rights akin to slavery as well as a barrier to social development, linked to high fertility, population growth, low nutrition levels of children, and ultimately to explosive demographic pressures on a stagnant labor market. This in turn leads to high levels of child labor; it perpetuates the low socioeconomic status of girls sustaining low parental interest in their education. This results in low per capita GDP growth and prevents diversification into higher-productivity skills. Discontentment, the fodder for terrorism, is the end product of this poison, which is encoded directly into the nation's constitutional structure. Pakistan's reluctance to educate females is probably the most important reason Pakistan's fertility rate is 3.0 compared to India's 1.8.

Even when Musharraf agrees to loan conditions concerning social and poverty targets, he cannot ensure that they will be carried out, because the institutions that manage social budgets and implement the projects have atrophied and civil service weaknesses prevent the will of government from being carried out. Musharraf's government can only commit to meeting disbursement targets expressed as a percentage of GDP over a given time period, but considering the quality of the administrative apparatus at his disposal, he still has no credible way to meet performance targets.

Additionally, the new money was promised without an explicit commitment to cut "nonproductive expenditures," a code name for Pakistan's excessive military expenditures. Pakistan is not required to commit to explicit cuts from its defense budget, which is twice as large as the budget for health, education, and business development programs. Pakistan's military expenditures spent in the pursuit of largely unattainable goals bring Pakistan no assurances of security. They continue because the military is the best-organized, most powerful interest group in the nation. Pakistan, in fact, is often described as an army in search of a nation. Real security will only come once the nation can productively employ the skills of its population.

The Musharraf regime has revealed no competence in any of the reform areas signaled in this chapter, yet the success of the IMF program requires economic growth rates of 7 to 8 percent. How can an anemic economy and a government that fails to provide basic law and order achieve this? Pakistan's economic future offers few foreseeable scenarios from which the country can pay down its debts and still support a vibrant private sector needed to create jobs and opportunities. Government deficits drive real interest rates to levels that crowd out options for financing the private sector. Access to entrepreneurial start-up capital for the majority of the population is the lowest in Asia. Political uncertainties drive private capital out of the country into overseas bank accounts. Even a simple step like providing a sure and safe mechanism for the lower rungs of society to save and transfer money has not been undertaken. Instead, citizens depend on black-market money dealers who also fund terrorism.

"Pakistan terms" has become a euphemism for donor funding without accountability for policy objectives. Donor decisions to continue lending to Pakistan are based on the hope that assistance can be an incentive for leadership to concentrate on poverty reduction, sound fiscal management, implementation of the rule of law, and the creation of conditions for a sound democracy to emerge. IMF programs have failed in the past when recipient countries complied only with those programs they like while ignoring others. This failure is rarely benign; redistributing income toward the elite while failing to support economic growth often generates grievances and debts.

Consider the opening remarks in this chapter made by Pakistan's ambassador to the United States. In Pakistan, donors are supporting a government that is cynical and brazen enough to suggest that it must be bribed with better Paris Club terms to care about the welfare of its own people.

Like his military predecessor Zia ul-Haq, Musharraf seeks political support from the most backward rural regions, which have lost credibility with the nation's nascent urban economy. His isolation from the educated urban classes from which he emerged is one of the reasons Pakistan may eventually veer out of control. Urbanization could help the president develop a secular constituency for the state, but instead Musharraf alienates the urban classes that will be a majority in Pakistan by the end of the decade.

Seeking support from wherever he can get it, Musharraf, like Zia, is adding another contradiction into Pakistan's future by mixing theocracy with the promise of eventually reestablishing liberal democracy. Without a political constituency among the urban middle classes, he throws himself at fundamental religious leaders who despise him and who are the real constituents for continued unrest in Kashmir. This is ironic for a leader who leads a secular lifestyle and is known to be an unabashed drinker and smoker. Even his drinking partners do not want to toast him since they have no reason to trust him. His government continues to seek authority over Kashmir, yet it shows no convincing ability to govern the populations under its control. These inconsistencies only embolden religious leaders to believe they can topple the government through street power.

International donors believe generous terms to the military regime will make Pakistan more stable. Instead, more doubts exist since Musharraf has taken office about whether Pakistan will survive as a secular nation-state. Now that the secular parties have been neutralized and their leaders exiled, concerns are mounting that the country will suffer dismemberment or will have a fundamentalist revolution. A gap between the educated and the uneducated in Pakistan is growing so that two nations exist in Pakistan.

A Shakespearean dramatist is needed to capture the elements for monumental tragedy in the history of Pakistan. Consider the personal tragedy of Benazir Bhutto, whose life has been dedicated to avenging the political legacy of her father, who was hung by the generals. Elite fratricide has visited her own bedroom. While she was the prime minister, her brother Murtaza Bhutto was gunned down in front of his own home in full daylight. Most people in Pakistan believe that the powerless former prime minister shares her bed with her brother's killer. Benazir Bhutto's apparent inability to take action is emblematic of the breakdown of confidence

TABLE 8.2
Percentage of Marriages between Cousins (First Half of the 1990s)

Sudan	57
Pakistan	50
Mauritania	40
Tunisia	36
Jordan	36
Saudi Arabia	36
Syria	35
Oman	33
Yemen	31
Qatar	30
Algeria	29
Egypt	25
Morocco	25
United Arab Emirates	25
Iran	25
Bahrain	23
Turkey	15

Source: Todd (2002: 65).

in government action. That story is believed by many Pakistanis and has never been refuted. It should help us understand why where the elite is a law unto itself, people do not put their faith in elected leaders.

There is one final element that this dramatist must not ignore—incest. Pakistan has one of the highest recorded rates of endogamous marriages in the world. The level of endogamy varies throughout the Muslim world: it is 15 percent in Turkey, 25 percent in Iran, 25–35 percent on average in the Arab world, and Pakistan is close to the top at 50 percent.[64] (See table 8.2.) Does endogamy reflect or cause a complete breakdown of trust and the erosion of civic humanism? People turn to kinship and form intense bonds with family members in regions where the state cannot provide security or justice. It is practical to rely on family members when the courts cannot enforce business agreements, as families can ostracize disloyal members. The power of family networks provides an edge in illegal enterprises or mafia-like activities but weakens loyalties to the larger society.[65]

Societies that organize along bloodlines are less likely to adhere to abstract principles around which Western notions of civil society are based.

Does the soil for an impartial state based on civic ties exist when loyalty to family and community tower above loyalty to the state? Anthropologists associate endogamy with values like equality and community and disrespect for authority. Intense family bonds, once established, can contribute to the ineffectiveness or illegitimacy of government. How does the donor community intend to inculcate respect for global systems and formal, impartial institutions in such an inhospitable environment, in which loyalty to the larger society is subordinate to organization based on blood ties? The French sociologist Emmanuel Todd argued that diversity of family structures produces different state structures and that the construction of the institutions of civil society must reflect the diversity of family formations around the world. If that is true, the models of development that will work in Pakistan may have to be drawn from a completely different repertoire than those the donors presently employ. If Todd is correct, then so are Pakistanis who say, "Leave your assumptions at home and just bring us your money."

Pakistan lacks the constitutional foundations that give India political security. It lacks the security that China draws from its deliberate efforts at establishing a social equilibrium. It lacks the protection of property rights and sound fiscal and macroeconomic policies characteristic of East Asia's high-performing economies. It has virtually no public risk-mitigating capabilities to help its population coordinate and plan for the future. As a consequence, Pakistan's population depends on blood ties and not on the institutions of the state for stability in their lives. For all these reasons, Pakistan as a state is failing many of its people.

CHAPTER NINE

China's Capitalist Dream

BETWEEN HIERARCHY AND MARKET

THE IMPORTANCE of property rights in an efficient market economy seems like a cliché until one considers the People's Republic of China (PRC). Its success at capitalism without a firmly based system of private property rights baffles economic policy specialists. China's discretionary official-dom and opaque procedures for political succession, recruitment, and promotion are further causes of uncertainty that in normal circumstances have a significant negative effect on the prospect of economic growth. But China has a strength that is rarely acknowledged. Before opening its markets, China's leaders took measures to mitigate the kinds of social imbalances that undermine support for markets and distort public policy in, for example, Latin America and in South Asia. Efforts were made to provide access to health, education, and sanitation before liberalization, enabling a wide percentage of the population to benefit from new opportunities. China's development trajectory thus more closely resembles East Asia, where the social productivity gap was closed by deliberate government efforts to mitigate social risk. As a result, the economic opportunities that followed did not lead to class or ethnic-based struggle. China's population supports competition as an incentive to promote hard work as much as peers do in North America according to cross-national surveys of contemporary attitudes.[1] The contradictions in the management of China's market economy such as the absence of private property rights, have not thwarted growth because prior reforms created initial social conditions that were hospitable to liberalization of the economy.

If China were doing poorly it would be much easier for economists to explain. Yet its economic performance measured by GDP growth per capita surpasses the other regions. (See figure 9.1.) China's reforms have been viewed as an anomaly by mainstream economists who generally fail to appreciate that the behavior of economic agents is affected by sources of uncertainty that are independent of the market system. China's recipe works because it balances the need to increase the size of the economic pie with the need to address social equity and satisfy the interests of those already in power. Hence, social and political uncertainty is reduced, allowing China to successfully foster liberalization without privatization although it violates international best practice.

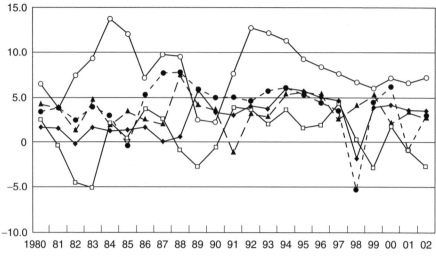

o China
♦ Developing Asia
● Developed Asia
▲ India
□ Latin America

Figure 9.1 Growth of GDP per Capita by Region, 1980–2002 (GDP growth –10.0 to 15.0)

Despite consistent progress toward more market-based enterprises, ownership arrangements in China remain unstable.[2] The reform process has benefited from trial and error, and many participants in various regions have learned to adapt during these trials.[3] Nevertheless, the small private sector has yet to develop adequate governance mechanisms to establish large efficient organizations. The absence of a clear boundary between the state and individuals prevents spontaneous and comprehensive privatization. This absence fosters complicated interactions between the government and managers, and a confusing blend of coordination mechanisms that fluctuate unpredictably between hierarchy and market result in corruption and the misuse of administrative power.

Today, almost every product bought or sold on the domestic market is exchanged at prices set by the market. Subsidies for most commodities have been slashed and prices for most products reflect market forces. Nicholas Lardy has established that market price formation went from zero to close to 100 percent in retail goods, from zero to just under 90 percent in producer goods, and from less than 10 percent to more than 95 percent in agricultural goods between 1978 and 2001. Average import tariffs went from higher than 50 percent to less than 20 percent.[4] Yet, China is only partly governed by market forces. The government continues to meddle in the management of the market. Institutional completion of the reform process has been arrested because strong vested interests in mixed ownership have been established that bar the PRC from establishing an efficient enterprise system based on explicit private ownership and manage-ment. The biggest obstacle remains the Communist Party's insistence on appointing the top enterprise managers. The party rewards loyalty by con-trolling the career paths of managers. If they manage without supervision, the party loses the authority to control resources and the loyalty of its agents. This pattern of managing the managers conflicts with the party's commitment to an economy governed by competition and guided by prices set by the market. The market for enterprise managers does not reflect the returns on the capital under management. This contradiction affects both allocative efficiency and the level of property-rights protection enjoyed by nongovernmental actors. Agents of the state stand a better chance of pro-tecting their rights than do the owners of privately held firms.

CHINA'S POLITICAL MARKETPLACE

Among developing nations, nowhere is there a greater passion for enter-prise development than in the People's Republic of China. No government in Asia today has more businesspeople in decision-making positions, and nowhere does business more fully occupy the minds and plans of the gov-ernmental elite.[5] No country in the world has done more to relieve domes-tic poverty. Nevertheless, China shares many basic characteristics of un-derdevelopment with other emerging regions. The foundations for a market economy are still weak, and many of the institutional sine qua nons of a market economy have yet to be firmly established.

Similar to other economies of East Asia, China contains many of the structural characteristics that have caused relationship-based exchange to prevail over arm's-length contracts, and bilateral monopolies to replace markets. With only 150,000 lawyers, law enforcement is inadequate, credi-tors' rights are difficult to defend, and administrative decisions replace liti-gation and contracts. The boundaries between the public and private sec-tors are unclear. The prevalence of public resources and transactions involving state entities renders private contract law essentially useless.

Accounting idiosyncrasies have yet to be standardized, as the number of trained accountants is inadequate. The nation's financial assets are con-centrated among a handful of government-owned banks that have ques-tionable balance sheets, and much of the debt is state owned. The state-owned enterprises are intertwined with the state-owned financial sector, forcing privately owned firms to depend on friends and retained earnings for funding. Public companies listed on China's stock markets do not rank among the nation's fastest-growing firms. As in most of the world's developing nations, China does not suffer from a shortage of rules and regulations. Governmental agencies can and do make rules, but procedures and venues for the appeal of regulatory decisions are rarely adequate and the rules are enforced erratically. Labor laws that seem liberal on paper often are highly restrictive in practice. Closing a firm is often easier than terminating workers.

Hindsight has led many analysts to associate the severity of East Asia's 1997 financial crisis to these same structural weaknesses that are now commonplace in China. Moreover, the Chinese are still engaged in an unresolved debate over the proper relationship of markets and government. That said, however, China remains the fastest-growing emerging market in the world. Explaining this paradox has led to creative modifications of applied economics and, most notably, to doubts about the importance of formal law in the early stages of development and to the view that best-practice institutions may not be the most appropriate goal of societies seeking to jump-start their economies and establish patterns of convergent wealth production.

From the bottom up and from the top down, Chinese government officials enjoy a vested, some would say an encompassing, interest in economic reform. Engaging the private interests of officials in developmental reform has facilitated China's rapid development. Unlike those of developing-country giants India and Indonesia, all levels of China's government own, direct, and invest in its reform process. Policy reforms and investment projects are not imposed by outside donor organizations; instead, China's leaders at all levels of the administrative structure engage in the process of economic reform up to the highest officials in the state. Early reforms in agriculture reflected local initiatives that proved successful and only later were endorsed by national-level leaders. The reform process has been interactive up and down the government hierarchy rather than following the top-down process in South Asia and Latin America.

The contrast with Indonesia and India strongly highlights this important difference in policy ownership. In Indonesia, throughout the Suharto period and continuing to the present, many projects and policies reflect the preferences of donor organizations and are carried out by international consultants. Local officials are typically more concerned with the private benefits they derive from a project than with overall project effectiveness. China engages the multilateral development organizations in limited policy dialogue and decides for itself which projects and which sectors to support.

India and China came to market opening from opposite directions. China's reform process owes its strength of purpose to its broad-based political foundations. In India, by contrast, technocrats from the Ministry of

Finance led reform, and only essentially technical reforms were implemented. In India, the unshackling of markets altered the rules of the political game and deprived politicians' access to sources of patronage and corruption. In China, by contrast, the markets gave officials access to corruption and wealth that they did not previously enjoy.[6] Ironically, despite divergent starting points, Asia's two giants may be converging toward the same equilibrium, in which "authorities . . . continue to meddle in a market that is only partially governed by market forces and at the mercy of government whim and intervention."[7] India arrived at this outcome through constitutionalism and excessive rules and regulations, whereas China arrived at the same outcome through an absence of constitutionalism, few rules, and relatively limited judicial independence. In both countries, a weak private sector depends on the discretion of official overseers.

China's transition has been a practical exercise of learning what works best and then expanding on these successes. Because market experiments are on a dual track with the state-owned sector, they do not require an ideological defense before they are introduced. Only successful examples influence government debates about general policy. This process of learning by doing has many advantages. Once a reform is selected, investors are assured that it will be sustained through government backing, further encouraging their willingness to invest.[8]

However, despite these virtues, many inconsistencies in China's reform strategy can be traced to what Susan Shirk called particularistic contracting, which gives government officials at every level the opportunity to gain political support from subordinates through generous contract terms exempt from state rules.[9] The reforms of China's planned economy began after Deng Xiaoping became the leader of China and helped establish his power by engaging the private incentives of the bureaucrats in market outcomes. Thus he established a broad-based coalition for reform that was consolidated by party secretaries who gained the gratitude and political support of their subordinates by plying them with special economic treatment.

Ad hoc initiatives drive the reform process and take the form of either fiscal contracting to provinces or profit contracting to enterprises.[10] These initiatives include special economic zones and the management of collective firms that offer local officials a menu of options to enrich themselves.[11] As Yingyi Qian put it, "These institutions work because they achieve two objectives at the same time—they improve efficiency on the one hand, and make reform compatible for those in power on the other."[12] "Particularistic contracting" allows aspiring leaders to gain power, championing reform by winning over groups who otherwise might have lost as a result of the reforms. Because the reforms follow a political rather than an economic logic, reform policies send mixed messages that often conflict with each other. As Shirk summed up, "Deng Xiaoping and his lieutenants . . . pushed up against the wall of the Chinese bureaucracy. Where they found loose stones, they pushed through: when stones would not move, they did not waste energy pushing." Reform proposals apply different rules to different enterprises on a case-by-case basis to meet the demands of local enterprise managers. A reform process of particularistic bargains that lacks a systematic framework of rules requires that each new transaction reinvent the rulebook. To avoid this, firms tend to cluster where a well-established deal path has already been laid: the first venture fund for science and technology in Nanjing was harder to set up than the twentieth such fund in the Shanghai region.

The particularistic process of buying local party support complicates the legal system with a maze of unclear, contradictory decrees and unco-ordinated initiatives, leading many policy specialists to infer that the disadvantages of the ad hoc arrangements in the long run can outweigh their advantages.

> A complicated grid has developed, leading to an accumulation of legal and bureaucratic regulations—and clandestine laws to test their effectiveness. Additional problems include . . . long consensus efforts to unite administrative players with contradictory interests. This penalized entrepreneurs, particularly those not plugged into power networks and foreigners unfamiliar with the legal and administrative climate.[13]

Since each expansion of the market increases the number of hands at the table, particularistic contracting deadlocks many profitable deals in exhausting negotiations. Each step in the reform enfranchises more players in the policy process and allows incumbents discretion over the creation of new enterprises. In China, the circle of insiders has become wide enough to include businesspeople, who were invited to join the Communist Party for the first time in 2002. Some interpret this as a sign that the party was finally making the ultimate concession to capitalism. Often called "the greatest leveraged buyout of all time," the PRC itself is being bought with the wealth of the business it has created. However, many downsides to expanding the inner circle exist; incumbent capitalists have veto power over the flow of future deals and can use their positions to veto reforms that threaten their already acquired positions.

Particularistic contracting also leaves a legacy of state organizations involved in profit-generating activities. Equipped with legitimate discretion, agencies get involved in profit-generating activities and use their power to regulate and make monetary gains for their often underfunded organizations. To accumulate extra-budgetary funds, agencies frequently impose charges, fees, fines, and impositions, shared in accord with hierarchical rank among agency members.[14] Some particularly entrepreneurial agencies generate profits by spinning off firms that depend on the political power of the parent agency. Sometimes influence is exerted more surreptitiously. A business seeking a license may be forced to hire a consulting firm that is itself owned by the officials who issue the license. Beijing tolerates off-budget financing because it lacks the capacity to supplement insufficient state budgets.[15] However, even when its origin is to assist in providing public goods, off-budget financing opens a Pandora's box of opportunities for corruption.

Piecemeal reforms result in a grid of exceptions that inspire departmental activism in the search for new deviant sources of funds. Off-budget funds, including surtaxes, levies, and user charges, grew from "2.6 percent of GDP in 1978 to more than 4 percent in 1996 and to perhaps 8–10 percent in subsequent budgets; most of these funds are in the hands of local government."[16] Off-budget accounts threaten fiscal stability with underreported fiscal deficits, compromised formal procedures, weakened transparency and accountability, and undermined government control over its agents. The resulting expansion of levies borne largely by small businesses in urban areas is a source of discontent that weakens government legitimacy. Minxin Pei commented, "collusive local officialdom is the principal source of China's governance crisis." The political center has few reliable tools to flush out corruption at the lower reaches of the party state.[17]

CHINA'S ELUSIVE PRIVATE SECTOR

China's growth is often described as stable incrementalism, a process in which new practices are introduced without the elimination of old practices. This has allowed new and old institutional arrangements to exist side by side, and caused the economy to move along two tracks at once. However, one track has consistently moved faster than the other.[18] China's leaders hope that a shrinking state sector will eventually be replaced by a new profit sector in a seamless, organic transition that mimics the industrial revolution in the West, with new industries growing alongside traditional crafts.

The for-profit commercial track is moving fast, but when the privately owned sector was officially recognized in 1999, a total of 1.3 million private companies were registered, employing 17.8 million people,[19] producing less than 10 percent of China's output,[20] and absorbing less than 5 percent of bank lending.[21] Many of these private entities do business with government-owned enterprises, and the government often is the consumer of their products or the supplier of their inputs so that the division between public and private is rarely transparent. As with most emerging markets, a low percentage of loan volume goes to small and medium-size enterprises, leaving firms in China dependent on familial ownership and financing.

China's private firms typically begin as family businesses managed by their owner, which eliminates the need to have a formal governance structure. Family structure provides group insurance against failure, misaligned loyalties, and a lack of trust. When CEOs also own the company, as is the case with most family ownership, the conflict between the principal and the agent is eliminated, and the perennial dilemma of ensuring that staff acts in the interests of owners is avoided. Communication in family firms is generally vertical and resembles communication in China's families. The decision maker at the top exercises great power, which allows important financial and operating information to be withheld from middle management. These characteristics of Chinese firms limit growth because a family only has so much talent within the small circles of trust. To grow, family firms sometimes create enterprise webs, linking with outside companies rather than increasing company size. These webs form industrial clusters of loose alliances that involve mutual agreements to share production, thereby curbing competition and fostering collusion.[22]

Chinese private firms are structured to survive; their small size allows nimble responses to market opportunities. With few loans on their balance sheets, they rarely suffer liquidity crunches during economic downturns and do not end up as victims of interfirm price wars caused by overcapacity. Business cycles do not easily affect their operations, and they can often absorb the impacts of recessions and depressions. Nevertheless, organizational minimalism has a downside; information and data about markets or costs are not publicized, and firms have fewer incentives to become open and transparent in their management practices. As a result, China's private sector attracts inadequate outside investment. Much outside investment comes from overseas Chinese who surmount cultural barriers to investment by using family ties.[23]

Chinese firms have strong incentives to misrepresent financial flows, numbers of assets and employees, and other information that is essential to would-be outside investors. Outsiders frequently have difficulty discerning who owns what, how decisions are made, and how the firm is controlled. Without accurate financial data on pretax profits, or on fixed and working capital, evaluating the rate of return on capital is difficult. A certified annual report by an outside accounting agency is a rarity, as many firms see little advantage in issuing audited financial statements. Because they are able to hide related party transactions, including loans and loan guarantees, investors are prevented from determining company liabilities. As a result, loans from the banking sector to the private sector are less than 5 percent of all loans. Furthermore, because the quality of a firm's balance sheet is difficult to determine, the government rarely allows private firms to list on the stock market, which further obstructs the path of growth. Even if it were easy to list on China's stock markets, the need for secrecy in the company accounts would make their shares unappealing to outside investors.

Firms that must survive by financing projects through retained earnings can excel in labor-intensive manufacturing sectors and in fast-changing, segmented, small markets such as textiles, apparel, timber, furniture, plastics, toys, and paper products. Such firms lack the capital necessary to enter sectors in which product lines have long gestation periods or require research, development, or name branding. Chinese private firms rarely enjoy brand-name recognition because firms avoid publicity and glamour to avoid being a target of opportunism by government officials.[24]

Since its introduction in 1979, China's private sector has developed into an essential component of the economy; however, without property-rights protection and stable government policies, it is hobbled by an absence of formality and predictability. Publicly owned firms engaged in the pursuit of commercial profits dominate the economy and enjoy benefits unavailable to private competitors. Small market niches, left vacant by the state sector, have been the private sector's principal opportunities for profit. For example, during the first twenty years of reform, township and village enterprises (TVEs) received greater property-rights protection than did privately owned enterprises because their local government owners help the central government maintain order and provide local public goods.[25] With government protection, township-owned operations could select longer-term investments. The government frequently looks the other way when state-owned enterprises violate intellectual property rights, and boundaries between public and private sectors are so informal that public policy and bureaucratic self-interest are tightly intertwined.

The International Finance Corporation's assessment of China's private sector is identical to that of other emerging markets. China's private firms

are typically owned by a single individual or a small group of people who know each other very well; they do not raise capital from the public; and debt capital plays an insignificant role in their financing. What they need most is to have the state eliminate the obstacles that it has been putting in their path. Indeed, local governments in China often interpreted new regulations as a signal allowing them to attack and interfere in private sector activities. However, unclear property rights have slowed the growth of many firms, and hybrid forms of ownership that resulted created perverse incentives, which have become a drain on the resources of enterprises and the government alike. The particularistic approach, as opposed to universally applicable rules, forced local officials and enterprise managers to concentrate on rent-seeking rather than economic returns. It led to collusion between local governments and enterprises, with the local governments acting as patrons rather than regulators. Moreover, the process made private entrepreneurs more susceptible to interference from local bureaucrats. The former reliance on personal connections in the relationship with the government has been transplanted to the market place and now dominates exchanges there. The highly particularistic nature of market transactions makes it difficult to gain reliable information about people, commodities, prices, and distribution channels.

The market has therefore become highly fragmented and relies on personal relationships for vital information.[26]

So what makes China different from countries in which the same structural restrictions prevent the economy from performing? Yingyi Qian asserts that China's success has come from the development of "second best" institutions that are most appropriate to the Chinese environment.[27] The no-name bank accounts are a perfect example. They diverge from international best practices but encourage citizens to deposit their savings in the state-owned banks, where the government can control their allocation. As a result of looser supervision, China's financial assets are far greater than those of India, where the banking system is governed by more exacting financial supervision that is more in accord with developed-country norms.

Conglomerates

Conglomerates commonly occur in Asia to help firms escape from the confines of family ownership. In China, private conglomerates are a rarity because the government rarely encourages the existence of organizations powerful enough to stand up to government authority. China's leaders learned from the experiences of their counterparts in South Korea, where a few large, indigenous conglomerates captured bureaucrats and politicians and where conglomerate operations became an alternative political base to one-party rule. With conglomerates, a small number of oligopolies will eventually threaten to surpass the state sector in its overall control of national resources—a reality that China's leaders are not prepared for. Restraining conglomerate growth inhibits the formation of an industrial oligarchy and helps China's economic reform take egalitarian roots without challenging party rule.

BLURRING PUBLIC AND PRIVATE

To understand the complexity of enterprise development in China, we must shift our gaze from the purely private sector, still in its infancy, to the mixed sector where a firm's governance is shared between the government and the market. China's government has been implementing reforms and restructuring state-owned enterprises (SOEs) for more than two decades. Of China's more than seven million enterprises, only 300,000 were classified as SOEs by September of 2002, with more than 51 percent of the shares held by municipal, provincial, or central governments. Forty thousand SOEs remain in the industry sector, and the contribution of the SOEs to gross domestic product fell from 58 percent in 1980 to 37 percent in 1994, declined again to 25 percent by 2000, and continues to fall. However, the government reports that SOEs continue to account for 55 percent of employment, 56 percent of value added, and more than two-thirds of the fixed assets of the industry sector.[28]

The overall financial performance of SOEs relative to private enterprises is weak due to (i) poor internal management subject to political interference, (ii) soft budget constraints, with subsidies given through the budget and loans directed through state-owned commercial banks (SOCBs), and (iii) overemployment associated with heavy social-welfare responsibilities. Despite their low efficiency, SOCBs are the main source of financing to SOEs.

In 1984, during the second phase of China's market reforms, the government adopted a contract responsibility system under which contracts were negotiated between SOE managers and government supervising agencies. The government proposed more substantive reforms ten years later to prevent the continuing interference of local governments in enterprise-level decision making. Beginning in the mid-1990s, the government initiated the divestment of state shares and retrenchments into smaller SOEs, and in the early 1990s, a process of "corporatization" started, transforming SOEs into limited liability companies under the Company Law and establishing a two-tier board of control. The government also started encouraging mergers and acquisitions to push management in the direction of commercial viability.

The experimental, step-by-step approach to SOE reforms has not produced clearly defined property rights. Although corporatization increased autonomy and decentralization through the formation of state asset operations corporations (SAOCs), the state holding companies (SHCs) have experienced no change in overall financial and operational performance. The proliferation of government departments controlling the SOEs has resulted in "too many owners" exercising de facto property rights without bearing any residual risks. The shift in ownership classification from being state-owned to being public or corporatized did not eliminate protection from competition and subsidies. Appointments in more than 80 percent of the SOEs still do not reflect merit, and management selection remains a key role of the party. Not surprisingly, the managers are generally government officials enjoying security of tenure, with salary schedules and job security on par with civil service restrictions and rarely contested by poor market performance. In a market economy, managers that bankrupt their companies are likely to be dismissed, but in China, financial and operational performance are rarely criteria for dismissing management. As a result, state assets are often poorly managed, and information about managerial contributions to firm performance is unavailable to would-be investors.

The poor operational and financial performance of SOEs over the years has led to deterioration in the portfolio quality of the SOCBs that lent to SOEs. SOEs account for more than half of the outstanding credit of SOCBs, equivalent to 128 percent of GDP. Neither the banks nor financial markets have a significant effect on the quality of firm governance; more than 95 percent of the one thousand enterprises listed on the Shanghai and Shenzhen Stock Exchanges are SOEs, and more than 70 percent of the shares issued are not tradable and are held directly or indirectly by the state.[29]

Chinese firms are often not what they seem. Variations in the combination of public and private make it difficult to determine where the private sector ends and the state sector begins.[30] Many hybrid forms have emerged to allow firms that were originally state-owned to engage in commercial activity. The creative ad hoc arrangements that have propelled the pace of China's market transition have also created opportunities for abuse and left behind a legacy of irregularities. Mixed governance provides many incentives for managers to divert the firm's resources to their own private use. Bureaucrats who enter business do not categorically quit the government and continue to exercise policy levers over sectors and firms in which they enjoy private benefits.

Because they are not owners and because their contracts rarely are performance based, managers have an incentive to consume or convert firm assets into their own private property. Asset stripping can take many forms. The blurring of state and nonstate sectors allows managers to move assets from state entities to nonstate entities, leaving the original firm with only liabilities. In such cases, the original firm may declare bankruptcy. Managers may lease assets to workers, keeping the profits of the firm in a nonstate spin-off and leaving the state firm with debts it cannot repay. State-owned firms frequently use their preferred access to loans to lend the funds to nonstate enterprises. The state does not have adequate information to observe or prevent the diversion of the firm's resources to the private use of firm managers.

To reduce abuse, the World Bank strongly advocates the separation of state control from what it calls "state cash flow rights." Cash flow rights could be turned into preferred nonvoting shares. According to a World Bank report, unified treatments of state and nonstate entities are essential:

The coexistence of different ownership forms has created additional incentives and opportunities for managers to realize private benefits from their control over state assets. With the rapid development of the non-state sector, managers and their relatives and friends often have their own businesses, which provide opportunities for diverting state assets to private benefits. A large body of anecdotal evidence indicates that asset stripping, or siphoning resources into structures where the controller has both majority control and income rights, is widespread.[31]

Despite the opaque boundaries between state and nonstate enterprises, China is a great success. Its two decades of rapid and sustained economic growth have created doubts about the essential role of property rights in development, as China seems to be enjoying the benefits of the price system without private ownership and without clear boundaries between ownership and control.[32]

Joseph Stiglitz explained that in any economy, the separation of ownership and control causes a conflict between the interests of the owners and those of the agents or managers.[33] Stiglitz cautioned that managers in mature market societies have mixed incentives because of disparate ownership, for example, when shareholders own the majority of a company. According to Stiglitz, the competition among firms, not the separation of ownership from management, compels managers to be concerned with the firm's performance as measured by returns on capital. Although return on capital to shareholders is not the direct concern of managers in China, they must avoid deficits that place a burden on state-owned banks. Firms with excessive deficits are likely to be sold off, depriving managers of their control rights. In a compelling paper, David Li and Francis Liu asked why government divests itself of state enterprises. They explored two hypotheses: one that privatization is driven by efficiency concerns and the other that government is motivated to stop subsidies to loss-making enterprises. They concluded in favor of the revenue theory. Later, we will explore the possibility that this same revenue imperative may push China to adopt innovations in governmental decision making.[34]

China has introduced the incentives of competition by making agencies and regions compete. This competition exists at all levels of enterprise management, beginning with town and village enterprises and extending all the way to the large state-owned industries that compete internally with foreign-invested companies.[35] Moreover, firms must compete in export markets for access to foreign currency, their most important source for future investment capital. As long as competition exists, the efficiency of enterprise management can be assessed. Stiglitz concluded, "it is not ownership that is crucial but the existence of competition." The benefits of market competition would be stronger in China if it was extended to the financial system. Without subsidies from the state-run banking system, the state-owned enterprise sector would face steeper pressure to operate according to market principles, but then bankruptcies and layoffs would become a fact of life, something the Communist Party wants to minimize.

In 1983, direct state subsidies ended. SOEs had to be funded by the banks. In replacing socialist grants with bank loans, the government hoped to control the amount and effectiveness of its capital expenditures. However, having limited experience in commercial lending, state banks funded underperforming projects on the basis of the central government's annual credit plan.

The government dealt with the problem of poor bank performance by creating more banks. Nevertheless, because the rationale for extending loans has not changed, the credit quality of the new banks resembles that of the original banks. Political lending continues, with government dictating the price of loans as well as their destination.[36] The *Economist* concluded, "All Chinese banks are, directly or indirectly, state-run, and the government, local or central, interferes both in appointment of managers and in lending. There is, therefore, no such thing as a market-driven, meritocratic Chinese bank."[37]

In general, banks play a socially useful role by monitoring the performance of the firms they finance by providing an early warning system when those firms are headed into difficulty. Banks that are directed by government to lend instead encourage excessively risky behavior. Clients will overborrow, and the banks will practice forbearance expecting government to absorb the excesses it has encouraged. With the bulk of lending going to the SOEs, and to targeted sectors in the form of policy loans shaped by government stimulus packages, portfolio quality in China is poor. The banking section is deeply troubled: the banking sector and its fragility is perhaps the largest threat to China's economic stability.[38] State-owned banks carry nonperforming loans that may equal 50 percent of their portfolio.

China's financial sector suffers from the legacy of central planning. The unhealthy state of the SOE sector prevents the restructuring of the banking sector, and the banks cannot be healthy until they are liberated from a need to subsidize value-destroying state enterprises. Before the banks seek out the most productive uses of capital for their savers, the incentives of bank managers to increase returns on the capital invested by diffuse shareholders will have to be reformed to resemble the incentives of the private market.

The biggest barrier to the development of a well-managed financial sector is that the government is the main provider of loans and is the main consumer of credit. To make the financial sector more transparent, the government needs to establish an infrastructure for credit and then step aside so that financial institutions will develop the tools to actively assess the creditworthiness of projects and distribute funds on a commercial basis. The percentage of bank financing that goes to the private sector is inadequate and cannot be expanded because the banks are already over-extended by the nonperforming loans they made to SOEs. This bad news for the banks could be turned into an advantage for the capital markets, which if properly managed could offer an attractive alternative.[39]

FINANCIAL REVOLUTION STILLBORN

During the early 1990s, the pace of China's nonbank financial reforms exceeded other necessary economic reforms such as privatization and bankruptcy reform. China's stock markets expanded rapidly after their inception in Shenzen on December 1 and Shanghai on December 19, both in 1990. New issues were often oversubscribed and could not meet ballooning demands. An early enthusiast, William Overholt reported:

> By August 1992, excitement over share investment had built up to the point where authorities were issuing certificates to the public for the right to buy future share issues; people had to buy these application forms and then accept whatever stock came along when it was their turn. Even in Shanghai, where excitement was less than in Shenzhen, it was not unusual for share purchase certificates to trade at 4,000 percent premiums to the original government charge.[40]

By the end of the decade, China had 1,300 listed companies (mostly public companies that enjoy A share status) and sixty million shareholders; domestic stock market capitalization at US$590 million made China's markets the fastest-growing in the world[41] and the second largest after Japan, dwarfing all other emerging markets. Listings of "red-chip" and H share companies on the Hong Kong Exchange accounted for 28 percent of Hong Kong market capitalization by 2000.

Rapid stock, bond, and futures market development offers a logical alternative to an ailing banking sector. A large role for capital markets would facilitate the next stages of market reform, including mass privatization, pension reform, financial sector restructuring, and technology. It can help enterprises distribute their profits equitably, enabling the transformation of state-owned industries into publicly held entities. An active stock market can facilitate the mergers and acquisitions needed to rationalize industry through consolidation so that domestic firms can compete internationally. Furthermore, China can manage its demographic time bomb by creating a public pension system and encouraging the placement of funds from that pension system into the market as institutional investments. China's technological ambitions can benefit from start-up capital and venture funding. Venture investors will be looking for an exit option such as initial public offerings on the capital markets, and with the World Trade Organization's accession, capital account liberalization will gradually open the domestic market to foreign institutional investors.

Ideologically compatible with the deeper goals of socialism, the concept of a nation of shareholders promotes market development while maintaining the vision of China's communist founders. An emerging middle class with financial independence will demand better governance both at a firm level and at a national level. Shareholders will demand greater accountability and transparency, and corporate governance in capital markets will allow the middle classes to diversify their investment portfolios. They will then demand better legal protection of their investments and, ultimately, better governance from their leaders.[42]

But the markets have yet to become a catalyst for broad-based social and economic reform; their great future has yet to materialize. At the onset of 2004, the financial markets were moribund after a thirty-month slump. The country's brokerages made a net loss for the whole of 2002, three out of four brokerages are in arrears in 2003, and the market is without genuine investors in 2004, with even less enthusiasm for new entries.

When China's freely traded shares are compared to those of its neighbors, China's market capitalization is the lowest in the region.[43] Since the government insists on being a majority owner, two-thirds of listed shares are nontradable. Investment companies that dodge government rules by holding multiple accounts open the vast majority of accounts. Sixty million shareholders are listed, but it is more likely that these shares have but two million owners. One company in India, Reliance, with its 2.4 million shareholders, has more individual shareholders than the entire stock markets of China. Reliance, which conducts its general meetings in a football stadium, grew into one of India's most successful exporters by offering shares to the public and by steady appreciation in the value of those shares. No Chinese company has been able to grow by mobilizing funds from diffuse shareholders. China's capital markets are weak at serving the financial needs of private business; only 1 percent of the listings on the Shanghai and Shenzhen Exchanges are private. Because private firms fail to meet disclosure standards the government erects laws barring private firms from listing. (See figure 9.2.)

Capital market development has hit a brick wall. Considering that provincial governments selected the first 1,300 listings according to a quota system, without reference to management quality or the market prospects of companies, investor value is overlooked and the selected companies

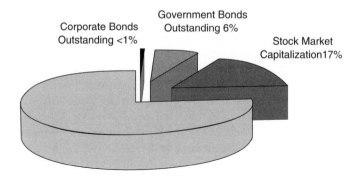

China

Corporate Bonds Outstanding <1%

Government Bonds Outstanding 6%

Stock Market Capitalization17%

Bank Assets 76%

India

Corporate Bonds Outstanding <1%

Government Bonds Outstanding 23%

Bank Assets 43%

Stock Market Capitalization 34%

Figure 9.2 Size and Composition of Financial Systems: China vs. India. Note: Financial assets are 269 percent of GDP in China, but in India only 166 percent

rarely put equity to effective use. Many specialists hold that the extent of government-held nontradable issues is the largest problem facing the market. The government maintains a majority share in most listed companies to prevent their privatization. Every time the government offers to sell its dominant holdings share prices plummet.

In developing economies, stock markets provide valuable information about company and sector well-being. China's real economy is posting 9 percent growth figures, yet the stock market is moribund. Why does this discrepancy exist? In an attempt to restore investor confidence, government has initiated a number of efforts to improve the quality of information, to support financial innovation, to facilitate the introduction of new products and services, and to contain value inflation, manipulation, and fraud. Along with these policy initiatives, highly qualified people now hold key positions. The terms and conditions for securities have improved, and the China Securities Regulatory Commission (CSRC) independently introduces international prudential standards. Nevertheless, most experts believe that the capital markets are not growing fast enough to meet China's needs and will not be able to step in if the banking sector fails. Since 2000, the total amount of funds raised in equity markets has been minimal.[44] Since 2003, the entire capital markets' combined growth was less than 5 percent of the amount by which the banks grew. China's peak year for the issuance of corporate bonds was 1992, and issuance has been going down while bank loans keep growing. The increase of loans relative to GDP is dramatic, with banks' share of total financial intermediation rising over 90 percent. China depends more on banks than before the Asian financial crisis, while the rest of East Asia is moving toward more diversified financial markets.

China's reforms do not go far enough to address the absence of minority shareholder rights and weak disclosure standards.[45] Most government measures have been artificial efforts to shore up prices to prevent losses from affecting state-owned enterprises and security houses that are the dominant players, along with the National Security Fund. Few companies are ever delisted, and insolvent security houses are not allowed to fail. Punishment for reckless or unscrupulous behavior is rarely meted out, despite the fact that most brokerage houses are losing money and many are accused of misappropriating customer deposits.

Important vested interests in China prevent the disposal of the government's dominant shares in the market. The strength of these vested interests, as Ba Shusong (of the cabinet's chief research center) has indicated, leads to incremental reforms that do not address the underlying causes of the market's poor performance. In this view the solution would be a clear timetable for government to dispose of the shares it owns. But as Ba explained to the *Financial Times*, incremental reforms do not address the underlying causes of the market's poor performance: "Perhaps our stock market is not a barometer of economic growth, but of the defects of our whole system."[46] Under the current system, monitors have no incentive to change the standards of prudential regulation or to eliminate the corrupt standards from which they personally benefit.

The emergence of strong shareholder control will not occur unless China's stock markets overcome another major hurdle. In a cross-national study of corporate governance, Mark Roe found that where the interests of managers could be tied to shareholders, strong shareholder rights emerged, yet when political officials interfered with managers, diffuse shareholding as a corporate governance structure was ineffective. The social goals of government make diffuse ownership less attractive for owners because they lose the ability to monitor and discipline managers. Roe concluded that when social agendas intervene in corporate decision making, managers end up aligned with employees against the interests of diffuse shareholders. The mechanisms that align U.S. managers with diffuse shareholders—incentive compensation, transparent accounting, and hostile takeovers—are generally harder to implement when social agendas intervene. In China, for example, managers are rewarded for output rather than profit. As in most strong social democracies, Chinese socialism will put a wedge between shareholders and management, making it difficult for companies to maximize shareholder returns. Following Roe's reasoning, Chinese minority shareholders will not find the kind of protection found by their counterparts in the United States and the United Kingdom. Roe's work provides little solace that the malaise of China's stock markets will be easy to overcome.[47]

China's Governance Dilemma

The classic commitment dilemma of autocracy is that the sovereign, being above the law, cannot police itself. Standing above the law, China's party-state lacks institutions to appropriately monitor its agents, which prevents government from providing impartial governance, regulation, and grievance resolution to protect the property rights of the nongovernmental sector.[48] Laws curtailing the power of the party are difficult to enforce without a countervailing authority such as a parliament, an independent bureaucracy, or judiciary to ensure compliance.[49]

Achieving third-party enforcement of contracts entails subjecting the party to independent oversight and distinguishing the interests of the party from those of the state. Investors need assurances that political bodies will not violate contracts or engage in practices that will randomly alter the wealth of participants. Constitutional reforms are needed to restrain the discretionary exercise of political power, but until a credible legal system exists, no substitute for the guarantees of central party officials will be available. The hindrances to complex impersonal exchange must be reduced via enhanced third-party contract enforcement. To create a firm foundation for a market economy, the party has no choice but to risk its power and tie its hands in exchange for rules of law.

Discipline in economic management is compromised by the long reach of government's "grabbing hand," which deftly employs a wide array of instruments from which to extract revenues from enterprises.[50] The government controls regulations for project approvals and can directly intervene in routine company decisions such as employment targets, wage determination, and investment decisions. Regulatory activities concerning standards and codes and the incidence of taxation are all areas over which the party has discretion and over which enterprise owners have no recourse. The *China Daily* reported, "As the institutions involved play the dual role of regulators and for-profit entities, they fiercely defend their vested interests against competitors. This greatly tarnishes the image of government institutions and their monopoly industries."[51]

Up until March of 2004 China's constitution encouraged party members to believe that one day, only socialist property would exist and that in an ideal world, government can do better than private ownership. That illusion was shattered by the decision of the People's Congress to recognize private property. Illicit profits and ill-gotten private fortunes derived from the appropriation of state assets, however, continue to arouse popular anger and misgiving in party ranks. Now that constitutional protection has been extended to private property, the government might be especially concerned to guarantee Article 13 of the constitution, which protects the rights of citizens to own only specific kinds of private property "lawfully earned income, savings, houses, and other property." The government hopes that in recognizing private property it will stem capital flight, estimated at $50 billion in 2002—equal to the sum of annual direct foreign investment.[52] However, as a result of this moral and ideological dilemma, income from private investment is still not safe from seizure. Now that constitutional protection of private property is written into the constitution, the question remains about how it will be enforced, considering the absence of a tradition of private contract-law enforcement.

Minxin Pei pointed to the multitude of signs that the state is unable to deliver public services. He asserted that an inability to discipline its agents, along with inadequate fiscal resources, prevents the party from effectively delivering public goods so that health, education, environmental protection, and protection from crime are all underprovided. Road fatalities, low social investment, crumbling public health facilities, environmental degradation, and worker accidents that occur because of unpoliced, bribe-paying workplaces are all indictments, according to Pei, of the party's inability to provide necessary order.[53] The public's most vocal complaints involve the lack of infrastructure services, including telecommunications, postal services, electric power, public transportation, and the gas supply. These "China-centric" concerns reflect the fact that the Chinese population has come to expect the delivery of services and infrastructure even to the humble sectors of the population. China's efforts at providing basic infrastructure to the poor is often more effective than efforts of other economies at the same income level. In fact, World Bank data reveals that electricity losses in China are lower than 10 percent, which is close to OECD standards and more efficient than other developing regions such as India, where losses are close to 25 percent.[54] Also the World Bank reports that hours per day of pipe water are much higher in Beijing than in other developing country capitals and that the percentage of water unaccounted for is much lower than among other developing country cities.[55]

The party must eventually confront a weakness that goes beyond inadequate physical infrastructure. To reduce corruption and to become more inclusive, it must offer more public policy and fewer private goods.[56] But can the party's dual roles be reconciled? Will reconciliation come in due time? It has launched numerous anticorruption campaigns that feature stiff fines for those indicted. It has sought to separate local and central tax administration, strengthen the central bank, and set up impartial supervisory and regulatory authorities, but providing a mixture of policy and private goods to supporters stretches its resources during a decade of shrinking governmental budgets. To win more support through better public policy, the party must curtail dispensing private goods (privileges, exemptions, off-budget accounts, subsidies, and discretion) to supporters. The PRC's distribution of private goods to maintain loyalty within the party's ranks conflict with its provision of public goods, including universal rules and sound macro policies.

Limited reform of legal systems, village elections, and admission of entrepreneurs into the party apparatus are all steps in the direction of being more inclusive and sensitive to the needs for good governance. These very positive steps risk weakening the legitimacy of the party by exposing its frailties, but they cannot stem the rising tide of corruption. Instead, partial reforms leave a residual fuel of grievances on the forest floor that one day can turn routine brush fires into giant conflagrations. Some party officials worry that the party is now providing the battering ram through partial governance reforms that China's population will eventually use to smash the fortress of party domination.

Part of the solution must be governance innovations, such as civic associations, to deal with professional standards, environmental and public health issues, and the provision of basic services in information and monitoring. The failure to take measures to deter the SARS outbreak reflected an absence of such institutions, but party sources have not yet openly recognized a larger role for civil society as a result of the outbreak. China has many institutions in nascent form, such as a People's Congress and local bodies that can help impose greater accountability. To create legitimacy for these institutions, legislators must make existing elections competitive or introduce direct elections.

CHINA'S UNDERLYING WEAKNESS

Rigid fiscal machinery forces the government to depend on sources of revenue that are inelastic and that cannot be expanded easily in the case of an emergency. The transfer of decision rights to local officials has resulted in less revenue for the center. The central government's revenue share of GNP fell from 35 percent to 20 percent by 1990. Although China's revenue reforms are ongoing, under present institutional arrangements China lacks a credible facility to deal with surprise. Since a growing percentage of the nation's resources are now under the control of provinces or of individuals, Chinese officials would have three options if faced with a surprise: to extort resources from resource holders through extraordinary levies using coercion when necessary; or to inflate the currency, risking the derailment of China's economic locomotive; or to negotiate with resource holders, which would open a path to some kind of formal political representation of creditors and taxpayers.

The growth of public debt requires a fundamental overhaul of the tax system. If China must resort to taxing the private wealth of individuals or corporations, it may find that compliance is questionable at just that moment when government is weakest. The government might require sources of extraordinary revenue to meet the demands for social services, unemployment compensation, severance for laid-off workers, war, a large-scale ecological disaster, or even an extreme health epidemic. At such a moment, the brittleness of the system will be exposed. The most likely short-term crisis scenario is a banking system meltdown that will require emergency government assistance.[57] China's financial assets as a percentage of its GDP are roughly equivalent to those of the United States. In both countries, financial assets are about 240 percent of GDP. But China's financial system is dominated by the banking sector in which four banks hold a 59 percent share of all banking assets. (See figure 9.3.) The "big four" therefore account for about half of the nation's financial assets, and their nonperforming loans are estimated to be as much as 40 percent of their asset base. China's equity market capitalization and bonds outstanding are a small percentage of the world total. (See table 9.1.) This makes China's economy particularly vulnerable to a possible meltdown of the financial sector.[58] Because the country's financial resources are heavily concentrated in four banks, if one of those should fail, there will be enormous consequences for the economy.

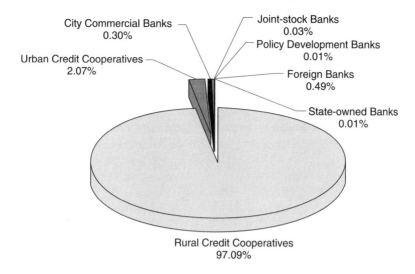

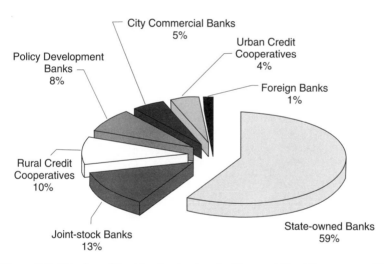

Figure 9.3 Number of Banking Institutions by Type and Total Percentage of Bank Assets Held by Type of Bank: China (2002). Note that 97 percent of banks are rural cooperatives, yet they hold only 10 percent of total bank assets. State-owned banks, on the other hand, comprise only 0.01 percent of banks, yet they hold the majority of bank assets at 59 percent. The author thanks James Barth (Milken Institute) for sharing the data used in this figure

TABLE 9.1
Regional Financial Assets as a Percentage of World Total. Note: China data from 1999

	World Total	Percent of Total Accounted for by:		
		China	Japan	United States
Population	6.1 billion	20.8	2.1	4.5
GDP	$31.1 trillion	3.7	13.6	32.7
Bank Assets	$36.9 trillion	5.3	16.2	15.7
Equity Market Capitalization	$27.8 trillion	1.9	8.1	49.6
Bonds Outstanding	$31.6 trillion	0.7	16.7	54.0

Environmental degradation, health issues, military modernization, and the outbreak of war cannot be ruled out, either. Moreover, China's current fiscal position is weaker than official data suggest because of many hidden contingent liabilities, which include pension liabilities and the quasi-fiscal operations of the banking system. As one IMF study indicates, unwelcome contingencies can come in various packages:

> At first glance, fiscal policy does not seem a pressing medium-term policy challenge for China. The measured debt stock is low, and the reported budget deficit is modest and easily financed. However, fiscal activity in China extends well beyond the state budget, and public finances will face a number of difficult challenges in the next few years. There is a sizable amount of quasi-fiscal debt in the form of non-recoverable loans in the banking system, the legacy of central planning. Further, although efforts are being made to limit the flow of new non-performing loans, through state-owned enterprise and financial sector reforms, the possibility that part of ongoing bank funding will become non-performing cannot be ruled out. The budget also faces heavy future expenditure demands for health and education, pension reforms, and the government's ambitious infrastructure program. As a result, a broader measure of China's public debt stock is larger than reported stock, and could grow further if corrective measures are not taken.[59]

China's government lacks a protocol to engage parties whose resources will be needed to cope with unforeseen future contingencies. What makes China an underdeveloped country is not weak purchasing power parity, or questionable GDP growth. Because of its ad hoc and uncertain budgetary process, China, like most developing countries, maybe unable to deal with a wide range of uncertainties. Coping with rapid change and future

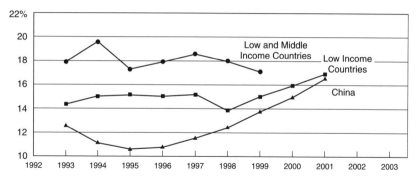

Figure 9.4 China: Government Revenue as a Percentage of GDP (10–22 percent).
Source: International Financial Statistics and World Development Indicators

dangers while remaining within the constitutional framework by which it is presently governed is China's greatest uncertainty.

Fiscal Imperatives on the Road to Democracy: From State Finance to Democracy?

It is widely believed among China specialists that a rapidly modernizing economy is likely to generate pressure for political change away from one-party rule. A persistently inadequate revenue base may open another path toward evolutionary change. Party officials hope that piecemeal reforms can stem the loss of revenue previously provided by state enterprises.[60] New tax legislation that simplifies collection has increased revenues, while partially enforced laws limiting corrupt lending practices are designed to prevent the growth of nonperforming loans. Since 1996, government revenue as a percentage of GDP has increased. (See figure 9.4.) But its deficit since that time has also increased. (See figures 9.5 and 9.6.)[61] The party hopes that economic growth will lead it out of these problems and that a growing revenue base and a growing economy will be the solution, which Ross Terrill called "saving Leninism with consumerism."[62] Will consumer growth be fast enough to provide the government with adequate sources of revenue?[63] Sequencing is another problem; the government needs revenue to build the regulatory infrastructure to keep growth on track. Without growth, there is no revenue to support needed regulation, but without revenue to support needed regulation, growth will be stymied.

Central state revenues have fallen by half since the late 1970s, from 30 percent of GDP to just over 18.72 percent in 2002. Compensating for the decline of tax revenues has fostered abuse and corruption through off–

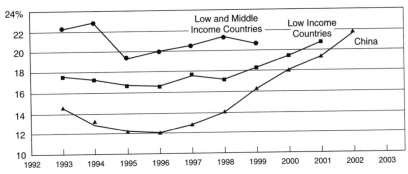

Figure 9.5 China: Government Expenditures as a Percentage of GDP (10–24 percent). Source: International Financial Statistics and World Development Indicators

balance sheet nontax receipts. The nontax, off-budget funds are often spent ineffectively and without supervision.

As the deficits of state-owned enterprises further erode the government's revenue base, fiscal necessity drives reforms to more market-oriented solutions. Ad hoc arrangements help smooth the transition path but are insufficient for the future. To restore China's troubled financial institutions, radical reforms must further compromise the Communist Party's authority. If the financial system is opened to the discipline of foreign ownership and banks are allowed to operate commercially without day-to-day party oversight, the party loses its remaining mechanisms of central control.[64] Beijing likes to use the banking system to preserve that part of the economy, state-owned or -managed enterprises, from which it derives the most direct political benefits. Privately owned banks would not share this objective and might draw savings away from the state banks, making the servicing of SOE debts more difficult for the shrinking state-owned banks.[65]

A stable market economy requires a government with a stable source of revenue. In this regard, democracy and fiscal solvency can both be steps along the same path. When representatives of society are legally empowered to tax, more taxes can be collected at lower cost. The path to fiscal stability commences when governments are able to bargain with constituencies for money to run the government.[66] China has yet to take the first steps along this path. Today the party has no means other than coercion to ensure that potential taxpayers support the fiscal needs of government.[67]

China's future fiscal solvency necessitates a stable mechanism to negotiate for needed revenues. The government's relationship with the provinces currently grants fiscal privileges that impede fiscal solvency. Particularistic

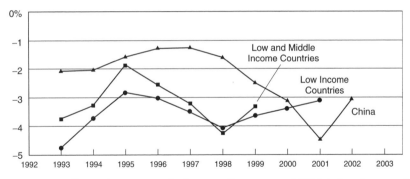

Figure 9.6 China: Government Budget as a Percentage of GDP (−5 to 0 percent).
Source: International Financial Statistics and World Development Indicators

contracting provides local governments with important sources of revenue that are not taxable by central authorities.[68] In order to gain secure
access to revenue in the provinces, a bargaining format is needed. In 1979
and 1980, Shanghai turned surpluses over to the central government that
was equal to more than half of its provincial GDP. After a new formula
was introduced in 1993, it paid only about 8.5 percent of its GDP. Consider Guangdong, a province that produces 40 percent of China's exports:
after 1993, the net remittances of the province declined to only 0.4 percent of GDP.[69] Officials in Guangdong argue that it should not matter
how much they turn over to the center since local public goods are locally
provided. It is widely assumed that the percentage of local GDP that various provinces pay to the central government varies significantly. Rather
than having arbitrary levies that may arise at any time, a regular process
for negotiating the size of the levies is essential. Economic rationality
needs a rule-bound system of regular negotiated levies conducted with
respect to the rights of revenue-generating firms.

The state will not have sufficient sources to finance the country's development needs without a stronger tax base to support further borrowing.
Since 1990, government revenues as a percentage of GDP have been much
lower than world averages and are considerably lower than the low- and
middle-income averages up till 1998. Since 1998, China has moved closer
to world averages. While the revenue base has increased, expenditures
have increased even more, making the accumulated budget deficits grow.
(See figures 9.4 and 9.5.)

China's most successful people generally do not pay taxes. In 2000,
Forbes magazine published the list of China's richest people. A govern-
ment newspaper, the *Jinhua Times*, later disclosed that only four of
Forbes's fifty were on the list of the country's largest private taxpayers.[70]
China's richest citizens are suspected of illegal activities, including tax

evasion, no matter how they manage their private affairs. Because their competitors do not act in accordance with the law, it makes little sense to develop good civic morals when it comes to paying taxes. In China, few people are even aware of what taxes to pay.[71]

Of the roughly $180 billion the central government collected in 2001, personal income taxes accounted for only $12 billion, or about 6.5 percent of this total. Developed countries are usually able to collect as much as 28 percent of the total in personal direct taxes, and in the United States, the figure is about 30 percent.[72] But in China, the reform process created a series of loopholes that must now be closed to everyone.

BETTING ON CHINA'S FUTURE: ARE THE CHINESE THE AMERICANS OF ASIA?

After the United States, China is the second-largest contributor to global growth. Together, the two economies account for more than half of world economic growth. In a curious way, these two countries may complement each other as future global and cultural leaders. Historical events have separated the citizens of both China and the United States from their respective pasts.

Americans physically divorced themselves from their ancestors by leaving their ancestral homes with little more than a suitcase in their hands. As immigrants, they cannot return to the homes of their ancestors and are geographically separated from the issues and relationships of the past. As the Mexican poet Octavio Paz has written, "the United States was not founded on a common tradition, as has been the case elsewhere, but on the notion of creating a common future."[73] The People's Revolution is the declaration of a deliberate and self-conscious separation from the past, an effort to tear the past out of the ground, destroy its physical and psychological traces to separate China from its "feudal" way of thinking, and sever identification with ancestral prejudices and predilections. Elites lost their privileges: the intelligentsia tasted the bitter fruit of the peasantry's misery, and much of the historic cultural infrastructure was destroyed.[74] Yet, the institutions of modern capitalism may actually take root where people have no grounding at all and instead try to create a common future. Thus, they base their sense of who they are on who they wish to become. In this sense, both the Chinese and the Americans perceive the future as means to control their own destiny.

I remember a breakfast I had with the mayor of Nanjing in which I was wearing a Buddhist wheel of life on the lapel of my jacket, a gift from a journalist who had interviewed me for a Shanghai newspaper. The mayor looked down at the traditional symbol of Buddhism on my lapel, something that would have been recognized as a Buddhist symbol anywhere in the world, and with complete cultural amnesia asked me what company I was representing. Though this symbol originated in the same province and just seventy miles from Nanjing—in the capital of Chinese Buddhism, Wuhu—he didn't know what it was.

This story attests to the fact that the Cultural Revolution makes China's returning to its past difficult. In India, where ancient religious, cultural, and ethnic divisions have not disappeared, rivalries from the past continue to tear India apart. Past suspicions, threats, and resentments are always just under the surface, ready to erupt in fresh bloodshed, which drives away many would-be sympathizers and investors. India's nationalism defies comprehension by idealizing, exalting, and even salvaging the past. On any given day, one can pick up a newspaper and read about people killing each other over a dispute that concerns a temple built two thousand years ago. China has walked away from ancient communal disputes and has tried to create a universal future for its citizens. China looks to the future and does not hold others responsible for its own destiny. Unlike the nationalism of the Middle East, South Asia, and Latin America, China does not use today's resources to fight yesterday's battles. The Chinese hold their own leaders responsible for where they are today and for where they are going. The legitimacy of China's government comes from what it accomplishes today for its own people.[75]

Conclusion: An Evolutionary Path Out of China's Developmental Contradictions

The Communist Party is driven by fiscal necessity to sever itself from one of its primary sources of revenue; the system of state ownership and central control. The financial burden posed to the government by the debts of the state-owned enterprise sector drives the reform process to more and more market-oriented governance systems. Unprofitable enterprises have to be dumped or transformed so they are off the balance sheet of the central government. The government tries to stop the hemorrhaging without surrendering decision rights over production. But where will it find a substitute form of revenue? Running the services of government via off-budget accounts opens the door to corruption and encourages the rent seeking of government agencies, undermining party legitimacy at all levels.

The need to devise effective fiscal policies may eventually lead China's policy makers to consider creating a format for building a consensus that enfranchises provinces as well as individual taxpayers with constitutional representation. The granting of purse-string control over policies to the agents of private wealth creation may eventually transform a nation of citizen-workers into a nation of citizen-creditors.

The questions most frequently asked by China watchers in the short and medium term are: Will the government solve the problem of nonperforming loans? Can the for-profit economy grow fast enough to provide the resources to liquidate the remaining SOE sector? Can SOEs be made more efficient? Is the traditional welfare system sufficient to protect workers who are shed by loss-making enterprises? Will the burgeoning private sector create enough jobs to absorb layoffs from SOEs? Does latitude exist to continue deficit budgets without provoking runaway inflation? Can the party complete the unfinished banking reforms and successfully reduce nonperforming loans to a manageable level? Even if all of these questions can be answered affirmatively, the People's Republic of China will eventually face far greater future challenge to its authority: Can the capacity of government be expanded to stabilize revenues and expenditures? In the near term, this question can be avoided, as the government faces no immediate constraints on its ability to borrow. National debt is less than 20 percent of GDP, and even if hidden liabilities such as nonperforming loans are added up, the short-run burden is still manageable. Reserves estimated at US$400 billion in 2003 are high. However, to be ready for unforeseen contingencies, the central government might have to contemplate new contracts with the provinces, with firms, and with individuals to further extend the state's legitimate powers to tax the growing profit sector of the economy. A stable source of tax revenues requires a new social contract in which firms and individuals provide tax revenues to the government in exchange for an environment in which firms can prosper. Can such an agreement be reached while preserving the monopoly political status of the party? Depending on how this question is answered, China may become a successful market economy or another transition disaster.

The status of property rights is another issue in limbo, but the notion that property rights do not exist in China misstates the issue. The party does an excellent job at defending the property rights of state-owned industries but fails to protect the interests of its competitors. Although complete privatization would enhance firm efficiency and provide broad benefits to the entire economy, the benefits to the Communist Party would be indirect.[76] Ultimately, the party faces the contradiction that it is not representative or inclusive enough to hold an encompassing interest in the nation's economic fortunes. To keep party loyalties in check, the government provides significant and very costly private goods in the form of privileges and exemptions to local officialdom. This conflicts with the party's broader mission to promote the public policy requirements for productivity growth, equity, and efficiency. Instability haunts the leadership because with every step they take to provide more policy goods, they dilute the value of the private goods dispensed to keep local officials loyal. To become more inclusive, the party faces the supreme irony that it must put at risk its undisputed status as China's unique representative.

In considering China's future prospects, policy makers emphasize sustaining China's new manufacturing industries rather than the challenges facing the government and the public sector. This emphasis is understandable in the short to medium term, while rapidly increasing trade and capital flows place China in the enviable position of being able to increase borrowing without provoking debilitating inflation. Cyclical variations in the terms of trade will no doubt place a burden on national finance, but in the short term this can be managed. Over the long term, the rise of a competitive marketplace will challenge the government to build institutional capacity for greater efficiency in tax collection. This will require the accumulation of political capability embedded in institutions. Over the long term, public debt management requires changing the norms of government so that a regular administrative tax apparatus can be constructed to avoid recurrent ad hoc renegotiations with the provinces. A weak institutional link between social consensus and growing government deficits is among China's greatest developmental challenges.

Will China change fast enough to avoid being trapped by its many contradictions? A government that feels the pressure to succeed or risk being ousted from power is more likely to keep on the course of reform and endure some of the costs to buy political longevity. Is China's leadership such a government? Can the Communist Party hope to survive if it fails at the very standard—economic modernization—it has set for itself? The fact that there is no comfortable answer to this question is China's best hope for the future. Much of the optimism or credibility of China's reform process comes from a belief among China's citizens that the party's potential to survive is sufficiently high to encourage husbanding the economic reform process to a successful conclusion.[77]

China's unfinished transition and its incomplete political commitment to economic policy reform has a political logic that reflects the exclusive political foundations of the Communist Party. To ensure the stability of those foundations, the party must provide private benefits to party members at the same time that it must invest more resources into supporting infrastructure for the private, nonparty market economy.

PART III

Conclusion

CHAPTER TEN

Mobilizing the State as Public Risk Manager

STANDARD ECONOMIC models envision a world where risks can be bought or sold in the marketplace. In such a world, all forms of social welfare can be optimized through market transactions, varying assessments of risk create opportunities for trade, and the most efficient managers bear risk.[1] Contemporary financial theory strongly affirms the view that divergent capacities to manage risk and different ideas of what constitutes risk create opportunities for trade and investment. But can this assumption be extended to households in the developing world?

In the early 1920s, Frank Knight established a distinction between measurable risks and immeasurable uncertainties. When most business uncertainties can be expressed numerically and the near-term future is both predictable and subject to forces that can be quantified, risk management through the market can be a profitable activity. A wide range of economic and social activities in developed countries can be optimized via market-based risk-management techniques that transfer risk to the best-suited managers. However, in most developing societies, many risks cannot be measured, and thus the optimal manager cannot be found.[2]

People living in developed countries depend on a wide range of market-based risk mitigators that encourage experimentation and investment. The specialization of financial services is well established. The decentralization and diversity of capital instruments enable people to match money with talent and new ideas, allowing companies to choose financing that best suits market structures. A series of specialized firms and operatives that span the entire economy exist to monitor market transactions, and provide linkages of information. Thus, a fully developed market economy can reconcile the different opinions and different capacity of people to manage risk.

The boundary between risk and uncertainty is mediated by institutions that allow people to reduce risks by trading with others who are capable of bearing those risks. Uncertainty can be a positive incentive for innovation in a developed economy, but when key institutions are absent, uncertainty inhibits innovation. Social relationships and methods of production are encased in tradition in developing countries because innovations yield uncertain "rewards," ranging from confiscation and censure to discrimination. In these countries, firms often doubt the accuracy of published information and are suspicious of authority. Compliance with prudential regulation cannot be assumed. Even in the most financially developed of East Asia's economies—Japan, Taiwan, and South Korea—firms rarely comply with international accounting standards. Are these firms acting irrationally by making themselves unattractive to creditors? To the contrary, developing-country firms that ignore international accounting standards are acting reasonably, considering the uncertain consequences they face for accurately disclosing assets.

Pervasive and deep uncertainty is the major reason why developing countries do not achieve their potential. Widely divergent estimates of outcomes make it difficult for unrelated parties to reach an agreement. The more uncertain a mutual endeavor appears, the less likely it is that agreements will be made for joint action. The three basic sources of uncertainty are:

1. *Economic.* Weak contract enforcement between market participants results in an inability to ensure against opportunism. Government protection of property rights in many developing countries extends only to the deals and property of those who are the linchpins of the regime and are essential to the political survival of the incumbent leader.

2. *Social.* In developing societies, social groups are typically unable to reach consensus about shared social priorities. They are frequently hobbled by an inability to identify mutually compatible and plausible beliefs and values. These failures may result from high degrees of inequality or ethnic and geographic diversity, both of which reduce common knowledge about the costs and benefits of policies. Uncertainty is present because fiscal targets to meet social goals become difficult to agree on. The divergent preferences of a polarized society make it hard to deliver services and formulate policy. When reform is uncertain, opposing parties harden their positions, thus increasing their differences and reducing the likelihood of compromise and reconciliation.

3. *Political.* A third source of uncertainty stems from an insufficient supply of institutions to ensure that leaders pursue social welfare and economic growth instead of personal gain. Economists are trained to believe that the final distribution of policy decisions represent the best analytical judgment about the social utility of a policy's outcome. Under conditions of autocracy, however, social goals may diverge from an autocrat's private utility. Autocrats often have little interest in the social consequences of a particular policy. Measurable evidence of social outcomes are ignored unless they further the well-being of the dominant coalition. For example, autocrats may inadequately su-

pervise the financial system, leaving institutions vulnerable to mismanagement. In times of financial distress, autocrats protect their private-sector friends rather than correcting systemic weaknesses.[3]

Uncertainty affects cooperation in the production of nontraded social goods, just as it impacts the traded sectors of an economy. Developed societies depend on voluntary organizations such as limited liability companies, political parties, or partnerships to manage common-pool resources, but in developing nations, households are reluctant to contribute to a common pool. A shortage of social institutions eliminates transparency and accountability and makes many collective goals unattainable; individuals instead maintain temporary goals and do not form enduring alliances outside their families. Thus, citizens are left vulnerable to the consequences of their poverty that is itself the result of a failure to control risks and to plan for the future. They must cope with hidden information, as public information is mistrusted and rarely used to improve their individual well-being.

THE GOVERNMENT AS UNIVERSAL RISK MITIGATOR

Much of the world's future wealth exists in developing countries. The potential value of eliminating risk in these nations is greater than the size of other risk-management systems, including the stock markets of New York, London, or Tokyo. To unshackle this wealth, however, one must consider the path that citizens of developed societies followed to create a capacity for public risk management. If developing societies can learn from these past experiences, they will be better able to design financial technology that increases the pace of economic development.

A modern market economy is supported by a wide range of risk-mitigating activities, some provided by the government, others by the private sector. Often, the two work hand-in-glove, with the government monitoring the integrity of privately provisioned services, and the private sector overseeing the effectiveness of government provisioning. Long-term risk management requires the stability of legal and civil institutions that can protect the public interest. However, the governments of developing countries are more often a source of institutional failure, distorting the calculation of market risk.

In most highly developed market economies, the government's role as public risk manager expands over time to cover a wide range of personal and social risks to supplement private mechanisms. To play this larger role, the government requires institutions for building consensus about how to augment, supervise, or even replace privately evolved mechanisms.

Without the capacity to equitably collect and then allocate public resources effectively, public support for expanded government risk management is difficult to obtain. As David Moss revealed in his sweeping history
of the government's role as public risk manager in the United States, a
long series of strategic interactions between government and organized
citizen groups preceded each increment in the government's risk-mitigating role.[4] The complicated intervention by lawmakers to reduce and reallocate risk is a story of a steadily evolving contractual relationship between the governed and their lawmakers, involving multiple, evolving
strategic interactions among legislators, law enforcers, and society, and
thousands of consecutive episodes of consensus building. As trust develops, society permits government officials to manage more and more risk.

According to Moss, governments adhere to the same risk-reduction
principles as the private sector. When governments reallocate risk by shifting it from one party to another or by spreading it across a wide number of
people, they act according to the same economic principles as the private
insurance market. Government product liabilities shift risk from individuals to manufacturers, its workers' compensation shifts risks from employees to employers, and deposit insurance spreads risk across all depositors.[5]
Moss concluded that although the government's role as universal risk
manager is still unfolding, a modern economy would not be possible if
the government were unable to act effectively as a mitigator of public risk.

The government's role in public risk mitigation has helped to make
industrialization possible by providing the market system with the ideological and moral underpinnings to keep worker insecurity from igniting
unrest and even rebellion. During the Great Depression of 1929, John R.
Commons, the intellectual founder of America's social security system,
warned that social security was required to avoid the provocation of class
war that erupted in Europe. Without the insurance provided to workers
under the Social Security Act, the demands of workers might have disrupted the evolution of the private marketplace, considerably reducing its
scope.[6] By mitigating social tensions caused by the abrupt swings in market fortunes, government intervention made much economic activity safe
for private investment, consolidating the basic framework of social relations needed to support the market system. Where does that leave developing countries that lack the political capacity to ensure that the market
can cater to a full range of human needs? Developed market economies
offer private parties many opportunities to avoid having to self-insure
against market risks. By contrast, the wellsprings of economic progress
in developing countries are blocked by pervasive risk. Incomplete markets
for risk represent one of the greatest failings of market economies in developing regions, and their absence is one of the reasons that market reforms
meet resistance.

Public Risk Management and the Survival of Capitalism

Risk-management policies were a mainstay of the Industrial Revolution. By reducing fundamental market risks, innovations such as limited liability companies, banking regulation, bankruptcy law, fixed exchange rates, and the predictable enforcement of property rights altered the behavior of individuals and lengthened the timeline for people's future plans. The availability of socially provisioned risk-management devices encouraged individuals to engage in productive, private risk-rewarding activities, eventually developing privately provisioned long-term risk-management vehicles including stocks, bonds, and insurance contracts.[7] Instead of choking the spirit of enterprise, the government's risk-management policies expanded and supported the private market for risk. It provided social protection to mitigate the social disruptions that could arise from downswings in the economy. It offered insurance to overcome risk-related failures in the private sector and helped surmount asymmetric information between buyers and sellers, thus increasing the scope and scale of the projects they undertook.

Risk-management institutions allow people to plan for their future, to form organizations, and to spread risk across many individuals. These institutions are not available in developing countries. When people have no way to deal with basic, first-order market risks, they cope by providing too much self-insurance, rendering their assets illiquid. They also engage in aversion strategies, avoiding activities that could provide long-term benefits for their families and for their societies. Or they may choose to transact only with individuals with whom they share prior connections or relationships to mitigate opportunism. Networks of interpersonal and interhousehold obligations exist as alternatives to the market to deal with routine household risks. Without institutions to ensure the quality of public information, savings do not end up in the formal banking system, and information about household assets and liabilities is hidden. A weak financial system results, which limits the market for goods and services. As Robert Shiller, an advocate of government-provisioned insurance against inequality, put it:

> The reduction of risks on a greater scale would provide substantial impetus to human and economic progress. Indeed, the progress that our society has achieved to date would not be so magnificent were it not for the kinds of risk management devices that evolved over time. If, for example, insurance did not exist, a vast variety of vital enterprises would have been considered too risky to even consider. Without our capital markets, we would not have so many of the corporations and partnerships, large and small, that produce so much of value for us.

Again, their work would often have been considered too dangerous to embark upon. Without existing financial technology, we would be living in a much less inspired world.[8]

Today, the citizens of developed countries spend more on social security than any other budget item, including national defense.[9] Yet, progress toward broad-based risk management was slow; only after the Great War in Europe and the Great Depression in the United States did the laboring classes effectively organize and demand insurance that necessitated a coordinated response by government. Essential to establishing a stable market system, social-security expenditures are a stage in the sequence of risk-mitigating roles played by governments, helping to reduce price volatility caused by the threat of civil and legal disruptions of order during economic downswings. Risk-management arrangements by the government on an increasingly large scale encourage individuals to engage in increasingly complex, future-oriented private transactions. As an example, the rise of private insurance markets depends on the expanded role of government statistics, regulation, and institutions such as the courts. The actuarial tables of private insurers are generally based on data collected by the government. This may be why private provisioning of health, accident, and social-security old-age insurance increases at the same time that government provisioning expands.

Market economies lacking competency in risk management enjoy only limited support from those who are most vulnerable to business cycles.[10] Such socially provided risk mitigation encourages complex social organizations outside of the family and increases the mobility of the workforce, whereas inadequate risk mitigation results in a risk premium. The price society pays in the complexity of organizations, the durability and duration of contracts, and the scope and scale of cooperation between contracting parties is a risk premium. Societies make progress toward building an inclusive market system as they develop increasingly sophisticated mechanisms to manage risk.

Essential to the government's role as risk manager is the ability to manage information and to provide information that identifies risk and that allows the costs and benefits of risk management to be calculated. Adequate information must exist for individuals to assess the effects of greater governmental intervention in terms of measurable probabilities. With each step toward government's expanded information access, citizens require assurances that information they disclose about private assets will not expose them to unscrupulous officials or become available to the general public.

The government depends on its capacity as tax collector to perform its role as risk manager. Unfortunately, most developing countries lack revenue-collection systems and consequently are unable to effectively provide social insurance. The first efforts to introduce an income tax in both nineteenth-century Great Britain and the United States failed because government was not trusted to acquire and process information in a fair and reliable manner. Initial efforts to collect information produced an inquisition that met widespread resistance, and those most able to pay ended up avoiding taxes altogether. Without a credible civil service, governments could not convince individuals that the greatly expanded informational capabilities would be used in an honest manner. Instead of catching evaders, government officials abetted their efforts in exchange for bribes, a situation comparable to that of today's emerging-market hopefuls. Doubts also existed about the ability of the fiscal system to use funds judiciously. A government that is not trusted to collect taxes in an impartial matter will not be trusted to provide risk insurance.

To provide confidence in its impartiality, governments had to protect property rights, ensure the existence of independent courts for the effective adjudication of disputes, and implement bankruptcy proceedings to provide secured transactions in the private marketplace. These measures necessitate a reliable and accountable public administration of independent bureaucratic operators who can act without prejudice in the application of universal standards. Today, citizens in developing countries frequently oppose introducing information technology that would reduce inequities in tax collection because the citizens lack confidence that such technology would be used exclusively for that purpose. The technology is affordable, but acquiring the trust necessary to believe in government's good intent is a much more costly and complicated process.

RISK MANAGEMENT AS A PUBLIC GOOD

When risk-management contracts are adequately insured, individuals will take action and engage in risky endeavors to improve their wealth. All members of society will benefit from such activity. Nevertheless, as Shiller put it, "These institutions require a sense of public commitment to a standard of risk sharing that must remain unchanged through time."[11] This standard requires a strong underlying social consensus. Extreme inequality in the distribution of resources within society can prevent a consensus about future plans. The failure to reach an agreement generally means that nontradable public goods will be in short supply. Inequality foments resentment and despair due to lost ambitions. Demoralization and despair are inevitable when income discrepancies have no connection to ability or rationality; unscrupulous behavior receives a moral rationale when people do not respect the social contract. In the extreme, lost ambitions engender crime and eventually lead to insurrection and terrorism.

Public-risk mitigation strengthens the market by mitigating the risks to households of engaging in anonymous market transactions, such as seeking employment outside of the family. Second, it mitigates the dangers of riots or uprisings during downswings, and by weakening the appeal of revolutionary ideologies, it makes the investment environment safer. Thus, a poor man's security becomes a rich man's security. Governments that undersupply public-risk management weaken the viability of the market system. Although this proposition seems incontestable, political leaders last longer when they manage their own risk at the expense of others in the economy, creating more stability for the insiders by adding risk to outsiders.

Millennium Development Goals

At the United Nations Millennium Summit in 2000, the nations of the world set measurable targets for reducing world poverty, disease, illiteracy, and other indicators of human misery. The first seven goals were stated in concrete, easily measurable terms. Each one has a specific numerical goal to be met by 2015. The millennium compact for development recognizes that one way to foster hope is to provide broad-based dividends to future growth through basic practical education along with basic health facilities for all. For example, primary school enrollment for girls should match that for boys by 2005. By 2015, the proportion of poor people in the world should be halved, and the chances of women dying in childbirth reduced by two-thirds as compared with 1990.[12]

Three years later, the UN's 2003 Human Development Index indicated disappointing progress toward meeting the millennium development goals. Since 1990, per capita GDP has fallen in fifty-four countries. The rate of hunger has increased in twenty-one nations; the morality rate of children under the age of five has risen in fourteen nations. Twenty-one countries had a lower overall score in human development. One bright spot is that only 23 percent of the global population lives on less than US$1 a day, compared with 30 percent in 1990, but most of this improvement is attributable to China. Excluding China in absolute terms, more people are poor than in 1990. Why is it that the leaders of 147 countries cannot accomplish a task for which collectively they easily have the resources?

Bueno de Mesquita and Root and Bueno de Mesquita et alia showed that domestic political incentives are an often-overlooked source of a high-quality socioeconomic infrastructure. Inclusive regimes with large winning coalitions, they demonstrated, foster healthier populations that live longer.

When the political system is dominated by a small coalition of cronies, relatives, or military officers, citizens do markedly worse on humanitarian indices than do their counterparts who live under more inclusive systems. Data on every measure of public well-being—including safe drinking water, public education, medical care, free trade, suppression of corruption and black marketeering, and attracting investment—reveal that inclusive regimes outperform exclusive polities. Moreover, even resource-poor inclusive societies usually offer more of these advantages than do autocratic countries lucky enough to possess some important or valuable resource.[13] Even life expectancy at birth can be correlated with the inclusiveness of a leader's governing coalition. Being lucky enough to be born in a polity that promotes inclusiveness can add nearly fourteen years to life expectancy. By contrast, the increase in per capita income adds but five years. This difference reflects both a government's spending priorities and the likelihood that competitive political systems encourage open market policies, contributing to economic growth. A comparison between Brazil and Jamaica offers a good illustration: Brazil's 1972 per capita income, after years of military rule, was $2,907. In the same year, Jamaica, a functioning, albeit narrowly based parliamentary democracy, enjoyed a per capita income of about the same size, $3,099. But Jamaica was four times more inclusive than Brazil, and its life expectancy was nearly a decade longer than that of Brazil. Similar evidence can be marshaled using other measures of social welfare, the equality of educational opportunity for women and men, and differences in infant mortality rates. Bueno de Mesquita and Root concluded with data indicating that when a governing coalition goes from exclusive to inclusive, human-development indicators show a marked improvement over the next three to five years. Inclusive governments tend to have deeper and broader capital markets because they are likely to develop institutions to strengthen their financial sector with appropriate fiscal policies and regulation.

Exclusive governments have an interest in contracting loans for projects from which the leadership clique draws benefits. Leaders take risky gambles with their country's finances knowing that the burden of risk lies with their citizens while the benefits of the loan are privately consumed. The debts tend to become the burden of citizens who rarely enjoy the benefits of growth or development.[14] The debt overhang of many developing nations reflects this misalignment of incentives. Greater inclusiveness—made possible by increasing the size of the winning coalition— similarly correlates with the transparency of revenue collection, measured by the percentage of tax revenue as a percentage of GDP and by the degree of distortion of tax collection, the volatility of annual growth rates, access to information measured by the number of radios, televisions, and newspapers per capita, and measures of social violence caused by civil war, guerilla war, civil unrest, and antigovernment riots. The inclusiveness of the governing coalition will influence the establishment of institutions needed for a civic community to function. Without such institutions, society exposes itself to risks that in many regards are comparable to existence in a state of nature, where life for most can be short, nasty, solitary, poor, and brutish, to paraphrase Hobbes.

THE BLACK BOX OF PUBLIC-SECTOR MANAGEMENT

The political economy of disappointment often has its origin in the arcane workings of civil service systems. Many countries have good laws on the books to cover a wide range of public-sector responsibilities, but by deliberate acts of omission, governments may allow the laws to languish and offenders to go unpunished. Laxity is tolerated and discipline is not enforced. Through benign neglect of law enforcement, leaders place a premium on loyalty by selectively protecting the interests of regime insiders. No risk-sharing contract will ever mitigate the effects of deliberate mismanagement by political leadership.

Irregularities in public-sector management can be a significant market-distorting activity.[15] Mismanagement keeps countries like Bolivia or the Philippines locked into near zero growth for extended periods of time, although it does not prevent productivity at levels substantially above subsistence. In such environments, remedial actions that can improve economic performance are easy to envision through the reform of administrative incentives and organizations. Improvements in fiscal management and administration will provide handsome dividends: increasing transparency within the budget process, ensuring competitive public procurement, and enhancing accounting and auditing are among the many short-term actions that allow governments to more effectively deliver services to citizens.[16] Medium-term follow-up actions include strengthening legal and regulatory frameworks, monitoring processes, and improving budget formulation. Freeing up fiscal resources to finance social programs is difficult, given the competing claims on the budget, hence the importance of improving collections and prioritizing expenditures and of making competing claims on the budget transparent.[17] These all sound like administrative exercises that do not require sophisticated technology. The English monarchy of the eleventh century was able to accomplish many of these tasks without information technology. Fixing broken systems of public-sector management is fundamentally a political act.[18]

Civil service reform is surprisingly cost efficient because in the best civil service systems, respect and status for providing good public service are their own rewards. Even societies without monetary resources can organize hierarchies of service to the state.

Mid-nineteenth-century Germany was poorer than England and France in large part because the unification of the German market came much later than in those two countries. Germany's lower per capita income did not prevent it from erecting a civil service system superior to that of England, the United States or France.[19] As Gary Miller observed, hierarchies "make it easy to trade off social acceptance and esteem against wealth."[20] A system established for the special education of the bureaucracy stressed moral fitness and opened government service to competitive examination. Special schools and universities were set up for those pursuing a career in the public administration of the law. Honors and emoluments kept the system attractive to capable individuals and allowed government to raise the bar for entrance. A career of service was rewarded with promotions and stability based on an objective, although rigid, notion of merit. Public recognition in front of one's peers had value in a society that shared a common strategic objective—catching up to more developed neighbors to the West. If not for the professionalization of the bureaucracy, the growth of the state would have produced more political patronage (as in Latin America), rather than more education, sanitation, and transportation (as in East Asia).

When private-sector employment alternatives exist, it becomes costly to maintain a high-quality bureaucracy. Once money is prevalent in an economy, the government must be sure that civil servants receive a share commensurate with the value they provide. At that point, good government must be paid for by the proceeds of an effective system of tax collection.

Public-Sector Management in U.S. History

The link between bureaucratic effectiveness and tax collection is one of the many daunting "chicken or egg" problems in development that economists aptly interpret as endogeneity problems or equilibrium traps. United States history provides a clue to help establish the trail of causality. In 1862, the United States introduced its first income tax but, like the United Kingdom, which tried it earlier, U.S. officials were unable to enforce it with any accuracy and rescinded it ten years later because of rampant tax evasion. The government had neither the technology nor the administrative apparatus to sustain the experiment.[21] A second experiment with income tax occurred in 1916 after the Civil Service Commission, established in 1883, had forty years to professionalize government employees. The second experience succeeded because a base of competence existed in the government, and because technological advances, which included the typewriter and the proliferation of printed forms, left a paper trail that allowed the government to catch evaders.

As in today's developing country democracies, the United States of the nineteenth century suffered the effects of a linkage among political patronage, a weak public service ethos, and high turnover following elections. An absence of transparent rules for hiring and firing ensured a shortage of qualified personnel within the civil service. Career structures were erratic, partisan influence was rampant, and a career path based on merit or quality of service had yet to be established. These deficiencies interfered with the government's ability to provide basic services in an impartial manner. Patronage in recruitment and appointments led to corruption in service delivery and weakened the capacity for regulation and revenue collection. Unlike most developing countries, governmental mismanagement in the United States did not have an impact on macroeconomic stability because the size of the government budget was a relatively small percentage of total GDP.[22]

A civil administration full of partisan office holders eroded confidence in the competence of government and made it difficult for the executive to build support for expanding the role of the federal government. Because the citizens lacked trust in the administration's fidelity to the public good, presidents promised to reduce expenditures rather than turn resources over to public service. The share of government costs to national income rose with improvements in public-sector management. Tax payments increased from 4 percent in 1860 to 23 percent in 1938; expenditures rose from 6 percent in 1890 to 26 percent in 1938.

After James Garfield's assassination by a disappointed office seeker in July 1881, his successor, Chester Arthur (a former political boss), signed into law the Pendleton Act, on January 16, 1883, establishing the Civil Service Commission. The act streamlined pay and career structures, helped eliminate shortages of qualified personnel, and enhanced incentives for senior staff to concentrate on filling their job responsibilities according to the letter of the law instead of to the whim of the political officials. Improved accountability and service delivery reduced corruption and partisan influence and allowed for the improvement of key functions, such as tax administration and the regulation of commerce. But the act did not ensure Arthur's reelection; his own party refused to give him a chance to run for office when his term was up, and Grover Cleveland was elected president. The bosses were not pleased with the loss of patronage opportunities.

In his inaugural speech on March 4, 1885, President Cleveland defended civil service reform: "Our citizens have the right to protection from the incompetency of public employees who hold their places solely as the reward of partisan service, and from the corrupting influence of those who promise and the vicious methods of those who expect such rewards."[23] The act initially classified 15,000 jobs of about 131,000 jobs in 1883, and by 1897 it had expanded to include 86,000, or almost half of all federal employees. Cleveland's patchwork of reforms, according to Stephen Skowronek, did not reverse the domination of the executive by the courts and the legislature.[24] It was Theodore Roosevelt (1900–1908) who reconstituted the institutional power relationship between the executive and Congress by bolstering the authority of the Civil Service Commission to make it a "strong, stable and professional arm of civil administration under executive control."[25] Under Roosevelt's guidance, the commission reclassified civil service positions to provide equal pay for equal work, upgraded compensation to compete with the private sector, regulated promotions within the service, and introduced a retirement plan that included governmental contributions to a pension fund. A comprehensive civil service career system resulted that was based on political neutrality, tenure in office, recruitment by special training or competitive examination, and uniform rules for promotion, discipline, remuneration, and retirement. These reforms altered the position of civil administration within the federal government, freed the executive from the domination of party bosses in Congress, and gave the executive the means to exercise independent control over the machinery of government. In this regard, Roosevelt did for the United States what Lee Kuan Yew and Park Chung Hee did for their respective nations, establishing executive capacity to effectively formulate and implement policy. A major difference between the American experience and that of East Asia was that the U.S. president had to overcome the power of lawmakers, party bosses, and judges to develop administrative capacity. In East Asia, the independent authority of the law and of legislative bodies has only just begun to be constituted and was not a barrier to the establishment of administrative authority.[26]

Once doubts about the capacity and impartiality of government were diminished, presidents could seek public support for expanding the role of the federal government. Eventually, the monitoring of service delivery provided watchdog agencies with evidence and data about the effectiveness of public services. As faith in government increased, and as more citizens began to identify their interests with the success of federal programs, it became easier to mobilize support for public debt issuances and eventually for direct citizen taxation. Only then could the next step toward socially provisioned risk management be taken. Administrations that are poor at public-sector management and that lack effective bureaucratic capabilities cannot manage complex systems of health insurance or social security, or guarantee pension benefits for the aged.

The experience of the United States suggests that administrative reform is critical to and dependent on revenue raising by the state; only after standards of civil service performance are established can the government assess and collect revenues from taxpayers.[27] The first national old-age insurance began in Bismarck's Germany in 1889, in large part because Germany's government alone among the Western powers had adequate civil service capacity. An astute contemporary observer in the *London Times* reported that Germany was able to take the lead in this experiment because "Nowhere is the ponderous, conscientious, plodding, incorruptible bureaucracy so effective and so cheap."[28] Eventually, a competent bureaucracy allowed the government to extend the range of social service to include social security and unemployment. Establishing a professional civil service channeled popular participation in politics away from patronage and toward the provisioning of social services. The system of state provisioning of social insurance, in turn, was the final nail in the coffin of traditional patronage politics.

To gain broad support for economic liberalization among the world's poor, human development priorities—such as education, health, child nutrition, and women's rights—must be added to the list of economic priorities, which includes trade, fiscal, monetary, and industrial policy. Economic reform would be more popular if complemented by reforms that directly touched people's lives and their daily household concerns. Thus, to establish political support at election time for the Indian reform process, Pranab Bardhan asserted:

> If the administrative mechanism of delivery of public services in the area of human development remains seriously deficient, as it is today in most states, chances of constructing a minimum social safety net are low, and without such a safety net any large-scale program of economic reform will remain politically unsustainable, not surprising in a country where the lives of the overwhelming majority of the people are brutalized by the lack of economic security.

Bardhan concluded that the incentives and organizations of public administration are essential to the success of economic reforms.[29]

TAXES: MOTHER TO ALL RISK MITIGATION

The state's role as risk mitigator is intimately connected to its ability to collect taxes, something a private-sector insurer is barred from doing. The government can spread risks much more widely over time and across more constituencies than the private sector can. The social security system, euphemistically referred to as a system of social contributions, is really a form of taxation.

Acquiring the administrative capacity for greater efficiency in tax collection is a challenge faced by many developing nations.[30] With the exception of East Asia's high performers, few developing countries have the administrative capability to measure income accurately. However, computer technology today makes the exercise considerably less expensive than it was for the United States in the early twentieth century.[31] Nevertheless, Latin America, India, China, and Pakistan cannot ensure that information technology is used to improve public-sector capacity. Class conflict arises whenever issues of public finance are raised in Latin America, the Philippines, or Pakistan, where the development of effective tax-collection machinery is feared as a step toward the legal redistribution of income.

When Citizens Are Creditors: Debt as Political Choice and the Myth of Debt Sustainability

Is there some sustainable level of debt that can be determined in accord with universally understood technical principles? Certainly the IMF would be delighted to discover such a formula. But should a universal formula for debt sustainability be a goal of international financial policy? Just as there are differences among individuals about how much debt they are willing to absorb, so too do differences exist among countries. The level of debt is a social choice; its essence is a bet that citizens make on their collective future. One household may choose to front-load debts while another prefers less consumption in order to be safer in the future. Who is right? The existence of a credible commitment to repay the debt is ultimately more important than the size of the debt as a percentage of GDP.[32] The credibility of a government's commitment to repay its debts determines the cost of capital that a government pays for its debts. Also critical from a political perspective is the composition of the debt and how it is shared among sectors of the population. The contributions of citizens are more effectively collected when mechanisms exist to enable broad participation in decisions about the future.

Despite a weaker economy, Great Britain was able to defeat Germany in two world wars because Britain's greater fiscal capability allowed it to support a higher level of debt as a percentage of GDP. Similarly, eighteenth-century Britain prevailed over the much larger French kingdom because the British Parliament funded the national debt through tax revenues that it mandated. Britain's debts enjoyed greater credibility of repayment, since Parliament stood behind the debt, allowing the British monarchy to borrow at a lower rate than the French. One of the sources of U.S. strength after World War II was the financing of war expenditures through a funded debt, linked directly to future tax receipts earmarked by Congress to pay off the debt. Congressional guaranties of repayment kept postwar interest rates low enough to resume rapid growth when the other combatants were crushed by the much higher cost of their post war credit. The funding of government debts by a legislative body that represents the national will to repay enabled Britain and the United States to project power that was far greater than that of nations with larger populations and more natural resources.

The Political Dimension of Public Debt: The Demise of the Citizen Creditor

Historians tend to identify strong leaders like Cromwell, Napoleon, or Bismarck as the great heroes of modern state-building while ignoring the real heroes: citizen taxpayers. Strengthening the connection between the private savings of citizens and the public debts of the state allows countries to prevail in the competition between nations. These great icons of European statecraft were tax-reform innovators who increased participation in tax collection.

When development resources must be found in the pockets of citizens, the national budget becomes a financial plebiscite on national objectives.[33] Deficits passed on to future generations loosen the relationship between taxpayer interests and government expenditures. Tax payments that engage the voluntary participation of citizens heighten their awareness of the use to which their money is put. When leaders depend on citizen savings to fund government functions, a layer of accountability is created. However, James MacDonald pointed out that the growing role of pension funds and investment funds in global public finance since the late 1970s creates a layer between public debt and citizen choice that insulates citizens from direct responsibility for the costs and benefits of public expenditures. The debts of nations become impersonal, MacDonald warned, because the citizen as creditor is being replaced by a faceless international or institutional investor: "the portion of public debts held by domestic financial intermediaries in recent years ranges from 37% in the United States to more than 77% in Japan."[34] The loss of accountability that results is especially severe in developing countries, where mechanisms for public scrutiny of spending are weak.

Assured that the sovereign will repay, foreign investors seem less concerned with how the funds they invest in developing nations serve the interests of citizens who seek a better life for themselves and for their children. The external investor does not question whether a particular investment is consistent with the well-being of people who must repay the debt, or whether the overall government budget will build human capital for the future. An external lender decides to lend based on one consideration, the feasibility of repayment, even if this means tearing down a nation's forests, as in the case of Thailand or the Philippines.

International lenders are not equipped to judge the effects of administrative management on a population's well-being.[35] They do not question whether the composition of budgetary expenditures is consistent with developmental objectives. They may look at the need for infrastructure as an investment opportunity without considering the politics of setting rates for distribution to the poor. By contrast, taxpayers are more likely to ask how the well-being and security of their household will be served. When citizens have no voluntary engagement in how leaders spend, a key element for forging citizen consensus is lost.

By making the sovereign responsible for the repayment of debts incurred to international organizations, international law may have created a mechanism that inadvertently weakens due diligence by creditor and taxpayer alike. Creditors bet that a sitting government will not risk an international moratorium for delinquency; as a result, due diligence is suspended, leaving no one to mind the store. Citizens of the developing countries become debtors with obligations that do not engage their voluntary mandate.[36] Consider the dilemma of Philippine President Macapagal-Arroyo, an American-trained PhD economist familiar with the fundamentals of economic development. She leads a country that has not experienced sustained economic growth in forty years. She faces a significant budgetary shortfall caused in part by many price-distorting subsidies that Filipinos depend on for basic services, such as electricity and consumer goods. Tax revenue stands at just 12.3 percent of GDP, yet efforts to overhaul the Bureau of Internal Revenue by giving it fiscal independence and the clout to pursue the moneyed delinquent elites has been defeated in the Senate. Borrowing to survive, the Philippines spent 42 percent of its tax revenues on debt service in 2003. Yet the 1.1 billion peso Macapagal Highway that bears the president's name wasted more than 600 million pesos, according to the political opposition. No wonder the president has a problem with taxpayer motivation. A government that squanders the taxes that it does collect cannot be expected to improve revenue collection. Citizens shrug their shoulders and look the other way at the waste, since international lenders accept the sovereign guarantee of the Philippines and continue to lend.

An assessment of the constraints on taxable capacity of the Philippine state must be made within a framework of broad assumptions concerning social structure and political institutions. Any efforts to increase current income payments will be met by resistance both from the poor, who do not receive basic services from government, and from the rich, who do not use publicly provided services. Governments that are unable to satisfy their population's indispensable needs find that their requests for more revenue are unwelcome. Without a solution to the present deadlock over revenue, the Philippine government cannot provide a minimum standard of social welfare for the poor, but a change in social structure is needed to surmount this impasse. Such a change means leading a revolution the government fears it could not control.

The Philippines is but one of many developing countries that is unable to accommodate modern economic growth without a long-term weakening of the social fabric of society. Growth is pregnant with conflict because it would disturb the preexisting relative positions of the dominant social groups. To prevent growth from stimulating social conflict, the political institutions of the Philippines must be reconfigured to make reelection depend on satisfying the population's basic needs.

Conventional accounts of economic reform typically eschew references to conflicts that may arise from rapid changes in the economic and social organization of a nation. However, economic growth is a venture into the unknown for any society; the full range of direct and related effects can never be known or fully anticipated in advance. When loyalty to the nation-state is weak and trust in the underlying institutions of a nation is doubtful, economic change is likely to expose the state's very survival to the risk of destabilizing conflict.

Shocks to the System: Chaos, Convention, or Transition

Volatile scenarios receive little attention when people contemplate the future. Theories about social change that assume a linear transformation are preferred. Consider China's disregard of the revenue-reducing effects of weak institutions. Weak revenue-raising institutions that foster uncertainty about responding to future macroeconomic shocks are blissfully ignored.[37] Policy analysts like straight-line projections. Contingencies that involve major changes in the structure of a particular society are shunned, and people who indulge in predicting such negative scenarios risk persecution. Bland optimism is a feature of those who succeed in the business of diplomacy. People want reassurances that they are on a straight path to a place they can predict and envision. News that gives pause is discounted. Business lobbies with the most at stake are the least willing to entertain scenarios of rapid change. For example, support for research of social or political fault lines may put a firm's income-producing assets in jeopardy, and firms will donate money to stifle such unwelcome prognoses.

The experts too often have a vested interest in continuity because expertise loses value whenever a regime changes power. Recall how the Middle East establishment missed the signs of the rapid crumbling of the shah's regime in Iran. United States State Department experts at the time considered Islam to be a moderating force in the Middle East that would put a lid on radical politics. Key U.S. officials continued to believe in the viability of the Marcos regime until a few weeks before popular unrest forced him to leave the Philippines. Just days before the Suharto regime in Indonesia collapsed, exposing its corruption to the world, the resident director of the World Bank denied allegations of gross impropriety by regime leaders. He was among the many Indonesia specialists that affirmed reasons why Suharto was indispensable to his country's future long after key constituents of the regime had doubts. There are few Soviet specialists who can claim to have foreseen the rapid disappearance of the Soviet Union. Such predictions were not in their interest, as their professional expertise lost much of its value the day the regime disappeared. Most plans for the future envision evolution without major surprises or fundamental transformations. Most social science ignores the danger of a crisis that can overwhelm the capacity of today's institutions.[38]

In developing societies, large sets of life-sustaining activities are unpredictable. People have a limited set of tools at their disposal to shape a future to their liking. Latent opportunities are hard to identify. Mechanisms to hedge against unpredictable dangers are unavailable. When tools for analysis and navigation of a future course are scarce, people respond by acting out short-term motives and gratifying immediate needs.

Just as households must insure themselves from shocks, countries too must prepare themselves for the unexpected. Developed societies derive their robustness from their adaptive capacity to cope with contingencies. Agreements exist about how to reach long-term strategic objectives. To ensure the survival of the group, these societies have a process to which they can return with certainty when dealing with unexpected outcomes. Thus they can harness existing capabilities to create new capabilities.

Social-risk sharing necessitates a consensus about the future. However, developing countries are particularly weak at involving multiple organizations or interest groups with different types of knowledge in collective decision making. Because developing societies are weak at collectively choosing from a range of alternative futures, they have few enduring commitments. To surmount this weakness, citizens welcome and even seek out strong leaders.

Autocracies often arise in developing countries as a response to an absence of consensus building.[39] Regimes with narrow constituencies typically result, concerned with only one possible future—that which affects the immediate prospects for the survival of the incumbent coalition. To members of the winning coalition, it does not matter if courts cannot be depended on to hand down impartial decisions. They can overcome rampant corruption by appealing to friendly executive action.

In the logic of autocracy, it does not matter that immense insurmountable debts are passed on to future generations so long as the winning coalition can exit with its share securely intact, frequently in foreign currencies held in foreign banks. In the historically significant transitions to greater citizen accountability—such as the American, British, or French Revolutions—it was debt that forced the hand of government compromise with constituents to build a better tax base. The funding of sovereign debts by international creditors weakens incentives for domestic oversight of investment decisions.

When regime foundations are narrow, multiple views of the future will be lacking, multiple sources about information will be stifled, and multiple organizations to help carry out the strategic objectives in the name of the collective body may even be banned. The models for the future advocated by autocrats usually contain simplistic and inadequate variables that lack adaptive strategies for using a wide range of available information. The only uncertainties addressed will be those of interest to the immediate set of incumbent stakeholders. Leaders will care about only one path to the future, that taken by coalition insiders or regime linchpins. New information will be hard to come by because a restrictive social base narrows sources of information. Arguments about the best policies to shape unpredictable futures are irrelevant, especially if the regime has no assurances that it will survive the near term; no surprise that such regimes are inherently unstable. When they fail, their collapse seems inevitable to everyone except those closest to senior leadership.[40]

No society can ensure an ideal future. Surprises are inevitable, but developed societies have the advantage of weathered decision-making methodologies to tackle uncertainty. They can forge appropriate policy solutions because of access to the sources and capabilities of broad constituencies within their society who see different dimensions of a problem and can make varied contributions to a solution. Being able to engage many parties with divergent knowledge and capabilities, their decision makers can test the consistency of information at their disposal.

A transition from achieving consensus about goals to implementing them is the final stage of organizational adaptiveness. A society must have conventions to take action despite differences about values and beliefs about the future. Once a strategy has been determined, consistent procedures are needed to translate plans into actions.

Developing societies frequently espouse great strategies—think of the many iterations of Pakistan 2015 and of Mozambique 2020—but few means of translating enlightened vision into mundane action. Vietnam sports a document that presents a plan to become a highly developed society by 2010, but the specific policies needed to facilitate this outcome are not listed in the document. A great lacuna of underdevelopment is an inability to go from aspiration to action, either in an individual or collective sphere.

In developing societies, decision makers do not enjoy a wide range of information about the present. Leaders may actually suppress scientific and social analysis and, as a result, have few competing strategies from which to make a decision. With no reliable method to deal with long-term and long-range policy making, developing societies are in constant danger of being overwhelmed by complexity and deep uncertainty. Their citizens cannot make credible promises to each other, to their children, or to their rivals in public life. Their policy makers lack the necessary information to decide on socially optimal actions and, once they have made a decision, they lack effective means to ensure implementation. Hence, compliance lags and the credibility of those actions they do undertake is weak.

An adaptive society requires mechanisms that allow citizens to define and bet on the future they collectively envision and to ensure the durability of commitments driven by that vision. Resilient societies have conventions to manage transitions and avoid chaos, allowing citizens to participate in the future plans of their government. This is the greatest safety net a nation can enjoy.

THE POLITICS OF INSTITUTIONAL CHANGE

After fifty years of mixed results, a World Bank vice president stated that the Bank was finally equipped to deliver infrastructure services: "how we do it has changed remarkably over recent decades. It's more about the private sector. It's about targeting services to the poor. It's more emphasis on building good regulatory capacity and investment climates. But we know how to do it."[41] When will political leaders, parties, and legislatures participate in the bank's expanded awareness and competency? When will bank staff concede that the creation of good institutions is about more than just the technical design of the right structures but also about the incentives of politicians?[42]

The views of this World Bank vice president are not business as usual, they represent a considerable degree of evolution since the 1980s and reflect the impact of institutional economics inspired by the work of Douglass North and other "new institutionalists" whose academic research in the 1990s prompted much discussion about structure and economic change. North's inquiries into the institutional foundations of economic growth taught economists the importance of assessing, measuring, and engineering institutions linked to economic performance.[43] Development, as a result, is understood less as a process of capital accumulation and more as a process of organizational change. But this change in emphasis is highly problematic for economists who generally understand markets better than they understand organizations. Legal and regulatory bodies with a role in the enforcement of property rights now routinely receive attention in developing-country reform packages. But these formal structures do not explain how the organization works. Why are the benefits of the rule of law, which have been obvious to political philosophers for hundreds of years, yet to be implemented in many of the world's poorest countries? Identifying the institutional deficiencies of the world's weakest economic performers is easy to do; ensuring the survival of new institutional structures is a different story.[44]

Political corruption and weak government are the main reasons why countries perform below their potential. In many of the world's poorest countries, bad economic policy and weak institutions are good for politics. A poor state of economic affairs helps leaders stay in office but does not necessarily promote growth and prosperity. Competing in public policy increases leaders' risks of being held to task for their performance. Leaders who embrace transparency risk that their own mistakes will also be transparent. Those who practice predictability will have few off–balance sheet favors to offer friends and cronies. Those who embrace accountability risk that their authority will be contested. Leaders who excel at providing public goods face greater dangers of losing office than those who create enduring loyalty machines by privately allocating resources to key supporters. Leaders with the longest record of longevity in office are frequently those who are most successful at gratifying their constituents with privileged access while denying the public of basic resources. With a small coalition to satisfy, a leader that acts in a discretionary manner to create economic uncertainty for the general economy can provide more private benefits for insiders. Leaders who make the public at large pay the price of their political longevity do not need enlightenment from Washington technocrats to open their eyes to the unforeseen consequences of their mistaken ways. They are willing to pay the price in economic stagnation for policies that help strengthen their grip on office. Reluctance to lose political support, much more frequently than ideological conviction, underlies the patterns and persistence of poor governance in developing countries. Appealing to ideology or to the goodwill or civic integrity of leaders is not the best way to change policy outcomes.[45] Lectures about the virtues of freedom or self-rule will do little to encourage good governance, compared with changing the social construction of power. When an economic crisis becomes a political crisis, it becomes a threat to political leadership. Unfortunately for the poor, multilateral intervention is more likely to occur when a balance-of-payments crisis occurs than in response to the slow erosion of infrastructure, education, or health facilities in rural communities.

The key to getting the incentives right for growth is to change the incentives of politicians. Strategically distributed private goods strengthen the loyalties of small winning coalitions. The channels that leaders use to direct resources to supporters can be used to benefit all citizens through policies that promote universal access to opportunity. However, if supporters are a small subset of the total population, the mix of private versus public goods can be heavily biased in favor of private goods. Since private goods are distributed to members of the leaders' coalitions whose support is needed, institutions to increase the size of the coalitions are essential to create demand for economic policies that foster growth and competition. Leaders who are compelled to draw their support from a broad pool of prospective supporters must dispense more resources to good policies to stay in office. For this reason, political competition has a greater effect on primary school enrollment than does increased spending in education. Thus, in contrast to the views of the World Bank spokesperson mentioned earlier, the existence of competitive political parties whose legitimacy depends at least in part on the support of the poor is essential to ensure that they benefit from public investment.

To address the impediments to institutional reform requires answers to two questions: why do some countries adapt more developmentally sound institutions and policies than do others, and what is the causal link between poor institutions and the personal utility considerations of incumbents? Economic policy reform must change the equation that renders bad economic policy into good politics. Tying the welfare of political leaders to the welfare of the majority will be development policy's greatest challenge.

The Sequencing of Economic Policy Reform

Economists frequently ask about the proper sequencing of reforms. Because macroeconomic reform determines a nation's credibility with international donors and investors, it takes precedence before other developments. This is understandable, as a macroeconomic crisis can bring the wheels of government to a grinding halt, and this priority reflects the increased interconnectedness of the international financial system. Nevertheless, with the resurgence of institutional economics in the 1990s, many policy specialists are persuaded that the old consensus had the wrong priorities. The right institutions are just as important in economic development as the right macroeconomic reforms. When it comes to determining the right institutions, one of the few consensus views held by transition specialists concerns the law, especially laws that protect property rights. But should the lawyers have the final say?

Financial resources for building legal capacity frequently accompany the assistance packages that international organizations offer developing and transitional countries. Large numbers of economic laws have been written and are now on the books, courts have been reformed, and regulatory agencies have been established where none existed in the past. Yet, despite investments in legal infrastructure, most developing countries perform well below expectations.[46]

Political and social forces can interfere with the institutions of justice. A law-based economy is administratively complex, resting on many organizations and conventions that are easily manipulated by those in power. The functioning of the organizations that implement the law are politically controlled. The application of law in a fair, reasoned, and predictable way is largely the result of the responsiveness of judges to their political masters. Law can easily be rendered ineffective by the meddling of politicians and by their interference in the selection of judges. Laws are often written in broad terms, and their interpretation and implementation depend on administrative directives from political authorities. The utility calculations of political masters explain why the law is upheld in one setting and not in another.

In developing countries, the announcement of a new constitution or a new set of rules to protect acquired wealth rarely reduces uncertainty about the security of those rights. The fact that Nigeria has a constitution modeled on that of the United States does not persuade anyone to invest there. Nor will a new set of banking regulations or bankruptcy codes erase underlying insecurity about policy continuity in Iraq or Afghanistan when extreme ethnic or social polarization is the source of the problem. If social polarization explains why societies fail to implement stable fiscal policies in the first place, it matters little whether the institutionalists, with their emphasis on the rule of law, or macroeconomists, with their emphasis on rationality, austerity, and the primacy of prices, are in charge. The construction of institutions to shape social forces is frequently left to the crude mallet of revolution or conquest.

So then what is the proper sequence of economic policy reform and which category of reforms needs to be in the driver's seat? Answers to these essential questions are needed to guide corrective action.[47] The domestic political process steers the process of institutional reform. Long-term economic and social change may underlie the process but it cannot be said to hold the steering wheel: the sequence of institutional change is in the hands of a nation's political leadership. This is why fixing institutions is rarely sufficient to ensure durable change. India, Pakistan, Malaysia, and Singapore all inherited similar civil service traditions from the British with similar reporting mechanisms and rules of service, but those systems function today with radically different levels of effectiveness and integrity. Laws and institutions are easily circumvented by political decisions about the composition of public expenditures and by strategies of stealth, obstruction, and indirection that can shift the operation of existing institutions away from their designated purpose, or they prevent adaptations to shifting external circumstances. Financial institutions, property rights, and tax compliance are maintained according to the coalitional support they provided to incumbent leadership. Economic institutions without political viability will not endure. This is why liberalization, stabilization, and privatization—established in Washington as the great policy objective of the transition years (1989–2001)—did not deliver stable outcomes. These great milestones of development policy ignored a lasting insight of Marxism: development is social transformation.

> Capital is a collective product, and only by the united action of many members, nay, in the last resort, only by the united action of all members of society, can it be set in motion.
>
> Capital is, therefore, not a personal; it is a social power.[48]

Our study rests on that same assumption: that the essence of economic reform is a change in the institutions of power to encourage more inclusive forms of cooperation. The ultimate social safety net is the mechanism by which citizens reach decisions cooperatively.

Uncertainty, Competition, and Collusion in Early Capital Accumulation

THE BOUNDARIES between competition and collusion are rarely as clear-cut as economic textbooks would have us believe. The boundaries are unstable and shift with economic evolution. To successfully grapple with them, new institutions and new analytical frameworks must be as mindful of society and politics as they are of economics.

Even in highly developed economies, what constitutes an unlawful act when doing business with friends, relatives, or neighbors is subject to continuous debate. The standards and mechanisms required to ensure a competitive market are frequently altered.

The conviction that competition produces the right incentives for growth is firmly established in economics. The collusive practices that flourish in developing societies, however, may actually improve their economic performance. During periods of economic development, we see intermediary organizations appear such as the guilds of early-modern Europe, the town and village enterprises of transitional China, and the holding companies of East Asia. Intermediary organizations that enhance coordination at one stage of development may hinder it later.

A society lacking organization beyond the family may benefit from the concentration of control of large enterprises among a few family groups. The ability to collude may be a form of social capital in societies that lack institutions for building trust and social reciprocity. Thus, what looks like a crony relationship to someone sitting in San Francisco or Geneva may actually provide cooperation and planning that otherwise would be unavailable in a developing society. Uncertainty about the reliability of partners and contracts renders the distinctions between capital and collusion that are common in modern economies inapplicable to the early stages of capital accumulation, when collusive relationships supplant missing market institutions.

Differences in the political and social organization of developing societies affect economic performance and cause divergent definitions of competition and collusion. Assumptions common to developed societies about the role of personal responsibility during the pursuit of economic advantage may not even apply to the agricultural communities that typify many preindustrial societies. Countries that begin the process of economic growth from different starting points require different advice about the social and political innovations they will need along the way.

Economic policy advice can confuse the goal with the means of getting there. The typical advice is an exercise in comparative statistics that attempts to bridge the gap in one transforming step between the advisors' home institutions and those of the developing-country client. But what the client needs are models of dynamic change to coordinate a multiperiod process of phases and sequences rather than invocations of international best practice. The no-name bank accounts of China deviate from international best practices, yet they outperform India's banking system because they keep money in the formal banking system, whereas the rule-bound Indian banks drive savings into the black market. As a result of China's more flexible, yet suboptimal system, its financial assets as a percentage of GDP are 269 percent, compared with only 166 percent in India. The exacting standards of evidence demanded by India's penal code transcend the capacity of its underfinanced, inadequately trained law enforcers, making felonies difficult to prosecute.

In the battle against third-world corruption, twenty-first-century New York City may have less to offer as a model than its battle against Tammany Hall in the nineteenth century, when legal institutions were weak and subjected to the influence of bribery. The difficult part of policy is getting the dynamics of change right.

Boundaries among the political, social, and economic realms shift as economies mature and, in the early stages of growth, may be highly amorphous, making it difficult to discriminate collusion from competition. Enforcing the distinctions between collusion and competition require the existence of organizations for consensus formation, which are often unavailable in the developing world. Growth can cause disruptions that reconfigure social and political structures and in turn make the existing stock of social capital obsolete. A consensus among different groups about who should bear the costs of change is often the most elusive component of the change process. Agreement on conventions for handling the unforeseen may be more difficult to attain than the change itself.

Acknowledgments

The debts I have acquired writing this book will require a lifetime to repay. Several intrepid souls were willing to stand in the front line and provide the critical insights that turned the crude early drafts into a book. At the very early stages of writing and conception, Stanley L. Engerman, Yi Feng, Robert Klitgaard, Gregory P. Lablanc, Nancy J. Overholt, and Henry Rowen were essential collaborators. I could not have launched this project without their generosity, insights, diligence, and expertise.

After many hours of discussion, Kenneth Arrow skillfully encouraged me to believe that I had something to add to the conception of risk and uncertainty in economics, a topic that he so thoroughly mastered and generously shared. His line-by-line attention greatly refined the substance and sequence of the ideas in this book. Following many fruitful years of dialogue, Bruce Bueno de Mesquita and I first published together ideas linking institutions and leadership, and that collaboration stands behind this book and makes its appearance throughout. The friendship, open exchange, and problem-solving skills of my Stanford colleagues Larry Diamond, Avner Greif, George Schultz, and Barry Weingast have encouraged my ventures in translating scholarship into policy and practice. Joe Stiglitz aided my appreciation of the role of information in economic development.

In the country chapters, I have shamelessly solicited and obtained the assistance of Albert Keidel, Nicholas Lardy, Robert Madsen, Minxin Pei, and Chunjuan Wei on China; Gautam Adhihari, Ashima Goyal, Ramkishen Rajan, Karti Sandilya, Shaijumon C. S., Manmohan Singh, and Sundaram Pachampet on India; Hassan Afzal, Nadeem ul-Haq, Fakhir Imam, Miftah Ismail, Eric Jenson, Jehangir Karamut, Muhammad Moshin Khan, Farooq Leghari, Hafiz Pasha, Tariq Siddiqui, and Mohammad Waseem on Pakistan; Paul Holden; Liliana Rojas-Suarez; and Anjali Kumar and numerous colleagues at the World Bank on Latin America. Under the auspices of John Page, Ed Campos and I collaborated on a book that still shapes my view on the role of government in the development of East Asia's tiger economies. The dozens of visits to the nations of East Asia make it impossible for me to list the many individuals who have helped me to form my views and who have provided resources to undertake my research.

My colleagues at Claremont Graduate University and Pitzer College created the supportive environment in which much of the writing was undertaken. I would particularly like to thank Thomas Borcherding, Arthur Denzau, Jacek Kugler, James Lehman, Lewis W. Snider, Thomas Willett, and Paul Zak. Colleagues James Barth, Judith Gordon, Peter Passel, Susanne Trimbath, and Glenn Yago at the Milken Institute extended support whenever needed.

Many thanks to the editors of *Asian Survey, Foreign Affairs, National Interest*, and the *Journal of Democracy* for helping me to develop some of the themes found in the book.

My service to the U.S. Department of the Treasury added clarity, precision, and purpose to the vision as no other experience could have done. I am especially grateful to Undersecretary John Taylor and others in the administration for the priceless opportunity of serving in the first year of a political administration when the president's agenda is still being formed.

Many dedicated individuals in the U.S. Department of State Bureau of Educational and Cultural Affairs merit recognition for organizing the speaking tours that enabled me to develop the themes of this study. One particular visit stands out. While I was lecturing on East Asian productivity growth at the University of Hanoi, a member of the faculty asked where his country could begin to establish a framework for capital markets. The following year I presented the first draft of this book as a series of class lectures to Vietnam's Institute of Foreign Relations, and together with my Vietnamese students we explored why mobilization for warfare seems to have little bearing on the ability to mobilize for investment and economic growth. Those discussions helped to crystallize many of the ideas found in this book.

Many Claremont students worked on this book. Cheryl Van Den Handel was project manager, helping in every aspect of production; Jessica Byers' editing was a revelation. The final stages of writing and research were funded by the Freeman Foundation. A special note of thanks goes to Tim Sullivan at Princeton University Press, whose creativity has been indispensable on substance, delivery, and audience.

Data Sources

Banking and Finance in China

- Milken Institute, International Monetary Fund: International Financial Statistics

Economic Freedom

Heritage Foundation

GDP Growth Rate

- World Bank, Asian Development Bank, International Monetary Fund, Bloomberg

Gini Index

- World Bank

Global Risk

- International Country Risk Guide

Governance

- World Bank

Human Development Indicator

- United Nations Human Development Programme

Income/Consumption Distribution

- World Bank World Development Indicators, United Nations Human Development Indicators, *Inequality in Latin America and the Caribbean* (World Bank 2004a)

Variables

Developing Asia
Gross national income per capita $745/annum or less:

- Cambodia, Indonesia, Laos, Vietnam

Developed Asia
Gross national income per capita $746/annum or more:

- Hong Kong, Malaysia, Philippines, Singapore, South Korea, Taiwan, Thailand

Latin America
Population 15 million or more:

- Argentina, Brazil, Chile, Columbia, Mexico, Peru, Venezuela

Western Europe

- Austria, Belgium, Denmark, France, Germany, Ireland, Italy, Netherlands, Portugal, Spain, Sweden, United Kingdom

Unless otherwise noted, all data are from 2001 from all sources.

Notes

1. On the role of capital adequacy models in development policy, see Easterly (2001).

2. Countries that have received the most aid on a per capita basis in Africa have grown less quickly than regions receiving less per capita aid, like China and East Asia.

3. Many languages do not have words that distinguish risk from uncertainty. Former socialist nations, for example, tend to view risk as insecurity to avoid rather than a probability to be managed through market diversification and hedging.

4. A. Przeworski et al. (2000: 257). Whether a political regime is democratic or autocratic systematically affects population growth rather than economic performance.

5. International financial institutions frequently evade this restriction against entering into the realm of politics indirectly via technocratic interventions that depend on narrow political foundations and end up with agreements that enjoy inadequate public support. Such agreements can be looked at as bribes to keep an unpopular regime in office.

6. Political leadership may agree to create institutions the donors like, but through functional diversion they allow the institutions to function in ways that deviate from their agreed-on purpose. To survive a financial crisis, leaders may agree to austerity packages with the IMF that enjoy little popular support.

7. Campos and Root 1996; Root 1996b, 1997, 2001b, 2002.

8. For example, political access distorts the price of assets by inflating their value to those with political connections while reducing its market price.

9. Probability theory assumes that people make decisions as if to maximize the mathematical expectation of gain. The original purpose of probability theory was to determine how a gambler should play in order to enjoy the best long-run odds.

10. Individuals will pool and spread risks in developing societies without using the market. According to Partha Dasgupta (1995: 202), "The need for trading risks in a world where there are few formal risk markets leads to a highly integrated network of interpersonal and inter-household obligations (including marriage ties) that anthropologists and economists have often observed in agrarian and pastoral societies in poor countries."

11. Distinguishing between risk and uncertainty is helpful in this discussion because it helps to highlight differences between developing and underdeveloped economies. However, asserting such differences conflicts with many recent trends in decision theory (Hirshleifer and Riley 1992). Most current scholarship refers to uncertainty as a form of risk or risk being a type of uncertainty. The difference between risk and uncertainty raises philosophical issues. Frank Knight reasoned that risk involves measurable possibilities, whereas uncertainty involves immea-

surable probabilities. An example of Knightian uncertainty is the probability that a cure for cancer will be found, as compared with the probability that a smoker diagnosed with cancer will die. The first is a matter of guesswork, for the latter tables and data exist to make the probability reasonably well known. Another example of Knightian uncertainty is a prediction about an outbreak of war as compared with a prediction that a certain candidate will be elected (Knight 1971). Luce and Raffia (1957) distinguished between risk and uncertainty as those probabilities that are knowable and those that are not, but they later repudiated their own view, finding the distinction to be unhelpful. For the treatment of risk and uncertainty in economics see Arrow (1996; 1964) and Borch (1968). On the role of government as risk mitigator, see Moss (2002), Arrow and Lind (1970), and Hirshleifer (1966).

Knight's work has only marginally influenced decision sciences. Today, formal decision sciences treat risk and uncertainty as the same and assume that decisionmakers have the option to make additional investments in information seeking. Standard capital asset-pricing models assume that shareholders can fully diversify against idiosyncratic risks. In general, most models assume perfect markets in which each investor has the same opportunities and can make the optimal investment in search costs. All trading is done at market-clearing prices. The notion that all decision makers have the option of informational action is unrealistic in developing countries. Risk-bearing assets can be disposed of through market-clearing mechanisms in developed economies, whereas in developing-country economies, a market solution or the means to refer to market prices to optimize risk mitigation strategies is not available. As a consequence, productive adaptation to information is constrained so that actors seek redistribution via political channels rather than through competition in the marketplace, making property rights politically contestable. Thus, in developing countries, the expectation is unrealistic that individuals can insure against negative outcomes or idiosyncratic market risks through diversification. Country-specific complexities in contracting will be reviewed in part II.

12. In economic parlance, uncertainty prevents potential investors from calculating the discount rate applied to net present value.

13. The average behavior of a large group of similar individuals will be more predictable than the behavior of a smaller group, or of any single member of the group.

14. In investing, the greater the variance, or the standard deviation around the average, the less the average return will signify the outcome. Diversification is the best insurance against variance, which can send the investor or country back to where it began. When trying to make a killing, the investor risks being killed.

15. For example, in developing societies, intergenerational care is provisioned through family rather than social resources.

16. Contractual arrangements for sharing risk include common stock and derivative securities, as well as trade, catastrophe, and life insurance.

17. Six months before the outbreak of violent opposition to the shah of Iran, U.S. State Department officials espoused the view that Islam was a force for stability for the region. The French thought unrest in Algeria was pacified at the very moment that violent outbreaks made remaining in the country untenable. Karl Marx overestimated the probability of insurrection in Western Europe's industri-

alizing societies and overlooked the instability faced by preindustrial societies like Russia. The different assessments of experts about social stability as well as actual disruptions are two related but independent sources of uncertainty.

18. No matter how dangerous the environment, some investors will develop specialized skills to operate there, e.g., the mafia in post-transition Russia.

19. Other forms of incorporation in which individuals relinquish their individual rights to terminate the collective entity include partnerships, professional guilds, nonprofit organizations, political parties, local governments, and the state. For example, business corporations that require limited liability can only be liquidated after a majority decision of the shareholders.

20. A self-determining entity possesses an independent legal personality to sue or be sued and to purchase or alienate property in its own name. This enables it to manage its common resources effectively. For example, during the Old Regime in France, village communities acquired a legal personality that allowed them to generate revenues through the management of collective properties. These revenues were used for local infrastructure, schools, and churches and significantly contributed to rural literacy, and eventually funded lawyers to challenge landlord exactions (Root 1987).

21. An irony exists in that voluntary organizations to reduce uncertainty will not form unless uncertainty about their management is reduced.

22. Mancur Olson (1982) paid attention to social costs arising from the perpetuation of residual institutions that have lost their social justification for continuation. But developing societies face an inability to form rather than terminate collective enterprises.

23. Bates (2001).

24. Social polarization based on ethnic or religious identity can limit public incentives to provide service delivery to rival groups. Some social groups will not want to pay for services that benefit other groups. Social polarization creates incentives for politicians to exclude from public services those outside of their ethnic coalition, so that ethnic heterogeneity is often coupled with the unequal provision of public services. Ethnic polarization frequently results in the systemic capture of services by a particular ethnic group or elite (Easterly and Levine 1997; Alesina, Baqir, and Easterly 1999).

25. These countries borrow internationally when interests rates are low, thus weakening their currencies and resulting in higher long-term costs to society.

26. A reliable tax base is needed to support a strong government bond market. Weak government bond markets, in turn, will result in weak private-sector markets. However, strong government debt markets do not ensure strong private markets.

27. Michael Bordo and Roberto Cortes-Conde (2001) make this point in their introduction to the edited volume Transferring Wealth and Power from the Old to the New World. Consensus and fiscal capacity in British history is explored in North and Weingast (1989).

28. Most discussions of probability are based on two views. Classical theory is frequency based; contemporary theory is subjectivist or Bayesian and finds frequentist views to be sterile. The first view refers to the frequency of the occurrence of an event, assuming a long-run frequency convergence as the number of trials increases. A coin toss fits this description, providing a discrete number of trials that are exchangeable in sequence. An accurate estimate of probability is possible

in the setting of a game, but in the real world, policy making rarely enjoys a relevant number of trials that allow estimates with accurate probability of the relationship between cause and effect. Events such as a coin toss have known starting points and a known number of relevant variables, but most real-world policy decisions lack such clarity. Policy makers rarely know which variable must be tested for traces of a particular cause. Thus, frequency-based models of probability, based on a discrete set of parameters, are not particularly helpful to policy makers. Instead, decision sciences have determined that a subjective view of probability is more realistic. The probability of an event occurring is determined by the beliefs of an individual rather than by a quantifiable number of discrete occurrences. The analysis shifts to measuring the frequency of information rather than the number of discrete occurrences of an event. The probability of an event is constantly altered as each participant gathers new information, and probability is determined by how each person views an event. Different people or the same person at different times may assign different probabilities to the same event, which describes the real world more accurately than a simple coin toss. In the long run, differences between values and empirical parameters are diminished.

29. When the necessary support base or coalition is broad, leaders will have to increase the supply of good policies, which reduces their resources for discretionary private subsidies. Chapter 3 attempts an explanation of this pattern.

30. Bueno de Mesquita et al. (2003: 51–57).

31. My thinking on this topic has been refined through my collaboration with Bruce Bueno de Mesquita elaborated in various coauthored projects (2000a, 2000b) and expanded on in chapter 3.

32. The kings of early-modern Europe created the foundations of the modern state by making the court into "a fountain of privilege" on which the fortunes of the national elites in trade, religion, agriculture, and the military all depended (Root 1994).

33. Such subsidies can always be revoked should power change hands.

34. Property-right enforcement requires that agents of the state control the rights to arbitration of property disputes.

35. Similarly, in insurance, risks must be independent of one another. Independence means that the cause of a loss-creating incident must be relatively independent of the actions of the policyholder. The absence of independence creates moral hazard. It also means that the risk can be attributed to a particular cause or event and not to some general movement of prices such as the collapse of the market or the outbreak of a war. There must also be a way to calculate the probability of a loss. It would be impossible, for example, to buy insurance against a change in fashion.

36. In their assessment of the risk-spreading aspect of government investments, Arrow and Lind (1970) observed that there are two types of reasons why markets for many kinds of insurance do not exist. "The first is the existence of certain moral hazards. In particular, the fact that someone has insurance may alter his behavior so that the observed outcome is adverse to the insurer. The second is that such markets would require complicated and specialized contracts which are costly" (366). Developing-country economies suffer from these generic barriers

to the formation of insurance markets as well as the special considerations indicated above in the text.

37. When there is a loss of transparency, investors will not be able to distinguish between the quality of economic management of particular firms, which is why there is a tendency in developing stock markets for the prices of all traded companies to rise and fall in tandem. This makes it difficult to selectively invest in well-managed companies and inspires herding behavior, since investors are unable to reach independent assessments of the quality of management at individual firms (Prasad et al. 2003; PricewaterhouseCoopers 2001). International equity investment avoids less-transparent countries; herding is more evident, as is capital flight during a financial crisis (Gelos and Wei 2002).

38. Markets for insurance against expropriation by government are unlikely because there exists no credible enforcement.

39. On several occasions, the World Bank has been prodded to provide insurance against administrative malfeasance, such as ex post contract violations, in the countries to which it lends but has so far never agreed. The central government of Russia has explored the idea of providing investors with insurance against malfeasance by local administrators.

40. A constitution provides a framework for voice to be exchanged for loyalty. Exit is another option but citizens rarely express their discontent with leaders by migrating because citizenship is not easily portable. Constitutions are ultimately unenforceable by a third party, so they must be self-enforcing to be durable.

41. Exploitation is compatible with capital formation, of course. Economic historians report many examples of plunderers who become investors, such as the Viking invaders of western Europe (France and Italy) in the eleventh century, or the British invaders of India in the eighteenth century. Whether plunder becomes investment depends on the institutions the plunderers develop for mastering risk.

42. Information access may produce a "winner-take-all" society that, although classless, is very unequal.

43. Shiller (2003).

44. A lemons discount occurs when the buyer is not sure whether the seller has inside information (e.g., a defect that is not visible) that allows the seller to overcharge the buyer. Imperfect information arouses skepticism about whether grounds for a mutually beneficial exchange exist (Akerlof 1970). Mutually productive bargains are impeded as a result.

45. World Bank definition.

46. Data are based on the Milken Institute Capital Access Index project directed by James R. Barth et al. (2002).

47. Financial deepening is the measure of currency outstanding in people's hands plus short-term deposits in banks divided by GDP. Loayza, Schmidt-Hebbel, and Serven (2000).

48. Innovative microcredit schemes operating at the grassroots level are in some regions helping to overcome the disconnect between resources and financing.

49. Prasad et al. (2003) illustrated how the quality of domestic institutions is essential for emerging economies to benefit from financial globalization.

50. Lempert, Popper, and Bankes (2003).

51. With fewer children, families will be able to invest more in the education of each.

52. Courts in the former Soviet Union, as in most developing countries, create certainties only for a small subset of the population.

53. Recognizing its connection to uncertainty, John Stuart Mill (1871) maintained that insecure property rights "mean uncertainty whether they who sow shall reap, whether they who produce shall consume, and they who spare today shall enjoy tomorrow" (531).

54. If not derived from their own mettle, elites like to justify their status by that of their ancestors. The nobility of Old Regime Europe rationalized their privilege on consideration of the military prowess of their ancestors.

CHAPTER TWO
SOCIAL FOUNDATIONS OF POLICY CREDIBILITY

1. The beneficiaries of economic policy reform may only accrue in the long run, and the political benefits go to future leaders, rather than those who initiate the process.

2. Dani Rodrik (1991: 229–42) argued that skepticism that reform will be successful leads economic actors to not support the reforms. By hedging, they thwart the prospects for successful reform.

3. See Levi (1997). Citizen consent, which is essential for effective tax collection and for resource mobilization for war, is predicated on perceptions of the fairness of government action. Standards of government trustworthiness elicit the citizen reciprocity needed to form norms of compliance, cooperation, and consent.

4. Olson's (1965; 1982) work challenged models of collective action held by both the left and the right. The left assumed that as objective conditions became ripe, class-consciousness would lead to collective action. The right believed that traditional clientelistic relationships would be superseded by ideology that would motivate common action. Olson pointed out that when individual costs exceed the benefits of joining, collective action becomes improbable. Individual rationality frequently works against collective action for political purposes.

5. The arguments in this chapter draw on a burgeoning theoretical literature on income distribution and growth. This literature has grown dramatically since the mid-1990s and represents a relaxation of the planned/decentralized dialectic that dominated policy studies during the cold war. The empirical literature has made fewer breakthroughs. The availability and quality of observations in the empirical literature are both disappointing and largely inconclusive, limited by the available cross-section data of income distribution. The data are reduced-form estimates that add income distribution variables to the set of independent variables of otherwise standard growth regressions. Aggregate data hide country specificity, and country data may hide inequalities within countries. Since they do not specify the channels by which income distribution affects decisions made by individuals, such as the level of human capital, there is little basis for policy-oriented deductions. A simplistic conclusion is that growth by itself will reduce inequality. Many Latin American countries (chapter 6) and Pakistan (chapter 8) grew with-

out combating income inequality. Perotti (1996) reviewed both the empirical and theoretical research on income distribution and growth. An inability to specify the institutional path that growth will follow to reach the poor is the weakness of this literature.

Efforts to identify a direct connection between income distribution and growth generally lack appropriate counterfactuals and do not provide an assessment of the underlying mechanisms or specific channels by which inequality influences development. Policy makers need to know which forces actually drive the observed outcomes. In the empirical section, East Asia and Latin America are compared, in an attempt to find a logical explanation linking inequality to policy continuity, bureaucratic performance, and the ability to implement a rule of law. Chapter 6 argues that inequality in Latin America makes confidence in reform unsustainable and prevents the impartial functioning of government agencies, especially the courts, so that the rule of law is not ensured. Latin American bureaucracies reflect rather than neutralize the inequality in society. Governments underfund agencies that are necessary to ensure equal access to justice. A mix of social expenditures to ensure that all social groups benefit from future growth does not occur. An effective method to quantify these discrepancies across world regions and relate them to GDP is absent in scholarship. Data to measure credible commitment, bureaucratic effectiveness, or rule of law even within the same society is difficult to come by; finding data that are comparable across countries is that much more difficult.

6. Unlike macroeconomic adjustments motivated by impending financial crisis, institutional reforms rarely carry a similar sense of urgency. The reform of operational institutions such as tax-collecting or customs agencies because it opens the door to future reforms might be a better way to begin than directly altering meta-institutions or rule-making bodies such as the judiciary, the parliament, or the executive.

7. Mancur Olson (1982: 75) argued that "countries whose distributional coalitions have been emasculated or abolished by totalitarian government or foreign occupation should grow relatively quickly after a free and stable legal order is established. This can explain the postwar "economic miracles" in the nations that were defeated in World War II, particularly those in Japan and West Germany." Olson went on to argue that "countries that have had democratic freedom of organization without upheaval or invasion the longest will suffer the most from growth-repressing organizations and combinations. This helps explain why Great Britain, the major nation with the longest immunity from dictatorship, invasion, and revolution, has had in this century a lower rate of growth than other large, developed democracies" (77–78). If Olson was entirely correct, Britain's growth in the 1990s would not surpass that of Germany and Japan. Hindsight has not sustained Olson's generalizations about the origins of the "British disease." Britain in the '90s grew faster than Japan or Germany without upheaval.

8. See Dornbush and Edwards (1991).

9. Root (1996b: 153, 154). The perception by some groups that they pay a high share of adjustment costs may lead to backsliding as soon as external pressures subside (Laban and Sturzenegger 1992; 1994). The inequality of income distribution delays economic stabilization (Alesina and Drazen 1991).

10. India introduced a number of liberal reforms in 1991, which altered the policy matrix governing the country's trade and foreign investment regime by tearing down protective tariff walls and simplifying industrial licensing rules. The completed reforms include an initial devaluation of the rupee and subsequent market determination of the exchange rate; abolition of import licensing, with the important exceptions of restrictions on imports of manufactured consumer goods and on foreign trade in agriculture; convertibility (with some notable exceptions) of the rupee on the current account; reduction in the number of tariff lines as well as tariff rates; and reduction in excise duties on a number of commodities. For a detailed account of India's reforms, see Srinivasan 1996: 14–15.

11. China's average tariff rate is 15.7 percent, India's 29.05 percent. India's 1999–2000 budget imposed a 4 percent levy on top of already-high tariff barriers. India requires import licenses on 715 products including liquor, passenger cars, and consumer electronics (O'Driscoll, Holmes, and O'Grady, 2002).

12. Subversive Marxist-Leninist political movements, assured of logistic, material, and intellectual support from the rise of revolutionary China, North Korea, and North Vietnam, swept over Asia, forcing leaders to acknowledge the importance of social equity. Latin American leaders, by contrast, had a powerful friend in Washington, which was committed to rooting out left-wing political movements. This friendship had the unintended consequence of freeing the region's leaders from anxiety about the equity implications of their policies. By mitigating the threat of subversion by the discontented, Washington relieved these governments of the obligation to produce economic benefits for their entire population, thus forestalling the economic gains accomplished through fundamental institutional reform that occurred throughout East Asia.

Although rarely acknowledged, China's radicalism may have inadvertently helped its neighbors find a path to growth with equity. With the future of their countries at risk, the 1960s produced a generation of leaders in East Asia that changed the region's relationship with the world by changing the domestic policy matrix that governed access to the market. Putting an end to nonproductive rent-seeking market oriented policies transformed Singapore, Hong Kong, Taiwan, and South Korea into the Asian Tigers, perched for high growth, taking over the export markets of the world in consumer durables, and making inroads into product lines as diverse as electronics, ships, cars, toys, and textiles. Trading companies became industrial conglomerates. Strong, unified market-oriented economies and societies were built where disorder and revolution threatened.

13. In a variety of models, Stiglitz (1973) illustrated the role of expectations in determining savings and shaping the society's path of long-run accumulation.

14. Surveys of three Central American countries in 1989 suggest the poor are often willing to accept the notion that their misery is a test by God (Sheahan and Iglesias 1998: 40).

15. Alesina and Rodrik (1994) showed that a lower median-to-mean ratio in the relative endowments of accumulable and nonaccummulable factors reduces growth. Empirical confirmation of a positive relationship between equality and subsequent economic growth can also be found in Clarke 1993 and Birdsall 1994.

16. Arguments linking inequality to credit-market imperfections that confine human capital to the owners of initial wealth can be found in Bruno, Ravallion,

and Squire (1998). The policy implication is that improving access to education and health benefits is Pareto improving.

17. The size of transfers is not a good indication of equity. Direct transfers are typically captured by the middle and top, instead of reaching the bottom. Even when they do reach their target, a net transfer to the poor depresses savings incentives. Alesina (1998) reported that a significant fraction of health and education expenditures are captured by the middle 40 percent. In Latin America, the top 20 percent appropriate the largest share. Housing subsidies in developing countries rarely reach the neediest (World Bank 1997: 59). In middle-income countries like Brazil, the government has resources to tackle poverty but social spending rarely reaches those who need it most. Joan Nelson (1989: 95–113) documented leakages of resources to groups other than targeted beneficiaries.

18. Glaeser, Sheinkmen, and Shleifer (2002) argued that judicial institutions that protect the poor mitigate the inequality of influence in developed societies.

19. Data for ninety-six countries indicate that a higher level of government employment results in lower government wages (World Bank 1997: 10; for data on Africa, see p. 95).

20. A shortage of key public services is the converse of an excess of rules; both impede smooth functioning of public institutions, and both leave room for influence. Convergence between China (with too few rules) and India (with too many) may result.

21. Chapter 7, "Why Not India?" illustrates all of the above distortions.

22. A compelling example is the preferential tax treatment of land in countries like Pakistan and the Philippines, where the success landowners enjoy in gaining preferential treatment of their landed assets leads them to shun industrial or commercial ventures. The resulting misallocation leads to slower growth and higher inequality.

23. Hellman and Kaufman (2004) measured the influence of perceived biases of public institutions on firm managers and found that the perception that public institutions are biased influences subsequent behavior by the firm. "The inequality of influence thus appears to generate a self-reinforcing dynamic in which institutions are subverted[,] further strengthening the underlying political and economic inequalities."

24. Robert Barro (1991) argued that when the median voter is distant from the average capital endowment in the economy, redistributive taxes will be likely. Voters will support a tax rate that is higher when the distribution of wealth is more unequal. A higher tax rate will constrain productive behavior. Similarly, Persson and Tabellini (1994) asked how income distribution affects changes in income and concluded that income inequality harms growth because it leads to policies that weaken property rights and thwart private appropriation of returns from investment. Equality, on the other hand, leads to less redistribution, more investment, and growth. Distributional conflict generates policies that reduce private appropriation from investment, resulting in less accumulation and less growth (Persson and Tabellini 1994: 600).

25. See Knott and Miller (1987) and Mead and Schwenninger (2003).

26. An example of this strategy is the regime of F. Marcos of the Philippines (Root 1996b: 111–38).

27. See Barro (1991) for correlation between economic growth and various education indicators, including expenditure and education; Easterly and Rebelo (1993) for the share of expenditures on education in total expenditures; Otani and Villanueva (1990) and Diamond (1989) for capital expenditures on education; and Clements and Levy (1994) for linkage between education expenditures and private investment.

28. An excellent example is the contrast between Kerala and Uttar Pradesh in India (Sen and Dreze 1999).

29. This idea is fully developed in Bueno de Mesquita et al. (2003).

30. In Brazil, most of the places in public universities go to students who have enough money to first attend private school. The poor go to dismal primary schools and, if they are lucky, will make it to private universities they cannot afford. In general, privately managed schools in Latin America perform better than publicly managed schools (Ferreira and Litchfield 1997). "Privately managed schools (in 12 Latin American countries) also have higher student retention and attendance rates than similar public schools" (Burki and Perry 1998: 89).

31. Bueno de Mesquita and Root (2000a: 235).

32. Kremer and Jayachandran (2002).

33. A large, open economic system can mitigate this tendency.

34. Public-choice theory predicts that to enhance political support, legislators are motivated to vote for spending projects in their districts so their voters will benefit from a wealth transfer while the costs are borne by all voters in the country. By the same token, legislators will resist tax increases that affect their constituencies (Buchanan, Rowley, and Tollison 1987).

35. World Bank (2002d: 103–4).

36. The legacy of Karl Marx has encouraged nations to believe that an alternative exists to the pattern of growth without equality in the example of nineteenth-century Europe. Countries that have understood his message have tried to be mindful about the distributive consequences of public policies.

37. Olson (1993) and McGuire and Olson (1996) argued that when few constraints limit the ruler's behavior, investors face a considerable risk of policy reversal driven by the ruler's own shifting distributional interests, by sudden concessions to populism, or, in extreme cases, revolution.

38. See Mahathir (1970) and Root (1996b: 65–90).

39. Laban and Sturzenegger (1992).

40. Brainard and Verdier (1994).

41. According to Alesina and Perotti (1996), Gupta (1990), Hibbs (1973), and Venieris and Gupta (1983, 1986), inequality leads to sociopolitical instability, such as violent protests, assassinations, and coups, undercutting investment and growth. Roberto Perotti (1996) argued that inequitable income distributions reduce a country's development prospects for two reasons. "First, it creates uncertainty regarding the political and legal environment. Second, it disrupts market activities and labor relations, with a direct adverse effect on productivity" (151).

42. See Putnam (1993: 111).

43. See Tocqueville (1960: 216).

44. See North (1990: 42–45).

45. In an article, which argued that "Public rent seeking attacks innovation, since innovators need government-supplied goods, such as permits, licenses, import quotas," the authors make plausible the assumption that as resources move into rent seeking, returns to innovation fall faster than do returns to rent seeking. One implication of this multiple equilibrium model is that lowering the fraction of innovators lowers returns to innovation (Murphy, Shleifer, and Vishny 1993: 412). In an analogous finding, Hellman, Jones, and Kaufman (2000: 4) show that returns to corruption are greater in highly corrupt countries. Where governments permit low levels of corruption, the returns to corrupt behavior are negligible. Corrupt firms grow at faster rates than other firms do when government is highly corrupt. The implication is that public-sector corruption engenders private-sector corruption.

46. The common assumption that inequality has a greater impact on policy in democracies incorrectly assumes that dictators are less subject, than democratically elected leaders, to political pressures. Alesina and Rodrik (1994) noted that even dictators are subject to political pressure, through riots or bribes. They postulated that inequality matters if it affects the desire for redistribution of a ruler's constituency.

CHAPTER THREE
POLITICS AND ECONOMIC STRUCTURE: THE ECONOMIC LOGIC OF AUTOCRACY

1. Many of the ideas in this chapter have been developed in dialogue and in previous work with Bruce Bueno de Mesquita (Bueno de Mesquita and Root 2000a; 2002b;, 2002). I would like to thank Bruce for allowing me to use jointly developed material in this chapter.

2. In an analogous argument, Arrow (1962a) hypothesized that in an emerging industry, the profitability of each firm depends on the accumulated experience in the industry.

3. On the public good properties of knowledge, see Arrow (1962a; 1962b), Dasgupta, Gilbert, and Stiglitz (1982), and Stiglitz (1999).

4. When information is dispersed, no one has an incentive to reveal anything because rents accruing from knowledge are lost. This is why firms may prefer trade secrets rather than patents. In politics, as in the marketplace, transparency is costly to those that gain rents from information.

5. Early-modern European kings demobilized their rural opponents by making the fortunes of all subjects depend on largess from the court. By judiciously targeting favors, the monarch could make or break the fortunes of even the most powerful subjects (Root 1994; Bates 2001).

6. Autocrats prefer to ration information. If they enjoyed absolute power they would not fear dissemination because they could make pareto-improving trades with their subjects. Autocrats, however, rarely have absolute power. Hence, rationing is the better option although economic performance of the economy will suffer, ultimately causing an autocracy to lose its resource base which is why autocracy is inherently unstable.

7. Bueno de Mesquita et al. (2003).

8. In Pakistan, the military accepts the support of religious extremists to compensate for the loss of its middle-class secular support.

9. Bueno de Mesquita and Root (2002).

10. All regimes protect property rights; they differ as to which rights are protected. For example, if the state owns all enterprises, it will protect its property rights by penalizing competitors or embezzlers. Autocrats may offer vigilant protection of the property owned by supporters while neglecting the rights of those from whom it does not draw direct political benefits.

11. There is no justification to devote output to the invention and production of new goods and services if uncertainty exists about the enforcement of rights to future streams of revenue derived from that activity.

12. Robert J. Shiller (2003) has written of a new financial order for macro markets. It envisions large international markets for long-term claims on national incomes and occupational incomes as well as for illiquid assets such as real estate. Some of these markets could be far larger, in terms of the value of the risks traded, than anything the world has yet experienced, dwarfing today's stock markets. Shiller contemplates a market for the combined gross domestic products of the entire world, a market for the sum total of everything of economic value. These markets would be potentially more important in the risks they deal with than any financial markets today, and they would remove pressures and volatility from our overheated stock market. Individual and institutional investors could buy and sell macro securities as they do stocks and bonds today (4–5). See also Shiller (1993) and Athanasoulis and Schiller (2000; 2001; 2002).

13. McKinnon (1973) analyzed credit repression.

14. Ultimately, making it hard for autocrats, or "illegitimate regimes" in general, to borrow is likely to be more effective than obstructing a country's trade via sanctions. Trade restrictions hurt ordinary people more than restrictions on sovereign borrowing would. Although borrowing usually leaves behind a legacy of odious debts for future regimes to pay off, the borrowed funds are likely to be enjoyed primarily by regime insiders. Kremer and Jayachandran (2002) concluded that if creditors anticipate that loans to illegitimate regimes might be sanctioned and not transferred to successor governments, fewer such loans would be made. Thus, they argued, establishing the right to write off odious debts would be highly beneficial by making it harder for governments that might eventually be overthrown from surviving.

15. World Bank (2003: 3).

16. For example, the government of Vietnam is willing to discuss civil service performance with international consultants, but compensation is off-limits.

17. Until public accountability is strengthened, much of the world's population will remain locked into unproductive social systems that are erected as a defensive response to official plunder.

18. Similarly the towns of western Europe in the Middle Ages built walls around market entrances so that traders would be unable to avoid taxation, whereas governments in many developing countries are persistently unable to do likewise.

19. Root (1987).

20. A good case study of deliberate mismanagement is provided by Kobb (2003: 11–24).

21. In Bangladesh, for example, the UNDP made fifty-three recommendations for public sector reform, the number reduced from an earlier USAID report that suggested 151 reforms. Only one reform was undertaken of the total. The Bangladeshi government then invited the World Bank to make an extensive study of public administration, the exact same ground covered by the previous two studies. At the end of the World Bank study, a universally lauded publication on how to make government work to serve the interests of the people was issued and served as the topic of an international conference in Dhaka. Like the previous three studies, this one was ignored by the next government, which then invited the Asian Development Bank to conduct an additional study again on the same topic of the previous three studies. Despite a consensus that the system of public administration was not working to serve the needs of the public, at no time did any of these organizations consider linking the continuation of aid to public administration performance, which each study concluded was a basic obstacle to the country's economic development. A seemingly transparent open round of studies, reports, and conferences successfully covered up the absence of reform.

22. Root, Hodgson, and Vaughn-Jones (2001).

23. World Bank (1998; 113). By the 1990s, nearly 50 percent of the continent's paved roads and 70 percent of unpaved roads were in poor condition.

24. People trapped in mismanaged polities are barred from enjoying the benefits of global technological change and prosperity in their own country and turn increasingly to global institutions for help; some may resort to terrorism. Getting countries to sign international covenants, or to be party to policies adopted by the development banks or WTO, is one way to drive local leaders to harmonize local conditions with international standards. The Millennium Pledge of the United Nations to reduce global poverty is one important milestone in the campaign to surmount the damage done by poor domestic leadership. However, multilateral solutions can rarely overcome the implementation failures of domestic institutions, for the simple reason that the quality of domestic institutions is critical to a country's ability to live up to the conventions that it has agreed to. Because of poor domestic institutions countries signing pledges to be good global citizens are often unable to live up to their commitments despite the goodwill of the minister whose signature appears on the agreement. Moreover, the international community cannot monitor or enforce compliance with the agreements. Systems of governmental compliance are protected by doctrines of sovereignty, protected from international intervention. The international community is an idea that is well worth nourishing, for it is the only hope that many of the world's people have of being part of global change. The real challenge and work, however, are mostly domestic; change must come from within the countries.

25. World Bank (2002: vii).

26. Institutional weaknesses are widely recognized to be the source of implementation failures in development. For example, the World Bank's *World Devel-*

opment Report 2003 argued that "many appropriate policies are known but not implemented because of distributional issues and institutional weaknesses." It pointed to distributional imbalances and institutional weakness to explain failures of implementation and sought a remedy in the enfranchisement or inclusion of the poor. This book takes the next step. The root cause of exclusion lies not in the institutions but in the incentives of leaders who maintain those institutions and who manage their use. Competent institutions that execute agreements and balance interests will exist when incumbents require such instruments to reveal their competence in public policy.

27. Frequently, banks under autocratic regimes serve as little more than the fiscal arms of the governing elite, specializing in the allocation of capital subsidies to favored groups. Financial links among high government officials, regulators, and governmental institutions facilitate the allocation of capital to projects that generate high returns for government officials and their supporters. The developmental impact of cheap loans made to political followers is rarely enough to destabilize a country's finances. However, untreated corrupt practices spread until the establishment of a sound financial system is impossible without a systemic political solution or regime change. Perhaps the greatest difficulty facing a government that wishes to change is that a reduction in political spoils may destabilize the very government that seeks reform. No reform will be possible if the result is to be chased out of office.

28. Bueno de Mesquita et al. (2003) developed indicators of coalition inclusiveness and of institutionally induced loyalty across almost every country in the world. Depending on the variable to be explained, their data span various subsets of the years from 1816 to 2000. For most factors of interest here (growth, per capita income, freedom, health, education), the data span thirty to fifty years.

29. One common way leaders build political support while ruining their countries is to use their control over economic regulation to deter entry into the market, reduce competition, and raise the costs of doing business for firms not politically favored. Trade restrictions make import licenses valuable. Protecting domestic industries creates rents for which local entrepreneurs are willing to pay. Subsidies to interest groups provide opportunities for government officials to collect side payments. Price controls are an attractive source of bribes, as businesses may be willing to pay government officials for access to inputs at below-market prices. Multiple exchange-rate and foreign-exchange allocation schemes create incentives for businesses to reward officials to obtain the foreign-exchange necessary for purchasing imports. Inevitably, foreign-exchange control makes access to foreign currency politically dependent, and the officials who handle these transactions and their clients become rich. Such policy instruments, once justified as mechanisms to correct market failures, allow governments to purchase political loyalty. By contrast, generally conducive policies for growth may give rise to new interests that raise the political cost of enforcing existing monopolies and privileges.

30. Kaushik Basu (2000) wrote, "Once we endogenize the state, so that agents of government are also part of the economy, with their own motivations and strategies, the role of advising becomes ambiguous. . . . The pervasive error of the advising economist is "futile" advising" (167, 169).

CHAPTER FOUR
AN AMAZING ECONOMY OF INFORMATION: THE FINANCIAL SYSTEM

1. Merton (1995). A financial system provides (1) a payment system, (2) a mechanism for pooling funds (pooling means that households do not have to invest their entire savings in their own businesses but can cover their risks by owning shares in the businesses of other households), (3) a way to transfer resources across time and space, (4) a way to manage uncertainty and control risk, (5) price information to allow the economy to allocate investment, and (6) a way to reduce problems that arise when one party has information not available to another party in a financial transaction (asymmetric information).

2. Economists once assumed that financial institutions arise when the need for services arises. Financial services were viewed as passive, permissive, or facilitating agents that followed the development of the real economy. An expanding literature establishes the importance of financial development for economic growth. Measures of the banking-sector and the size and liquidity of the stock market strongly correlate with gross domestic product and per capita growth (Levine 1997). Both the level of banking sector development and stock market development exert a positive influence on economic growth. See King and Levine (1993a; 1993b), Levine and Zervos (1998), Levine, Loayza, and Beck (2000), Neusser and Kugler (1998), Rousseau and Wachtel 1998, Demirguc-Kunt and Maksimovic 1998, Rajan and Zingales (1998b). Rajan and Zingales (1998a) showed that industries that depend on external financing grow faster in countries with well-developed financial systems. This finding has important implications for developing countries like Brazil, China, and India that want to succeed in research and knowledge-intensive production. Firms grow faster when they avail of an active stock market and large banking sector (Demirguc-Kunt and Maksimovic 1998).

3. Distinguishing the financial system from the real sectors of the economy requires great analytical subtlety. The financial sector is responsible for allocating capital and the real sector for using capital. But where to draw the line becomes murky. When a bank takes deposits and makes loans, this seems to be part of the financial sector, but if a firm goes directly to investors, does the financial sector play a role then? What if a firm is self-financed, using its own retained earnings to supply its investment capital? Distinguishing financial institutions from financial markets is similarly complex. Under the simplest definition, financial intermediaries are firms. But is Lloyd's a market or a firm? Is the New York Stock Exchange a market or a firm? Just as some scholars, like Douglass North (1990) and Avner Greif (2003) call markets institutions, a case can also be made to refer to institutions as markets.

4. Rajan and Zingales (2003: 6–7).

5. Not as important for technology start-ups as for operations that have a steady cash flow (hotels, giant department stores, and phone service providers).

6. Particularly important for tech start-ups because of the industry's intense cyclicity.

7. Black and Gilson (1998: 243–77).

8. How can an entrepreneur get confirmation that a project is a good one? Opinions are cheap and have little value when their beholders have no stake in the out-

come. By attracting outside investment, an entrepreneur can gain feedback that is likely to be more accurate than simply by asking opinions. Of course, getting good advice means disclosing the true character of the project. If uncertainty exists about property rights, an entrepreneur would never be able to release enough information to get good investment advice or to attract enough diverse interest to take advantage of the lower cost of capital that goes with diversification.

9. Stiglitz (1994: 212).

10. Private firms are unlikely to pay for fixed costs associated with developing information from which they will not derive economic benefit. They may see their client base shrink if they disseminate information that potential clients do not approve. Market participants frequently have incentives to hide information or to provide misleading information so that one party may gain from the mistakes of another.

11. World Bank (2003: 9).

12. Lempert, Popper, and Bankes (2003) are developing high-powered computation tools for long-term policy analysis that can distinguish between risk and uncertainty, dispensing with subjectivist Bayesian methods.

13. A milestone in the recognition of the importance of the financial system for growth is the World Bank's *World Development Report of 1989; Finance and Development*, associated with the intellectual leadership of Millard Long.

14. World Bank definition.

15. Data are based on the Milken Institute Capital Access project directed by Barth et al. (2002).

16. Antoine van Agtmael made this suggestion at a conference on the future of domestic capital markets in developing countries (Litan, Pomerleano, and Sundararajan 2003: 512).

CHAPTER FIVE
CLOSING THE SOCIAL PRODUCTIVITY GAP IN EAST ASIA

1. In the past twenty years, more than two-thirds of countries in all parts of the world and at all stages of development have undergone a financial crisis.

2. Crisis stricken countries are Korea, Indonesia, Malaysia, Thailand, and the Philippines. Taiwan's economy has shown signs of weakness after the bursting of the U.S. technology bubble. Singapore and Hong Kong have been resilient.

3. Economist (8 Feb. 2003: 5).

4. Technocratic insulation is defined as "the ability of economic technocrats to formulate and implement policies in keeping with politically formulated national goals with a minimum of lobbying for special favors from politicians and interest groups" (Campos and Root 1996: 267).

5. Many citizens in the developing world have the misfortune of being served by bureaucracies recruited through political patronage. A bloated, poorly paid, and ineffective state sector poses no constraint on executive discretion. Effectiveness is not well served, since the officials have a strong incentive to use their politically acquired positions to collect private rents.

6. Significant variation exists across the region in the extent of competence: in Singapore, the entire bureaucracy; in Indonesia, just the core economic strategy team (Campos and Root 1996: chap. 4).

7. The proactive role of bureaucrats in extracting maximum export performance is reported in Westphal (1990: 45–46), Rhee, Ross-Larson, and Pursell (1984: 22), and Rodrik (1997: 428–30).

8. For examples of the role played by institutions in using business collaboration productively, see Campos and Root (1996: 76–109), and Root (1996b).

9. "Although Asia (including Japan) accounts for over half of mankind, one-third of the world's GDP and one quarter of its exports, the region's share of worldwide equity-market capitalisation is only 16%—or merely 5% without developed Japan" (Economist, 8 Feb. 2003: 5).

10. On the role of stock markets in creating a market for corporate control, see Jensen and Meckling (1976); Jensen (1983; 1991; 1998; 2002).

11. Gerschenkron (1962).

12. The region's overreliance on bank finance was eloquently captured in Alan Greenspan's (1999) "spare-tire" speech: "This leads one to wonder how severe East Asia's problems would have been during the past eighteen months had those economies not relied so heavily on banks as their means of financial intermediation. . . . Had a functioning capital market existed, the outcome might well have been far more benign. . . .The lack of a spare tire is of no concern if you do not get a flat. . . . East Asia had no spare tires."

13. Banks have both advantages and disadvantages relative to markets. Despite considerable and very stimulating debate, economists have yet to determine which exogenous variables lead one set of institutions to be superior to the other or why at one point in time banks are better or worse than alternative financing. Answers that dwell on stages of development have been particularly inconclusive. The influence of financial structure on corporate decision making is well explained in Stulz (2001).

14. The letter of intent between the government of Korea and the IMF note that "the limitation of Korea's system of detailed government intervention at the micro level has become increasingly apparent. In particular, the legacy of government intervention has left an inefficient financial sector and a highly leveraged corporate sector that lack effective market discipline" (available at http://www.imf.org/external/np/loe/120397.htm; cited in Metzger 2006).

15. Leff (1978).

16. Rahman (2000) found that a majority of firms from Japan and Southeast Asia failed to meet international accounting standards. Lax lending standards resulted from governmental involvement in the region's banking systems. Powerful government ministries urged investments in preferred sectors with little regard for their creditworthiness. Connected lending was rampant, in which ordinary loan appraisal standards were overlooked when banks lent to their own proprietors or to affiliated business. The skills to effectively supervise the system were in low demand, as government encouraged forbearance in the hope that new lending would drive problem loans away. Without exception, crisis countries had volumes of non-performing loans that were not reflected in official accounts.

17. I would like to thank Greg Lablanc for sharing his work on these disparities.

18. Root (2001b: 9–14).

19. Systems of contract enforcement exhibit path dependence (North 1990; Greif 2003).

20. Berle and Means (1932/1991: 114).

21. This process is well described by Heilbroner and Singer (1999: 173–93). Also excellent on this process are Temin (1964); Strassman (1981); Noble (1977); Chandler (1977); Rosenberg (1982); Evans (1948); and Tedlos (1991).

22. Berle and Means (1932/1991: 6–7).

23. Although differences in accounting, transparency, and corporate law exist between German/Japanese–type financial institutions and U.S./U.K. models, all share the basic institutions needed for effective financial intermediation: they can enforce contracts effectively and ensure quality public administration (Barth et al. 2001:116–23). Thus, although Japan differs from the United States in the owner-ship structure and financial structure of its large privately owned firms, it shares a fundamental institutional infrastructure, unlike the developing-country exam-ples to be explored in the following chapters.

24. For example, members of a Japanese *keiretsu* are united by small percent-age of shares that are cross-held, and by the exchange of the board of directors and employees between member companies. The companies typically share com-mon goals and form business strategies jointly, top executives meet regularly, and the companies participate in joint investment. They will often buy each other's products, and they receive favored treatment from member banks. These banks are permitted by law to own equities and can have seats on the board of directors in member companies. A dominant central organization such as a trading com-pany is another common feature. Vertical industrial *keiretsu* have received the most attention in the literature on management because they are considered to have given Japan an edge in manufacturing. In the vertical *keiretsu*, member firms belong to the same industry and carry out different functions along the value-added chain: they have significant cross-ownership of equity and cooperate closely in a particular geographic proximity (Prowse 1992).

25. For a detailed description of equity cross-ownership and common board membership in Southeast Asia, see Kunio (1988). Groups comprising diverse busi-nesses initiated by a single family are characteristic of Indonesia. Twenty-five polit-ically connected groups account for revenues of more than $60 billion in 1995, when GNP was estimated to be $200 billion (Fisman 2001: 1101).

26. Hoshi and Kashyap (2001).

27. Root, Abdollahian, and Kugler (1999).

28. In a study of nine East Asian economies, Claessens, Djankov, and Lang (2000) found that voting rights frequently exceed cash flow rights typically through pyramid structures and cross-shareholdings. The result is that in more than two-thirds of the firms, a single shareholder has effective control over the firm. Deviations of one share, one vote are not unique to East Asia. In the United States shareholders can achieve control rights that exceed cash flow rights through ownership of common shares that carry high numbers of votes. The shares that carry superior voting rights trade at a premium.

29. Joh (2000a) documented that controlling blockholders in Korean firms are more effective when they have high cash flow ownership.

30. "Profits may be shifted from a parent corporation to a subsidiary in which the controlling group have a large interest. Particularly profitable business may be diverted to a second corporation largely owned by the controlling group. In many other ways it is possible to divert profits that would otherwise be made by the corporation into the hands of a group in control. When it comes to the question of distributing such profits as are made, self-seeking control may strive to divert profits from one class of stock to another, if, as frequently occurs, it holds interest in the latter issue" (Berle and Means 1932/1991: 115). Such abuses by owners were made difficult in the United States by laws and judicial interpretations, which are only beginning to find their way into practice in South Korea or China today. Because jurisprudence provides only weak protection for Asian shareholders, there is a strong preference among Asians for the state to play a direct role in oversight and/or ownership of large enterprises.

31. Evidence that diversified firms invest inefficiently by making investments that are inconsistent with returns on capital can be found in Scharfstein (1998), Rajan, Sevaes, and Zingales (2000), and Ahn and Denis (2002). Investment that is less sensitive to cash flow in firms that belong to the same group can be found in Hoshi, Kashyap, and Scharfstein (1991). Shin and Park (1999) and Perotti and Gelfer (1998) make the same finding for Russian firms that belong to financial investment groups.

32. Williamson (1985: 76) claims that incentives in nonintegrated supplier relationships are higher powered than incentives within firms. Baker, Gibbons, and Murphy (1997: 3) support this assertion by showing how incentives in firms are provided through bonuses based on subjective performance assessments. Because the firm owns the asset, an employee has no recourse if the firm refuses to pay a bonus. When services are contracted from outside the firm, the employee is an independent contractor who owns the asset and can extract payment through bargaining. This reduces the temptation not to pay the bonus.

33. Toyota and Nissan typically own 20–50 percent of the equity of their largest suppliers. Toyota owns equity in fifty of its 310 suppliers. American manufacturers do not and cannot take similar stakes.

34. Evidence exists that *keiretsu* membership reduces the costs of financial distress by mitigating free-rider and information asymmetry problems in negotiation with creditors. Hoshi, Kashyap, and Scarfstein (1991) show that *keiretsu* members, as well as firms with ties to a main bank, invest more in productive assets and sell more products in financial distress than do other Japanese firms.

35. Root, Abdollahian, and Kugler (1999).

36. The general thrust of these reforms are improvements in the transparency of listed companies, accountability of management to shareholders, protection of minority shareholders, elimination of related-party transactions between controlling shareholders and their companies. Company laws, commercial codes, securities market laws and regulations, stock exchange listing rules, and competition or antimonopoly and fair-trade laws were amended. The goal is to open corporate decision making to scrutiny by shareholders and the investing public, to encourage professional management and decision making on market criteria, and to reduce the domination of the economy by a few corporate groups. The success of these

reforms has varied significantly across the countries according to their precrisis institutional capacity.

37. A letter of intent is an accompaniment to the loan documents that is not an enforceable treaty with consequences for noncompliance.

38. Metzger (2003).

39. Chui, Titman, and Wei (2001) examined the impact of financial liberalization on firms and tested whether financial reforms hurt politically connected firms relative to independent firms. They found that connected families in Indonesia were not hurt by financial liberalization.

40. Root (1996b: 108).

41. Using data from Indonesia, Raymond Fisman (2001) measured the relationship between connectedness and firm value. Indonesia's centralized and stable political structure under Suharto made it possible to construct an index of political connectedness. Fisman constructed an event study to measure the extent of firm profitability that relied on connections. The events included adverse rumors about the state of Suharto's health along with returns of firms with differing degrees of political exposure. Fisman wrote: "First, I show that in every case the returns of politically dependent firms was considerably lower than the returns of less dependent firms. Furthermore the magnitude of this differential effect is highly correlated with the net return on the Jakarta Stock Composite Index. Over the corresponding episode, a relationship that derives from the fact that the return on the JSCI is a measure of the severity of the rumor as perceived by investors. . . . [W]ell-connected firms will suffer more, relative to less-connected firms, in reaction to a more serious rumor. My results suggest that a large percentage of a well-connected firm's value may be derived from political connections" (1095–96).

42. See Root (1996b: 108–10). That legacy caused the electoral loss suffered by his hand-picked successor, Habibie.

43. Root (2001g: 32–35).

44. Conversation with Megawati, APEC Business Forum, October 2002.

45. Root (2000c).

46. The last round of vote buying usually takes place on the night before the election, which is known as "dog barking night" because villagers are visited by so many vote buyers that their dogs bark the whole night (Pinto-Duschinsky 2002: 74).

47. Campaign financing in the United States, according to one study, has not grown faster than national income and has hovered around 0.01 percent of GDP since 1912 (Ansolabehere, Gerber, and Snyder 2001).

48. Taking differences in income into account, elections in the Third World can cost forty-four times more per capita than all the elections—state, local, and federal—that took place in the United States in 1996. A general overview of the question of money and politics can be found Pinto-Duschinsky (2002).

49. Ironically, the weapons used in the battle against corruption can be too effective. How can democracy bring stability to the region if government after government is prevented from serving out its term? When implementing institutions are weak, anticorruption legislation can be used idiosyncratically for political purposes. If government after government fails, then democracy too can fail.

50. On democracy in Thailand, see McCargo (2002), Bunbongkarn (1999), Callahan and McCargo (1996), Phongpaichit and Baker (2002), and Nelson (2002).

51. Root (1996b: 105–9).

52. Root, Abdollahian, and Kugler (1999).

53. See World Bank (1993), and Campos and Root (1996).

54. They need institutions that make it costly to engage in corruption. They need watchdog agencies and multiple layers of accountability that allow government agencies to scrutinize one another and that allow the electorate and civil society to monitor the officials of the state. The judicial system must be able to impose penalties without interference by money or influence. Citizens must be assured that public accounts will be subject to independent, systematic, and regular reviews. Legislators must have the tools to assess and design legislation. Independent electoral commissions must safeguard voting procedures. Tax collection must be fair, predictable, and comprehensive, with proper legal processes and grievance procedures in place. The media must be credible, and independent and professional organizations must be able to ensure that their members derive their stature from the integrity with which the serve the public. Of course the region's policy makers have become fluent in the institution-building mantra. The remaining task is to create more inclusive political coalitions with sources of wealth that are independent of government favor.

55. Root (2002: 113–26).

56. Yusuf and Evenett (2002) defined a strategy for resumed competitiveness in knowledge-intensive manufacturing and services but emphasized that future competitiveness will depend on stronger domestic and regional institutions and improved regional coordination. Open trade and investment regimes can provide a new round of competitiveness if Asians implement appropriate policy measures.

57. In Indonesia, the New Order's three national development plans (Repelita I, II, and III) built rural infrastructure, reducing the inequality in the distribution of income. This plan supported self-sufficiency in rice production and irrigation facilities. The second and third five-year plans added social infrastructure as well. Importantly, Indonesia allocated a substantial share of the profits from its oil to poverty-reducing programs. By the late 1970s, the proportion of the population living below the poverty line fell from 60 percent to 40.1 percent, the Gini index fell from .40 in the late 1960s to .30 in the late 1980s (Campos and Root 1996: 65–66).

58. For example, the Kuomintang (KMT), needing the support of the native Taiwanese, used land reform to gain their support. Rent ceilings limited rent to 37.5 percent of the annual crop yield and a "land-to-the-tiller" program required landowners to sell excess land to the government, which redistributed it to small holders. The KMT also established uniform weights and measures, engineering standards, and social surveys to reduce costs to small farmers. Price information was disseminated to peasants, and marketing channels were provided to reduce rents extracted by middlemen. Village councils were created to discuss local land and management issues. As a result, the number of landowners increased and the number of tenants decreased. Importantly, income inequality declined (Campos and Root 1996, 53–54). Singapore established the Housing and Development Board in 1960 to ensure home ownership for all citizens. In 1993, the government sold shares of its newly privatized Singapore Telecom stocks to citizens at half the market price, again the goal being to make every Singaporean a shareholder in the nation's growth.

59. To allay labor tensions, Singapore's government created the National Wage Council to decide nationwide wage increases. All three parties—business, labor, and government—have veto power, so agreements represent all stakeholders.

60. Datt and Walker (2004: 77).

61. Bankruptcy laws were quickly reformed in each of the crisis countries (Korea in February 1998, Indonesia in April 1998, and Thailand in October 1998) but the reforms are slow in implementation and have been largely ineffective in many cases (Metzger, 2003).

62. In order to deliver stability in East Asia and improve the quality of life for the region's populations, democracy must create favorable conditions for bolstering political accountability and transparency. East Asian countries need reforms that will strengthen the integrity of their civil services, judiciaries, organs of public finance and procurement, and systems of campaign financing. Broader information access will help by eroding the disproportionate powers of elites. A more equitable distribution of political power should be the end result. As the economic base of the elites weakens, winning elections the old way—through jobbery and payoffs—will become more difficult.

This tendency has already become apparent in local elections in the Philippines, where several well-heeled incumbents have run out of resources trying to drive away well-funded challengers. Once the resources of the wealthy minority are exhausted, leaders who want to sustain a large following will have to offer policies that produce benefits for broad segments of the population. East Asia's leaders will become competent in economic policy once political competition compels them to reach for political coalitions too broad to be held together with bribes and personal favors.

63. Phongpaichit and Baker (2004).

64. Financial markets in New York and London, because of their global reach, and their closer conformity with market fundamentals, more effectively allocate regional savings than do regional institutions. Hong Kong and Singapore's leadership in regional finance has done more to link East Asian economies with advanced economies than to promote regional integration. With the improvement in information and communication, the benefits to local firms of local information diminish while the gap in expertise that favors New York and London markets grows. Progress must be made in harmonizing legal systems for protecting minority stockholders, regulatory systems, tax treatments of cross-border flows, banking standards, auditing disclosure, and regional corporate governance to avoid a period of the generic, predictable, and recurrent crisis.

CHAPTER SIX
THE PRICE OF EXCLUSION: LATIN AMERICA'S EXPLOSIVE DEBT

1. An example of risk sharing that has beneficial public components are government bonds that can be sold to wealthy people for the development of infrastructure that benefits all.

2. Data were compiled for the Latin American countries with a population exceeding fifteen million: Argentina, Brazil, Chile, Columbia, Mexico, Peru, and Venezuela.

3. World Bank (2004a: 1). Gini coefficients for Latin America are inconsistent measures of inequality because the data are not collected in the same manner using the same criteria across regions or from year to year within the same region. Additionally, gaps exist during which the data was not collected for several years or more (Mungaray and Van Den Handel, 2004).

4. World Bank (2004a: 11).

5. The difference between risk allocation (workers' compensation) and distribution (food stamps) are not always clear-cut. Redistribution is introduced to change expected outcomes by transferring wealth. Risk allocation makes outcomes more certain by pooling resources.

6. Barham (2002: 49).

7. The era of market reforms has not delivered what was advertised. Critics can point to the fact that from 1960 to 1980, income per person increased 75 percent but from 1980 to 2000, it grew by 7 percent.

8. In an extensive cross-country analysis, Kaufman and Kraay (2002) found little evidence that general economic development improves the quality of institutions.

9. Dependence on short-term finance makes firms especially vulnerable to unanticipated shocks. Access to a mix of long-term debt or equity could soften the impact of sudden downturns.

10. Although Brazil has a primary surplus of 3.765 percent, interest rate payments on the debt have exploded to more than 9 percent of GDP, resulting in an overall budget deficit of 5 percent. About a third of the domestic debt is indexed to changes in the exchange rate in order to protect investors against currency loss. When the *real* depreciates against the dollar, the government's debt payments rise automatically. Moreover, most of this debt is short term and is indexed to the dollar, which leaves Brazil highly exposed to the vagaries of capital flows, like most of the regional economies. Shifting to longer-term maturities would carry an initial significant risk, which the countries are barred from doing because that would push them below the 3.675 percent surplus required. They then find themselves in cycles of short-term optimizing. Clearly, debt markets overall are inadequate supervised.

11. On Latin America's capital markets, see Edwards (1995: 200–251).

12. See Burki and Perry (1998).

13. For an excellent discussion of the factors essential to establishing an economic and institutional environment for private-sector development in Latin America, see Holden and Rajapatirana (1995).

14. See Holden (1997).

15. Calculation from IFS (2004).

16. UNDP (2004).

17. See Cavallo 1997. Also, see Ratliff and Fontaine (1990; 1993) and Murphy and Moskovits (1997).

18. This account of Argentina's collapse is drawn from the excellent journalism of Hector Tobar in the *Los Angeles Times* (2003).

19. Except for Peru and Mexico, no Latin American country has enjoyed a successful land registration program. Documenting small landownership in Mexico was difficult until Alvaro Obregon expropriated large landholdings in 1920, distributing *ejido* plots to communities in perpetuity in legislation in 1921–22 (Levy and Bruhn 2001). This first effort to deed small holdings to families was discontinued by President Salinas in the late 1980s.

No Latin American nation protects secured transactions. A convenience that makes extrajudicial enforcement simple in the United States—not to require a court case to prove the validity of debt to settle secured transactions—is illegal throughout the continent. Moreover, new reforms in Latin America rarely stipulate that old commercial legislation must be superseded. Without negotiable assets, clear title, or based on the contract enforcement rule of law, investors do not have a vision of the end condition of their investments or assurances that the market will drive activities to the highest-valued best use.

20. Brazil's new government will be able to avert Argentina's fate and avert a fiscal crisis by imposing tax increases and spending cuts, which no recent government has attempted.

21. For example, poor teacher training, outdated methods, inadequate materials, and low student motivation are not necessarily altered by increased budgets but they do hobble educational reform.

22. See Murphy, Libonatti, and Salinardi (1995: 18).

23. Using survey data contained in the International Country Risk Guide (ICRG) and the Business Environmental Risk Intelligence (BERI), the index of bureaucratic effectiveness is highly correlated with the "unexplained" portion of East Asia's high performers growth rate (excluding Indonesia). This suggests that bureaucratic effectiveness has made a significant marginal contribution to the economic performance of the East Asia's high performers (Keefer and Knack 1993). Using a different data set, Mauro (1995) also investigated the effect of bureaucratic credibility (with a related but different measure) on growth after controlling for political instability. He found that it has a significant effect on economic growth.

24. Some as yet very incomplete moves toward legal reform have been taken in Latin America. See Ratliff and Buscaglia (1997), and Buscaglia, Ratliff, and Cooter (1997).

25. Edwards (1998: 46–47).

26. See Edwards (1998: 47).

27. See Murphy, Libonatti and Salinardi (1995: 30–32, 42, 48–49, 53–54); and Yáñez and Letelier (1995: 168–72).

28. See the comments of nineteenth century Argentine writer and president Domingo Faustino Sarmiento in Waisman (1987: 39). One very bright star in Latin America' s future is that relatively successful reforms have, with the single exception of Chile, come in democratic or somewhat democratic environment. McGuire (1997) and others argued that change through democratic means makes the Latin American experience look good in comparison with East Asia. In most cases, elected presidents appointed a powerful economic reformer as economy minister and the reformer, in turn, comes with a team of like-minded "followers" developed over a period of years. This suggests the process itself is not internally

democratic. Waterbury (1993) argued that "the crucial factor is the public backing of the team by the head of state" (27). Nevertheless the reforms were conducted outside of normal bureaucratic circles by politically appointed officials.

29. Leopoldo Solís, quoted in Waterbury (19)93: 9 and Murphy (1994: 12–17).

30. Graham and Naim (1998: 341).

31. Critics have argued that the East Asian state-led model only reallocates the cost of capital and that direct state support of the banking sector may in the long run diminish the incentives for the private sector to develop risk-mitigating capabilities. If companies cannot go bankrupt and if there are no penalties for default, then risk does not exist. As a transition model, it is still unknown if a road map can be found eventually leading from the East Asian model to a U.S./U.K.–type financial system.

32. Not being secure against the dangers of regional insurrection, East Asia's elites felt compelled to support wealth-sharing mechanisms that provided dividends from growth to the entire population.

33. Lora and Londono (1998: 96).

34. The famous inverted U of Kuznets, which postulates that distribution worsens during early development to improve later. Kuznets's (1966) work was based on time-series data for England. Ahluwalia (1976) found strong support "for the proposition that relative inequality increases substantially in the early stages of development with a reversal of this tendency in the later stages" (338). A recent affirmation of the theseis of high inequality in early growth is Forbes (2000). A reexamination of the data by Anand and Kanbur (1993a; 1993b) provides reversal of the Kuznets U hypothesis.

35. Campos and Root (1996).

36. Lora and Londono (1998: 96).

37. UN Report on Democracy and Development in Latin America (2004).

CHAPTER SEVEN
WHY NOT INDIA? NEW CENTURY, NEW COUNTRY

1. Between 1994 and 2003, India's software exports increased from US$128 million to US $10 billion (India, Ministry of Technology 2003).

2. Some economists forecast that as a producer of manufactured goods and provider of services, India will put pressure on other regional low-income economies such as Indonesia, the Philippines, and Vietnam, and that it will force its more advanced neighbors China, South Korea, Taiwan, and Japan up the technological chain.

3. The average annual rate of growth between 1951 and 1981was 3.5 percent.

4. Rajiv Gandhi in 1985 initiated the process of liberalization by opening telecom, computers, and electronics to private investment.

5. The power subsidy to the agricultural sector alone is estimated to be $6 billion a year, or about 25 percent of India's deficit, and is twice the annual public spending on health and irrigation (World Bank (2002a).

6. The examples of ineffective economic administration are from *India Today* (2001).

7. In the 2002 Forbes list of the world's top 200 small-cap companies, thirteen were Indian.

8. Whereas special economic zones in China have attracted significant foreign investment, India's experiments have not been as successful because units are not allowed access to domestic markets until they pay prevailing duties on finished goods.

9. O'Driscoll, Holmes, and O'Grady (2002: 227).

10. The A. T. Kearney/Foreign Policy Magazine Globalization Index includes a ranking of sixty-two countries for fourteen variables grouped in four baskets: Economic Integration, Personal Contact, Technological Connectivity, and Political Engagement. Globalization Index 2004, in *Foreign Policy* (2004).

11. In 1950, India's share of world trade was 1.78 percent; in 1994, it was 0.61 percent after reaching a nadir of 0.53 percent in 1991 (India, Ministry of Finance, 1997).

12. The pre-independence Congress Party under Mahatma Gandhi espoused an ideology that cut across social barriers.

13. Because the Congress Party controlled much of that sprawling governmental structure, the Congress elite could readily channel those economic resources to build and sustain political support. The economic development implications of using scarce economic resources for political ends, or, for that matter, of adapting to local power structures and thus forgoing any reforms that might adversely affect the influential "big men," probably were negative. Nevertheless, those strategies were political in motivation and, when judged by political criteria, were quite successful. They helped Congress build and sustain a sprawling network of supporters across India (Kohli 1990: 186).

14. See Weiner (1957; 1967). This chain linked the party's national leaders with landowning members of the local elite who derived their legitimacy from an association with the nationalist symbols of the Congress Party and, "more important, by cultivating their image of being problem-solvers within the local community. Although their organization for problem-solving was like machine politics anywhere, the use of public resources at the discretion of the local elite had not yet come to be viewed as corrupt and self-seeking behavior." The so-called "big men" "received political offices or access to governmental resources in return for using their local influence to mobilize electoral support for Congress. That chain of important individuals stretching from village to state and eventually to the national capital, welded by bonds of patronage, was one central feature of Congress's success until the 1960s" (Kohli 1990: 186).

15. The term "demand groups" is used in Rudolph and Rudolph (1987).

16. Das (2000: 145). "The original aim of reservations was to accelerate the rise of the backward castes. It is now a sectarian tool used by backward castes to demand a share of patronage" (Das 2000: 147). The National Democratic Party (NDP), the Democratic Labor Party (DLP), and the Socialist Republican Party (SRP) in Kerala are caste-based Parties. The Rashtriya Janadadal (RJD) in Bihar and the Samajvadi Party (SP) in Uttar Pradesh are also caste-based parties. Rajni Kothari wrote: "Caste has a major influence in politics. Political parties are selecting their candidates on the basis of the prominent caste in a particular constituency" (Kothari 1970).

17. Voting in India does not seem to reflect awareness of major issues or the intention to maintain or change specific policies—which is contrary to the description sometimes made of voters in the United States. Indian voters do not vote prospectively in expectation of certain policy outcomes (Meyer 1989: 1121).

18. "Since 1951 India has had over 100 political parties, most growing out of the will of a handful of people with only a local base. Others were confined to a linguistic region and only a few were organized across state boundaries. There have been thousands of individual defections, dozens of party splits and mergers, and frequent electoral alliances" (Meyer 1989: 1113).

19. Kohli (1990: 196–97).

20. "Public sector industry has absorbed 55 percent of the planned investment and controls 70 percent of fixed assets. The share of the public sector has increased from 10 percent of the gross domestic product in 1960 to 15 percent in 1970 to 21 percent in 1980" (Kochanek 1987: 1281).

21. Ethnic solidarity intensifies the competition for spoils. Marathis were discriminated against in both education and jobs, especially government jobs, in a state controlled by the Kannadigas. (Kholi 1990: 97). They demanded the town be transferred to Maharashtra.

22. Since the economy was growing slowly, the incumbent party could not simply offer more. Competing parties could not offer more, either; instead they specialized in shifting the flow of spoils to create new coalitions. This meant that one party built its support base by encroaching on the spoils allotted to rivals.

23. Politicians controlled access to licenses to land, which they auctioned off to wealthy tycoons in exchange for kickbacks that were used to buy votes from poor ethnic voters. The economic consequences were relatively benign in the United States because unlike India, the U.S. government exercised limited direct control over the economy.

24. On bloc voting see Bueno De Mesquita and Root (2000b: 10–11).

25. Kohli (1990: 124–25).

26. McDonald (1995: 78).

27. Schenk (1986: 117).

28. Economists have viewed corruption as a form of price discrimination that helps get more goods produced. For example, if an expediter ensures that those with the highest valued usage get to the head of the line at an airport check-in, the bribe payers can then use the time they saved to employ their talents to create more goods for society.

29. The Santhanam report in 1964 confirmed this observation (India, Ministry of Home Affairs 1964b).

30. The most dramatic change in the character of public service occurred when Indira Gandhi was the leader of the Congress Party (1969–84). In attempting to create a "committed" civil service, she initiated a process of deinstitutionalization. Once the rules were bent, and the institutional controls were removed to accommodate "committed" socialists, venal motives took over, and personal aggrandizement replaced ideology. India's democracy under Indira Gandhi entered a new era, in which the poor became an interest group to be courted. Social prestige no longer automatically translates into political power as a result of Indira's legacy. The lower two-thirds have displaced the upper castes at

both the state and national levels in the half-century since independence. One national cabinet—Deve Gowda and I. K. Gujiral in the mid-1990s—included almost entirely lower-caste members.

31. In Old Regime France, venality, referred to the buying and selling of public offices as private property which in some cases can improve performance (Root 1994).

32. The police captain is a key patronage position. The local political boss requires a loyal chief of police, since the police decide which laws to enforce and which public to serve. A captain enjoying the support of the political boss has little to fear and many opportunities to exploit.

33. The Vohra Committee Report of the Indian government, which assesses the linkages between electoral politics and the administrative apparatus, asserts: "there has been a rapid spread and growth of criminal gangs, armed senas, drug Mafias, smuggling gangs, drug peddlers and economic lobbies in the country which have, over the years, developed an extensive network of contacts with the bureaucrats/government functionaries at the local levels, politicians, media persons and strategically located individuals in the non-state sector. Some of these Syndicates also have international linkages, including the foreign intelligence agencies" (India, Ministry of Home Affairs 1993). "Criminals can also help politicians gain and retain power by capturing poll booth, organizing demonstrations or stirring up violence. In exchange, politicians can help them avoid prosecution. Criminals became even more involved in politics when they began to realize the nature of the immunity that political power granted them," wrote Jason Overdorf in the *Far East Economic Review*. In Uttar Pradesh, "[i]n the 2002 state assembly elections, more than a sixth of the 5,539 candidates had police records" (*Far East Economic Review* 2003a: 56). Politicians like to have both the police and the criminals in their pockets.

34. Even in Kerala, where literacy is high by national standards, management appoints teachers and usually after receiving a hefty bribe. The state pays the salary (Prabhash 2003).

35. In the Indian system, the holders of elite positions viewed themselves as cultivated men, not technocratic specialists; education formed the basis of social esteem. This was attacked as a continuation of traditional feudal, theocratic, and patrimonial domination.

36. After independence, the bureaucratic basis of governmental authority was gradually submerged by older traditions of patrimonial authority, an evolution, opposite that followed by the West, where state authority shifted from the patrimonial to the bureaucratic over the course of a long evolution. The rules governing India's bureaucratic institutions were often compromised by commerce and association with other forms of social authority that had deep roots in India's traditions.

37. Bhambri (1972).

38. One civil servant reported: "politicians are moved by a determination not to allow officials to stand between them and the exploitation of even the details of administration for political-cum-personal ends. In the war of benefits and concessions for clients, the dividing line between the policy-making and field administration has been eroded. The bureaucratic fort has given way and officials are

adjusting themselves to new ways even to the extent of doing and saying what might please political masters. This abdication is leading to blurred roles of the two wings. The one abets the other's corruption" (Jain 1998: 806).

39. The evolution to public authority followed a trajectory that was opposite that of Europe and East Asia, where bureaucratic authority first emerged as a tool of government to challenge patrimonial assumptions and structures. For example, in France bureaucracy emerged as a way for the king to circumvent the authority of the landed nobility (Root 1987). The process was reversed in India, which began with a bureaucratic administrative system, based on abstract rules in a society characterized by personalism and communalism. Over the course of time, both money and patronage supplanted the rule by impersonal bureaucratic rules.

40. Weber (1961).

41. Knott and Miller (1987).

42. Postings were used by the British to limit officials from creating local coalitions that could be used to increase their power at the expense of London's control. Transfers were also used to prevent the official from acquiring a vested personal interest in the local economy.

43. The IAS comprises state cadres. During the course of a career, a member might work for the central government on deputation (reverting back to the state cadre). Serving a state government, an IAS officer was formally under state control; however, service rules were made by the central government and these could not be altered or interpreted without central support. An officer could appeal to the central government, against local authorities, if service rights had been infringed. The rules of service could be used to tie up in red tape activities that the officer does not favor.

44. Dreze (2003).

45. The IAS collector had literally thousands of enumerated powers as head of the magistracy, revenue collection, other government departments, and urban and rural local authorities. In exercising these powers, the IAS collector engaged centrally in the political process of the district. A prime indicator of this was the fact that every collector received a steady stream of "pressure" from local, and not-so-local, politicians to use his or her powers to allocate scarce resources in a manner beneficial to particular interests (Potter 1986: 222).

46. Another linchpin of local administration, the Chief Secretary, must also be drawn from IAS.

47. In Rajastan during one year, 40,000 transfer orders were carried out in the education department alone. Fees help explain this merry-go-round. Each transfer cost its bearer 1,000 to 3,000 rupees. The post of a superintendent engineer went for 50,000 rupees (Zwart 1994: 81).

48. Vittal (2000).

49. Police stations are repeatedly auctioned; officers of rank will bid for the rights based on the corruption prospects.

50. In the early 1980s, transfer policies laid down norms calling for postings of three years, but numerous independent studies reveal that this is not followed. One study shows that 80 percent of IAS officers held posts for less than two years, and a majority stayed for less than one year; only 20 percent stayed for two or more years (Potter 1986: 218).

51. The transferring authority is accountable for transfer decisions only to the immediate officer; no justification for one assignment rather than another need be given to anyone else. Who the transfer officer is depends on the rank of the transferee and on the distance of transfer. Procedures do not exist by which individuals are entitled to be consulted or even to express their preferences. No reasons need be given and no appeal procedure is available (Wade 1985).

52. Wade (1985: 485). Canal managers are under pressure to behave almost exactly contrary to the ostensible objectives of their job: instead of reducing water uncertainty, they artificially increase it if they wish to maximize bribe revenue; instead of maintaining the canals in good condition, they leave large stretches of the canal unmaintained so as to save maintenance funds for other uses. Agricultural officers are under pressure, if they wish to have congenial postings, to adulterate the special inputs they are given charge of, so as to be able to sell the balance on the black market and to approve the substandard seeds or fertilizers of private dealers.

53. Potter (1986: 161).

54. United Press International (2003).

55. Lower-court judges, prosecutors, and police are widely suspected of corruption, and in the higher courts, legal delays are endemic. Even if the Supreme Court ensures prosecution, it could take decades and achieves little, so that probity even where it tends to be concentrated rarely provides results.

56. The largest mutual fund in India, the Unit Trust of India (UTI), bought undesirable shares of companies at the behest of politicians who received kickbacks from the companies that were purchased. One politician forced UTI to invest in companies owned by a sibling.

57. All major banks and insurance companies were nationalized in 1969, and these accounted for more than 90 percent of the financial sector's assets by the early nineties (Srinivasan 1996).

58. Based on a survey of 2,000 business executives from forty-nine countries (*India Today*, 1996a: 97).

59. Campos and Root (1996).

60. In 1964, this weakness was recognized by a national committee set up to investigate corruption. The Santhanam Committee "agreed with the view that association of recognised bodies of commerce in decision-making can greatly reduce issue of licenses to spurious firms who have no standing in a particular commercial activity or industry." This is so because those in the field would know the bona fides of a firm in that field, while it is possible that a supervisor or inspector of the government can be duped by the false credentials of a bogus firm. Again, licenses should not be issued to those firms who are not admitted to a particular trade guild or chamber of commerce. Another step to curb corruption would be for the government to enter into direct negotiations with business organizations (Gopinath 1982). The committee's report took notice of frequent unrecorded meetings between executives of commercial firms and senior government officials.

61. For example, it is reputed that during the 1950s and 1960s, important business houses had "captured" certain members of Parliament. "Members of the FICCI are generally understood to have well-established contacts with the Congress hierarchy, with bribes being passed under the table to party coffers in ex-

change for political favors. Most business houses, moreover, maintain "liaison offices" in New Delhi that wine, dine, and probably bribe bureaucrats and senior politicians to facilitate licensing and access to other resources the government controls" (Kohli 1990: 325–326).

62. Kochanek (1974: 327–28).

63. Kochanek (1987: 1283).

64. Import substitution was based on a broad consensus that domestic production of import-competing goods should satisfy the domestic market under incentives provided, regardless of the level of protection against imports. Even import prohibitions were acceptable.

65. Observation of China's rapid growth was a key to converting the Indian planning commission to a strategy of openness.

66. One of the problems with doing business with government-owned entities is that they seem more solvent than they are in fact. Major discrepancies are known to arise in the accounts of public-sector firms that are notorious for being able to avoid the annual scrutiny of auditors; however, deregulation compels government firms to show a profit. India's central bank, the Reserve Bank of India, has been ineffectual in monitoring the activities of banks under its supervision. The inspectors are highly competent but their reports are submitted to a superior who is not subjected to outside accountability. Sensitive information can often be withheld, since everything is secret. Often the directors of the central bank have conflicting interests, as they also serve as directors of the banks they oversee. All this means that firms never know where they stand when they deal with the government (*Grant's Asia Observor* 1996: 9).

67. During the 1970s, ministers were known to insinuate that a particular industry or trade might be nationalized to encourage the flow of contributions (Kochanek 1987: 1290–92). Even India's largest private conglomeration faced the threat of public bashing. Indira Gandhi's minister of industry, George Fernandez, a prominent labor leader, threatened to break up the big private holdings, such as the Birlas, and talked of nationalizing India's most successful steel firm, Tata Iron and Steel Company (TISCO) (Waterbury 1993: 58). Nationalization of foreign investment was a worldwide phenomenon, not unique to India, that peaked around 1975 and vanished in the early eighties (Kobrin 1984).

68. "It would appear that by the early 1970s the whole apparatus of control and regulation of industry has acquired a momentum of its own. It was seen that the scope for conferring or denying favors meant considerable accretion of power and patronage to the political system . . . [resulting in] the emergence of the combined and powerful vested interests of politicians, bureaucrats and businessmen" (Waterbury 1993: 57). See also Marathe (1986: 18–19).

69. Laws protecting shareholders of Indian companies lack teeth, and regulatory bodies rarely play the role of watchdogs. The staff of India's Securities and Exchange Commission is inadequate and undertrained. Few are lawyers. When investigative agencies are weak and understaffed, corporate fraud cannot be effectively prosecuted. Companies cannot be expected to provide realistic information to oversight boards when the books are cooked to avoid restrictive laws (*India Today* 1996b: 105).

70. *Grant's Asia Observor* (1996).

71. In the family holding company, the majority of shares are owned by the family; only with difficulty can shareholders monitor firm performance.

72. See Fukuyama (1995) for a discussion of the commonalities in firm organization of the world's industrial leaders.

73. A distinctive feature of the private corporate sector of India is the dominant position enjoyed by a relatively small number of large, family-controlled business houses. The top thirty-seven houses were drawn predominantly from families who belonged to the major traditional trading communities of India (Kochanak 1987: 1281).

74. These tend to be vertically integrated; multiproduct oligopolies designed to minimize competitive pressures from clients and suppliers, spreading risk through diversification in various sectors. Diversification dominates specialization in research and development. Eclectic diversification is often a response to special deals made available in specific sectors.

75. Das (2000: 167).

76. Above all, economists and donor organizations believe that corruption is a political problem, and the cure is liberalization. Cutting red tape is the first step, followed by simplifying procedures to narrow the opportunities for petty graft. Trade liberalization, it is hoped, will wipe out opportunities for big-time graft, characterized by collusive arrangements between large firms and government.

77. Srinivasan (1996: 14–15). Many observers consider these reforms easy compared with the reforms that lie ahead. The first wave of reforms does not mean job losses for organized labor and do not threaten subsidies that are defended by powerful lobbies. The long list of reforms still necessary include amending the labor laws, closing the fifty-eight public-sector enterprises that are chronically ill and trimming the rest, closing loss-making bank branches, privatizing the insurance sector, reducing the number of public-sector employees, increasing oil prices, imposing user fees for public utilities, and allow 100 percent foreign ownership of business ventures. The next round of reform—tackling education, agriculture, infrastructure, banking, labor laws, and public enterprises—must be openly conducted, as these reforms will impinge on India's masses. The full engagement of the community and the cooperation of many groups will be needed this time.

78. Root (1996b).

79. World Bank (2003).

80. Similarly, much of the opposition campaign in India's 1989 national election was based on Rajiv Gandhi's alleged involvement in a scandal that involved kickbacks on a government contract (Bofors).

81. The reluctance in 1996 of the new government in Maharashtra to accept a deal with Enron consummated by the previous state government is a well-publicized example of how reform can be politically contested when it is not institutionally secure. Enron demanded a risk premium to enter a market that had experienced considerable policy uncertainty. That premium was renegotiated as soon as a rival political party assumed office. The renegotiations created additional policy uncertainty that will make future investments of a similar scale unlikely.

82. Root (1994).

83. Traditionally in the economic literature, uncertainty has not been viewed as a powerful explanatory factor in neoclassical investment and growth models,

which rarely analyzed the impact of volatility on economic activity. However, recent empirical studies indicate that volatility can adversely restrict investment. Ramey and Ramey (1995) demonstrated a strong negative correlation between volatility in real GDP and the average rate of growth using cross-country evidence. Others have found a negative relationship between various volatility measures and private investment; see Aizenmen and Marion (1993), and Hausmann and Gavin (1995). Alesina et al. (1992) identified adverse growth effects of political instability in developing countries after controlling for other variables. Aizenman and Marion (1993) have argued that underinvestment will occur in the absence of a commitment mechanism. For example, populist political pressures have created volatility in India by weakening institutional commitment mechanisms. Investment subsidies needed to overcome policy uncertainty are made unsustainable through these pressures. Tax concessions offered to multinationals are another example; they are made in many developing countries but are one such measure that rarely finds support in India.

84. World Bank (2003: 34). The survey included taxes and regulations, financing, policy instability, inflation, exchange rate, corruption, street crime, anticompetitive practices, organized crime, infrastructure, and the judicial system. Only in South Asia was corruption ranked as the number one constraint.

85. World Bank (2003: 51).

86. Transparency International (2002).

87. World Bank (2003: 37, fig. 2.13).

88. Economists have queried if society does not profit when channels exist to buy one's way out of excessive permits and regulations through corruption. Trying to satisfy the regulations might divert more resources to unproductive uses (World Bank 2003: 52–53).

89. India's only bout of authoritarian emergency rule lasted from 1975 to 1976 when civil liberties and personnel rights were suspended. Indira Gandhi ended up being ousted from office in 1977.

90. Jenkins (1999: 274).

91. Das (2000: 227). He wrote, "The biggest failing is that no one has tried to sell the reforms to the people. As such, the perception has grown that reforms help the rich and hurt the poor" (222).

92. Barro (2000: 209–231).

93. International Business Risk in 2003 assigned both countries a risk rating of 6.0, with 10 being the highest risk (Jarvis 2003).

94. Octavio Paz (1997) observed that "universal sovereignty, democracy, the party system, equality before the law, human rights and freedom of religion are the legacy of the British Raj. The great absence in classical India was a universal state. The three great historical empires—the Maurya, Gupta, and Mughal—never ruled the entire subcontinent. The political history of India was always that of rival monarchies in perennial conflict with one another. . . . The peoples of India shared a civilization with common values, but they lived in permanent war with one another" (94).

95. Studies that rank trust across societies usually rank China ahead of other nations with its income level, despite the fact that China lacks a rule-based system

of property rights and its leaders rule without elections. The trust its leadership has earned seems to come from its commitment to the elimination of deprivation.

96. Dreze and Sen (2002).

97. Women in particular benefited from China's pre–market-opening reforms. Female literacy is almost twice as high as India's, Chinese women enjoy higher life expectancy and their share of the total labor force is 50 percent higher than in India (Sen and Dreze 1999: chapter 4, 81).

98. See Sen and Dreze (1999: 4, 57–86).

99. Chile, Latin America's most successful reformer, increased social services only after the market-opening reforms of Pinochet.

CHAPTER EIGHT
PAKISTAN ON THE EDGE

1. The Paris Club is an informal group of creditor governments.

2. Haq (1995).

3. Robert Bates (1995) argued that policies that appear economically irrational might be politically rational. The literature in political science generally takes the position that bad policies occur when they are more politically expedient than good policies. This book extends this logic to poor institutions. The economic literature views inappropriate government policy as the root cause of poor development performance. The argument of this book is that bad institutions, like bad policies, are chosen because of their distributional effects.

4. Javed Burki (1974) described Pakistan's governing elite as being committed to passive policies to stay in power. "I regard the present political elite in Pakistan to belong to the passive category as did the other constitutional regimes in the country's history. Passive policies are aimed at preventing any erosion of existing support" (1127).

5. To preserve this coalition, no government since 1981 has allowed national census taking. Pakistan's population has increased significantly and has become more urban since that time.

6. The creation of an independent Muslim homeland was an objective of the Muslim League, founded in 1906.

7. Jinnah "had shown a tendency toward insisting that his orders be followed without question. He had also shown that those who disagreed with him were likely to be subject to penalties" (Baxter 2001: 128).

8. Callard (1957: 67). Thirty years later, the same description could be given. "The political parties are little more than alliances of the oligarchy that have been formed for the sole purpose of retaining power in some form or the other. Issues and ideas are not discussed on any political platform nor is a division in the Assembly or among the parties along ideological or rational lines. Votes both inside and outside the legislatures are being bought. Allegiances continue to be switched not because a major issue of public interest is involved but only because of narrow self-interest. Cabinet and other positions are not being awarded according to merit or the ability of the individual to perform. These positions are rewards to be handed out by the government. The politicians appear to lack an understanding of the

central concept of democracy that they have been elected for a reason—to run the country on behalf of the people as their representatives. The only purpose that the politicians appear to have is to make as large a personal fortune for themselves as possible" (Samad 1993: 181). The introduction of a national legislature chosen by popular vote did not solve Pakistan's accountability deficit.

9. Arif (2001: 91).

10. After Jinnah's death in 1948, the Muslim League was divided over the definition of an Islamic state. The two sections of Pakistan could not agree on representation within a central assembly. Representation of minority religious groups and the selection of a national language proved equally divisive. The Constituent Assembly was dismissed in 1954, and the second assembly produced a constitution in 1956. The title of governor-general changed to president but the duties remained essentially the same: the chief executive exercised decisive control over the government.

11. During this period, politicians virtually forfeited the right of transferring CSP officers from one job to another.

12. The policy is criticized for exacerbating ethnic and ideological polarization.

13. Ayub's economic policies reflected a strategy of building coalitional support from a political elite that was not only small but drawn from an extremely narrow social base: the "combined Muslim bureaucratic, military, and political elites totaled no more than a few hundred people. This extremely small consolidated elite was superimposed on a largely rural, agrarian society dominated by kinship ties, tribal and religious loyalties, and patron-client relationships. . . . There was practically no urban middle class, the business community was insignificant and largely refugee in origin, and the urban middle class was small and politically weak. There was therefore no really organized group to challenge the new ruling coalition even if it had chosen to do so. Thus, the distribution of power in the new system focused on the relationship among the governing elite groups" (Kochanek 1983: 47–48).

14. Foreign assistance played a significant role between 1959–60 and 1967–68, providing 35 percent of total development expenditures and 48 percent of total imports (LaPorte 1975: 113). Much of that aid was tied to purchasing supplies from donor countries.

15. Khan (1980: 196).

16. Husain (1990: 13–14).

17. In an address to the West Pakistan Management Association in April 1968, the chief economist of the planning commission, Mahbudal Haq, coined the phrase the "lucky twenty" for the families that had direct control of the bulk of large-scale business and commerce and indirect control of much else (LaPorte 1975: 93). Their control allegedly included 80 percent of banking and 97 percent of insurance. Subsequently, scholars have expanded the list to about thirty-five families. As noted, these families often entered into joint business ventures with retired military or civil service leaders who could provide political contacts and licenses to secure foreign exchange.

18. Most of these families were migrants from India who brought their wealth and acumen with them (Haq 1976: 5–6).

19. LaPorte (1975: 127).

20. The People's Party Manifesto cited the need to redress "[a]ll the forms of oppression by authority and by those who exercise the power on account of their riches; . . . every government of this country has followed the policy of concentrating expenditure in the domains that benefit the privileged classes (Wolpert 1993: 110).

21. Looney (2001: 203).

22. Zulfiquar Ali Bhutto, chair of the People's Party, became the first elected president of Pakistan in the 1970 election. Civilian rule was restored on December 20, 1971, and an interim constitution was established in 1972. A permanent constitution, enforced in April 1973, named Bhutto prime minister. The manifesto of the Pakistan People's Party stated, "The present system of administration is a legacy of colonial rule; any modifications introduced were to promote the interest of groups holding the lever of power within the government and administration; the administration thus became its own master. The representative regime will need a different structure of administration" (Pakistan People's Party 1970: 27).

23. Reserved posts were abolished, uniform pay scales were established for all cadres, the all Pakistan Services were abolished and replaced with a single unified civil service. The members of the abolished CSP were assigned to one or more independently constituted subcadres. Lateral recruits into the Central Superior Services were established and amalgamated into the regular service. Horizontal movement was introduced. Theoretically, technical officers could head ministries or departments. Heads of Department and Secretary posts were open to all on the basis of merit.

24. The service tribunal was available only after internal remedies were exhausted, including redress through one's superiors in the service; officers could only go to a tribunal three months after the submission of grievances.

25. Conversation with Hamid L. Sharif, Asian Development Bank (1996).

26. Mahmood (1990: 62).

27. At the normal rate of recruitment of about fifty to one hundred a year, it would take more than a decade to dilute the effects of Bhutto's action.

28. Mahmood (1990: 63).

29. Burki (1974: 1133).

30. Bhutto started by nationalizing ten basic industries, which allowed the government to influence wages as well as prices. He ended with the takeover of all private banks, which allowed the government to control who received credit and on what terms.

31. New labor legislation led to a significant increase in real industrial wages. "The wages of unskilled workers in a government-controlled enterprise is now 60 percent higher as compared with 1969" (Burki 1135).

32. He impounded the passports of leading industrialists and then proceeded to confiscate their properties. This included thirty-one industrial units in ten basic categories: iron and steel, heavy engineering, heavy electrical, basic metals, motor vehicles, heavy chemicals, basic chemicals, petrochemicals, cement, utilities (electricity, gas, and oil). In March 1972, thirty-two life insurance companies were added to the list, and in January 1974, private banks. The control of assets of the large-scale manufacturing sector dropped from 41.7 percent to 31 percent for thirty-nine houses. Although the level of economic concentration weakened, the

top houses still controlled 40 percent of private assets and more than 45 percent of the private domestic assets (Kochanek 1983: 98).

33. Quoted in Burki (1974: 1133). Salik wrote: "The party remained for him only a legitimizing instrument or merely a conduit for coming into power. He reached the terrible stage where one feels that the party needs him rather than he the party. At one stage, he declared: 'I am the People's Party and they are all my creatures.' He was right in the sense that everything emanated from him. He nominated the office-bearers of all party organizations. He distributed favours. He granted recognition to party leaders and threw them out of circulation at will. The same autocratic trend characterized his behaviour as head of government. He sacked whom he wanted and elevated whom he liked. He even indulged in self-aggrandizement without much regard for rules and regulations. As one observer put it, he treated Pakistan as his personal estate. Thus, the difference between the PPP and the government became indistinguishable. Favours were showered from government sources on the favourite party workers—import licenses, permits for ration depots, loans from financial institutions, and even cash grants from government coffers. The party work suffered as the party workers got addicted to easy favours and as the party leaders assumed bureaucratic roles in nationalised institutions. By 1977, PPP had lost its effectiveness as an instrument of political participation. It ceased to be a platform for articulation and aggregation of national demands. In less than a decade of its founding, it deteriorated from a promising political institution to the handiwork of an autocrat. Elections were never held within PPP to elect its own office-bearers" (Salik 1997, 133).

34. Under Ayub, the allocation of rents for political purposes, rewarding supporters, buying off opponents, and ensuring support of key groups was not as economically costly as it later became under Bhutto's broader political base, when private goods had to be disbursed to cope with ethnic diversity and to accumulate resources to fight elections. This led to the polarization of politics according to ethnic identity.

35. Husain (1990: 356).

36. Looney (2001: 208).

37. Looney (2001: 223).

38. Husain (1990: xiii).

39. Anticorruption agencies have themselves been notoriously corrupt. Despite legislation that provides stern punishment and specifies minimum procedural delays for holding inquiries, no major cases of corruption have been successfully prosecuted.

40. In 1969, the CSP held 93 percent of all posts of joint secretary and above. By 1973, the comparable figure was reduced to 44 percent (Kennedy 1987: 103). The positional dominance of the CSP continues to decline as CSP cohorts at the senior level reach retirement age. The CSP no longer recruits, and its size relative to the bureaucracy is declining (Kennedy 1987: 105).

41. The officer corps of the Pakistan army was another essential member of the governing coalition. Pakistan had only four lieutenant colonels, forty-two majors, and 114 captains at independence. This corps received 60 percent of the total government expenditures from 1948 to 1959 (Kochanek 1983: 46).

42. Burki (1969: 242). In some developing countries, Malaysia being a prime example, the party controlled enough resources to make itself the source of patronage. In Pakistan, where the party organization is generally weak and the party controls few resources directly, politicians depend on the bureaucratic hierarchy to distribute spoils.

43. Zia reappointed several CSP officers dismissed by Bhutto and repositioned former CSP officers at key points within the bureaucracy. Nevertheless, the institutional control of the CSP has weakened. The lineal descendant of the CSP, the DMG, does not dominate the bureaucracy to the extent the CSP did. Nevertheless, a classless bureaucracy and unified service are goals that are as far from being achieved in 1997 as they were in 1973.

44. Witness the efforts of the Sharif government to fight constitutional battles rather than to concentrate on governance.

45. In the 1960s, very few provincial secretaries enjoyed a high pay scale; now most provincial secretaries are in the upper echelons.

46. Provinces are divided into divisions comprised of two to four districts, which consist of *tehsils* of 100–150 villages. The executive power of the government in a district reposes in the deputy commissioner.

47. For example, by 1958 twenty-six out of eighty, or 32.5 percent, of the assembly members were ministers.

48. According to the consensus of the jurists, independence of the judiciary means "[t]hat every judge is free to decide matters before him in accordance with his assessment of the facts and his understanding of the law without improper influence, inducement or pressure, direct or indirect, from any quarter or for any reason" (Ali et al. 1997: 92).

49. Ali et al. (1997: 174). A study conducted for the Asian Development Bank concluded: "The system of justice can no longer protect citizens from the excesses of the rich and powerful. Often, well-connected individuals interfere openly in the functioning of the judicial and police system. They frustrate criminal investigations, harass honest officials, and generally encourage and support oppressive and criminal behavior amongst government officials" (Jensen 1997).

50. Goodnow (1964: 133).

51. For example, the 1992 accounts were being audited in 1997.

52. Waseem (1994: 171–88). For example, even when the planning board was set up to be more independent of the CSP than other sections of the central secretariat, its recommendations had to be scrutinized by the CSP, allowing the revision of recommendations that might undermine CSP influence. The British tradition of secrecy in all governmental matters was carefully guarded: CSP officers could withhold information at will. The most important posts, including personnel and finance, were occupied by CSP officers, who through their control of information could influence virtually any governmental decision.

53. LaPorte (1975: 165).

54. Revenue-sharing rules in which proceeds are shared between local and national governments are one way to induce local officials to reveal local information.

55. See Root (1989) and North and Weingast (1989).

56. In practical terms, the decision making in this field was the preserve of the planning commission; the department of investment, production, and supplies; the licensing boards; and the chief controller of imports and exports (Waseem 1994: 171–88).

57. Corrupt bureaucrats can influence the rate of return on capital invested by asking bribes. Bribery affects competition by reducing the number of producers and thereby reducing the number of products available. By altering profit margins, bribery induces exit of firms and the loss of consumer surplus associated with consumption (Romer 1994, Bliss and DiTella 1997).

58. Samad (1993: 109).

59. A war of attrition pits rival families against each other in a struggle to dominate the small domestic market. "This struggle involved individual competition among the top families for the limited benefits available in a relatively small Pakistani market. The major families, allegedly twenty-two, fought among themselves in the process of building their own personal empires. They succeeded in securing positions in key allocation agencies in the system which controlled these benefits" (Kochanek 1983: 79).

60. Wintrobe (1997: 20–39).

61. After much lip service about the need to reduce corruption, restore the rule of law, recover defaulted loans from leading industrialists, revive the economy and restore grassroots political power, much remains frozen. Aqil Shah (2002) reported that "General Musharraf has set about the business of ruling by centralizing power, militarizing civilian institutions, and suppressing political activities. The drive against corruption has so far mostly targeted the regime's political opponents, leaving out the military officers and judges. Structural reforms announced with much fanfare remain either half-implemented or stalled as the regime drags its feet on policy changes that might threaten special interest groups" (74).

62. Looney (2001: 220).

63. Events in Afghanistan allow Pakistan to seek additional multilateral and bilateral financing on concessional terms, including grants from bilateral donors and an extension of the Saudi oil grant.

64. By contrast, marriage to a first or second cousin occurs less than 1 percent of the time in the United States. Todd (2002: 64–65).

65. Salter (2002).

CHAPTER NINE
CHINA'S CAPITALIST DREAM: BETWEEN HIERARCHY AND MARKET

1. www.worldvaluessurvey.org.

2. For an excellent institutional analysis, see Chen (1995).

3. "China's gradual and partial path of industrial reform was not determined by a few top officials. Industrial reform evolved from sequences of decisions made by tens of thousands of enterprises and millions of administrator, managers, and workers. The large number of participants and the extended duration of the re-

form process, which gave people ample time to evaluate alternatives and reconsider their initial views, eventually built a constituency for market-directed change that was far stronger than any official announcement could have achieved" (Jefferson and Rawski 1999: 85–86).

4. Cumulative foreign direct investment reached US $500 billion and imports as a share of GDP went from less than 12 percent to 30 percent between 1990 and 2003. If imports and foreign-affiliate domestic shares are combined, the total jumps from 30 to almost 50 percent of GDP by 2003. Product markets between 1990 and 2004 are clearly more open and competitive, but the market for financial services and for managers tell a different story (Nicholas Lardy, 2002: 24–25).

5. With one important caveat: China does not encourage business associations.

6. A number of scholars link the authority of the Communist Party system in China to a clientelistic and patronage-based logic. Walder (1986) and Oi (1989) have written about the creation of patron-client ties by factory managers and village leaders through their distribution of benefits to workers. Nathan (1973) and Pye (1982) have analyzed the clientelistic ties that underlie political factions within the Communist Party. On bureaucratic agencies' pursuit of their own organizational interests, see Lampton (1987), Lieberthal and Oksenberg (1988) and Hamrin (1990). It is widely acknowledged that local government is dominated by patronage politics.

7. Jarvis (2003: 63).

8. The development of the private sector has been cyclical rather than consistent. China's leaders never envisioned it to be a driver of growth. Reform experiments are followed by campaigns to ratify regulations needed to anchor the experiment in practice and win broad acceptance. Backpeddling frequently follows these campaigns of ratification.

9. "Carrying out economic reforms during a period of leadership succession meant that contending leaders used reform policies to extend new powers and resources to various groups within the selectorate. In addition, they adopted policies in the form of particularistic contracts to claim credit for their generosity to specific individuals and groups—in other words, to generate patronage. They recognized that they won more political support by granting ad hoc contracts to particular organizations and localities than by setting uniform rules. By the same logic, leaders were reluctant to enforce restrictions that hurt particular individuals or groups." Particularistic policies build and sustain a clientalistic support network "by enabling the contenders for national office to claim credit (and personal loyalty) from particular ministry and provincial leaders for giving them special deals and their own patronage opportunities" (Shirk 1993: 89–90).

10. On how gradualism and decentralization were used to build support from below, see McMillan and Naughton (1992), and Dewatripont and Roland (1995).

11. Enterprise managers who provide workers with housing, hospitals, and schools become powerful even when overall firm profits disappear. Soft budget constraints encourage firm expansion even if the firm fails to cover its cost of capital. The skylines of China's urban centers have been transformed virtually overnight by apartment and office blocks that are built by state enterprises and are often disposed of below their costs.

12. Qian (2003: 305).

13. Dahlman and Aubert (2001: 53).

14. Economics literature distinguishes between top-down and bottom-up corruption. Top-down corruption is concentrated at a central level of government that then monitors lower-level activities. Bottom-up corruption refers to decentralized actions by lower-level officials. China enjoys both types of corruption. See Cheung (1998a and 1998b), Rose-Ackerman (1999), and Waller, Verdier, and Gardner (2002).

15. On organizational corruption, see Lu (2000: 273–94).

16. Yusuf and Evenett (2002: 48).

17. Pei (2002a; 2002b) emphasized the incompatibility between one-party rule and market-oriented reforms.

18. The logic of the dual-track approach to liberalization is compellingly explored in Qian (2003). He explained, "The first implication of the dual-track approach is political: it represents a mechanism for the implementation of a reform without creating losers. The introduction of the market track provides the opportunity for economic agents who participate in it to be better off, whereas the maintenance of the plan track provides implicit transfers to compensate potential losers from the market liberalization by protecting the status quo rents under the preexisting plan" (307).

19. See Studwell (2002: 341).

20. See Dahlman and Aubert (2001: 58).

21. *Economist* (2001).

22. Schlevogt (2003).

23. An extensive literature explores overseas Chinese management: see Cai (1997), Chan (1982), Lee (1996), Leung (1995), Mackie (1992), Montagu-Pollock (1991), Redding and Wong (1986), Redding (1990), Schlevogt (1998), Turpin (1998), Weidenbaum (1996), and Weidenbaum and Hughes (1996). These sources use primarily descriptive interviews, newspaper citing, or historical accounts. For a theory of ethnically homogeneous middlemen and contract uncertainty, see Landa (1994). The assessment presented here of the management practices of private enterprises on the mainland is based primarily on Schlevogt (2002); Tenev, Zhang, and Brefort (2002); and Gregory, Tenev, and Wagle (2000). These sources employ a survey-based approach.

24. The prevalent patrimonial model of company management may prevent firms from growing in size and complexity. In the normal corporate life cycle, firms originate as family-owned businesses; some will evolve into closely held corporations in which ownership and management have not been separated. At this early stage, investors are related to the company. Mature firms become publicly traded corporations that must be able to attract investors that have no links to the company. The earlier in its developmental cycle that a firm shifts to professional management, the more quickly it will be assured of sustaining high growth and of surviving. Chinese firms are severely constrained from evolving to this stage because to succeed in China, firms must keep their financial structure and record opaque to prevent government audits.

25. The number of TVEs has plunged since the late 1990s, mostly because this form of ownership has lost its former advantages. Many of these firms were more

private than collective and were converted to private ownership, a process some-times called "taking off the red hat." These were private firms that sought the protections through registering as TVEs but when the advantages eroded they converted to private ownership.

26. International Finance Corporation (2000: 13).

27. For instance, China allowed no-name bank accounts, to encourage people to channel money into the state-owned banks. New no-name accounts have been prohibited. If it insisted on knowing the source of deposits, fewer deposits would be made and the state would have less access to private savings. Township and village enterprises are another second-best solution. Instead of trying to regulate private companies that can be taxed to provide revenues for public goods such as schools and hospitals, the government allows townships to operate commercial enterprises and provide public goods out of the proceeds of their commercial activities.

28. Data from this section are from Asian Development Bank (2002).

29. After a twenty-year slide that began in the early 1980s, a sharp decline in the profitability of the state sector has been reversed. Although profits are on the rise, they do not stand up to private-sector rates because of a tendency in the state-owned sector to maintain employment through wasteful inventory accumulation. The SOEs continue to receive support from the government for capital invest-ments. During the Asian financial crisis, the share of SOEs in the industrial sector rose in value-added terms from 47 percent in 1997 to 58 percent in 1998. The government also launched a three-year SOE bailout program at the end of 1998 to sustain the weak large and medium-size SOEs and encouraged debt-to-equity swaps to transfer their long-standing SOCB debts held by asset management com-panies. However, the ratio of value added to fixed assets has steadily declined from 60 percent in 1994 to 37 percent by 2000, and operating profits declined from 13 percent of the total assets in 1994 to 10 percent by 2000. Over the same period, the private-sector enterprises maintained their value added at one-to-one against fixed assets and increased their operating profits from around 15 percent to 17 percent of total assets.

30. State-owned companies in transition are referred to as collectives when 50 percent of the shares are still state owned; ownership data in this sector are often murky. Frequently, collectives benefit from government support and bank credit making them indistinguishable from state enterprises. Yet some are actually pri-vate firms, controlled by a single owner that assumes the designation "collective" to avoid regulations. These "red hat" collectives are actually private businesses leased to individuals who then run the collective as a private firm by paying the collective a fixed rent. This arrangement frequently ends with the lessee using the profits gained from leasing to become an owner. Others are state enterprises by another name.

Domestic owners who seek benefits that are sometimes afforded to foreign in-vestors may own foreign-registered companies. Some private firms adopt the structure of state-owned enterprises and appoint political board members, which politicizes decision making without providing effective managerial incentives.

Most publicly listed state-owned companies in which the state has retained dominant ownership are referred to as state-controlled shareholding companies but listing rarely ends state control. On average, the government takes a 70 percent interest in listed companies. In many listed companies, the party makes senior appointments. Since 1996, many of the industrial enterprises that were once listed as state owned turn up as joint stock companies in the nonstate sector but remain state liabilities. Listed companies are often included in the statistics of the market sector but are still government controlled (Studwell 2002: 339).

31. Tenev, Zhang, and Brefort (2002).

32. What remains unclear is whether owners have defensible streams of income without the formal, registered property rights necessary to defend interests in court.

33. Stiglitz (1993: 109–38).

34. Li and Liu (2001).

35. Qian and Weingast (1995) have emphasized that the beneficial effects of market competition are most strongly felt at the level of township and village enterprises due to the incentives they face. "First, the structure of these firms affords residual claim rights to township and village governments, which are eager to build up their revenue base under fiscal decentralization. Second, two forms of limits were imposed on the township and village governments. The first was a hard budget constraint. Because state banks set up branches only down to the county level, and because the only formal financial institutions in rural areas are Rural Credit Collectives, which are subject to tight regulation, access to credit by township and village governments and their enterprises has been limited. Unlike the state sector, TVEs may go bankrupt and lay off workers. Second, these governments do not have the authority or capability to use administrative means to protect their enterprises such as erecting trade barriers to keep out competition" (18).

36. Studwell (2002): The government throws money at the state-owned sector in the hope it will become market driven and that the private economy will grow in scale.

37. *Economist* (2003a: 67).

38. Nicholas Lardy (1998) has forcefully drawn attention to China's troubled banking sector. He estimates bad loans to be around $500 billion, or 50 percent of the total. The loan losses incurred by state banks are not legally a liability of the government, but the government may eventually be called on to cover them, at which time they may pose substantial future demands on public finance.

39. The financial sector is dominated by the banking sector. Chinese enterprises rely heavily on bank loans, which are equivalent to 120 percent of GDP.

40. See William Overholt (1994: 149–181) for a prescient assessment of China's capital markets. Overholt was one of the first Western authors to document the depth of China's commitment to market reforms. Share trading began in 1984 when seven state enterprises in Shanghai were permitted to issue public shares (167). From the beginning, Chinese officials were faced with a public demand for shares that vastly exceeded any foreseeable supply. By late 1990, Shenzhen had only five listed companies but sixteen brokers (170–71).

41. For the most extreme capital market optimism, see Hu (2001), who expects China's domestic stock market to reach approximately $2 trillion by 2010.

42. The optimists have argued that corporate governance reform threatens authoritarian regimes by removing assets and employment from state control by

making managers accountable to public markets (Shinn and Gourevitch 2002). But there is an alternative hypothesis to consider. Shareholders may also fear the chaos or paralysis that democracy has brought to neighbors like Indonesia or the Philippines. In both of those countries, Chinese business interests are rarely in alignment with forces for greater democracy. When Chinese officials consider the advantages of democracy they are more likely to consider the example of Indonesia since the fall of Suharto rather than what early-modern England gained in the way of a sound basis for public finance. Democracy in Indonesia does not give much encouragement to China's aspirations to be a great power. Indonesia's democracy is not creating new institutions, it is not making progress on law reform, and it is not adding to Indonesia's diplomatic stature within the region. There seems to be little hope that elected officials can create a domestic coalition to increase the pace of economic reform; economic reform seems IMF driven rather than domestically driven. Indonesia's democratic leaders have had no visible influence in neighboring Myanmar. Indonesia's foreign policy seems to lack an investment component.

43. *Far East Economic Review* (2003b: 47).

44. China's domestic corporate bond market as percentage of total bank loans to private sector has increased slightly since 1997.

45. Roe (2003).

46. *Financial Times* (2003).

47. The ratio of bank loans to GDP is about 160 percent in China.

48. In a widely publicized corruption case in the city of Shenyang, Liaoning Province, the *Washington Post* reported how one important suspect escaped interrogation because his father was a Poliburo member. "Others won immunity by using their ties to senior officials from Liaoning who are now based in Beijing." Two whistle-blowers were jailed and a journalist who reported the case was sentenced to nine years in prison (Pomfret 2002a).

49. "Attacks on corruption reflect a power struggle within the party, for no government agency has the power to impose discipline at the problem's source. Patronage and personnel relations, on which civil service appointments depend, make efforts to cleanse the bureaucracy from the inside unlikely. By insisting on hegemonic control over personnel, the party has weakened the government's ability to stem moral decay from within. Because the party will not allow an authority to stand above it, external sanctions on party members that abuse their power do not exist. The other Chinese societies (Hong Kong and Singapore) created corruption control authorities that stand outside political control as a means of stemming corruption. The Control Yuan that supervises official behavior in Taiwan is an independent branch of the government. Singapore and Hong Kong have both endowed their corruption control boards with autonomy from the civil service (Campos and Root 1996). In China, however, officials can short-circuit corruption investigations by appealing to their protectors in the party hierarchy" (Root 2000e: 391–92).

50. Unable to make a full commitment to the protection of private property, resources suffer poor husbandry. Instead of increasing the returns on capital invested, managers govern in their own private interests and those of the bureaucracy.

51. Zhou, Tianyong (2002).

52. This account of private property in China is derived from the *Far East Economic Review* (2003a: 29–31).

53. Melanie Manion (1994) calculated that in local bureaus and licensing offices, the probability of encountering clean licensing officials is less than 0.5 percent. John Pomfret (2002a) wrote in the *Washington Post*, "Corruption is routinely the top complaint of people queried in internal government polls, surpassing worries about unemployment, government officials said." John Burns (1994) found that only a small number of corruption complaints against party officials ever lead to convictions. Of more than 700,000 reports of corruption only one vice-ministerial-level official was convicted during the first half of the 1990s.

54. World Bank (2003: 175).

55. World Bank (2003: 160).

56. On the economic toll of corruption, see Wei (1997); he emphasized that its arbitrary character destroys economic value.

57. The liabilities of China's largest banks are not listed as government liabilities. But since most of these liabilities result from policy lending under the directives of government, they can be construed as contingent government liabilities if a banking crisis occurs.

58. In anticipation of weak future sources of tax revenue, a robust government bond market is inhibited, which creates a weak foundation in bond markets. The percentage of external funds raised by firms through bonds is less than 1 percent. Bond markets must be backed by law-based resolution of possible nonpayment.

59. Daniel et al. (2003: 113). The authors also flagged the potential fiscal burden of the pension system, which must struggle with the long-term problem of a rapidly aging population. China is unique among developing countries in that it faces a demographic profile similar to that of developed countries as a result of its population-limitation policies. The short-term problem of providing pensions to SOE employees adds to the fiscal burden, which is not reflected in official fiscal statistics. Lending to local governments is also not reported in the official state budget.

60. "State enterprises contributed 80 percent or more of 'adjusted budgetary revenues' in every year during 1978–87: state industry accounted for 73 percent of profits and profit taxes from all state enterprises" (Sicular 1992). "Prior to the reforms, Chinese State industry contributed 75 percent of budgetary revenues and, after netting out all industrial investment, contributed 5.9 percent of GNP to the budget (1978) figures. By the end of the decade [1980s], however, the system of collecting revenues through industrial enterprises was simply not working any more at either the central or local level. The net budgetary surplus provided by state enterprises had declined to only 0.4 percent of GNP" (Shirk 1993: 152).

61. "Revenue collection fell from about 31 percent of GDP in 1979 to about 13 percent in 1995, before recovering to about 16 percent in 2000. The official budget for 2000 estimates revenues of 17.2 percent of GDP, expenditures of 20.4 percent of GDP, and an overall deficit of 3.2 percent. The revenue decline after 1979 was in large part due to the separation of the financial accounts of the SOEs from the budgetary accounts. Since the mid 1990s, however, both revenue and expenditure have rebounded, and the budget deficit widened in response to the Asian Crisis" (Daniel et al. 2003: 114–15).

62. Terrill (2003).

63. An IMF study concluded: "Strong growth alone will not solve China's public debt problem. Even with average real annual growth of 7–8 percent of GDP, timely reforms are needed to ensure fiscal sustainability" (Daniel et al. 2003: 118).

64. In the first half of 2003, the collapse of two deals that would have opened the way to badly needed financial restructuring reveals how painful a step this would be for the party.

65. The new government is taking a more hesitant attitude toward foreign investment. In the spring of 2003, it withdrew support from two deals close to being consummated with foreign investors. First, the Shenzhen government pulled back from a deal that would transfer shares under its control to Newbridge, giving Newbridge a controlling interest. Then, another foreign investor, Hang Seng, a unit of HSBC, was denied a minority share in China's first wholly private bank, Minsheng Bank (McGregor 2003a).

66. Bordo and Cortes-Conde (2001: 1–19).

67. Levi (1997).

68. "The form of fiscal decentralization policies, namely, particularistic contracts negotiated by the center with each provincial government, gave central politicians the opportunity to win the gratitude and the political support of officials from the provinces. Sharing formulas tilted toward the provinces left the central treasury short of funds. The central government shifted many of its spending responsibilities to local governments—including public works expenditures and subsidies to food and consumer goods" (Shirk 1993: 151).

69. During the 1990s, some provinces retained nearly 90 percent of local revenues, and about 70 percent of provinces retained 100 percent of marginal local revenue (Qian 2003: 316). Rich provinces tended to contribute a smaller portion of their GDP in taxes after 1993, when a new formula was introduced that rebated 30 percent of any increase after 1993. Subsidies to poor regions declined abruptly due to this formula, which is particularly favorable to newly wealthy provinces (Khan and Riskin 2000).

70. See Studwell (2002).

71. Before 2003, Chinese citizens were allowed to conceal business transactions by using anonymous bank deposits. Bank depositors did not have to present identification or register real names. This deprived the state of information about the financial wealth of individuals stored in bank deposits. Qian (2003) made the ingenious argument that allowing individuals to hold revenue without government observation provided incentives for individuals to engage in wealth-generating activities. The government, Qian asserted, collected quasi-fiscal revenues from the state banking system by imposing restrictions on domestic interest rates. This, according to Qian, represented a welfare-enhancing trade-off for its loss of potential income taxes, which it does not have the capacity to collect. By denying itself information about the wealth of depositors, "predation," he asserted, is credibly constrained while the government's revenue is not drastically reduced (319–20).

72. Goodman (2002: E7).

73. Paz (1997: 79).

74. The crucible of China's post-Mao culture is cities of immigrants. Shanghai, Hong Kong, and Shenzhen—three of the powerhouse centers of the new China— are all cities of immigrants that were created during the twentieth century.

75. Compare the handling of the separation of Taiwan and China to the dispute between Pakistan and India over Kashmir. Taiwanese invest in China knowing that they are endowing their greatest enemy with the means to one day destroy them. China's entry into the World Trade Organization will likely strengthen investment ties between China and Taiwan. Confidence exists on both sides that this dispute can be resolved to the mutual benefit of both parties and that it will not be resolved until both parties benefit from the resolution. It is in this spirit that China inspires confidence and draws the money and respect that is denied other developing regions. The expectation of armed conflict between China and Taiwan is lower than that between India and Pakistan.

76. The public economy of the cities, like the army and the bureaucracy, is a key pillar of party support, hence reducing urban unemployment is a political objective in which the SOEs play a major role. By virtue of the social costs borne by the state enterprises, a ready rational for losing money is available.

77. Grossman and Noh (1990) argued that if an incumbent ruling elite enjoys high survival probability, it will act as an agent of its citizens to promote economic policy. McGuire and Olson (1996) similarly argued that monarchy, as an institution, by increasing the potential survival of the ruling elite, promotes more stable, less predatory economic policies. Olson thus explained the enduring popularity of monarchy.

CHAPTER TEN
MOBILIZING THE STATE AS PUBLIC RISK MANAGER

1. See Vose (2000), Glickman and Gough (1990), Fischhoff et al. (1993), and Bedford and Cooke (2001).

2. Daniel Ellsberg (2001) wrote that the tools of economics "remain the best available for analyzing problems of scarce resources, for evaluating merits and costs of alternative programs in terms of diverse objectives. Yet these tools, concepts, models, criteria, as yet are least developed to deal with uncertainty. And in those very fields where pre-decision analysis is at its highest premium—fields like foreign aid and military research and development, where major current investments and commitments must be made to further national objectives in a distant future—uncertainty is the central fact" (16).

3. The severity of Indonesia's financial crisis of 1997 has been attributed to the vacillation of President Suharto who tried to rescue cronies in the early stages of financial distress instead of seeking to restore viability to the banking sector. In Thailand, by contrast, regime cronies were widely dispersed throughout the polity and had ties to a diverse network of political decision makers. The Thai bailout operations were aimed at saving the banking sector instead of focusing narrowly on those favorites with political connections to the president, as in Indonesia (Desai 2003: 250–51).

4. Moss (2002) wrote: "a wide range of seemingly unrelated initiatives—from limited liability law to federal disaster relief—actually had more in common than a standard political history would suggest. All share a common policy objective, the logic of risk management" (9).

5. Moss (2002) separated risk management into policies that reduce and reallocate risk. Reduction refers to the outright prohibition or control of risky activities. He also distinguished between policies that redistribute risk from those that reallocate risk: "Whereas redistributive policies are enacted to change expected outcomes (by transferring resources from rich to poor), risk allocation policies are put in place to make an individuals' expected outcomes more certain (often by pooling resources among those with comparable levels of risk)" (19).

6. Extreme stock volatility during the 1919–39 interwar period is often attributed to a fear about social unrest and a violent challenge to the status quo. Hans-Joachim Voth (2003) related the extreme volatility of stock prices during the Great Depression to investor concerns about the survival of the capitalist system. Using panel data on riots and demonstrations, Voth argued that political instability was behind the great fall in stock prices during the interwar years. Again in 1972, a heightened risk of revolution depressed asset values on the world's leading stock markets. In a similar vein, Acemoglu and Robinson (2000) argued that capital owners mitigated worker disaffection by extending political franchise. These extensions, they postulate, were implicit promises of future redistribution.

7. Markets provide people living in developed economies with insurance policies on thousands of small risks in life. In underdeveloped economies, such insurance can generally be found only in social relationships.

8. Shiller (2003: 9).

9. For example, in Germany, a national health insurance program appeared in 1883, an accident insurance scheme was introduced in 1884, a compulsory national old-age insurance plan supported with health and accident insurance by employer and employee contributions was installed in 1889. "Total public spending sextupled from 1880 to 1913 in absolute terms, rising from 10 percent of GNP to around 17 percent. Total public debt has risen by more than seven times in absolute terms and had nearly tripled in relative ones, to around 55 percent of GNP" (Macdonald 2003: 375). The first national program of unemployment insurance was introduced in 1911 in Britain. Workers' compensation was introduced in the United States in 1911, and by 1920 all but six states had adopted it. Like many countries, the United States did not introduce unemployment insurance until 1935. More than 56 percent of the workforce in Western Europe enjoyed pension insurance by 1935, and 47 percent had health insurance coverage (Rajan and Zingales 2003).

10. Social security and welfare in developed economies typically include compensation for loss of income to the sick and temporarily disabled; payments to the elderly, the permanently disabled, the unemployed, family, maternity, and child allowances, and the cost of welfare services to care for the disabled, the aged, and children. Social welfare is now the single largest expense in most developed-country budgets. Traditionally, all these activities were provided through family and clan.

11. Shiller (2003: 271).

12. The goal is to eliminate extreme poverty between 1990 and 2015, by halving the number of people whose income is less than US $1 a day. Gender disparity in primary and secondary education will be eliminated by 2005 and in all levels of education by 2015. Child mortality is to be reduced by two thirds by 2015. The maternal mortality ratio is to be reduced by three-quarters between 1990 and 2015. The loss of environmental resources will be reversed and the spread of major diseases halved. By contrast, the question of governance is raised timidly without specific targets: "Develop further an open rules-based, predictable, nondiscriminatory trading and financial system. Including a commitment to good governance, development, and poverty reduction—both nationally and internationally" (http://www.developmentgoals.org). The question of why some governments are more successful than others at providing essential public goods for development is never posed. No link is suggested between domestic political competition and institutions that encourage the development of a quality socioeconomic infrastructure. How can a consensus about governance be reached when the very people who have robbed them of a future represent the poor people of the world? The failures strongly reflect neglected standards of governance as well as trade barriers against the exports of agricultural goods by rich nations.

13. El Salvador and Jamaica are two excellent examples of relatively poor but inclusive societies with above-average social welfare (as demonstrated by their low infant mortality rates and their high-quality drinking water). By contrast, during their nondemocratic years, Mexico and Brazil had above-average income levels, but performed poorly on the same indicators (Bueno de Mesquita and Root, 2002).

14. Bueno de Mesquita et al. (2003) posited that if the government is organized so that the selectors, of the governing coalition are a small subset of an elite group of certified selectors such as from a large body of card-carrying members of a party, even greater loyalty from the small circle of winners can be extracted, because a small winning set will fear losing their benefits to other credentialed party members.

15. Governments today rarely practice outright confiscation, as was common in the 1970s, when Mao Zedong, Gamal Abdul Nasser, and Indira Gandhi led a long list of tyrants who grabbed what they wanted and then asked the courts they controlled to make their seizures legal. A potent tool of tyranny, although less of a headline grabber, is government control over access to finance through the nationalization of the banking system. Governments also can control private business by nationalizing firms or sponsoring cartels over distribution and production. These measures by themselves are not inherently bad; it is the use to which the tools are used that produce generally horrendous outcomes. Abuses of capital controls once allowed governments to oppress their citizens and do grave economic harm. International economic consensus has trimmed these levers. Complete capital-account liberalization is now recognized to be as dangerous as an excess of control. Today, countries are counseled to pursue sensible capital controls with appropriate regulatory constraint.

16. For example, introducing functionally based in-year reporting and integrated financial management systems that ensure all government expenditures are accounted for is something that most developing countries can learn to do.

17. See World Bank (2000).

18. Possible remedies to increase bureaucratic capacity include contracting out services, instituting anticorruption programs, surveying civil servants and the users of services, linking recruitment and promotion to performance, and establishing an independent body to oversee the civil service. In Japan, the National Personnel Authority, a cabinet-level body, oversees and insulates the bureaucracy from inappropriate political influence. It sets pay scales and promotion policies, administers civil service exams, and makes most political appointments. In Malaysia, the chief secretary of the civil service has cabinet-level status so that he or she can stand up to politically appointed officials, defend civil service protocol, and protect career staff from the unfavorable actions of politicians.

19. Germany's advantage in administration was insufficient to overcome its weak financial machinery, which is one reason it suffered consecutive defeats at the hands of the better-financed English and American forces during the First and Second World Wars.

20. Miller (1992: 9).

21. Trade taxes accounted for half of public revenues in the United States in the early twentieth century and more than 90 percent before 1870. Taxes on trade are highly distortionary because they shelter domestic production and do not engage direct citizen participation in fiscal choices. They can be collected with limited citizen supervision. Not surprisingly, economic development generally increases tax revenue as a percentage of GDP while reducing taxes on trade as a percentage of total government revenue (World Bank 2002a: fig. 5.4).

22. The financially crippled federal government did not cause an uncivil society, because community-driven approaches to the delivery of social services were strongly encouraged by public leaders and substituted for weak governmental capacity. Social status often required a visible contribution to public charity. Private voluntary organizations, often church based, were important albeit inadequate providers of social services.

23. Whitney (1982: 179).

24. Stephen Skowronek (1982) argued that the American state was party dominated and lacked national centers of authority commensurate with the national scope of social interactions. The strength of courts and parties prevented the emergence of national administrative power in the nineteenth century. The Pendleton Civil Service Act in 1883 initiated a civil service career system, but Skowronek emphasized that the creation of an effective administrative power to surmount the power of party bosses had to wait until the reforms of the early twentieth century. The Civil Service Commission recast the foundations of national power. "An insulated administrative realm might now drive a wedge between the party and government and force the parties themselves to adopt the responsible posture exemplified in the independent reform movement itself" (67).

25. Skowronek (1982: 249).

26. Ironically, the centerpiece of the good-government movement in the United States was the creation of a strong independent civil service, yet the good-government movement advocated by development policy agencies of already developed nations generally overlooks this essential component of governmental capacity.

27. Before the twentieth century, the British and U.S. governments trailed the private sector in bureaucratic capacity. Ironically, in the late nineteenth century,

making government more businesslike meant making it more bureaucratic, whereas today it carries the opposite connotation.

28. Shiller (2003: 261).

29. Bardhan (2003).

30. Consider the dilemma faced by Vietnam. Many analysts have suggested that Vietnam increase its share of direct taxes from 30 to 50 percent of total tax revenue. This would relieve government dependence on distortionary trade tariffs, which are often at 30 percent or more, far higher than acceptable norms. Moreover, the amount and use of this revenue is only weakly reported. But increasing direct taxes is difficult for several reasons: (1) the tracking of corporate and personal income is prevented by incomplete accounting systems and limitations in auditing; (2) experience and skill in tax collection is lacking; (3) tax discipline among households is lax; (4) the recording of transactions, disclosure, and income statements are rare and cash transactions are the norm; (5) coordination among governmental authorities is not smooth, therefore the capacity to value taxable income is weak (Binh and Pham 2002: 84). This weakness justifies continued dependence on trade taxes and fees, which give the government money for which it does not have to account to the public or to any elected or independent bodies. Membership in the WTO will force a change, since Vietnam will be compelled to lower tariff rates. At that time, the government may have to develop sources of revenue for which it can be held to account by citizens.

31. Information technology offers governments a means to create institutions of trust at a far lower cost to the general population than has ever been possible in the past.

32. On credible commitment, see Root (1989; 1994), North and Weingast (1989), and Borner, Brunett, and Weder (1995).

33. A budget translates a government action program into financial terms. By matching expenditures with revenues the budget converts strategy into action.

34. Macdonald (2003: 473). Macdonald warned that the marriage between public credit and democratic government has been severed by the rise of international financial mediation. Foreign investment in domestic debt removes the citizen creditor from direct engagement in debates about the distribution of taxes, thus weakening an essential pillar of taxation. Judging from recent elections in California, it seems that citizens know the buck eventually stops with them.

35. The underlying shallowness of financial markets in developing countries reflects the fact that borrowing by the government is not backed by tax payments. Today, in developed and developing countries alike, the creditors are frequently far away in the headquarters of foreign banks or distant international organizations. This pattern takes us back to the early days of state finance, when the debt holder was mainly professional. In premodern Europe, elite networks of bankers and financiers handled the sovereign's debts. In eighteenth-century England, most state debt was held by the Bank of England or the East India Company. In the United States, most of the debt sold by the government to finance the War of 1812 was purchased by Europeans, whereas the debt to finance the Civil War was purchased mostly by banks. Citizen finance was a concept that arose primarily to fund the two World Wars.

36. Another perversity in developing-country finance is that government debts frequently were acquired by state-owned companies that raised their own financing abroad. The government, which owns the oil company, then distributes the loans in the form of patronage or rents. If the company was private, it could be taxed by the government and distributed as spoils. It is not the taxpayers of Angola, Iraq, or Mexico that owe the debt, yet they are required to pay it back.

37. The United States, for example, faces the prospects of having to increase taxes dramatically to pay contingent future Social Security and Medicare benefits. Well-established and familiar institutions and procedures based on citizen consent exist to deal with significant trade-offs that must be considered. Predictable procedures do not exist in China to deal with possible unforeseen liabilities, such as its pension obligations.

38. For example, the study of revolution, an integral part of social development, is not part of the mainstream curriculum in development studies.

39. On the political economy of hierarchy, see Miller (1992: 15–74).

40. Wintrobe (1997) explained this process.

41. World Bank (2004b).

42. A World Bank (2002b) study of the post-Soviet transition revealed a strong correlation between political systems and economic reform: where political coalitions are inclusive, institutional investments paid off, but where governing coalitions are small and exclusive, institutional reform withered. "Competitive democracies have made the greatest progress in implementing market-oriented reforms, while the noncompetitive regimes have made the least progress." The study concluded: "The concentration of political power appears to be an important determinant of the extent of state capture in transition economies. . . . Inclusive process for creating political institutions and the broad range of political groups that could compete for power in the new system enhanced the capacity of government to make credible commitments that the promised gains of economic reform would not be expropriated or otherwise restricted to particular vested interests." The study argued that in the early stages of transition, political choices drive economic reform (World Bank (2002b: 103–10). "In competitive democracies economic reforms have generally progressed across the board despite differences in the sequences of reform measures across countries. Similarly, noncompetitive political systems have generally made little or no progress in all of the key areas of economic reform. . . . In contrast, the concentrated political regimes and war torn regimes have tended to advance rapidly in liberalization and privatization with much slower progress in the institutional reforms to support effectively functioning markets, generating higher variance in their reform scores" (World Bank 2002b: 105). Challenging conventional thinking that considers political stability as a goal in itself, the World Bank study found that "the regular succession of different coalition governments created genuine competition among groups for political influence. That led to equally fierce competition over rents, quickly dissipating any efforts to concentrate rent flows and preventing theft on a massive scale" (World Bank (2002b: 107).

43. The experience of transition has taught economists not to take for granted the institutions of capitalism already present in advanced economies. This awareness has shifted the focus of transition studies increasingly toward an institutional

perspective in which contract theory, political economy, law and economics, and regulation theory have all contributed to a shift in emphasis away from markets and price theory.

44. Donors have been faulted for not paying sufficient attention to institutions during the post-Soviet transition. However, this charge ignores the millions of dollars that were spent on legal reform and institution building. In Russia, assistance programs led to the adaptation of a wide range of corporate, commercial law, and financial regulations. Even so, enforcement continues to be the real problem.

45. Public officials are not empty receptacles waiting to be filled by the recommendations of the wise. Both advisers and officials are engaged in a strategic interaction in which both parties are individual agents with their own agenda (Basu 2000: 166–81).

46. See Carothers (2003).

47. The direction of causality linking economic and political change is difficult to untangle. Policy choices shape the configuration of social groups and strengthen political constituencies, which suggest the closely interrelated nature of political and economic reform. An economic reform that increases entry and open trade generally builds support for greater accountability by political leaders for economic performance. Work by Bueno de Mesquita et al. (2003) and the World Bank (2002b), among others, suggests that with available knowledge, a stronger case can be made for identifying the direction of causality from political to economic choices. A World Bank (2002b) study mentioned earlier concluded: "That while the pace and direction of economic reform may have reinforced initial choices about the structure of the political system, economic reforms have yet to decisively shift the course of political transition" (105). Hellman (1998) was the first to document that "winner take all" reforms in Russia empowered a small circle of winners to subvert the institutions of the state to enhance their political and economic influence. The greatest challenge will be to unify into one coherent body of knowledge the three sources of uncertainty that are impediments to the coherence of exchange in human society. This means unifying what the scientific academy has separated into discrete and independent study areas and integrating the knowledge that each in isolation has assembled. Thinking about the interplay and complementarities of social, political, and economic forces is inhibited by institutional subdivisions within the academy.

48. Marx and Engels (1998).

References

Acemoglu, D., S. Johnson, and J. Robinson. 2001. "The Colonial Origins of Comparative Development." *American Economic Review,* 91(5): 1396–1401.

Acemoglu, D., and J. A. Robinson. 2000. "Why Did the West Extend the Franchise? Democracy, Inequality and Growth in Historical Perspective." *Quarterly Journal of Economics,* 115(4): 1167–99.

Ahluwalia, M. S. 1976. "Inequality, Poverty and Development." *Journal of Development Economics,* 3(4): 307–42.

Ahn, S., and D. Denis. 2002. "Internal Capital Markets and Investment Policy: Evidence from Corporate Spinoffs." Working paper, Purdue University.

Aizenman, J., and N. Marion. 1993. "Policy Uncertainty, Persistence and Growth." *Review of International Economics,* 1 June: 145–63.

Akerlof, G. 1970. "The Market for Lemons: Quality Uncertainty and the Market Mechanism." *Quarterly Journal of Economics* 84: 488–500.

Alesina, A. 1998. "The Political Economy of Macroeconomic Stabilizations and Income Inequality: Myths and Reality," in V. Tanzi and K.-y. Chu (eds.), *Income Distribution and High Quality Growth,* 299–326. Cambridge, Mass.: MIT Press.

Alesina, A., R. Baqir, and W. Easterly. 1999. "Public Goods and Ethnic Divisions." *Quarterly Journal of Economics,* 114(4): 1243–84.

Alesina, A., and A. Drazen. 1991. "Why Are Stabilizations Delayed?" *American Economic Review,* 81(5): 1170–88.

Alesina, A., S. Ozler, N. Roubibi, and P. Swagel. 1992. "Political Instability and Economic Growth." Working Paper No. 4173, National Bureau of Economic Research, Cambridge, Mass.

Alesina, A., and R. Perotti. 1996. "Income Distribution, Political Instability, and Investment." *European Economic Review* 40(6): 1203–28.

Alesina, A., and D. Rodrik. 1994. "Distributive Politics and Economic Growth." *Quarterly Journal of Economics,* 109(2): 465–90.

Anand, S., and S.M.R. Kanbur. 1993a. "Inequality and Development: A Critique." *Journal of Development Economics,* 41(1): 19–43.

———. 1993b. "The Kuznets Process and the Inequality-Development Relationship." *Journal of Development Economics,* 40(1): 25–52.

Ansolabehere, S., A. Gerber, and J. M. Snyder Jr. 2001. "Corruption and the Growth of Campaign Spending," in G. Lubenow (ed.), *A User's Guide to Campaign Finance Reform.* Lanham, Md.: Rowman & Littlefield.

Arif, K. M. 2001. "The Role of the Military in Politics: Pakistan 1947–97," in H. Malik (ed.), *Pakistan: Founder's Aspirations and Today's Realities.* Oxford: Oxford University Press.

Arrow, K. J. 1962a. "The Economic Implications of Learning by Doing." *Review of Economic Studies,* 29(3): 155–73.

Arrow, K. J. 1962b. "Economic Welfare and the Allocation of Resources for Invention," in R. R. Nelson (ed.), *The Rate and Direction of Inventive Activity: Economic and Social Factors.* Princeton: Princeton University Press for the National Bureau of Economic Research.

———. 1964. "The Role of Securities in the Optimal Allocation of Risk Bearing." *Review of Economic Studies,* 31(2): 91–96.

———. 1979. "Pareto Efficiency with Costly Transfers." *Economic Forum,* 10(1): 1–3.

———. 1996. "The Theory of Risk-Bearing: Small and Great Risks." *Journal of Risk and Uncertainty,* 12(2–3): 103–11.

Arrow, K. J., and R. C. Lind. 1970. "Uncertainties and the Evaluation of Public Investment Decisions." *American Economic Review,* 60(3): 364–78.

Asian Development Bank. 2002. "Technical Assistance to the People's Republic of China for Improving Corporate Governance and Financial Performance of State-Owned Enterprises." Technical Assistance Report No. TAR:PRC 32132, September, Washington, D.C.

Athanasoulis, S., and R. J. Shiller. 2000. "The Significance of the Market Portfolio." *Review of Financial Studies,* 13(2): 301–29.

———. 2001. "World Income Components: Measuring and Exploiting Risk Sharing Opportunities." *American Economic Review,* 91(4): 1031–54.

———. 2002. "Defining Residual Risk-Sharing Opportunities: Pooling World Income Components." *Research in Economics,* 56(1): 61–84.

Baker, G., R. Gibbons, and K. J. Murphy. 1997. "Implicit Contracts and the Theory of the Firm." Working Paper No. 6177, National Bureau of Economic Research, Cambridge, Mass.

Bardhan, P. 2003. "The Politics of Economic Reform in India," in Pranab Bardhan, *Poverty, Agrarian Structure, and Political Economy in India.* New Delhi: Oxford University Press.

Barham, J. 2002. "Will Prudence Prevail?" *Latin Finance,* November: 48–50.

Barro, R. J. 1991. "Economic Growth in a Cross Section of Countries." *Quarterly Journal of Economics,* 106(2): 407–43.

———. 2000a. "Democracy and the Rule of Law," in B. Bueno de Mesquita and H. L. Root (eds.) *Governing for Prosperity.* New Haven: Yale University Press.

———. 2000b. "Inequality and Growth in a Panel of Countries." *Journal of Economic Growth,* 5(1): 5–32.

Barth, J. R., D. McCarthy, T. Phumiwasana, S. Trimbath, and G. Yago. 2002. "Missing Markets: Global Barriers to Financing the Future." Global Capital Access Index, Milken Institute, Santa Monica, Calif.

Barth, J. R., D. E. Nolle, H. L. Root, and G. Yago. 2001. "Choosing the Right Financial System for Growth." *Journal of Applied Corporate Finance,* 13(4): 116–23.

Barth, J. R., T. Phumiwasana, and G. Yago. 2002. "The Foreign Conquest of Latin American Banking: What's Happening and Why?" Policy Brief No. 32, November. Milken Institute, Santa Monica, Calif.

Basu, K. 2000. *Prelude to Political Economy: A Study of the Social and Political Foundations of Economics.* New York: Oxford University Press.

Bates, R. H. 1995. "Macropolitical Economy in the Field of Development," in J. E. Alt and K. A. Shepsle (eds.), *Perspectives on Positive Political Economy*. Cambridge: Cambridge University Press.

———. 2001. *Prosperity and Violence: The Political Economy of Development*. New York: W. W. Norton.

Baxter, C. 2001. "Political Development in Pakistan," in H. Malik (ed.), *Pakistan: Founder's Aspirations and Today's Realities*. Oxford: Oxford University Press.

Bedford, T., and R. Cooke. 2001. *Probabilistic Risk Analysis: Foundations and Methods*. Cambridge: Cambridge University Press.

Berle, A. A., and G. C. Means. 1932/1968. *The Modern Corporation and Private Property*. New York: Harcourt, Brace & World.

Bhambhri, C. P. 1972. *Administrators in a Changing Society*. Delhi: National Publishing House.

Binh, T., and C. D. Pham (eds.). 2002. *The Vietnamese Economy: Awakening the Dormant Dragon*. London: RoutledgeCurzon.

Birdsall, N. 1994. "Inequality, Exports, and Human Capital in East Asia: Lessons for Latin America," in C. I. Bradford Jr. and R. Sabot (eds.), *Redefining the State in Latin America*. Paris: OECD Development Centre and Inter-American Development Bank.

Black, B. S., and R. J. Gilson. 1998. "Venture Capital and the Structure of Capital Markets: Banks versus Stock Markets." *Journal of Financial Economics*, 47: 243–77.

Bliss, C., and R. DiTella. 1997. "Does Competition Kill Corruption?" *Journal of Political Economy* 105(5): 1001–23.

Borch, K. H. 1968. *The Economics of Uncertainty*. Princeton: Princeton University Press.

Bordo, M. D., and R. Cortes-Conde (eds.). 2001. *Transferring Wealth and Power from the Old to the New World: Monetary and Fiscal Institutions in the 17th through the 19th Centuries*. Cambridge: Cambridge University Press.

Borner, S., A. Brunett, and B. Weder. 1995. *Political Credibility and Economic Development*. Basingstoke, U.K.: Palgrave Macmillan.

Brainard, S. L., and T. Verdier. 1994. "Lobbying and Adjustment in Declining Industries." *European Economic Review*, 38(3–4): 586–95.

Bruno, M., M. Ravallion, and L. Squire. 1998. "Equity and Growth in Developing Countries: Old and New Perspectives on the Policy Issues," in V. Tanzi and K. Chu (eds.), *Income Distribution and High-Quality Growth*. Cambridge: MIT Press.

Buchanan, J. M., C. K. Rowley, and R. D. Tollisson (eds.). 1987. *Deficits*. Oxford and New York: Basil Blackwell.

Bueno de Mesquita, B. 2000. "Political Institutions, Political Survival and Policy Success" in B. Bueno de Mesquita and H. L. Root (eds.), *Governing for Prosperity*. New Haven: Yale University Press.

Bueno de Mesquita, B., and H. L. Root. 2000a. "Improving the Effectiveness of Donor Assisted Development," in B. Bueno de Mesquita and H. L. Root (eds.), *Governing for Prosperity*. New Haven: Yale University Press.

Bueno de Mesquita, B., and H. L. Root. 2000b. "When Bad Economics Is Good Politics," in B. Bueno de Mesquita and H. L. Root (eds.), *Governing for Prosperity*. New Haven: Yale University Press.

———. 2002. "Political Roots of Poverty: The Economic Logic of Autocracy." *National Interest*. Summer: 27–37.

Bueno de Mesquita, B., A. Smith, R. M. Siverson, and J. D. Morrow. 2003. *The Logic of Political Survival*. Cambridge: MIT Press.

Bunbongkarn, S. 1999. "Thailand's Successful Reforms." *Journal of Democracy*, 10(4): 54–68.

Burki, S. J. 1969. "Twenty Years of the Civil Service of Pakistan: A Reevaluation." *Asian Survey*, 9(4): 239–54.

———. 1974. "Politics of Economic Decision Making during the Bhutto Period." *Asian Survey* 14(12): 1126–40.

Burki, S. J., and G. E. Perry. 1998. *Beyond the Washington Consensus: Institutions Matter*. Washington, D.C.: World Bank.

Burns, J. P. 1994. "Civil Service Reform in China." *Asian Journal of Political Science*, 22(2): 44–72.

Buscaglia, E., W. Ratliff, and R. Cooter (eds.). 1997. *The Law and Economics of Development*. Stamford, Conn.: JAI Press.

Cai, P. H. 1997. "Chinese Family Enterprises." *Wenhui Bao* (Shanghai), 15 October.

Callahan, W. A., and D. McCargo. 1996. "Vote-Buying in the Thai Northeast: The Case of the July 1995 Election." *Asian Survey*, 36(4): 376–92.

Callard, K. 1957. *Pakistan: A Political Study*. New York: Macmillan.

Calvo, G. A., and F. S. Mishkin. 2003. "The Mirage of Exchange Rate Regimes for Emerging Market Countries." Working Paper No. w9808, June, National Bureau of Economic Research, Cambridge, Mass.

Campos, J. E., and H. L. Root. 1996. *The Key to the Asian Miracle: Making Shared Growth Credible*. Washington, D.C.: Brookings Institution.

Carothers, T. 2003. "Promoting the Rule of Law Abroad: The Problem of Knowledge." Working Paper No. 34, Carnegie Endowment for International Peace, Washington, D.C.

Cavallo, D. 1997. *El peso de la verdad*. Buenos Aires: Planeta.

Chan, W.K.K. 1982. "The Organizational Structure of the Traditional Chinese Firm and Its Modern Reform." *Business History Review*. 56(2): 218–35.

Chandler, A. Jr. 1977. *The Visible Hand: The Managerial Revolution in American Business*. Cambridge, Mass.: Belknap.

Chen, D. 1995. *Chinese Firms between Hierarchy and Market: The Contract Management Responsibility System in China*. New York: St. Martin's.

Cheung, S.N.S. 1998a. "The Curse of Democracy as an Instrument of Reform in Collapsed Communist Economies." *Contemporary Economic Policy* 16(2): 247–49.

———. 1998b. "Deng Xiaoping's Great Transformation." *Contemporary Economic Policy*, 16(2): 125–35.

Chui, A.C.W., S. Titman, and K.C.J. Wei. 2001. "Corporate Groups, Financial Liberalization and Growth: The Case of Indonesia," in A. Demirgüç-Kunt and R. Levine (eds.), *Financial Structure and Economic Growth: A Cross-Country Comparison of Banks, Markets, and Development*. Cambridge: MIT Press.

————. 2003. "Intra-Industry Momentum: The Case of REITs." *Journal of Financial Markets* 6: 353–87.

Claessens, S., S. Djankov, and L.H.P. Lang. 2000. "The Separation of Ownership and Control in East Asian Corporations." *Journal of Financial Economics*, 58(1): 81–112.

Clarke, G.R.G. 1993. "More Evidence on Income Distribution and Growth." *Journal of Development Economics* 47(2): 403–27.

Clements, B., and J. V. Levy. 1994. "Public Education Expenditure and Other Determinants of Private Investment in the Carribean." Working Paper WP/94/122, October, International Monetary Fund, Washington, D.C.

Dahlman, C. J., and J. E. Aubert. 2001. *China and the Knowledge Economy: Seizing the 21st Century.* Washington, D.C.: World Bank.

Daniel, J., T. Richardson, R. Singh, and G. Tsibouris. 2003. "Medium-Term Fiscal Issues," in W. Tseng and M. Rodlauer (eds.), *China: Competing in the Global Economy.* Washington, D.C.: International Monetary Fund.

Das, G. 2000. *India Unbound.* New York: Anchor Books.

Dasgupta, P. 1995. *An Inquiry into Well Being and Destitution.* New York: Oxford University Press.

Dasgupta, P., R. Gilbert, and J. Stiglitz. 1982. "Strategic Considerations in Invention and Innovation: The Case of Natural Resources." *Econometrica*, 51(5): 1439–48.

Datt, G., and T. Walker. 2004. "Recent Evolutions of Inequality in East Asia," *Applied Economic Letters*, 11: 75–79

Demirguc-Kunt, A., and V. Maksimovic. 1998. "Law, Finance, and Firm Growth." *Journal of Finance*, 53(6): 2107–37.

Desai, P. 2003. *Financial Crisis, Contagion, and Containment: From Asia to Argentina.* Princeton: Princeton University Press.

De Soto, H. 2000. *The Mystery of Capital: Why Capitalism Triumphs in the West and Fails Everywhere Else.* New York: Basic Books.

Dewatripont, M. and G. Roland. 1995. "The Design of Reform Packages under Uncertainty." *American Economic Review*, 85(5): 1207–23.

Diamond, J. 1989. "Government Expenditures and Economic Growth: An Empirical Investigation." Working Paper WP/89/45, May, International Monetary Fund, Washington, D.C.

Diamond, L. 1999. *Developing Democracy: Toward Consolidation.* Baltimore: Johns Hopkins University Press.

Diamond, L., M. F. Plattner, and A. Schedler. 1999. *The Self-Restraining State: Power and Accountability in New Democracies.* Baltimore: Johns Hopkins University Press.

Dornbusch, R., and S. Edwards (eds.). 1991. *The Macroeconomics of Populism in Latin America.* Chicago: University of Chicago Press.

Dossani, R., and M. Kenney. 2001. "Creating an Environment: Developing Venture Capital in India." Working Paper No. 173, Berkeley Roundtable on International Economy, University of California, Berkeley.

Drèze, J. 2003. "Hunger amidst Plenty," http://www.indiatogether.org/2003/dec/pov-foodsec.htm.

Drèze, J. and A. Sen. 2002. *India: Development and Participation.* New York: Oxford University Press.

Easterly, W. 2001. *The Elusive Quest for Growth.* Cambridge: MIT Press.

Easterly, W., and R. Levine. 1997. "Africa's Growth Tragedy: Policies and Ethnic Divisions." *Quarterly Journal of Economics,* 112(4): 1203–50.

Easterly, W., and S. Rebelo. 1993. "Fiscal Policy and Economic Growth: An Empirical Investigation." *Journal of Monetary Economics,* 32(3): 417–58.

Economist. 2001. "Economist Intelligence Unit: China." February.

———. 2003a. "Banking in China." 8 March: 67.

———. 2003b. "The Weakest Link: A Survey of Asian Finance." 8 February: 3.

Edwards, S. 1995. *Crisis and Reform in Latin America: From Despair to Hope.* New York: Oxford University Press.

———. 1998. "The Latin American Economies at the End of the Century," in *Jobs and Capital: Economic and Political Conditions and Prospect: A Global Survey.* 7(1) 44.

Ellsberg, D. 2001. *Risk, Ambiguity and Decision.* New York: Garland.

Evans, G. H. 1948. *Business Incorporations in the United States 1800–1943.* General Series No. 49, National Bureau of Economic Research, Cambridge, Mass.

Far Eastern Economic Review. 2003a. "The Untouchables." 27 March: 29–31: 54–56.

———. 2003b. "Wake Up Call: China's Future Depends on Better Stock Markets." 20 November: 44–48.

———. 1995. "Demolitions Zealot: Civil Servant's Mandate Is to Raze Corruption." 18 May: 78.

Ferreira, F.H.G., and J. A. Litchfield. 1997. "Poverty and Income Distribution in Chile: 1987–94." Report No. 681–59, World Development Report Office, World Bank, Washington, D.C.

Financial Times. 2003. 16 December.

Fischhoff, B., S. Lichtenstein, P. Slovic, S. L. Derby, and R. Keeney. 1993. *Acceptable Risk: A Critical Guide.* Cambridge: Cambridge University Press.

Fisman, R. 2001. "Estimating the Value of Political Connections." *American Economic Review,* 91(4): 1095–1102.

Forbes, K. J. 2000. "A Reassessment of the Relationship between Inequality and Growth." *American Economic Review,* 90(4): 869–87.

Foreign Policy. 2004. "Measuring Globalization: Globalization Index," April–May: 54–57.

Fukuyama, F. 1995. *Trust: The Social Virtues and the Creation of Prosperity.* New York: Free Press.

Gelos, G., and S. Wei. 2002. "Transparency and International Investor Behavior." Working Paper No. w9260, October, National Bureau of Economic Research, Cambridge, Mass.

Gerschenkron, A. 1962. *Economic Backwardness in Historical Perspective: A Book of Essays.* Cambridge: Harvard University Press.

Glaeser, E., J. Sheinkmen, and A. Shleifer. 2002. *The Injustice of Inequality.* Manuscript, Harvard University.

Glickman, T., and M. Gough (eds.). 1990. *Readings in Risk.* Baltimore: Johns Hopkins Press.

Goodman, P. 2002. "China's Wealthy Facing Income Tax Crackdown." *Washington Post*, 22 October: E7.

Goodnow, H. F. 1964. *The Civil Service of Pakistan: Bureaucracy in a New Nation*. New Haven: Yale University Press.

Gopinath, P. K. 1982. "Corruption in Political and Public Offices: Causes and Cure." *Indian Journal of Public Administration*, 28(4): 897–918.

Graham, C., and M. Naim. 1998. "The Political Economy of Institutional Reform in Latin America" in N. Birdsell et al. (eds.), *Beyond Trade Offs: Market Reform and Equitable Growth in Latin America*. Washington, D.C.: Brookings Institution.

Grant's Asia Observer. 1996. "False Profits." 14: 5–9.

Greenspan, A. 1999. "Do Efficient Financial Markets Mitigate Financial Crises?" Speech given before the 1999 Financial Markets conference of the Federal Reserve Bank of Atlanta, 19 October, Sea Island, Ga. (available at www.federal reserve.gov/boarddocs/speeches/1999/19991019.htm).

Gregory, N., S. Tenev, and D. Wagle. 2000. *China's Emerging Private Enterprises: Prospects for the New Century*. Washington, D.C.: International Finance Corp.

Greif, A. 1993. "Contract Enforceability and Economic Institutions in Early Trade: The Maghribi Traders' Coalition." *American Economic Review*, 83(3): 525–48.

———. 2003. "Institutions and Impersonal Exchange: The European Experience." Department of Economics, Stanford University.

Grossman, H. I., and S. J. Noh. 1990. "A Theory of Kleptocracy with Probabilistic Survival and Reputation." *Economics and Politics*, 2: 157–71.

———. 1994. "Proprietary Public Finance and Economic Welfare." *Journal of Public Economics*, 53: 187–204.

Gupta, D. 1990. *The Economics of Political Violence*. New York: Praeger.

Hamrin, C. L. 1990. *China and the Challenge of the Future: Changing Political Patterns*. Boulder, Colo.: Westview.

Haq, M. 1976. *The Poverty Curtain: Choices for the Third World*. New York: Columbia University Press.

———. 1995. *A New Vision of Economic and Social Justice*. Lahore, Pakistan: Progressive Publishers.

Hausmann, R., and M. Gavin. 1995. "Overcoming Volatility," in *Economic and Social Progress in Latin America*. Washington, D.C.: Inter-America Development Bank.

Heilbroner, R., and A. Singer. 1999. *The Economic Transformation of America*. Fort Worth: Harcourt Brace College Publishers.

Hellman, J. S. 1998. "Winners Take All: The Politics of Partial Reform in Post-communist Transitions." *World Politics*, 50(2): 203–34.

Hellman, J. S., G. Jones, and D. Kaufmann. 2000. "Seize the State, Seize the Day: State Capture, Corruption, and Influence in Transition." Working Paper No. 2444, World Bank Institute, Washington, D.C.

Hellman, J. S., and D. Kaufmann. 2004. "Inequality of Influence," in S. Rose-Ackerman and J. Kornai (eds.), *Building a Trustworthy State in Post-Socialist Transition*. New York: Palgrave.

Hibbs, D. 1973. *Mass Political Violence: A Cross-Sectional Analysis.* New York: Wiley.

Hirshleifer, J. 1966. "Investment Decision under Uncertainty: Applications of the State-Preference Approach." *Quarterly Journal of Economics,* 80(2): 252–77.

Hirshleifer, J., and J. G. Riley. 1992. *The Analytics of Uncertainty and Information.* Cambridge: Cambridge University Press.

Holden, P. 1997. "Collateral without Consequence: Some Causes and Effects of Financial Underdevelopment in Latin America." *Financier,* 4(1): 12–21.

Holden, P., and S. Rajapatirana. 1995. "Unshackling the Private Sector: A Latin American Story." Policy Report No. 019, World Bank, Washington, D.C.

Hoshi, T., and A. Kashyap. 2001. *Corporate Finance and Government in Japan.* Cambridge: MIT Press.

Hoshi, T., A. Kashyap, and D. Scharfstein. 1991. "Corporate Structure, Liquidity, and Investment: Evidence from Japanese Industrial Groups." *Quarterly Journal of Economics,* 106(1): 33–60.

Hu, F. 2001. "Das Kapital: Capital Markets Are Transforming China." Paper, May, Goldman Sachs Group, Hong Kong.

Husain, I. 1990. *Pakistan: The Economy of an Elitist State.* Karachi: Oxford University Press.

India, Ministry of Finance. 1997. *Economic Survey.* New Delhi.

India, Ministry of Home Affairs. 1964a. *Report of the Committee on Prevention of Corruption.* New Delhi.

———. 1964b. *The Santhanam Report.* New Delhi.

———. 1993. *Vohra Committee Report.* New Delhi.

India, Ministry of Home Affairs, Administrative Vigilance Division. 1964. *Tenth Annual Report.* New Delhi.

India, Ministry of Information Technology. 2003. *Annual Report,* 2002–2003. New Delhi.

India Today. 1996a. "Striking Murky Deals." 30 November: 97–104.

———. 1996. 30 November: 105.

———. 2001. 17 August.

International Finance Corporation. 2000. *China's Emerging Private Enterprises: Prospects for the New Century.* Washington, D.C.: IFC.

International Monetary Fund. 2004. *International Financial Statistics 2004.* CD-ROM.

Jain, A. K. (ed.). 1998. *The Economics of Corruption.* Boston: Kluwer Academic.

Jarvis, D. (ed.). 2003. *International Business Risk: A Handbook for the Asia-Pacific Region.* Cambridge: Cambridge University Press.

Jefferson, G. H., and T. G. Rawski. 1999. "China's Industrial Innovation Ladder: A Model for Endogenous Reform," in G. H. Jefferson and I. Singh (eds.), *Enterprise Reform in China: Ownership, Transition, and Performance.* Oxford: Oxford University Press.

Jenkins, R. 1999, *Democratic Politics and Economic Reform in India.* Cambridge: Cambridge University Press.

Jensen, E. G. 1997. "An Agenda for Effective Governance." Manuscript, October, Asian Development Bank, Washington, D.C.

Jensen, M. C. 1983. "The Market for Corporate Control: The Scientific Evidence." *Journal of Financial Economics*, 11(1–4): 5–50.

———. 1991. "Corporate Control and the Politics of Finance." *Journal of Applied Corporate Finance*, 4 Summer: 13–33.

——— (ed.). 1998. *Foundations of Organizational Behavior.* Cambridge: Harvard University Press.

———. 2002. "Value Maximization, Stakeholder Theory, and the Corporate Objective Function," in J. Andriof, S. Waddock, S. Rahman, and B. Husted (eds.), *Unfolding Stakeholder Thinking: Theory Responsibility and Engagement.* Sheffield: Greenleaf.

Jensen, M. C., and W. H. Meckling. 1976. "Theory of the Firm: Managerial Behavior, Agency Costs, and Ownership Structure." *Journal of International Economics* (3): 305–60.

Joh, S. W. 2000a. "Control, Ownership, and Firm Performance: The Case of Korea." Research Paper No., 1264, presented at the Econometric Society World Congress, Korea Development Institute, Seoul.

———. 2000b. "Microdynamics of Industrial Competition." Working paper, Korea Development Institute, Seoul.

Keefer, P., and S. Knack. 1993. "Why Don't Poor Countries Catch Up? A Cross National Test of an Institutional Explanation." Working Paper No. 60, Institutional Reform and the Informal Sector, University of Maryland, College Park.

Kennedy, C. H. 1987. *Bureaucracy in Pakistan.* Karachi: Oxford University Press.

Khan, A. R. and C. Riskin. 2000. *China: Income Distribution and Poverty in the Age of Globalization.* New York: Oxford University Press.

Khan, M. M. 1980. *Bureaucratic Self-Preservation: Failure of Major Administrative Reform Efforts in the Civil Service of Pakistan.* Bangladesh: University of Dhaka Press.

King, R. G., and R. Levine. 1993a. "Finance and Growth: Schumpeter Might Be Right." *Quarterly Journal of Economics* 108(3): 717–38.

———. 1993b. "Finance, Entrepreneurship, and Growth: Theory and Evidence." *Journal of Monetary Economics*, 32(3): 513–42.

Klitgaard, R. 1991. *Adjusting to Reality: Beyond "State versus Market" in Economic Development.* San Francisco: ICS Press.

Knight, F. H. 1971. *Risk, Uncertainty, and Profit.* Chicago: University of Chicago Press.

Knott, J. H., and G. J. Miller. 1987. *Reforming Bureaucracy: The Politics of Institutional Choice.* Englewood Cliffs, N.J.: Prentice-Hall.

Kobb, D. 2003. "Corruption in Tanzania: Counting and Franchise Bidding," in J. McClaren (ed.), *Institutional Elements of Tax Design and Reform.* Washington D.C.: World Bank.

Kobrin, S. J. 1984. "Expropriation as an Attempt to Control Foreign Firms in LDCS: Trends from 1960 to 1979." *International Studies Quarterly*, 28(3): 329–48.

Kochanek, S. A. 1974. *Business and Politics in India.* Berkeley and Los Angeles: University of California Press.

———. 1983. *Interest Groups and Development: Business and Politics in Pakistan.* Oxford: Oxford University Press.

Kochanek, S. A. 1987. "Briefcase Politics in India: The Congress Party and the Business Elite." *Asian Survey* 27(12) Dec.: 1278–1301.

Kohli, A. 1990. *Democracy and Discontent: India's Growing Crisis of Governability.* Cambridge: Cambridge University Press.

Kothari, R. 1970. *Caste in Indian Politics.* London: Routledge.

Kray, A. 2002. "Growth without Governance." Policy Research Working Paper No. 2928, Washington, D.C.: World Bank.

Kremer, M., and S. Jayachandran. 2002. "Odius Debt." Working Paper No. w8953, May, National Bureau of Economic Research, Cambridge, Mass.

Kunio, Y. 1988. *The Rise of Ersatz Capitalism in South East Asia.* New York: Oxford University Press.

Kuznets, S. 1942. "National Income and Taxable Capacity." *American Economic Review.* 32(1): 37–75.

———. 1966. *Modern Economic Growth.* New Haven: Yale University Press.

Laban, R., and F. Sturzenegger. 1992. "La Economia Politica de los Programmas de Estabilization," *Colección Estudios CIEPLAN,* 36 (Dec.): 441–66.

———. 1994. "Fiscal Conservatism as a Response to the Debt Crisis." *Journal of Development Economics,* 45 (Nov.): 305–24.

Lampton, D. M. 1987. *Policy Implementation in Post-Mao China.* Berkeley: University of California Press.

Landa, J. T. 1994. *Trust, Ethnicity, and Identity: Beyond the New Institutional Economics of Ethnic Trading Networks, Contract Law, and Gift-Exchange.* Ann Arbor: University of Michigan Press.

LaPorte, R. Jr. 1975. *Power and Privilege: Influence and Decision Making in Pakistan.* Berkeley: University of California Press.

Lardy, N. R. 1998. *China's Unfinished Economic Revolution.* Washington, D.C.: Brookings Institution.

———. 2002. *Integrating China into the Global Economy.* Washington, D.C.: Brookings Institution.

Lee, J. 1996. "Culture and Management: A Study of Small Chinese Family Business in Singapore." *Journal of Small Business Management,* 34: 63–67.

Leff, N. 1978. "Industrial Organization and Entrepreneurship in the Developing Countries." *Economic Development and Cultural Change,* 26(4): 661–75.

Lempert, R. J., S. W. Popper, and S. C. Bankes. 2003. *Shaping the Next One Hundred Years: New Methods for Quantitative, Long-term Policy Analysis.* Santa Monica: Rand Corp.

Leung, F.F.L. 1995. "Overseas Chinese Management: Myths and Realities." *East Asian Executive Reports,* 17: 6–13.

Levi, M. 1997. *Consent, Dissent and Patriotism.* Cambridge: Cambridge University Press.

Levine, R. 1997. "Financial Development and Economic Growth: Views and Agenda." *Journal of Economic Literature,* 35(2): 688–726.

Levine, R., N. Loayza, and T. Beck. 2000. "Financial Intermediation and Growth: Causality and Causes." *Journal of Monetary Economics,* 46(1): 31–77.

Levine, R., and S. Zervos. 1998. "Stock Markets, Banks, and Economic Growth." *American Economic Review* 88(3): 537–58.

Levy, D. C., and K. Bruhn. 2001. *Mexico: The Struggle for Democratic Development*. Los Angeles: University of California Press.

Li, D. D., and F. T. Liu. 2001. "Why Do Governments Dump State Enterprises? Evidence from China." Manuscript prepared for the 12th Annual East Asian Seminar on Economics, Hong Kong University of Science and Technology, Kowloon, Hong Kong.

Lieberthal, K., and M. Oksenberg. 1988. *Policymaking in China: Leaders, Structures and Processes*. Princeton: Princeton University Press.

Litan, R. E., M. Pomerleano, and V. Sundararajan. 2003. *The Future of Domestic Capital Markets in Developing Countries*. Washington, D.C.: Brookings Institution.

Loayza, N., K. Schmidt-Hebbel, and L. Servén. 2000. "What Drives Private Saving across the World?" *Review of Economics and Statistics*, 82(2):161–81.

Looney, R. E. 2001. "Pakistan's Economy: Achievements, Progress, Constraints, and Prospects," in H. Malik (ed.), *Pakistan: Founders' Aspirations and Today's Realities*. Oxford: Oxford University Press.

Lora, E., and J. L. Londono. 1998. "Structural Reforms and Equity," in N. Birdsell et al. (eds.), *Beyond Trade Offs: Market Reform and Equitable Growth in Latin America*. Washington, D.C.: Brookings Institution.

Lu, Xiaobo. 2000. "Booty Socialism, Bureau-preneurs, and the State in Transition: Organizational Corruption in China." *Comparative Politics*, 32(3): 273–94.

Luce, R. D., and H. Raffia. 1957. *Games and Decisions: Introduction and Critical Survey*. New York: Wiley.

Macdonald, J. 2003. *A Free Nation Deep in Debt: The Financial Roots of Democracy*. New York: Farrar, Straus and Giroux.

Mackie, J.A.C. 1992. "Overseas Chinese Entrepreneurship." *Asia-Pacific Economic Literature* 6(1): 41–64.

Mahathir, M. 1970. *The Malay Dilemma*. Singapore: Times Books International.

Mahmood, S. 1990. *Bureaucracy in Pakistan: An Historical Analysis*. Lahore: Progressive.

Manion, M. 1994. "Corruption by Design: Bribery in Chinese Enterprise Licensing." Manuscript, Faculty of Social Sciences, Lingnan College, Hong Kong.

Marathe, S. 1986. *Regulation and Development: The Indian Policy Experience of Controls over Industry*. London: Sage.

Marx, K., and F. Engels. 1998. *The Communist Manifesto*. London: Verso.

Mauro, P. 1995. "Corruption and Growth." *Quarterly Journal of Economics* 110(3): 681–712.

McCargo, D., (ed.). 2002. *Reforming Thai Politics*. Copenhagen: Nordic Institute of Asian Studies.

McDonald, H. 1995. "Demolitions Zealot: K. J. Alphons." *Far Eastern Economic Review*, 4 May: 78.

McGregor, R. 2003a. "Newbridge Capital China Deal Near Collapse." *Financial Times*, 12 May.

———. 2003b. "Stock Exchanges: Seriously Out of Step with the Economy." *Financial Times*, 16 Dec. 4.

McGuire, J. 1997. "Rethinking Development in East Asia and Latin America." Working paper, Pacific Council on International Policy/Center for International Studies, University of Southern California, Los Angeles.

McGuire, M. C., and M. Olson. 1996. "The Economics of Autocracy and Majority Rule: The Invisible Hand and the Use of Force." *Journal of Economic Literature*, 34(1): 72–96.

McKinnon, R. 1973. *Money and Capital in Economic Development*. Washington, D.C.: Brookings Institution.

McMillan, J., and B. Naughton. 1992. "How to Reform a Planned Economy: Lessons from China." *Oxford Review of Economic Policy*, 8 (Spring): 130–43.

Mead, W. R., and S. Schwenninger (eds.). 2003. *The Bridge to a Global Middle Class: Development, Trade and International Finance*. Boston: Kluwer Academic.

Merton, R. 1995. "A Functional Perspective of Financial Intermediation." *Financial Management*, 24: 23–41.

Metzger, G. 2006 (forthcoming). "International Financial Institutions, Corporate Governance and the Asian Financial Crisis," in T. Heller (ed.). *The Ecology of Corporate Governance: The East Asian Experience*. Available at http://ssrn.com/abstract=382840.

Meyer, R. C. 1989. "How Do Indians Vote?" *Asian Survey*, 29(12): 1111–22.

Mill, J. S. 1871. *Principles of Political Economy*. London: Longmans, Green, Reader and Dyer.

Miller, G. J. 1992. *Managerial Dilemmas: The Political Economy of Hierarchy*. Cambridge: Cambridge University Press.

Montagu-Pollock, M. 1991. "All the Right Connections: Chinese Management Has Amazing Advantages over 'Modern' Methods." *Asian Business*, 27(1): 20–24.

Moss, D. 2002. *When All Else Fails: Government as the Ultimate Risk Manager*. Cambridge: Harvard University Press.

Mungaray, M. and C. Van Den Handel. 2004. "Economic Growth and Democracy in Latin America." Unpublished manuscript, School of Politics and Economics, Claremont Graduate University, Claremont, Calif.

Murphy, K. M., A. Shleifer, and R. W. Vishny. 1993. "Why Is Rent-Seeking So Costly to Growth?" *American Economic Review*, 83(2): 409–14.

Murphy, R. L. 1994. "Commentary," in Fundacion de Investigaciones Economicas Latino Americanas, "La Experencia del Asia Oriental." Documento de Trabajo No. 40: 12–17. Buenos Aires, Argentina.

Murphy, R. L., O. Libonatti, and M. Salinardi. 1995. "Overview and Comparison of Fiscal Decentralization Experiences," in R. L. Murphy (ed.), *Fiscal Decentralization in Latin America*. Washington, D.C.: Inter-American Development Bank.

Murphy, R. L., and C. Moskovits. 1997. "Decentralization, Inter-Governmental Fiscal Relations and Macroeconomic Governance: The Case of Argentina." Working paper, August, Foundation for Latin American Economic Research, Buenos Aires, Argentina.

Nathan, A. J. 1973. "A Factionalism Model for CCP Politics." *China Quarterly*, 53 (January–March): 34–66.

Nelson, J. M. 1989. "Overview: The Politics of Long Haul Economic Reform," in J. M. Nelson et al. (eds.), *Fragile Coalitions: The Politics of Economic Adjustment*. New Brunswick, N.J.: Transaction.

Nelson, M. 2002. "Thailand's House Elections of 6 January 2001: Thaksin's Landslide Victory and Subsequent Narrow Escape," in M. Nelson (ed.), *Thailand's New Politics: KPI Yearbook, 2001*. Bangkok: White Lotus.

Neusser, K., and M. Kugler. 1998. "Manufacturing Growth and Financial Development: Evidence from OECD Countries." *Review of Economics and Statistics* 80(4): 636–46.

Noble, D. F. 1977. *America by Design: Science, Technology and the Rise of Corporate Capitalism*. New York: Knopf.

North, D. C. 1990. *Institutions, Institutional Change, and Economic Performance*. Cambridge: Cambridge University Press.

———. 1991. "Institutions." *Journal of Economic Perspectives*, 5(1): 97–112.

North, D. C., and B. R. Weingast. 1989. "Constitutions and Commitment: The Evolution of Institutions Governing Public Choice in Seventeenth-Century England." *Journal of Economic History* 49(4): 803–32.

O'Driscoll, G. P., Jr., K. R. Holmes, and M. A. O'Grady. 2002. "Index of Economic Freedom." Washington, D.C: Heritage Foundation.

Oi, J. 1989. *State and Peasant in Contemporary China: The Political Economy of Village Government*. Berkeley: University of California Press.

Olson, M. 1965. *The Logic of Collective Action*. Cambridge: Harvard University Press.

———. 1982. *The Rise and Decline of Nations: Economic Growth, Stagflation, and Social Rigidities*. New Haven: Yale University Press.

———. 1993. "Dictatorship, Democracy, and Development." *American Political Science Review*, 87(3): 567–76.

Olson, R. D. 1965. "Mayan Affinities with Chipaya of Bolivia II: Cognates." *International Journal of American Linguistics* 31: 29–38.

Otani, I., and D. Villanueva. 1990. "Long Term Growth in Developing Countries and Its Determinants: An Empirical Analysis." *World Development*, 18(6): 769–83.

Overholt, W. H. 1994. *The Rise of China: How Economic Reform Is Creating a New Superpower*. New York: Norton.

Pakistan People's Party. 1970. *Election Manifesto*. Lahore: Classic.

Paz, O. 1997. *In Light of India*. New York: Harcourt, Brace.

Pei, M. 2002a. "China's Governance Crisis." *Foreign Affairs*, 81(5): 1–18.

———. 2002b. "Beijing Drama: China's Governance Crisis and Bush's New Challenge." Policy Brief No. 21, Carnegie Endowment for International Peace, Washington, D.C.

Perotti, E. C., and S. Gelfer. 1998. "Investment Financing in Russian Financial-Industrial Groups." William Davidson Institute Working Papers Series 242, University of Michigan Business School, Ann Arbor.

Perotti, R. 1996. "Growth, Income Distribution and Democracy: What the Data Say." *Journal of Economic Growth*, 1: 149–87.

Persson, T., and G. Tabellini. 1994. "Is Inequality Harmful for Growth?" *American Economic Review*, 84(3): 600–621.

Phongpaichit, P., and C. Baker. 2002. "Plulto-Populism: Thaksin, Business and Popular Politics in Post-Crisis Thailand," in E. Hedman and J. Sidel (eds.), *Populism in Southeast Asia: The Threat and Promise of New Politics*. New Haven: Yale University Press.

———. 2004. *Thaksin: The Business of Politics in Thailand*. Thailand: Silkwood.

Pinto-Duschinsky, M. 2002. "Financing Politics: A Global View." *Journal of Democracy*, 13(4): 69–86.

Pomfret, J. 2002a. "One Corrupt City Reflects Scourge Plaguing China." *The Washington Post*, 6 March.

———. 2002b. "Chinese Capitalists Gain New Legitimacy." *Washington Post*, 29 September.

Potter, D. C. 1986. *India's Political Administrators, 1919–1983*. Oxford: Clarendon.

Prabhash J. 2003. "Gram Sabha as an Instrument of State Civil Society Synergy: The Kerala Experience," in R. Balasubramaniyan and R. Shanmugaswamy (eds.), *Governability and Governance in South Indian States*. Chennai: University of Madras.

Prasad, E., K. Rogoff, S. Wei, and M. A. Kose. 2003. "Effects of Financial Globalization on Developing Countries: Some Empirical Evidence." Occasional Paper No. 220, International Monetary Fund, Washington, D.C.

PricewaterhouseCoopers. 2001. "Investigating the Costs of Opacity: Deterred Foreign Direct Investment." http://www.opacity-index.com.

Pritchett, L. 2003. "A Toy Collection, a Socialist Star, and a Democratic Dud? Growth Theory, Vietnam, and the Philippines," in D. Rodrik (ed.), *In Search of Prosperity: Analytic Narratives on Economic Growth*. Princeton: Princeton University Press.

Prowse, S. D. 1992. "The Structure of Corporate Ownership in Japan." *Journal of Finance*, 47(3): 1121–40.

Przeworski, A., M. E. Alvarez, J. A. Cheibub, and F. Limongi. 2000. *Democracy and Development: Political Institutions and Well-Being in the World, 1950–1990*. Cambridge: Cambridge University Press.

Putnam, R. 1993. *Making Democracy Work*. Princeton: Princeton University Press.

Pye, L. 1982. *The Dynamics of Chinese Politics*. Cambridge: Oelgeschlager Gunn and Hain.

Qian, Y. 2003. "How Reform Worked in China" in D. Rodrik (ed.), *In Search of Prosperity: Analytic Narratives on Economic Growth*. Princeton: Princeton University Press.

Qian, Y., and B. R. Weingast. 1995. *China's Transition to Markets: Market-Preserving Federalism, Chinese Style*. Stanford: Hoover Institution Press.

Qian, Y., and J. Wu. 2003. "China's Transition to a Market Economy: How Far Across the River?" in N. C. Hope, D. T. Yang, and M. Y. Li (eds.), *How Far Across the River: Chinese Policy Reform at the Millennium*. Stanford: Stanford University Press.

Rahman, M. Z. 2000. "Accounting Standards in the East Asia Region." Paper presented to the 2nd Asian Roundtable on Corporate Governance, OECD and World Bank, Hong Kong.

Rajan, R. 2002. "The Great Reversals: The Politics of Financial Development in the 20th Century." Unpublished working paper, University of Chicago.

Rajan, R., H. Servaes, and L. Zingales. 2000. "The Cost of Diversity: The Diversification Discount and Inefficient Investment." *Journal of Finance*, 55: 35–79.

Rajan, R., and L. Zingales. 1998a. "Financial Dependence and Growth." *American Economic Review*, 88(3): 559–87.

———. 1998b. "Which Capitalism? Lessons from the East Asia Crisis." *Journal of Applied Corporate Finance*, 11(3): 40–48.

———. 2003a. "The Great Reversal: The Politics of Financial Development in the Twentieth Century," *Journal of Financial Economics* 69: 5–50.

———. 2003b. *Saving Capitalism from the Capitalists: Unleashing the Power of Financial Markets to Create Wealth and Spread Opportunity.* New York: Random House.

Ramey, G., and V. A. Ramey. 1995. "Cross-Country Evidence on the Link between Volatility and Growth." *American Economic Review*, 85(5): 1138–51.

Ratliff, W., and E. Buscaglia. 1997. "Judicial Reform: The Neglected Priority in Latin America." *Annals of the American Academy of Political and Social Science*, 550 (March): 59–71.

Ratliff, W., and R. Fontaine. 1990. *Changing Course: The Capitalist Revolution in Argentina.* Stanford: Hoover Institution Press.

———. 1993. *Argentina's Capitalist Revolution Revisited: Confronting the Social Costs of Statist Mistakes.* Stanford: Hoover Institution Press.

Redding, G. and G.Y.Y. Wong, 1986. "The Psychology of Chinese Organizational Behaviour," in M. H. Bond (ed.), *The Psychology of the Chinese People.* Hong Kong: Oxford University Press.

Redding, S. G. 1990. *The Spirit of Chinese Capitalism.* Berlin: De Gruyter.

Rhee, Y. W., B. Ross-Larson, and G. Pursell. 1984. *Korea's Competitive Edge: Managing the Entry into World Markets.* Baltimore: Johns Hopkins University Press.

Rodrik, D. 1989. "Promises, Promises: Credible Policy Reform via Signaling." *Economic Journal*, 99(127): 756–72.

———. 1991. "Policy Uncertainty and Private Investment in Developing Countries," *Journal of Development Economics* 36(2): 229–42.

———. 1997. "The 'Paradoxes' of the Successful State." *European Economic Review*, 41(3–5): 411–42.

Roe, M. J. 2003. *Political Determinants of Corporate Governance: Political Context, Corporate Impact.* New York: Oxford University Press.

Romer, P. 1994. "The Origins of Endogenous Growth." *Journal of Economic Perspective* 8(1): 3–22.

Root, H. L. 1987. *Peasants and King in Burgundy: Agrarian Foundations of French Absolutism.* Berkeley: University of California Press.

———. 1989. "Tying the King's Hands: Credible Commitments and Royal Finance during the Old Regime." *Rationality and Society* 1(4): 386–90.

———. 1994. *The Fountain of Privilege: Political Foundations of Markets in Old Regime France and England.* Berkeley: University of California Press.

———. 1995. "Has China Lost Its Way? Getting Stuck in Transition." Essays in Public Policy Series, Hoover Institution, Stanford University.

Root, H. L. 1996a. "Corruption in China: Has It Become Systemic?" *Asian Survey* 36(8): 741–57.

———. 1996b. *Small Countries, Big Lessons: Governance and the Rise of East Asia*. London: Oxford University Press.

———. 1997. "Transparency and China's Aspirations." *Asian Wall Street Journal*, January 13.

———. 1999a. "Rethinking Global Economic Incentives: How Mismanagement Keeps World Leaders in Office." Policy brief, 29 October, Milken Institute, Santa Monica, Calif.

———. 1999b. "Self-Inflicted Wounds." *National Interest*. Winter: 105–8.

———. 2000a. "Improving the Effectiveness of Donor-Assisted Development," in B. Bueno de Mesquita and H. L. Root (eds.), *Governing for Prosperity*. New Haven: Yale University Press.

———. 2000b. "Korea's Recovery: Don't Count on the Government." Policy brief, 30 May, Milken Institute, Santa Monica, Calif.

———. 2000c. "Removing Estrada Will Not Save the Philippines." *International Herald Tribune*, November 21: 8.

———. 2000d. "Suharto's Tax on Indonesia's Future," in F. J. Richter (ed.), *The East Asian Development Model: Economic Growth, Institutional Failure and the Aftermath of the Crisis*. London: Macmillan.

———. 2000e. "Transparency and China's Aspirations," in B. Chen, J. K. Dietrich, and Y. Feng, *Financial Market Reform in China: Progress, Problems and Prospects*. New York: Westview.

———. 2000f. "When Bad Economics Is Good Politics," in B. Bueno de Mesquita and H. L. Root (eds.), *Governing for Prosperity*. New Haven: Yale University Press.

———. 2001a. "Do Strong Governments Produce Strong Economies?" *Independent Review*. 5(4): 565–73.

———. 2001b. "East Asia's Bad Old Ways: Reforming Business by Reforming the Environment." *Foreign Affairs*, 8(2): 1–5.

———. 2001c. "How to Get Ahead Again." The 5th Column. *Far Eastern Economic Review*, 26 April: 31.

———. 2001d. "Invisible Hand: A Thirst for Funds Drives Change." *Asian Wall Street Journal*, 26 April.

———. 2001e. "Public Administration Reform in Sri Lanka." *International Journal of Public Administration*, 24(12): 1357–79.

———. 2001f. "Thailand Moving Forward into the Past." *Asian Wall Street Journal*, 8 February.

———. 2001g. "What a Way to Reform: Indonesia Is Inching towards Political and Economic Change." *International Economy*, March–April: 32–35.

———. 2002. "What Can Democracy Do for East Asia?" *Journal of Democracy*, 13(1): 113–26.

Root, H. L., M. A. Abdollahian, and J. Kugler. 1999. "Economic Crisis and the Future of Oligarchy," in L. Diamond and D. C. Shin (eds.), *Institutional Reform and Democratic Consolidation in Korea*. Stanford: Hoover Institution Press.

Root, H. L., G. Hodgson, and G. Vaughan-Jones. 2001. "Public Administration Reform in Sri Lanka." *International Journal of Public Administration*, 24(12): 1357–78.

Root, H. L., and N. Nellis. 2000. "The Compulsion of Patronage: Political Sources of Information Asymmetry and Risk in Developing Country Economies," in B. Bueno de Mesquita and H. L. Root (eds.), *Governing for Prosperity*. New Haven: Yale University Press.

Rose-Ackerman, S. 1999. *Corruption and Government: Causes, Consequences and Reform*. Cambridge: Cambridge University Press.

Rosenberg, E. S. 1982. *Spreading the American Dream: American Economic and Cultural Expansions, 1890–1945*. New York: Hill and Wang.

Rousseau, P. L., and P. Wachtel. 1998. "Financial Intermediation and Economic Performance: Historical Evidence from Five Industrial Countries." *Journal of Money, Credit, and Banking*, 30(4): 657–78.

Rudolph, L., and S. Rudolph. 1987. *In Pursuit of Lakshmi: The Political Economy of the Indian State*. Chicago: University of Chicago Press.

Salik, S. 1997. *State and Politics: A Case Study of Pakistan*. Lahore: al-Faisal Nashran.

Salter, F. K. (ed.). 2002. *Risky Transactions: Trust, Kinship and Ethnicity*. Oxford: Berghahn.

Samad, A. 1993. *Governance, Economic Policy and Reform in Pakistan: Essays in Political Economy*. Lahore: Vanguard.

Scharfstein, D. S. 1998. "The Dark Side of Internal Capital Markets II: Evidence from Diversified Conglomerates." Working paper, National Bureau of Economic Research, Cambridge, Mass.

Schenk, H. 1986. "Corruption . . . What Corruption? Notes on Bribery and Dependency in Urban India," in P. M. Ward (ed.), *Corruption, Development and Inequality*. London: Routledge.

Schlevogt, K. A. 1998. *Powers and Control in Chinese Private Enterprises: Organizational Design in the Taiwanese Media Industry*. Boca Raton, Fla.: Universal.

———. 2002. *The Art of Chinese Management: Theory, Evidence, and Applications*. New York: Oxford University Press.

Sen, A., and J. Dreze. 1999. *The Amartya Sen and Jean Dreze Omnibus: Comprising Poverty and Famines, Hunger and Public Action, India: Economic Development and Social Opportunity*. New York: Oxford University Press.

Shah, A. 2002. "Democracy on Hold in Pakistan." *Journal of Democracy*, 13(1): 67–75.

Sheahan, J., and E. Iglesias. 1998. "Kinds and Causes of Inequity in Latin America," in N. Birdsell et al. (eds.), *Beyond Trade Offs: Market Reform and Equitable Growth in Latin America*. Washington, D.C.: Brookings Institution.

Shiller, R. J. 1993. *Macro Markets: Creating Institutions for Managing Society's Largest Economic Risks*. New York: Oxford University Press.

———. 2003. *The New Financial Order: Risk in the 21st Century*. Princeton: Princeton University Press.

Shin, H., and Y. S. Park. 1999. "Financing Constraints and Internal Capital Markets: Evidence from Korean Chaebols." *Journal of Corporate Finance*, 5:169–91.

Shinn, J., and P. Gourevitch. 2002. "Reputations at Risk: Corporate Governance and American Foreign Policy." Mimeo, Council on Foreign Relations, Washington, D.C.

Shirk, S. L. 1993. *The Political Logic of Economic Reform in China*. Berkeley: University of California Press.

———. 1994. *How China Opened Its Door: The Political Success of the PRC's Foreign Trade and Investment Reforms*. Washington, D.C.: Brookings Institution.

Sicular, T. 1992. "Public Finance and China's Economic Reforms." Discussion Paper No. 1618, Harvard Institute of Economic Research, Cambridge, Mass.

Skowronek, S. 1982. *Building a New American State: The Expansion of National Administrative Capacities, 1877–1920*. New York: Cambridge University Press.

Srinivasan, T. N. 1996. "Indian Economic Reforms: Background, Rationale, Achievements, and Future Prospects," in G. Rosen (ed.), *India's New Economic Policy: Liberalization and Regionalization*. Stamford, Conn.: JAI Press.

Stiglitz, J. E. 1973. "Recurrences of Techniques in a Dynamic Economy," in J. Mirrlees, (ed.), *Models of Economic Growth*. New York: Macmillan.

———. 1994. *Whither Socialism?* Cambridge: MIT Press.

———. 1999. "Knowledge as a Global Public Good," in I. Kaul, I. Grunberg, and M. A. Stern (eds.), *Global Public Goods: International Cooperation in the 21st Century*. New York: Oxford University Press.

Strassman, W. P. 1981. *Risk and Technological Innovation*. London: Methuen.

Studwell, J. 2002. *The China Dream: The Quest for the Last Great Untapped Market on Earth*. New York: Grove.

Stulz, R. 2001. "Does Financial Structure Matter for Economic Growth? A Corporate Finance Perspective," in A. Demirguc-Kunt and R. Levine (eds.), *Financial Structure and Economic Growth*. Cambridge: MIT Press.

Tedlos, R. 1991. *The Rise of the American Business Corporation*. Poststrasse: Harwood Academic.

Temin, P. 1964. *Iron and Steel in the Nineteenth Century*. Cambridge: MIT Press.

Tenev, S., C. Zhang, and L. Brefort. 2002. *Corporate Governance and Enterprise Reform in China: Building the Institutions of Modern Markets*. Washington, D.C.: World Bank and International Finance Corp.

Terrill, R. 2003. *The New Chinese Empire: And What It Means for the United States*. New York: Basic.

Tocqueville, A. de. 1960. *Democracy in America*, vols. 1–2. P. Bradley (ed.), New York: Vintage.

Todd, E. 2002. *Après l'empire: Essai sur la décomposition du système americain*. Paris: Gallimard.

Transparency International. 2002. *Corruption Perception Index*, http://www.transparency.org/cpi/2002/cpi2002.en.html.

Turpin, D. V. 1998. "Challenge of the Overseas Chinese." Mastering Global Business Series, part 2, *Financial Times*, 2 June: 8.

United Nations Development Programme. 2004. *Democracy in Latin America: Towards a Citizens' Democracy*. New York: UNDP.

United Press International, 2003. "Bureaucratic Corruption Worries India." October 9, 2003, http://quickstart.clari.net/qs_se/webnews/wed/ct/Uindia-corruption.Rbe3_DO9.html.

Venieris, Y., and D. Gupta. 1983. "Socio-Political Instability and Economic Dimensions of Development: A Cross-Sectional Model." *Economic Development and Cultural Change*, 31(4): 727–56.

———. 1986. "Income Distribution and Socio-Political Instability as Determinants of Savings: A Cross-Sectional Model." *Journal of Political Economy*, 94(4): 873–83.

Vittal, N. 2000. "Some Unexplained Sums," *Bulletin of Lok Sevak Sangh* (India), February 28, 2000.

Vose, D. 2000. *Risk Analysis: A Quantitative Guide*. New York: Wiley.

Voth, H. J. 2003. "Stock Price Volatility and Political Uncertainty: Evidence From the Interwar Period." Manuscript, Massachusetts Institute of Technology.

Wade, R. 1982. "The System of Administrative and Political Corruption: Canal Irrigation in South India." *Journal of Development Studies*, 18(3): 287–328.

———. 1985. "The Market for Public Office: Why the Indian State Is Not Better at Development." *World Development* 13(4): 467–97.

———. 1988. "The Management of Irrigation Systems: How to Evoke Trust and Avoid Prisoner's Dilemma." *World Development*, 16(4): 489–500.

Waisman, C. H. 1987. *Reversal of Development in Argentina*. Princeton: Princeton University Press.

Walder, A. 1986. *Communist Neo-traditionalism: Work and Authority in Chinese Industry*. Berkeley: University of California Press.

Waller, C. J., T. Verdier, and R. Gardner. 2002. "Corruption: Top Down or Bottom Up?" *Economic Inquiry*, 40(4): 688–703.

Waseem, M. 1994. *Politics and the State in Pakistan*. Islamabad: National Institute of Historical and Cultural Research.

Waterbury, J. 1993. *Exposed to Innumerable Delusions: Public Enterprise and State Power in Egypt, India, Mexico, and Turkey*. Cambridge: Cambridge University Press.

Weber, M. 1961. "Bureaucracy," in H. H. Gerth and C. W. Mills (eds.), *From Max Weber: Essays in Sociology*. New York: Oxford University Press.

Wei, S. J. 1997. "Why is Corruption So Much More Taxing than Taxes? Arbitrariness Kills." Working Paper No. 6255, National Bureau of Economic Research, Cambridge, Mass.

Weidenbaum, M. 1996. "The Chinese Family Business Enterprise." *California Management Review*, 38: 141–56.

Weidenbaum, M., and S. Hughes. 1996. *The Bamboo Network: How Expatriate Chinese Entrepreneurs Are Creating a New Superpower in Asia*. New York: Free Press.

Weiner, M. 1957. *Party Politics in India: The Development of a Multi-Party System*. Princeton: Princeton University Press.

———. 1967. *Party Building in a New Nation: The Indian National Congress*. Chicago: University of Chicago Press.

Weingast, B. R. 1997. "The Political Foundations of Democracy and the Rule of Law." *American Political Science Review* 91(2): 245–63.

Westphal, L. E. 1990. "Industrial Policy in an Export-Propelled Economy: Lessons from South Korea's Experience." *Journal of Economic Perspectives* 4(3): 41–59.

Whitney, D. C. 1982. *The American Presidents*. Garden City, N.Y.: Doubleday.

Williamson, O.E. 1985. *The Economic Institutions of Capitalism*. New York: Free Press.

Wintrobe, R. 1997. *The Political Economy of Dictatorship*. Cambridge: Cambridge University Press.

Wolpert, S. A., 1993. *Zulfi Bhutto of Pakistan*. New York: Oxford University Press.

World Bank. 1989. *World Development Report of 1989: Finance and Development*. Washington, D.C.: World Bank.

———. 1993. *The East Asian Miracle: Economic Growth and Public Policy*. New York: Oxford University Press.

———. 1997. *World Development Report: The State in a Changing World*. New York: Oxford University Press.

———. 1998. *Assessing Aid: What Works, What Doesn't and Why*. New York: Oxford University Press.

———. 2000. *Reforming Public Institutions and Strengthening Governance*. Washington, D.C.: World Bank.

———. 2002a. *Civil Serivce Reform: Strengthening World Bank and IMF Collaboration*. Washington, D.C.: World Bank.

———. 2002b. *Public Policy for the Private Sector*. Washington D.C.: World Bank.

———. 2002c. *Transition: The First Ten Years: Analysis and Lessons for Eastern Europe and the Former Soviet Union*. Washington, D.C.: World Bank.

———. 2002d. *World Development Report 2002: Building Institutions for Market*. Washington, D.C.: World Bank.

———. 2003. *World Development Report 2003: Sustainable Development in a Dynamic World: Transforming Institutions, Growth, and Quality of Life*. Washington, D.C.: World Bank.

———. 2004a. *Inequality in Latin America and the Caribbean: Breaking with History?* Washington, D.C.: World Bank.

———. 2004b. *Making Infrastructure Work for the Poor*. DevNews Media Center, http://web.worldbank.org/WBSITE/EXTERNAL/NEWS/0,,contentMDK: 2003505~menuP.

Yáñez, J. H., and L. S. Letelier. 1995. "Chile," in R. L. Murphy (ed.), *Fiscal Decentralization in Latin America*. Washington, D.C.: Inter-American Development Bank.

Yasin, M. and T. Banuri. 2003. *Dispensation of Justice in Pakistan*. Oxford: Oxford University Press.

Yusuf, S., and S. Evenett. 2002. *Can East Asia Compete? Innovation for Global Markets*. New York: Oxford University Press.

Zhou, Tianyong. 2002. "Build Up Credible Government." *China Daily*.

Tobar, H. 2003. "The Good Life Is No More for Argentina." *Los Angeles Times*, 18 February A1.

Zwart, F. de. 1994. *The Bureaucratic Merry-go-round: Manipulating the Transfer of Indian Civil Servant*. Amsterdam: Amsterdam University Press.

Index

Note: Page numbers in *italic* type refer to figures or tables.